RECLAIMING CONVERSATION

RECLAIMING CONVERSATION

The Power of Talk in a Digital Age

SHERRY TURKLE

PENGUIN PRESS

NEW YORK

2015

PENGUIN PRESS
An imprint of Penguin Random House LLC
375 Hudson Street
New York, New York 10014
penguin.com

Copyright © 2015 by Sherry Turkle
Penguin supports copyright. Copyright fuels creativity, encourages diverse voices,
promotes free speech, and creates a vibrant culture. Thank you for buying an authorized edition
of this book and for complying with copyright laws by not reproducing, scanning, or distributing
any part of it in any form without permission. You are supporting writers and allowing
Penguin to continue to publish books for every reader.

Selection by Louis C.K. on pages 59–60. Used by permission of Louis C.K.

ISBN: 978-1-59420-555-2
Export Edition ISBN: 978-1-10198-046-0

Printed in the United States of America
1   3   5   7   9   10   8   6   4   2

Designed by Michelle McMillian

To Rebecca, Kelly, and Emily,
with thanks for all the kitchen table conversations

Contents

I had three chairs in my house; one for solitude,
two for friendship, three for society.
—HENRY DAVID THOREAU, *Walden*

We had talk enough, but no conversation.

—SAMUEL JOHNSON, *The Rambler (1752)*

The Case for Conversation

The Empathy Diaries

Twelve-year-olds play on the playground like eight-year-olds. . . .
They don't seem able to put themselves in the place of other children.

—THE DEAN OF THE HOLBROOKE MIDDLE SCHOOL,
COMMENTING ON AN "EMPATHY GAP"
AMONG STUDENTS*

Why a book on conversation? We're talking all the time. We text and post and chat. We may even begin to feel more at home in the world of our screens. Among family and friends, among colleagues and lovers, we turn to our phones instead of each other. We readily admit we would rather send an electronic message or mail than commit to a face-to-face meeting or a telephone call.

This new mediated life has gotten us into trouble. Face-to-face conversation is the most human—and humanizing—thing we do. Fully present to one another, we learn to listen. It's where we develop the capacity for empathy. It's where we experience the joy of being heard, of being understood. And conversation advances self-reflection, the conversations with ourselves that are the cornerstone of early development and continue throughout life.

But these days we find ways around conversation. We hide from each other even as we're constantly connected to each other. For on our

---

* Holbrooke is a fictitious name. In this book I disguise the identities of all individuals I cite and of all institutions I visited–schools, universities, businesses. I use real names when I draw from the public record or cite words delivered in a public forum. For more on my method, see note on pp. 369–370.

screens, we are tempted to present ourselves as we would like to be. Of course, performance is part of any meeting, anywhere, but online and at our leisure, it is easy to compose, edit, and improve as we revise.

We say we turn to our phones when we're "bored." And we often find ourselves bored because we have become accustomed to a constant feed of connection, information, and entertainment. We are forever elsewhere. At class or at church or business meetings, we pay attention to what interests us and then when it doesn't, we look to our devices to find something that does. There is now a word in the dictionary called "phubbing." It means maintaining eye contact while texting. My students tell me they do it all the time and that it's not that hard.

We begin to think of ourselves as a tribe of one, loyal to our own party. We check our messages during a quiet moment or when the pull of the online world simply feels irresistible. Even children text each other rather than talk face-to-face with friends—or, for that matter, rather than daydream, where they can take time alone with their thoughts.

It all adds up to a flight from conversation—at least from conversation that is open-ended and spontaneous, conversation in which we play with ideas, in which we allow ourselves to be fully present and vulnerable. Yet these are the conversations where empathy and intimacy flourish and social action gains strength. These are the conversations in which the creative collaborations of education and business thrive.

But these conversations require time and space, and we say we're too busy. Distracted at our dinner tables and living rooms, at our business meetings, and on our streets, we find traces of a new "silent spring"—a term Rachel Carson coined when we were ready to see that with technological change had come an assault on our environment. Now, we have arrived at another moment of recognition. This time, technology is implicated in an assault on empathy. We have learned that even a silent phone inhibits conversations that matter. The very sight of a phone on the landscape leaves us feeling less connected to each other, less invested in each other.

Despite the seriousness of our moment, I write with optimism. Once aware, we can begin to rethink our practices. When we do, conversation is there to reclaim. For the failing connections of our digital world, it is the talking cure.

"They Make Acquaintances, but Their Connections Seem Superficial"

In December 2013, I was contacted by the dean of the Holbrooke School, a middle school in upstate New York. I was asked to consult with its faculty about what they saw as a disturbance in their students' friendship patterns. In her invitation, the dean put it this way: "Students don't seem to be making friendships as before. They make acquaintances, but their connections seem superficial."

The case of the superficial acquaintances in middle school was compelling. It was of a piece with what I was hearing in other schools, about older students. And so it was decided that I would join the Holbrooke teachers on a faculty retreat. I brought along a new notebook; after an hour, I wrote on its cover "The Empathy Diaries."

For that's what the Holbrooke teachers are thinking about. Children at Holbrooke are not developing empathy in the way that years of teaching suggested they would. Ava Reade, the dean of the school, says that she rarely intervenes in student social arrangements, but recently she had to. A seventh grader tried to exclude a classmate from a school social event. Reade called the remiss seventh grader into her office and asked why it happened. The girl didn't have much to say:

> [The seventh grader] was almost robotic in her response. She said, "I don't have feelings about this." She couldn't read the signals that the other student was hurt.
>
> These kids aren't cruel. But they are not emotionally developed. Twelve-year-olds play on the playground like eight-year-olds. The way they exclude one another is the way eight-year-olds would play. They don't seem able to put themselves in the place of other children. They say to other students: "You can't play with us."

They are not developing that way of relating where they listen and learn how to look at each other and hear each other.

The Holbrooke teachers are enthusiastic users of educational technology. But on their retreat, they follow what some call the precautionary principle: "Indication of harm, not proof of harm, is our call to action." These teachers believe they see indications of harm. It is a struggle to get children to talk to each other in class, to directly address each other. It is a struggle to get them to meet with faculty. And one teacher observes: "The [students] sit in the dining hall and look at their phones. When they share things together, what they are sharing is what is on their phones." Is this the new conversation? If so, it is not doing the work of the old conversation. As these teachers see it, the old conversation taught empathy. These students seem to understand each other less.

I was invited to Holbrooke because for many decades I have studied children's development in technological culture. I began in the late 1970s, when a few schools were experimenting with personal computers in classrooms or special computer laboratories. I work on this question still, when many children come to school with a tablet or laptop of their own, or one their school has issued.

From the beginning, I found that children used the digital world to play with issues of identity. In the late 1970s and early 1980s, children used simple programming as an expressive medium. A thirteen-year-old who had programmed a graphical world of her own said: "When you program a computer, you put a little piece of your mind into the computer's mind and you come to see yourself differently." Later, when personal computers became portals to online games, children experimented with identity by building avatars. The particulars changed with new games and new computers, but something essential remained constant: Virtual space is a place to explore the self.

Also constant was the anxiety of adults around children and machines. From the beginning, teachers and parents worried that computers were *too* compelling. They watched, unhappy, as children became lost in games and forgot about the people around them, preferring, at long stretches, the worlds in the machine.

One sixteen-year-old describes this refuge: "On computers, if things are unpredictable, it's in a predictable way." Programmable worlds can be made exciting, but they also offer new possibilities for a kind of experience that some began to call friction-free. Newton's laws need not apply. Virtual objects can be made to simply glide along. And you, too, can glide along if that's how things are programmed. In virtual worlds, you can face challenging encounters—with scoundrels and wizards and spells—that you know for sure will work out in the end. Or you can die and be reborn. *Real people, with their unpredictable ways, can seem difficult to contend with after one has spent a stretch in simulation.*

From the early days, I saw that computers offer the illusion of companionship without the demands of friendship and then, as the programs got really good, the illusion of friendship without the demands of intimacy. Because, face-to-face, people ask for things that computers never do. With people, things go best if you pay close attention and know how to put yourself in someone else's shoes. Real people demand responses to what they are feeling. And not just any response.

Time in simulation gets children ready for more time in simulation. Time with people teaches children how to be in a relationship, beginning with the ability to have a conversation. And this brings me back to the anxieties of the Holbrooke teachers. As the Holbrooke middle schoolers began to spend more time texting, they lost practice in face-to-face talk. That means lost practice in the empathic arts—learning to make eye contact, to listen, and to attend to others. Conversation is on the path toward the experience of intimacy, community, and communion. Reclaiming conversation is a step toward reclaiming our most fundamental human values.

Mobile technology is here to stay, along with all the wonders it brings. Yet it is time for us to consider how it may get in the way of other things we hold dear—and how once we recognize this, we can take action: *We can both redesign technology and change how we bring it into our lives.*

A Partisan of Conversation

I have spent my professional life as a student of conversation, trained as a sociologist, a teacher, and a clinical psychologist. These vocations have made me a partisan of conversation because they have taught me to appreciate the work that conversation can do—from Socratic classrooms to small talk around water coolers.

My mentor, the sociologist David Riesman, called these vocations "the talking trades." He was right. They rely on conversation and they approach it with high expectations. Each has an answer to the question: What is the work of conversation?

Sociologists and anthropologists use conversation to make sense of the web of relationships at home, at work, and in public life. When things go right, the social scientist's interview becomes an open, easy exchange. This often happens after trust has been established, when the researcher's notebook has been closed, when people who only a few minutes earlier had been "participants" in "your study" realize that there is something in this for them. Your question becomes their question as well. A conversation begins.

In the classroom, conversations carry more than the details of a subject; teachers are there to help students learn how to ask questions and be dissatisfied with easy answers. More than this, conversations with a good teacher communicate that learning isn't all about the answers. It's about what the answers mean. Conversations help students build narratives—whether about gun control or the Civil War—that will allow them to learn and remember in a way that has meaning for them. Without these narratives, you can learn a new fact but not know what to do with it, how to make sense of it. In therapy, conversation explores the meanings of the relationships that animate our lives. It attends to pauses, hesitations, associations, the things that are said through silence. It commits to a kind of conversation that doesn't give "advice" but helps people discover what they have hidden from themselves so they can find their inner compass.

Conversations in these traditions have a lot in common. When they work best, people don't just speak but listen, both to others and to themselves. They allow themselves to be vulnerable. They are fully present and open to where things might go.

You don't need to be in the talking trades to recognize the work conversation can do. I have asked people of all ages and circumstances to tell me about their most important conversations—with children, with friends, with spouses, partners, lovers, and colleagues. It was a question people wanted to answer. They offered the conversation when they fell in love, when they realized that their parents were vulnerable and needed their care, when they understood that their children were no longer children. They offered the conversation when they were confirmed in a career choice because a mentor gave them a chance to run with a quirky idea.

With all of this in mind, when I hear lovers say that they prefer to "talk" by editing a text on their smartphones, when I hear families say that they air their differences on email to avoid face-to-face tension, when I hear corporate vice-presidents describe business meetings as "downtime for emptying your inbox," I hear a desire for distraction, comfort, and efficiency. But I also know that these moves won't allow conversation to do the work it can do.

The Virtuous Circle

We are being silenced by our technologies—in a way, "cured of talking." These silences—often in the presence of our children—have led to a crisis of empathy that has diminished us at home, at work, and in public life. I've said that the remedy, most simply, is a talking cure. This book is my case for conversation.

I begin my case by turning to someone many people think of—mistakenly—as a hermit who tried to get away from talk. In 1845, Henry David Thoreau moved to a cabin on Walden Pond in Concord, Massachusetts, to learn to live more "deliberately"—away from the crush of random chatter. But the cabin furniture he chose to secure that ambition suggests no simple "retreat." He said that in his cabin there were "three chairs—one for solitude, two for friendship, and three for society."

These three chairs plot the points on a virtuous circle that links conversation to the capacity for empathy and for self-reflection. In solitude we find ourselves; we prepare ourselves to come to conversation with something to say that is authentic, ours. When we are secure in ourselves we are able to listen to other people and really hear what they have to say. And then in conversation with other people we become better at inner dialogue.

Of course, this virtuous circle is an ideal type, but taking that into account, it works. Solitude reinforces a secure sense of self, and with that, the capacity for empathy. Then, conversation with others provides rich material for self-reflection. Just as alone we prepare to talk together, together we learn how to engage in a more productive solitude.

Technology disrupts this virtuous circle.

The disruptions begin with solitude, Thoreau's first chair. Recent research shows that people are uncomfortable if left alone with their thoughts, even for a few minutes. In one experiment, people were asked to sit quietly—without a phone or a book—for fifteen minutes. At the start of the experiment, they were also asked if they would consider administering electroshocks to themselves if they became bored. They said absolutely not: No matter what, shocking themselves would be out of the question. But after just six minutes alone, a good number of them were doing just that.

These results are stunning, but in a way, not surprising. These days, we see that when people are alone at a stop sign or in the checkout line at the supermarket, they seem almost panicked and they reach for their phones. We are so accustomed to being always connected that being alone seems like a problem technology should solve.

And this is where the virtuous circle breaks down: Afraid of being alone, we struggle to pay attention to ourselves. And what suffers is our ability to pay attention to each other. If we can't find our own center, we lose confidence in what we have to offer others.

Or you can work the circle the other way: We struggle to pay attention to each other, and what suffers is our ability to know ourselves.

We face a flight from conversation that is also a flight from self-reflection, empathy, and mentorship—the virtues of Thoreau's three chairs. *But this flight is not inevitable. When the virtuous circle is broken, conversation cures.*

For there is good news. Despite the pull of our technology, we are resilient. For example, in only five days at a summer camp that bans all electronic devices, children show an increased capacity for empathy as measured by their ability to identify the feelings of others by looking at photographs and videos of people's faces. In my own research at a device-free summer camp, I hear what this resiliency sounds like.

At a nightly cabin chat, a group of fourteen-year-old boys talk about a recent three-day wilderness hike. One can imagine that not that many years ago the most exciting aspect of that hike might have been the idea of "roughing it" or the beauty of unspoiled nature. These days, what makes the biggest impression is time without a phone, what one boy calls "time where you have nothing to do but think quietly and talk to your friends." Another boy uses the cabin chat to reflect on his new taste for silence: "Don't people know that sometimes you can just look out the window of a car and see the world go by and it's wonderful?"

Crossroads

Just as some people will ask, "Why a book about conversation? We're talking all the time," some will say, "Why bring up the negative? You must know about all the wonderful new conversations that happen on the net!" I do know. I've gone to a reunion of my sixth-grade class from PS 216 Brooklyn that could never have happened if not for Facebook. Texts from my daughter, when she was twenty-three, made her seem closer to home even when she took a job on another coast. These from fall 2014: "Hi! I REALLY like *Life After Life*!" "Where do I get challah?" "My roommate and I are going to the party as Elsa and Anna from

Frozen." All of a sudden, with no warning, on my phone, in my hand, there will be a reference to a book or a food or a Halloween costume that reminds me of our intimacy and infuses my day with her presence. This is pleasurable and to be cherished. The problem comes if these "reminders" of intimacy lead us away from intimacy itself.

Most relationships are a blend of online and off-line interaction. Courtships take place via text. Political debates are sparked and social movements mobilize on websites. Why not focus on the positive—a celebration of these new exchanges?

Because these are the stories we tell each other to explain why our technologies are proof of progress. We like to hear these positive stories because they do not discourage us in our pursuit of the new—our new comforts, our new distractions, our new forms of commerce. And we like to hear them because if these are the only stories that matter, then we don't have to attend to other feelings that persist—that we are somehow more lonely than before, that our children are less empathic than they should be for their age, and that it seems nearly impossible to have an uninterrupted conversation at a family dinner.

We catch ourselves not looking into the eyes of our children or taking the time to talk with them just to have a few more hits of our email. Will we summon our attention if, a decade later, fearful of being alone but anxious about attachment, our children show us what it looks like to pay the price? It makes no sense to "match" this disturbing possibility with a happy story about Facebook friendship or Twitter exchanges. This isn't a game in which we can cross our fingers and hope that the good will outweigh the bad. We want to take the good and also make the changes necessary so that we don't pay a price that no technology is worth.

Generations

I remember the generation that first encountered networked personal computers in the 1980s and 1990s. These were machines you "went to" when you wanted to play games, or write, or work with spreadsheets, or send email. Computers offered aids to productivity and many new pleasures—but they did not suggest that text might displace talk.

Only a few years later, there would be cohorts of children who grew up with smartphones, social media, and chatty digital assistants. Today, these children, no longer children, are our teachers, businesspeople, doctors, and parents.

When these new generations consider the idea of a "flight from conversation," they often ask, "Is that really a problem? If you text or iChat, isn't that 'talking'? And besides, you can get your message 'right.' What's wrong with that?" When I talk with them about open-ended conversation, some ask me to specify its "value proposition." Some tell me that conversation seems like "hard work," with many invitations, often treacherous, to imperfection, loss of control, and boredom. Why are these worth fighting for?

Many of the things we all struggle with in love and work can be helped by conversation. Without conversation, studies show that we are less empathic, less connected, less creative and fulfilled. We are diminished, in retreat. But to generations that grew up using their phones to text and message, *these studies may be describing losses they don't feel.* They didn't grow up with a lot of face-to-face talk.

Of course, across the generations, there are those who do not need to be convinced of the value of conversation. But even these partisans of conversation often surprise me. So many of them seem defeated. They say the future has overtaken them. A filmmaker who graduated from college in 2009 tells me that was the year conversation died. I am particularly struck by parents who say they want their children to stop texting at dinner but don't feel they can object when the phones come out. They fear they are too late with their admonishments, that they will be left behind if they don't embrace the new.

I am describing more than a flight from conversation. This is a flight from the responsibilities of mentorship. Technology enchants; it makes us forget what we know about life. The new—any old new—becomes confused with progress. But in our eagerness, we forget our responsibility *to* the new, to the generations that follow us. It is for us to pass on the most precious thing we know how to do: talking to the next generation about our experiences, our history; sharing what we think we did right and wrong.

It is not enough to ask your children to put away their phones. You have to model this behavior and put away *your* phone. If children don't learn how to listen, to stand up for themselves and negotiate with others in classrooms or at family dinner, when will they learn the give-and-take that is necessary for good relationships or, for that matter, for the debate of citizens in a democracy? Reclaiming conversation begins with the acknowledgment that speaking and listening with attention are skills. They can be taught. They take practice and that practice can start now. In your home, in a classroom, at your job.

Stepping Up, Not Stepping Back

There are at least two audiences for this book. One audience needs to be persuaded that a flight from conversation suggests a problem and not an evolution. And it is a problem with a solution: If we make space for conversation, we come back to each other and we come back to ourselves.

And for the audience that feels defeated, whose members mourn an "inevitable" flight from conversation and see themselves as bystanders, I make another case: This is the wrong time to step back. Those who understand how conversation works—no matter what their ages—need to step up and pass on what they know.

We can step up in our families and friendships, but there are also the public conversations of Thoreau's third chair. These conversations, too, need mentors. Here I think of teachers and students: The classroom is a social space where students can see how thinking happens. College faculty are often shy about asking students to put away their devices in classrooms. Only a few years ago, most professors told me that they didn't want to be their students' "nannies," that this "policing" job was not for them. But we have learned that a student with an open laptop will multitask in class. And we have learned that this will degrade the performance not only of the student with the open machine but of all the students around him or her. These days, faculty are less deferential. Many begin the semester by announcing a device-free classroom policy or specifically set aside class time for "tools down" conversation.

I have met CEOs who now make a point of instructing employees to work out disagreements and apologize to each other *in person*. A new manager, in his mid-thirties, admits that he shies away from face-to-face conversation but is inspired by a weekly "all hands" meeting in his company that is reserved for "just talk." The new manager is insecure about what he can express, but he says of the weekly meeting: "That's a place where I'm learning to have a conversation." In another company, a manager begins her team's meetings by having all laptops and cell phones put into a basket at the door. She's tired of meetings where people do their email.

Beyond school and workplace, there is the public square.

In the media, one often hears a distinctive phrase: "We have to have a national conversation." But the pundits who say it have become accustomed to quick cuts, partisan bickering, and dropping the subject—be it war or weather or racism—when the next news cycle hits. They are also accustomed to talking about news with a "crawl" of unrelated stories scrolling under their images on the screen. That crawl under the news began during the Iran hostage crisis of 1981. No matter what the news, Americans wanted instant updates on the American prisoners in Iran. The hostage crisis ended; the crawl that divides our attention remains. A more satisfying public conversation will require work. But it's important not to confuse the difficult with the impossible. If we commit ourselves, it's work we know how to do.

Does the Exception Make the Problem Go Away?

The problem I sum up as a "flight from conversation" doesn't always capture our attention (the technology does!), so it's easy to defer thinking about it. People are still together talking—this looks like conversation—so we may not notice how much our lives have changed. In this way, the flight from conversation is something like climate change: We feel safe in our homes day to day and we usually aren't thinking about "thirty years from now." And in the case of both climate change and conversation, there is the temptation to think that an exception means the problem isn't real or will go away.

Weather patterns may be changing across the planet in alarming ways, but then you are faced with a beautiful sunny day, one of the most beautiful days you have ever seen, and somehow this makes it easier to put the problem out of mind. Similarly, we now rarely give each other our full attention, but every once in a while, we do. We forget how unusual this has become, that many young people are growing up without ever having experienced unbroken conversations either at the dinner table or when they take a walk with parents or friends. For them, phones have always come along.

I often speak to audiences of parents and many describe their difficulties in talking to their children. And then someone will raise a hand and say, "My son loves to talk and he is sixteen years old." As if this means the case is closed.

But the case is not closed. We have not assessed the full human consequences of digital media. We want to focus on its pleasures. Its problems have to do with unintended consequences. To take the measure of these, I follow a path suggested by Thoreau's three chairs: a first for solitude, a second for friendship, and a third for society.

Thoreau said that when conversation became expansive, he brought his guests out into nature. This image leads me to think of a "fourth chair": conversations that Thoreau could not have envisaged. I look at how we have built a "second nature," an artificial nature, and try to enter into dialogue with it. We have built machines that speak, and, in speaking to them, we cannot help but attribute human nature to objects that have none.

We have embarked upon a voyage of forgetting. It has several stations. *At a first, we speak through machines* and forget how essential face-to-face conversation is to our relationships, our creativity, and our capacity for empathy. *At a second, we take a further step and speak not just through machines but to machines.* This is a turning point. When we consider conversations with machines about our most human predicaments, we face a moment of reckoning that can bring us to the end of our forgetting. It is an opportunity to reaffirm what makes us most human.

The Moment Is Right to Reclaim Conversation

In 2011, when I published *Alone Together*, a book critical of our inattention to each other in our always-connected lives, I knew I was describing complications that most people did not want to see. As a culture, we were smitten with our technology. Like young lovers, we were afraid that too much talking would spoil the romance. But now, only a few years later, the atmosphere has changed. We are ready to talk. When we have our mobile devices with us, we see that we turn away from our children, romantic partners, and work colleagues. We are ready to reconsider the too-simple enthusiasm of "the more connected we are, the better off we are."

Now, we begin to take the measure of how our communications compel us. We have learned that we get a neurochemical high from connecting. We recognize that we crave a feeling of being "always on" that keeps us from doing our best, being our best. So we allow ourselves a certain disenchantment with what technology has made possible.

We recognize that we need things that social media inhibit. My previous work described an evolving problem; this book is a call to action. It is time to make the course corrections. We have everything we need to begin. We have each other.

The Flight from Conversation

My guess—and I think this will be debated for a long time—is that humans are very communicative, and so the fact that you're talking to more people with shorter bursts of communication is probably net neutral to positive.

—ERIC SCHMIDT, EXECUTIVE CHAIRMAN OF GOOGLE

Don't all these little tweets, these little sips of online connection, add up to one big gulp of real conversation?

—STEPHEN COLBERT, ACTOR AND COMEDIAN

These days, we want to be with each other but also elsewhere, connected to wherever else we want to be, because what we value most is control over where we put our attention. Our manners have evolved to accommodate our new priorities. When you're out to dinner with friends, you can't assume that you have their undivided attention. Cameron, a college junior in New Hampshire, says that when his friends have dinner, "and I hate this, everyone puts their phones next to them when they eat. And then, they're always checking them." The night before at dinner he had texted a friend sitting next to him ("'S'up, dude?") just to get his attention.

Cameron's objection is common, for this is the reality: When college students go to dinner, they want the company of their friends in the dining hall and they also want the freedom to go to their phones. To have both at the same time, they observe what some call the "rule of three":

When you are with a group at dinner you have to check that at least three people have their heads up from their phones before you give yourself permission to look down at *your* phone. So conversation proceeds—but with different people having their "heads up" at different times.

I meet with Cameron and seven of his friends. One of them, Eleanor, describes the rule of three as a strategy of continual scanning:

> *Let's say we are seven at dinner. We all have our phones. You have to make sure that at least two people are not on their phones or looking down to check something—like a movie time on Google or going on Facebook. So you need sort of a rule of two or three. So I know to keep, like, two or three in the mix so that other people can text or whatever. It's my way of being polite. I would say that conversations, well, they're pretty, well, fragmented. Everybody is kind of in and out. Yeah, you have to say, "Wait, what . . ." and sort of have people fill you in a bit when you drop out.*

The effect of the rule of three is what you might expect. As Eleanor says, conversation is fragmented. And everyone tries to keep it light.

Even a Silent Phone Disconnects Us

Keeping talk light when phones are on the landscape becomes a new social grace. One of Eleanor's friends explains that if a conversation at dinner turns serious and someone looks at a phone, that is her signal to "lighten things up." And she points out that the rule of three is a way of being polite even when you're not at the dinner table. When "eyes are down" at phones, she says, "conversation stays light well beyond dinner."

When I first planned the research that would lead to this book, my idea was to focus on our new patterns of texting and messaging. What made them compelling? Unique? But early in my study, when I met with these New Hampshire students, their response to my original question was to point me to another question that they thought was more important. "I would put it this way," says Cameron. "There are fewer conversations—not with the people you're texting, but with the people around you!" As he says this, we are in a circle of eight, talking together, and heads are going down to check phones. A few try not to, but it is a struggle.

Cameron sums up what he sees around him. "Our texts are fine. It's what texting does to our conversations when we are together, that's the problem."

It was a powerful intuition. What phones do to in-person conversation *is* a problem. Studies show that the mere presence of a phone on the table (even a phone turned off) changes what people talk about. If we think we might be interrupted, we keep conversations light, on topics of little controversy or consequence. And conversations with phones on the landscape block empathic connection. If two people are speaking and there is a phone on a nearby desk, each feels less connected to the other than when there is no phone present. *Even a silent phone disconnects us.*

So it is not surprising that in the past twenty years we've seen a 40 percent decline in the markers for empathy among college students, most of it within the past ten years. It is a trend that researchers link to the new presence of digital communications.

Why do we spend so much time messaging each other if we end up feeling less connected to each other? In the short term, online communication makes us feel more in charge of our time and self-presentation. If we text rather than talk, we can have each other in amounts we can control. And texting and email and posting let us present the self we want to be. We can edit and retouch.

I call it the Goldilocks effect: We can't get enough of each other if we can have each other at a digital distance—not too close, not too far, just right.

But human relationships are rich, messy, and demanding. When we clean them up with technology, *we move from conversation to the efficiencies of mere connection.* I fear we forget the difference. And we forget that children who grow up in a world of digital devices don't know that there is a difference or that things were ever different. Studies show that when children hear less adult talk, they talk less. If we turn toward our phones and away from our children, we will start them off with a deficit of which they will be unaware. It won't be only about how much they talk. It will be about how much they understand the people they're talking with.

Indeed, when young people say, "Our texts are fine," they miss something important. What feels fine is that in the moment, so many of their moments are enhanced by digital reminders that they are wanted, a part of things. A day online has many of these "moments of more." But as digital connection becomes an ever larger part of their day, they risk ending up with lives of less.

I'd Rather Text than Talk

For many, a sentiment has become a litany, captured by the phrase "I'd rather text than talk." What people really mean is not only that they like to text but also that they don't like a certain kind of talk. They shy away from open-ended conversation. For most purposes, and sometimes even intimate ones, they would rather send a text message than hear a voice on the phone or be opposite someone face-to-face.

When I ask, "What's wrong with conversation?" answers are forthcoming. A young man in his senior year of high school makes things clear: "What's wrong with conversation? I'll tell you what's wrong with conversation! It takes place in real time and you can't control what you're going to say."

This reticence about conversation in "real time" is not confined to the young. Across generations, people struggle to control what feels like an endless stream of "incoming"—information to assimilate and act on and interactions to manage. Handling things online feels like the beginnings of a solution: At least we can answer questions at our convenience and edit our responses to get them "right."

The anxiety about spontaneity and the desire to manage our time means that certain conversations tend to fall away. Most endangered: the kind in which you listen intently to another person and expect that he or she is listening to you; where a discussion can go off on a tangent and circle back; where something unexpected can be discovered about a person or an idea. And there are other losses: In person, we have access to the messages carried in the face, the voice, and the body. Online, we settle for simpler fare: We get our efficiency and our chance to edit, but we learn to ask questions that a return email can answer.

The idea that we are living moments of more and lives of less is supported by a recent study in which pairs of college-aged friends were asked to communicate in four different ways: face-to-face conversation, video chat, audio chat, and online instant messaging. Then, the degree of emotional bonding in these friendships was assessed both by asking how people felt and watching how they behaved toward each other. The results were clear: In-person conversation led to the most emotional connection and online messaging led to the least. The students had tried to "warm up" their digital messages by using emoticons, typing out the sounds of laughter ("Hahaha"), and using the forced urgency of TYPING IN ALL CAPS. But these techniques had not done the job. It is when we see each other's faces and hear each other's voices that we become most human to each other.

Much of this seems like common sense. And it is. But I have said that something else is in play: Technology enchants. It makes us forget what we know about life.

We slip into thinking that always being connected is going to make us less lonely. But we are at risk because it is actually the reverse: If we are unable to be alone, we will be more lonely. And if we don't teach our children to be alone, they will only know how to be lonely.

Yet these days, so many people—adults and children—become anxious without a constant feed of online stimulation. In a quiet moment, they take out their phones, check their messages, send a text. They cannot tolerate time that some people I interviewed derisively termed "boring" or "a lull." But it is often when we hesitate, or stutter, or fall silent, that we reveal ourselves most to each other. And to ourselves.

"My Tiny God"

I'm not suggesting that we turn away from our devices. To the contrary, I'm suggesting that we look more closely at them to begin a more self-aware relationship with them.

So, for example, I have a colleague, Sharon, thirty-four, who describes herself as "happily texting" since 2002. But she is taken aback when she hears a friend refer to her smartphone as "my tiny god." The comment makes Sharon wonder about her own relationship with her phone. Are there ways in which she treats her own phone as a god? Perhaps.

As Sharon talks with me, it becomes clear that her main concern is how social media is shaping her sense of herself. She worries that she is spending too much time "performing" a better version of herself—one that will play well to her followers. She begins by saying that all interactions, certainly, have an element of performance. But online, she feels involved in her performances to the point that she has lost track of what is performance and what is not.

> I spend my time online wanting to be seen as witty, intelligent, involved, and having the right ironic distance from everything. Self-reflection should be more about, well, who I am, warts and all, how I really see myself. I worry that I'm giving up the responsibility for who I am to how other people see me. I'm not being rigorous about knowing my own mind, my own thoughts. You get lost in your performance. On Twitter, on Facebook, I'm geared toward showing my best self, showing me to be invulnerable or with as little vulnerability as possible.

Research tells us that being comfortable with our vulnerabilities is central to our happiness, our creativity, and even our productivity. We are drawn to this message, weary, it would seem, of our culture of continual performance. Yet life on social media encourages us to show ourselves, as Sharon puts it, as "invulnerable or with as little vulnerability as possible." Torn between our desire to express an authentic self and the pressure to show our best selves online, it is not surprising that frequent use of social media leads to feelings of depression and social anxiety.

And trouble with empathy. Research shows that those who use social media the most have difficulty reading human emotions, including their own. But the same research gives cause for optimism: We are resilient. Face-to-face conversation leads to greater self-esteem and an improved ability to deal with others. Again, *conversation cures*.

To those with Sharon's doubts, this book says you don't have to give up your phone. But if you understand its profound effects on you, you can approach your phone with greater intention and choose to live differently with it.

Pro-Conversation

So, my argument is not anti-technology. It's pro-conversation. We miss out on necessary conversations when we divide our attention between the people we're with and the world on our phones. Or when we go to our phones instead of claiming a quiet moment for ourselves. We have convinced ourselves that surfing the web is the same as daydreaming. That it provides the same space for self-reflection. It doesn't.

It's time to put technology in its place and reclaim conversation. That journey begins with a better understanding of what conversation accomplishes and how technology can get in its way. As things are now, even when people are determined to have in-person conversations, their plans are often derailed. Across generations, people tell me, "Everyone knows you shouldn't break up by text. That's wrong. A breakup deserves a face-to-face conversation." But almost everyone has a story to tell in which they or a friend broke up a relationship by text or email. Why? It's easier.

We are vulnerable, compelled and distracted by our devices. We can become different kinds of consumers of technology, just as we have become different kinds of consumers of food. Today, we are more discerning, with a greater understanding that what tempts does not necessarily nourish. So it can be with technology.

A ten-year-old in New York tells me that he and his father never talk alone, without the interruptions of a phone. I ask his father, forty, about this. The father admits, "He's right. On Sunday morning, when I walk with my son to get the newspaper, I don't go out without my phone." Why is that? "Because there might be an emergency." So far, no emergencies have come up, but on the walk to the corner store, he takes calls.

The real emergency may be parents and children not having conversations or sharing a silence between them that gives each the time to bring up a funny story or a troubling thought. A counselor at a device-free camp describes a common experience that the staff is having. If you go on a walk in the woods with a camper who has been acting up (perhaps getting into fights, perhaps bullying younger boys in the dining hall), an hour can go by in silence. Sometimes two. "And then," the counselor says, "and then, there will be the question. And then, there will be the conversation."

The Three Wishes

Our mobile devices seem to grant three wishes, as though gifts from a benevolent genie: first, that we will always be heard; second, that we can put our attention wherever we want it to be; and third, that we will never have to be alone. And the granting of these three wishes implies another reward: that we will never have to be bored. But in creative conversations, in conversations in which people get to really know each other, you usually have to tolerate a bit of boredom. People often struggle and stumble when they grapple with something new. Conversations of discovery tend to have long silences. But these days, people often tell me that silence is a "lull" from which they want to escape. When there is silence, "It's good to have your phone. There are always things to do on your phone." But before we had our phones, we might have found these silences "full" rather than boring. Now we retreat from them before we'll ever know.

I said that I began my research planning to investigate the sentiment "I'd rather text than talk." Technology makes possible so many new kinds of connections—on email, text, and Twitter, just for a start. I thought I would explore what makes them appealing and unique.

But soon my interviews—across generations—put another issue at center stage. What people say to each other when they are together is shaped by what their phones have taught them, and indeed by the simple fact that they have their phones with them. The presence of always-on and always-on-you technology—the brute fact of gadgets in the palm or on the table—changes the conversations we have when we talk in person. As I've noted, people with phones make themselves less vulnerable to each other and feel less connected to each other than those who talk without the presence of a phone on the landscape.

In the midst of our great experiment with technology, we are often caught between what we know we should do and the urge to check our phones. Across generations, we let technology take us away from conversation yet yearn for what we've lost. We reach for a moment of correction, an opportunity to recapture things we know by heart. When we invest in conversation, we get a payoff in self-knowledge, empathy, and the experience of community. When we move from conversation to mere connection, we get a lot of unintended consequences.

By now, several "generations" of children have grown up expecting parents and caretakers to be only half there. Many parents text at breakfast and dinner, and parents and babysitters ignore children when they take them to playgrounds and parks. In these new silences at meals and at playtime, caretakers are not modeling the skills of relationship, which are the same as the skills for conversation. These are above all empathic skills: You attend to the feelings of others; you signal that you will try to understand them. Children, too, text rather than talk with each other at school and on the playground. Anxious about the give-and-take of conversation, young people are uncertain in their attachments. And, anxious in their attachments, young people are uncertain about conversation.

These days, the first generation of children that grew up with smartphones is about to or has recently graduated from college. Intelligent and creative, they are at the beginning of their careers, but employers report that they come to work with unexpected phobias and anxieties. They don't know how to begin and end conversations. They have a hard time with eye contact. They say that talking on the telephone makes them anxious. It is worth asking a hard question: Are we unintentionally depriving our children of tools they need at the very moment they need them? Are we depriving them of skills that are crucial to friendship, creativity, love, and work?

A high school senior tells me he fears any conversation that he cannot edit and revise. But he senses its worth. "For later in life I'll need to learn how to have a conversation, learn how to find common ground." But for now, he is only wistful. He says, "Someday, someday soon, but certainly not now, I'd like to learn to have a conversation." His tone is serious. He knows what he does not know.

The Pilot in the Cockpit

Walking through a campus library or almost any office, one sees the same thing: people in their own bubbles, furiously typing on keyboards and tiny touch screens. A senior partner at a Boston law firm describes a scene at his office: Young associates lay out their suite of technologies: laptop, tablet, and multiple phones. And then they put their earphones on. "Big ones. Like pilots. They turn their desks into cockpits." With the young lawyers in their cockpits, the office is quiet, a quiet that does not ask to be broken.

The senior partner realizes that the junior associates retreat to their cockpits in the name of efficiency. But he says that if they end up not interacting with their colleagues, the fallout will be more damaging than what they gain from doing "all of those emails." He worries that life in the cockpit leaves the junior associates isolated from ongoing, informal conversations in the firm. He wants reassurance that the new recruits are part of the team. He believes that in the end, success at his firm demands a commitment to in-person collaboration.

There are times in business when electronic exchanges are the only choice. But in the law firm where the "pilot" works, many are *actively finding ways around face-to-face conversation*. There, the young recruits are forthright about wanting to avoid even the "real-time" commitment of a telephone call. And the senior partner says that the strategy of hiding from conversation "is catching," rapidly crossing generations. In fact, it is an older lawyer who first tells me that he doesn't like to interrupt his colleagues because "they're busy on their email," before he corrects himself: "Actually, I'm the one; I don't want to talk to people now. It's easier to just deal with colleagues on my phone." He, too, has become a "pilot." The isolation of the cockpit is not just for the young.

And we use technology to isolate ourselves at home as well as at work. I meet families who say they like to "talk problems out" by text or email or messaging rather than in person. Some refer to this practice as "fighting by text." They tell me that electronic talk "keeps the peace" because with this regime, there are no out-of-control confrontations. Tempers never flare. One mother argues that when family members don't fear outbursts, they are more likely to express their feelings.

A woman in her thirties lists the advantages of online disagreements with her partner: "We get our ideas out in a cooler way. We can fight without saying things we'll regret." And she adds another benefit: Fighting by text offers the possibility of documentation. "If we fight by text, I have a record of what was said."

In all of these cases, we use technology to "dial down" human contact, to titrate its nature and extent. People avoid face-to-face conversation but are comforted by being in touch with people—and sometimes with a lot of people—who are emotionally kept at bay. It's another instance of the Goldilocks effect. *It's part of the move from conversation to mere connection.*

At home, at school, at work, we see a flight from conversation. But in these moments of flight, there are moments of opportunity. We can reclaim conversation. Consider dinner.

Table Manners 2.0

Young people tell me it would be nice to have the attention of their friends at meals but that this has become an unrealistic expectation. Social norms work against it, plus "you don't really want to give up what's coming in on your phone." For anyone who grew up with texting, "continuous partial attention" is the new normal, but many are aware of the price they pay for its routines.

I interview college students who text continuously in each other's presence yet tell me they cherish the moments when their friends put down their phones. For them, what counts as a special moment is when you are with a friend who gets a text but chooses to ignore it, silencing his or her phone instead. For one woman, a college sophomore, "It's very special when someone turns away from a text to turn to a person." For a senior man, "If someone gets a text and apologizes and silences it [their phone], that sends a signal that they are there, they are listening to you."

A junior admits that she wants to ask her friends to put away their phones at meals but she can't do it because she would be socially out of line. "It's hard to ask someone to give you their undivided attention." She elaborates: "Imagine me saying, 'I'm so happy to see you, would you mind putting your phone away so that we can have a nice breakfast conversation?' And they would think, 'Well, that's really weird.'" Asking for full attention at a meal, she says, "would be age inappropriate."

What is "age appropriate" is that "rule of three," the mealtime strategy where you make sure that enough people are participating in a group conversation before you give yourself permission to look at your phone. Young people recognize that full attention is important, yet they are unwilling to give it to each other. They treat their friends the way that made them feel so bad when they were growing up with distracted parents—parents on phones.

Some young people accept their vulnerability to being distracted and try to design around it. They come up with a dinner game, usually played at a restaurant. It recognizes that everyone wants to text at dinner, but that the conversation is better if you don't. The game is called "cell phone tower." All the dinner guests take their phones and place them in a pile in the center of the table. No phones are turned off. The first person to touch a phone when it rings pays for the meal.

Why do you need a game to force you to pay attention to your friends? One college junior says that "rationally" she knows that if she sends a text to a friend during the dinner hour, it is reasonable that she won't get a reply until after dinner. And that's fine. But if someone sends *her* a text during dinner, she can't relax until she has responded. She says, "I tell myself, 'Don't read it at the table!' But you want to read it, you do read it; it's a weird little pressure to have."

This comment about the "weird little pressure" to respond immediately to a dinnertime text reminds me of a conversation I had with a student in one of my undergraduate seminars—a class on memoir—who came to office hours to tell me that although she felt committed to the seminar, she had been checking her phone during class time. She had been feeling guilty—in the class, after all, students had been telling their life stories—and she wanted to talk to me about her texting. She said she felt "compelled" to check her messages. Why? All she could offer was that she needed to know who was reaching out to her, who was interested in her. Her formulation: "We are not as strong as technology's pull." Phones exert a seductive undertow. The economies of the "cell phone tower" help individuals swim against the tide.

In all of this, there is no simple narrative of "digital natives" at ease in the world they grew up in. On the contrary. The story of conversation today is a story of conflict on a landscape of clear expectations.

Indeed, when college students talk about how they communicate today, they express seemingly irreconcilable positions. In a group of college juniors, one man goes from saying "All of my texting is logistical. It's just a convenience" to admitting that he can't follow most dinner conversations because he feels such pressure to keep up with his phone. Another makes wistful remarks about the future of communication, such as "Maybe something new will be invented." The implication is that this "something new" might be less distracting than what he has now. Two women say that they don't look forward to what they have now being in their future—but they can't imagine alternatives. One man suggests that maybe there isn't a problem at all: Humans are "co-evolving" with their phones to become a new species. But his note of optimism ends when he jokes about being "addicted to texting" because it "always feels safer than talking." He throws up his hands: "It's not my fault, my mother gave me my first phone." Advertisers know their customers. I look up at a sign in a San Francisco subway station for a food delivery service that will deliver from a wide range of restaurants in the Bay Area. It reads, "Everything great about eating combined with everything great about not talking to people!"

"I'm Sorry," Hit Send

In this atmosphere, we indulge a preference to apologize by text. It has always been hard to sit down and say you're sorry when you've made a mistake. Now we have alternatives that we find less stressful: We can send a photo with an annotation, or we can send a text or an email. We don't have to apologize to each other; we can type, "I'm sorry." And hit send. But face-to-face, you get to see that you have hurt the other person. The other person gets to see that you are upset. It is this realization that triggers the beginning of forgiveness.

None of this happens with "I'm sorry," *hit send*. At the moment of remorse, you export the feeling rather than allowing a moment of insight. You displace an inner conflict without processing it; you send the feeling off on its way. A face-to-face apology is an occasion to practice empathic skills. If you are the penitent, you are called upon to put yourself in someone else's shoes. And if you are the person receiving the apology, you, too, are asked to see things from the other side so that you can move toward empathy. In a digital connection, you can sidestep all this. So a lot is at stake when we move away from face-to-face apologies. If we don't put children in the situations that teach empathy (and a face-to-face apology is one of these), it is not surprising that they have difficulty seeing the effects of their words on others.

The "empathy gap" starts with young children and continues throughout life. A graduate student in economics comments on what is missing when her friends apologize by text. She calls it an "artificial truce."

> *The texted "I'm sorry" means, on the one hand, "I no longer want to have tension with you; let's be okay," and at the same time says, "I'm not going to be next to you while you go through your feelings; just let me know when our troubles are over." When I have a fight with my boyfriend and the fight ends with an "I'm sorry" text, it is 100 percent certain that the specific fight will come back again. It hasn't been resolved.*

The "I'm sorry" text is a missed opportunity. These opportunities can be seized. Parents can insist that their children's apologies be done in person. One mother explains that her always-connected son, now thirteen, had a habit of canceling family plans by sending an email or text to announce his intentions. She has changed the rules. Now, if he wants to cancel a plan—say, dinner with his grandparents—he has to make a phone call to break the date.

That real-time telephone call teaches that his proposed actions will affect others. His mother says, "He can hear how my mother made the roast chicken and it's already in the oven. He can hear that his grandfather has already bought the syrup to make ice cream sundaes." In sum, he can hear that he is expected and that his presence will be missed. She adds that since the new rules have gone into effect, there has rarely been a cancellation.

In-person apologies are no less potent in business settings. Managers tell me that a big part of their job has become teaching employees how to apologize face-to-face. One CEO says he cries out in frustration, even to longtime employees, "Apologize to him. Face-to-face. You were wrong. Say you are sorry." Another tells me that in business, not being able to say you're sorry face-to-face is "like driving a car but not knowing how to go in reverse." Essentially, it means you can't drive. In his view, he is working with a lot of people who need driving lessons.

"I Would Never Do This Face-to-Face. It's Too Emotional."

When we move from conversation to connection, we shortchange ourselves. My concern is that over time we stop caring—or perhaps worse, we forget there is a difference. Gretchen is a college sophomore who doesn't see a difference. She sits in my office and tells me she is having a hard time concentrating on her coursework. It's roommate trouble. She's been flirting with a roommate's ex-boyfriend. She started out meaning no harm, but things escalated. Now the ex-boyfriend is using her as a weapon against her roommate. When we speak, Gretchen is distracted. Her grades are a disaster. I ask her if she wants to talk to someone in the counseling center. She says no, she needs to make things right with her roommate. What her roommate needs to hear, says Gretchen, is her apology and "the honest truth." Gretchen adds, "That is what will restore my concentration."

I ask Gretchen if she is comfortable going home now; it's close to dinnertime and her roommate is probably at the dorm, no more than a ten-minute walk from my office. Gretchen looks confused as though my question has no meaning. "I'm going to talk to her on Gchat," she says. "I would never do this face-to-face. It's too emotional."

I was taken aback when Stephen Colbert—as his "character," a right-wing blowhard political talk show host—asked me a profound question during an appearance on his show: "Don't all these little tweets, these little sips of online connection, add up to one big gulp of real conversation?" My answer was no. Many sips of connection don't add up to a gulp of conversation.

Connecting in sips may work for gathering discrete bits of information or for saying "I am thinking about you." Or even for saying "I love you." But connecting in sips doesn't work so well for an apology. It doesn't work so well when we are called upon to see things from another's point of view. In these cases, we have to listen. We have to respond in real time. In these exchanges we show our temperament and character. We build trust.

Face-to-face conversation unfolds slowly. It teaches patience. We attend to tone and nuance. When we communicate on our digital devices, we learn different habits. As we ramp up the volume and velocity of our online connections, we want immediate answers. In order to get them, we ask simpler questions; we dumb down our communications, even on the most important matters. And we become accustomed to a life of constant interruption.

Interruptions? "This Is My Life."

On a balmy evening in June, I interview a group of twenty-five young people, from eighteen to twenty-four, who are in Boston for a summer study program. During our two hours together they tell me that if I really want to know how they communicate, I should be in their group chat. They are having it on an application for their mobile phones called WhatsApp. They invite me into their group, I accept, and our meeting continues. Now we are together in the room and online. Everything changes. Everyone is always "elsewhere" or just getting on their way. With everyone on the app, people switch rapidly between the talk in the room and the chat on their phones. At least half of the phone chat takes the form of images—cartoons, photos, and videos—many of which comment on the conversation in the room. As the students see it, images connect them, equal to any text or any talk.

In the room, the topic turns to how hard it is to separate from family and high school friends during college. But it is hard for this discussion to go very far because it is competing with the parallel activity of online chat and image curation.

Yet I see how happy these students are. They like moving in and out of talk, text, and images; they like the continual feed. And they like always having someplace *else* to go. They say that their greatest fear is boredom. If for a moment students don't find enough stimulation in the room, they go to the chat. If they don't find the images compelling, they look for new ones. But sharing an image you find on the web is a particular kind of participation. You don't turn to your own experience, but pull instead from external sources. You express yourself but can maintain a certain distance.

As all of this is going on, I remember saying to my daughter when she was three, "Use your words." At first I wonder at my association. I appreciate the pertinence (and the wit!) of the students' shared images, but to me, going to the images is also a way for these young people to slip away from our group conversation just as it becomes challenging. When things get complicated, it's easier to send a picture than to struggle with a hard idea. And another child-raising truism comes to mind, this one in my grandmother's voice: "Look at me when you speak to me." We teach children the outward manifestations of full attention because we hope that by working backward from behavior we can get them to a more profound feeling state. This is the feeling state of attachment and empathic connection. We don't ask children to use their words or to look at us to make them obedient. We want words to be associated with feelings. Eye contact is the most powerful path to human connection.

The students who invited me onto WhatsApp said I could understand them best if I shared their app. But once we shared WhatsApp, their faces were mostly turned down, eyes on their phones.

On this June evening, in the mash-up of talk, texts, and images, the students keep returning to the idea that digital conversations are valuable because they are "low risk." The students talk about how, when they are online, they can edit messages before sending them. And whether the text is to a potential employer or a romantic prospect, if it's important, they often ask friends to go over their writing to help ensure they are getting it "right." These are the perks of connection. But in conversations that could potentially take unexpected directions, people don't always try to get things "right." They learn to be surprised by the things they say. And to enjoy that experience. The philosopher Heinrich von Kleist calls this "the gradual completion of thoughts while speaking." Von Kleist quotes the French proverb that "appetite comes from eating" and observes that it is equally the case that "ideas come from speaking." The best thoughts, in his view, can be almost unintelligible as they emerge; what matters most is risky, thrilling conversation as a crucible for discovery. Notably, von Kleist is not interested in broadcasting or the kind of posting that social media would provide. The thrill of "risky talk" comes from being in the presence of and in close connection to your listener.

The idea that risky talk might be exciting is far from my students' minds during our evening on WhatsApp. In fact, someone in the group says that one of the good things about sending images is that it makes communication even *less* risky than sending edited texts. Like text, images can be edited. They can be cropped and passed through the perfect filter. And the more you manipulate them, he says, the more you can keep them ambiguous and "open to interpretation." He sees this as a good thing because you can't be hurt if you haven't declared yourself. But if you haven't declared yourself, you haven't tried out an idea. Or expressed a feeling. Declaring and defending yourself is how you learn to be forthright. It is a skill that helps in both love and politics.

In Boston, once the group is both talking out loud and attending to WhatsApp, all communications are constantly interrupted. Phones interrupt talk; talk interrupts phones. I ask everyone how they feel about these interruptions and my question hardly seems to make sense. This group doesn't experience the intrusions of WhatsApp as interruption. One young man says, commenting on the buzz, "This is my life."

In the new communications culture, *interruption is not experienced as interruption but as another connection.* Only half joking, people in their teens and twenties tell me that the most commonly heard phrase at dinner with their friends is "Wait, what?" Everyone is always missing a beat, the time it takes to find an image or send a text.

When people say they're "addicted" to their phones, they are not only saying that they want what their phones provide. They are also saying that they don't want what their phones allow them to avoid. The thing I hear most is that going to your phone makes it easier to avoid boredom or anxiety. But both of these may signal that you are learning something new, something alive and disruptive. You may be stretching yourself in a new direction. Boredom and anxiety are signs to attend more closely to things, not to turn away.

We don't live in a silent world of no talk. But we drop in and out of the talk we have. And we have very little patience for talk that demands sustained attention. When talk becomes difficult or when talk turns to quiet, we've given ourselves permission to go elsewhere. To avoid life's challenges and boring bits.

Life's Boring Bits

A college senior has a boy in her dorm room. They're in bed together. But when he goes to the bathroom, she takes out her phone and goes on Tinder, an app where she can check out men in the area who might be interested in meeting—or more. She says, "I have no idea why I did this—I really like this guy. . . . I want to date him, but I couldn't help myself. Nothing was happening on Facebook; I didn't have any new emails." Lying there in bed, waiting for her lover to come out of the bathroom, she had hit one of life's boring bits.

When I share this story with people under thirty, I usually get shrugs. This is how things are. A dull moment is never necessary. And you always want to know who is trying to reach you. Or who might be available to you. But the sensibility in which we want a constant stream of stimulation and expect to edit out life's "boring bits" has also come to characterize their elders.

A young father, thirty-four, tells me that when he gives his two-year-old daughter a bath, he finds it boring. And he's feeling guilty. Just a few nights earlier, instead of sitting patiently with her, talking and singing to her, as he did with his older children, he began to check email on his phone. And it wasn't the first time. "I know I shouldn't but I do," he says. "That bath time should be a time for relaxing with my daughter. But I can't do it. I'm on and off my phone the whole time. I find the downtime of her bath boring."

In a very different setting, Senator John McCain found himself feeling restless on the floor of the Senate during hearings on Syria. So he played poker on his iPhone to escape the feeling. When a picture of his game got into the press, McCain tweeted a joke about being caught out. "Scandal! Caught playing iPhone game at 3+ hour Senate hearing—worst of all I lost!"

Escaping to something like video poker when you come to a moment of boredom has become the norm. But when senators are comfortable saying that going "elsewhere" is normal during a hearing on the crisis in Syria, it becomes harder to expect full attention from anyone in any situation, certainly in any classroom or meeting. This is unfortunate because studies show that open screens degrade the performance of everyone who can see them—their owners and everyone sitting around them.

And we have to reconsider the value of the "boring bits" from which we flee. In work, love, and friendship, relationships of mutuality depend on listening to what might be boring to you but is of interest to someone else. In conversation, a "lull" may be on its way to becoming something else. If a moment in a conversation is slow, there is no way to know when things will pick up except to stay with the conversation. People take time to think and then they think of something new.

More generally, the experience of boredom is directly linked to creativity and innovation. I've said that, like anxiety, it can signal new learning. If we remain curious about our boredom, we can use it as a moment to step back and make a new connection. Or it offers a moment, as von Kleist would have it, to reach out and speak a thought that will only emerge in connection with a listener.

But now we turn away from such reverie and connection. The multitasking we can do on our digital devices makes us feel good immediately. What our brains want is new input—fresh, stimulating, and social. Before technology allowed us to be anywhere anytime, conversation with other people was a big part of how we satisfied our brains' need for stimulation. But now, through our devices, our brains are offered a continuous and endlessly diverting menu that requires less work.

So we move away from the slower pace, where you have to wait, listen, and let your mind go over things. We move away from the pace of human conversation. And so conversations without agenda, where you discover things as you go along, become harder for us. We haven't stopped talking, but we opt out, often unconsciously, of the kind of conversation that requires full attention. Every time you check your phone in company, what you gain is a hit of stimulation, a neurochemical shot, and what you lose is what a friend, teacher, parent, lover, or co-worker just said, meant, felt.

Does Technology Make Emotions Easy?

Clifford Nass was a cognitive psychologist and communications professor at Stanford University who also worked as a "dorm dad," living in a freshman dorm as a counselor and academic adviser. Nass describes how he tried to connect with one freshman by talking to her about his own high school emotional ups and downs. The student's response was that she and her friends were beyond those kinds of worries. Nass was surprised. Teenage angst was over? That's exactly what the freshman was saying, and she had a theory of why: Social media had stepped in to smooth things out. Her summation: "Technology makes emotions easy."

This freshman's comment inspired Nass to explore the relationship of online life and the emotional life of teenage girls. Was this young woman's intuition correct? In short, the answer was no. Technology does not make emotions easy. Social media can make emotional life very hard indeed.

Nass compared the emotional development of young women who considered themselves "highly connected" with those who spent less time online: The highly connected young women did not have as strong an ability to identify the feelings of other people or, indeed, to identify their own feelings. They felt less accepted by peers and did not have the same positive feelings from interacting with friends as those who used social media less frequently. Online life was associated with a loss of empathy and a diminished capacity for self-reflection.

This is not really surprising. If you are only partially present, it's easy to miss out on the emotional and nonverbal subtext of what people are saying to you. And you are not focusing on your own feelings either.

For Nass, the emotional tone of social media is another possible source of trouble. When students go online, some of what appeals to them is that they meet a world of good news. Facebook, Nass reminds us, has no "thumbs-down." You can feel disappointed if something you share doesn't get the number of positive reactions you want, but you train yourself to post what will please.

So, on social media, everyone learns to share the positive. But Nass points out that negative emotions require more processing in more parts of the brain. So if you spend a lot of time online—responding to positive emotions—you won't get practice with this more complex processing. As a result, says Nass, your reaction time will be slowed down. This may be what happens to frequent users of social media: They can't respond quickly to others or to themselves. When they respond slowly to others, they "seem insensitive and uncaring." When they respond slowly to themselves, they lose crucial capacities for self-reflection.

Nass worries that in the "thumbs-up" world of online life, young people learn the wrong life lessons. Among the wrong lessons they learn: First, negative emotions are something that unsuccessful kids have rather than normal parts of life that need to be addressed and coped with; second, it is natural to allow distraction and interruption to take you away from other people.

This is a lot of bad news. But here again, there is good news as well: Conversation cures. Nass compares the parts of the brain that process emotion to a muscle: They can atrophy if not exercised, and can be strengthened through face-to-face conversation. Nass says, "The one positive predictor of healthy emotional interactions as well as feelings of social success (statements such as 'people my age understand me' and 'I feel accepted by my friends'): lots of face-to-face communication." Nass sums it up: "Technology does not provide a sentimental education." People do.

Technology Does Not Provide a Sentimental Education

Reclaiming conversation begins with reclaiming our attention. These days, average American adults check their phones every six and a half minutes. We start early: There are now baby bouncers (and potty seats) that are manufactured with a slot to hold a digital device. A quarter of American teenagers are connected to a device within five minutes of waking up. Most teenagers send one hundred texts a day. Eighty percent sleep with their phones. Forty-four percent do not "unplug," ever, not even in religious services or when playing a sport or exercising.

All of this means that during the dinner hour, the typical American family is managing six or seven simultaneous streams of information. Scattered about are laptops, tablets, phones, a desktop, and of course, in the background, a television, perhaps two. College students who are using any form of media are likely to be using four at a time. If students are on Facebook, they are also on Netflix, a music blog, and their class reading. What happens to conversation here? We want it to be something to which we can pay attention in the same way that we pay attention to other things—that is, we want it to be something we can drop in and out of. Something like the "crawl" on the bottom of a cable news screen.

Again, we live in a world of unintended consequences. Hyperconnected, we imagine ourselves more efficient, but we are deceived. Multitasking degrades our performance at everything we do, all the while giving us the feeling that we are doing better at everything. So it makes us less productive no matter how good it makes us feel. And recall technology's deficiencies as a "sentimental education": Frequent multitasking is associated with depression, social anxiety, and trouble reading human emotions.

What is most hopeful is our resiliency. If children develop problems with self-esteem and empathy when they turn to screens at an early age, conversation, remarkably, seems able to reverse it. So, instead of doing your email as you push your daughter in her stroller, talk to her. Instead of putting a digital tablet in your son's baby bouncer, read to him and chat about the book. Instead of a quick text if you find a conversation going stale, make an effort to engage your peers.

But the talking cure is no simple matter. For one thing, we are wired to crave instant gratification, a fast pace, and unpredictability. That is, we are wired to crave what neuroscientists call "the seeking drive," the kind of experience that scrolling through a Twitter feed provides. And people who chronically multitask train their brains to crave multitasking. Those who multitask most frequently don't get better at it; they just want more of it. This means that conversation, the kind that demands focus, becomes more and more difficult.

A twenty-four-year-old young woman who works at a start-up tells me that she is no longer able to focus on one thing or one person at a time. And that's the problem with conversation; it asks for a skill she no longer can summon. "If I try to do one thing, I'm not good. I pick my nails off. I can't do it. I physically can't do one thing." At first her multitasking made her feel like Wonder Woman. Now she feels she needs help.

One college junior describes her "problem with conversation" in similar terms. It rules out multitasking, and multitasking is how she copes with life: "When you deal with people face-to-face, you are only seeing one of them at a time. When I get used to messaging with my Facebook groups, talking to one person at a time seems slow." After college, she took a break from Facebook. She deleted the app from her laptop and her phone. She was off Facebook for only a few weeks, but she says the experience "calmed" her. "I am less impatient with people," she says. "And for the first time I know I can be alone."

We could say we are "addicted to multitasking," but this is not the most helpful way to frame the problem. Our phones are part of our media ecology. We have to find a way to make our lives better with our phones. I prefer to think in terms of technological affordances—what technology makes possible (and often attractive and easy)—and human vulnerabilities. If you are addicted, you have to get off your drug. If you are vulnerable, you can work to be less vulnerable.

Thinking in terms of technological affordances and human vulnerabilities positions us to design for vulnerability. I meet with an inventor who observes that when people engage with smartphones, they are compelled into a new kind of vigilant behavior. "They want to make sure they're not missing anything," he says, "so they keep interacting with their devices." He makes this intriguing suggestion: "What if we designed a smartphone interface that made it easy for us to do a specific task (such as messaging a friend or family member) and then, instead of encouraging us to stay connected as long as possible, would encourage us to disengage? The interface would be designed to reduce our usage, and make spending more time on our phone a deliberate action." The point is not to make connection impossible or difficult. But it should demand intention; it should not be something the system helps you slide into. He says, "So instead of a phone that keeps us mesmerized, we may want to build a phone that lets us attend to our business and then gradually releases us because that is what is best for us."

We can design technology that demands that we use it with greater intention. And in our families, we can create sacred spaces—the living room, the dining room, the kitchen, the car—that are device-free. We can do the same thing at work—for certain meeting spaces and classes. We can plan for a future in which the design of our tools and our social surroundings encourages us to be our best. As consumers of digital media, our goal should be to partner with an industry that commits to our using their products, of course, but also to our health and emotional well-being.

"They Look like Deer Caught in the Headlights. They Don't Want to Have Another Conversation."

Conversation implies something kinetic. It is derived from words that mean "to tend to each other, to lean toward each other," words about the *activity of relationship*, one's "manner of conducting oneself in the world or in society; behavior, mode or course of life." To converse, you don't just have to perform turn taking, you have to listen to someone else, to read their body, their voice, their tone, and their silences. You bring your concern and experience to bear, and you expect the same from others.

When we express our anxiety about conversation, we express our anxiety about our ability to do all of this. A sixteen-year-old boy tells his mother that he has just received a text from his best friend. His friend's father has died. He tells his mother that he has texted his friend to say he is sorry. His mother, almost uncomprehending, asks, "Why didn't you call?" She is thinking about consolation. The boy says, "It isn't my place to interrupt him. He's too sad to talk on the phone." The boy assumes that conversation is intrusive even at moments that beg for intimacy.

I tell this story to a twenty-one-year-old college senior who has been working with me at my home every day for months, organizing my papers for an archive. She says that she wouldn't call me if she heard that there had been a death in my family. She says that she *knows* I would be more comforted by a call, that it would mean more to me. But she echoes the sentiments of the sixteen-year-old boy. She says, "Anything having to do with the voice feels like an interruption."

One high school senior talks about a plan to put himself on a self-improvement program. He is going to "force himself" to use the telephone. I ask him why. "It might," he says, "be a way to teach myself to have a conversation . . . rather than spending my life in awkward silence. I feel like phone conversations nowadays will help me in the long run."

This is a poignant admission. This young man acknowledges that for all his many hours a day texting and messaging, he has not learned how to listen and respond. At news of a death, he, too, would send an email. These days, there are college courses on conversation. The curriculum includes how to pay attention to someone on a date. How to disagree with someone politically. It is an acknowledgment that students are comfortable going to bed with each other but not talking to each other. They will know each other's sexual preferences but not if their partner has a widowed father or an autistic sister. They may not even know if their partner has siblings at all.

Employers have come to appreciate the vulnerability of the new generations. Some businesses explicitly screen for an ability to converse. A vice-president at a large pharmaceutical company tells me her strategy for hiring new recruits. "It's very simple," she says. "I have a conversation with them."

Most applicants are prepped for one conversation. And then at the end, I tell the potential recruits that their homework is to organize what we've discussed and from that make an agenda of interesting themes for our next conversation . . . hopefully tomorrow or the day following. They are stunned. They look like deer caught in the headlights. They don't want to have another conversation. They were hoping for some follow-up emails.

The Three Chairs

In the chapters that follow, I look at the kinds of conversation Thoreau envisaged when he described the three chairs in his cabin. The story begins with *one-chair conversations*, those of solitude. Solitude does not necessarily mean being alone. It is a state of conscious retreat, a gathering of the self. The capacity for solitude makes relationships with others more authentic. Because you know who you are, you can see others for who they are, not for who you need them to be. So solitude enables richer conversation. But our current way of life undermines our capacity for solitude.

I've said that, these days, being alone feels like a problem that needs to be solved, and people try to solve it with technology. But here, digital connection is more a symptom than a cure. It expresses but it doesn't solve the underlying problem—a discomfort with being alone. And, more than a symptom, constant connection is changing the way people think of themselves. It is shaping a new way of being. I call it "I share, therefore I am." We share our thoughts and feelings in order to feel whole.

In order to feel more, and to feel more like ourselves, we connect. But in our rush to connect, we flee solitude. In time, our ability to be separate and gather ourselves is diminished. If we don't know who we are when we are alone, we turn to other people to support our sense of self. This makes it impossible to fully experience others as who they are. We take what we need from them in bits and pieces; it is as though we use them as spare parts to support our fragile selves.

If you don't have practice in thinking alone, you are less able to bring your ideas to the table with confidence and authority. Collaboration suffers. As does innovation, which requires a capacity for solitude that continual connection diminishes.

A love of solitude and self-reflection enables sociability. Many think of Thoreau as a recluse. He was anything but. In fact, his friends joked that he could hear the Emerson family dinner bell from his cabin in the woods. Thoreau's *two-chair conversations* are with friends, family, and romantic partners.

These days, parents complain that children won't talk to them because they are so busy with their phones at mealtime; children have the same complaints about their parents. Parents respond that children don't have the "standing" to make this kind of complaint. During meals, children go to their phones. We are at an odd standoff with neither side happy.

In a television commercial for Facebook, a large, gregarious family sits down to a meal. It is a Norman Rockwell moment. In our positive associations to family dinner, myth and science come together. We know that for children the best predictor of success later in life is the number of meals shared with their families. The dinner in the Facebook commercial looks like one of those dinners that everyone knows they are supposed to love.

Just as the viewer locks on to this image of unconditional "good," the narrative is disrupted. An older woman at the table—let me call her "boring Auntie"—begins a painfully dull story about trying to buy a chicken at the market. A teenage girl at the table does the predictable: She pulls out her phone and goes onto Facebook. Immediately, the scene is populated with scenes from her newsfeed: A friend plays the drums, another performs ballet, yet others are in a snowball fight. The teenager is no longer at dinner. She is elsewhere.

We once taught our children to ignore a ringing phone at dinner. We became annoyed if telemarketers interrupted us. Now, Facebook suggests that it may be a good thing to interrupt dinner *ourselves*.

And then there are *three-chair conversations*, conversations in the social world. Here I begin with examples from the world of work. I look at my own kind of workplace, the world of education, and also the business and corporate world. I saw striking commonalities between education and business, between the dynamics of classrooms and offices. I found conversation to be at the heart of the learning culture and I learned that conversation is good for the bottom line.

And both domains face similar threats to their cultures of conversation. In classrooms and offices, the cultural expectation for multitasking subverts conversation and constant interruption threatens achievement. Just as we go to dinners with friends that are not quite dinners together, we go to classes that are not quite classes and work meetings that are not quite meetings. What these not quite encounters have in common is that we all feel free to be on some device and to let our minds wander.

And, most recently, in both education and at work, conversation is challenged by new experiments that use technology to engage people from a distance. So, for example, there is the hope that online courses will make remote learning more "efficient" in ways that can be measured. One unexpected result of the online experiments has been to make the value of teachers and students talking face-to-face ever more clear. A teacher "live" in front of a classroom gives students an opportunity to watch someone think, boring bits and all. That teacher is a model for how thinking happens, including false starts and hindsight. There has been a parallel development in the workplace: Many of the firms that encouraged employees to work at home are calling them back to the office in order to have a more collaborative and productive workforce.

Of course, in many businesses, remote work is the cost-saving rule. I interview an executive, Howard Chen, who is the creator of a social media site for a multinational corporation. He is passionate about the necessity for advanced social media in his company because it has decided to close down local offices. In their place is a new system called "hoteling." When people need the resources of an office, they bring their computer to a building where an automated system assigns them a room. When they get there and plug in their computer, a virtual telephone pops up on the screen. That is their company line for the day. They are "at work."

So when Chen goes to the office, there are no regular colleagues around, no community at all. But this is all the more reason for him to be excited about the new social network he has designed. He dreams that it will restore life to his work environment, now stripped so bare of familiar objects and people. On the day I meet him, we are in a new hotel space. He responds to his unfamiliar physical surrounds by extolling the "sociability" of his social media. With only a few keystrokes he can call up an international database of all employees and their interests. This, he hopes, can be the basis for online conversations and new connections. He says, "Yeah, if you're a soccer fan, you can talk to all the other soccer fans in the company. How cool is that?" But as an aside, he says that recently he has been feeling rather sad:

Last week I was sitting there and I finished doing something and I looked around and you could hear a pin drop. And I'm, like, this is ghastly. It's just horrible. So I took out my iPhone and I recorded the silence for a minute to show my wife. This is what it sounds like, or doesn't sound like, at work.

We work so hard to build our online connections. We have so much faith in them. But we must take care that in the end we do not simply feel alone with our devices.

This is all the more important because although the flight from conversation affects us as individuals, it also changes our life in communities. Here I consider three questions about politics and social policy on our new digital landscape.

First, the Internet gives us the possibility of sharing our views with anyone in the world, but it also can support information silos where we don't talk to anyone who doesn't agree with us. Studies show that people don't like posting things that their followers won't agree with—everyone wants to be liked. So technology can sustain ever more rigid partisanship that makes it hard to talk, enabling us to live in information bubbles that don't let in dissenting voices.

Second, when politics goes online, people begin to talk about political action in terms of things they can do online. They are drawn to the idea that social change can happen by giving a "thumbs-up" or by subscribing to a group. The slow, hard work of politics—study, analysis, listening, trying to convince someone with a different point of view—these can get lost. The Internet is a good start, a place to bring people together. But politics continues in conversation and in relationships developed over time. I have said that technology gives us the illusion of companionship without the demands of friendship. Now I worry that it can also give us the illusion of progress without the demands of action.

Third, digital communication makes surveillance easier. The corporations that provide us with the means to talk on the net (to text, email, and chat) take our online activity as data. They declare ownership of it and use it, usually to better sell things to us. And we now know that our government routinely makes a copy of our communications as well. The boundaries have blurred between private communication and routine surveillance, between private communication and its repackaging as a commodity. So, in addition to the question *What is intimacy without privacy?* I consider another: *What is democracy without privacy?*

The Fourth Chair

And I think of a "fourth chair." I've said that when conversation got expansive, Thoreau took his guests into nature. I think of this as his fourth chair, his most philosophical one. These days, the way things have gotten philosophical causes us to confront how we have used technology to create a second nature, an artificial nature. For so long we have assumed that the conversations that matter are the conversations we have with other people. In recent years, this idea has been challenged by computer programs that seduce us not by their smarts but by their sociability. I explore proposals for new, more intimate conversations with "socially" competent machines—a development with the potential to change human nature itself. For me, our *fourth-chair conversations* are ones that Thoreau could not have envisaged: We are tempted to talk not only through machines but to them, with them.

At first, we met Siri, a digital companion always ready to engage. But that was just the beginning. As I write these words, the media is full of stories about the launch of the first "home robots" who are there to be always-available "best friendly companions" by acting as though they understand what you are saying when they exchange pleasantries through the magic of simulated feelings. Have we forgotten what conversation is? What friendship is? Is talking to machines companionship or abandonment?

We lose our words. *Intelligence* once meant more than what any artificial intelligence does. It used to include sensibility, sensitivity, awareness, discernment, reason, acumen, and wit. And yet we readily call machines intelligent now. *Affective* is another word that once meant a lot more than what any machine can deliver. Yet we have become used to describing machines that portray emotional states or can sense our emotional states as exemplars of "affective computing." These new meanings become our new normal, and we forget other meanings. We have to struggle to recapture lost language, lost meanings, and perhaps, in time, lost experiences.

At one conference I attended, the robots were called "caring machines," and when I objected, I was told we were using this word not because the robots care but because they will take care of us. Caring is a behavior. It is a function, not a feeling. The conference participants seemed puzzled: Why did I care so much about semantics? What's wrong with me?

It is natural for words to change their meaning over time and with new circumstances. *Intelligence* and *affective* have changed their meaning to accommodate what machines can do. But now the words *caring, friend, companionship*, and *conversation*?

A lot is at stake in these words. They are not yet lost. We need to remember these words and this conversation before we don't know how to have it. Or before we think we can have it with a machine.

We paint ourselves into a corner where we endanger more than words.

I talk of our having arrived at a "robotic moment," not because we have built robots that can be our companions but because we are willing to consider becoming theirs. I find people increasingly open to the idea that in the near future, machine companionship will be sufficient unto the day. People tell me that if a machine could give them the "feeling" of being intimately understood, that might be understanding enough. Or intimacy enough.

The ironies are substantial. We turn toward artificial intelligence for conversation just at the moment that we are in flight from conversations with each other.

More generally, in our fourth-chair conversations, we imagine ourselves in a new kind of world where machines talk to each other to make our lives easier. But who will we become in this world we call friction-free where machines (and without our doing any talking at all!) will know what we want, sometimes even before we do? They will know all about our online lives, so they'll know our taste in music, art, politics, clothes, books, and food. They'll know who we like and where we travel.

In that world, your smartphone will signal your favorite coffee shop as you set out in the morning to get a latte, which of course will be waiting for you when you arrive, exactly as you want it. In the spirit of friction-free, your phone will be able to reroute and guide you so that you can avoid your ex-girlfriend and see only designated friends on your path. But who said that a life without conflict, without being reminded of past mistakes, past pain, or one where you can avoid rubbing shoulders with troublesome people, is good? Was it the same person who said that life shouldn't have boring bits? In this case, if technology gives us the feeling that we can communicate with total control, life's contingencies become a problem. Just because technology can help us solve a "problem" doesn't mean it was a problem in the first place.

Paths Forward

I explore the flight from conversation in digital culture by looking at big questions and small details. I begin with the conversations of solitude, romance, friendship, and family life and end with our desire to chat with robots. I report on the current state of conversation in schools, universities, and corporations, looking at children as they develop and adults as they love, learn, and work. In every case, I describe our vulnerability to settling for mere connection—why it tempts—and I make the case for reclaiming the richness of conversation.

Reclaiming conversation won't be easy. We resist: It sometimes seems that we want to be taken away from the conversations that count. So I go to meetings where laptops are open and phones turned on. Yet the participants admit that constant interruptions are interfering with group work. When I ask the participants why they all continue to bring their devices to meetings, they say, "For emergencies." I inquire further, and they admit that it's not so much about emergencies—they're bored, or they see an opportunity to double down on their emails. And other reasons come up: Some feel so much pressure to outsmart their peers that when they feel they can't, they turn to their phones, pretending to do something else more "urgent" than anything that could be going on in the meeting. And sometimes the idea of "emergencies" on their phones is a strategy to step away from each other and their differences, to defer them for another day, another meeting.

And sometimes, I am told, they actively want to avoid the spontaneity of conversation. The desire for the edited life crosses generations, but the young consider it their birthright. A college senior doesn't go to his professors' office hours. He will correspond with his teachers only through email. The student explains that if he sees his professors in person, he could get something "wrong." Ever since ninth grade, when his preparations to go to an Ivy League college began in earnest, he and his parents have worked on his getting everything "right." If he wasn't getting enough playing time on a team, his father went in to see the coach. When his College Board scores weren't high enough, he had personal tutors. He had no interest in science, but his high school guidance counselor decided that a summer program in neurobiology was what he needed to round out his college application. Now he is three years through that Ivy education and hoping for law school. He is still trying to get things right. "When you talk in person," he says, "you are likely to make a slip."

He thinks his no-office-hours policy is a reasonable strategy. He tells me that our culture has "zero tolerance" for making mistakes. If politicians make "slips," it haunts them throughout their careers. And usually they make these mistakes while they are talking. He says, "I feel as though everyone in my generation wants to write things out—I certainly do—because then I can check it over and make sure it is okay. I don't want to say a wrong thing."

Studying conversation today brings forth many comments like these. They encourage a fresh look at our cultural expectations of getting everything "right." And a fresh look at what we accomplish when we communicate perfection as a value to our children. Studying conversation suggests that it is time to rediscover an interest in the spontaneous. It suggests that it is time to rediscover an interest in the points of view of those with whom we disagree. And it suggests that we slow down enough to listen to them, one at a time.

These are not easy assignments. But I am hopeful about our moment. Some of the most "plugged in" people in America find conversation blocked and struggle for ways to reclaim it. Corporations devise strategies for workplace teams built on face-to-face meetings. They ask employees to take a break and not check their email after business hours. Or they insist that employees take a "smartphone-free" night during the business week. One CEO sets up pre-workday breakfasts where there are no phones or scheduled meetings. Others begin the day with technology-free "stand-up meetings." There are new corporate programs for emotional self-help in an age of overconnection: I meet executives on technology "time-outs," Sabbaths, and sabbaticals.

Even Silicon Valley parents who work for social media companies tell me that they send their children to technology-free schools in the hope that this will give their children greater emotional and intellectual range. Many were surprised to learn that Steve Jobs did not encourage his own children's use of iPads or iPhones. His biographer reports that in Jobs's family, the focus was on conversation: "Every evening Steve made a point of having dinner at the big long table in their kitchen, discussing books and history and a variety of things. No one ever pulled out an iPad or computer." Our technological mandarins don't always live the life they build for others. They go to vacation spots deemed "device-free" (that don't allow phones, tablets, or laptops). This means that America has curious new digital divides. In our use of media, there are the haves and have-nots. And then there are those who have-so-much-that-they-know-when-to-put-it-away.

Sometimes people sense that there is a flight from conversation but want technology to restore it for them. When I give talks about the importance of conversation for young children, sometimes teachers in the audience will come up at the end of my presentation to say that they wholeheartedly agree ("Kids can't talk anymore") but go on to tell me how they are using messaging on the iPad to try to increase student sociability. Apps for sociability may increase sociability on apps; what children are missing, however, is an ease with each other face-to-face, the context in which empathy is born. Indeed, empathy, too, will have its own technologies: The researcher who found a 40 percent decrease in empathy in college students over the past twenty years has begun to develop apps for smartphones to encourage empathic habits.

Clearly, her finding about the decrease in empathy did not feel like something she wanted to accept. It felt like something that called for action. But does a decrease in teenage empathy suggest the need for an empathy app? Or does it suggest that we make more time to talk to teenagers?

Sometimes it seems easier to invent a new technology than to start a conversation.

Every new technology offers an opportunity to ask if it serves our human purposes. From there begins the work of making technology better serve these purposes. It took generations to get nutrition labels on food; it took generations to get speed limits on roads and seat belts and air bags into cars. But food and transportation technology are safer because all of these are now in place. In the case of communications technology, we have just begun.

In every encounter, we need to use the right tool for the job. Sometimes face-to-face conversation is not the right tool for a particular job. But having the whole person before you is reliably the best way to begin. It gives you the most information to decide which communication tools you need as you move forward. But what I've found is that once people have texting, chat, and email available, they stick with them even when they suspect that these are not the right tools for the job. Why? They are convenient. They make us feel in control. But when we allow ourselves to be vulnerable and less in control, our relationships, creativity, and productivity thrive.

We are at a crossroads: So many people say they have no time to talk, really talk, but all the time in the world, day and night, to connect. When a moment of boredom arises, we have become accustomed to making it go away by searching for something—sometimes *anything*—on our phones. The next step is to take the same moment and respond by searching within ourselves. To do this, we have to cultivate the self as a resource. Beginning with the capacity for solitude.

One Chair

Solitude

I Share, Therefore I Am

You need to build an ability to just be yourself and not be
doing something. That's what the phones are taking away.
The ability to just sit there. That's just being a person.

—LOUIS C.K., ACTOR AND COMEDIAN

In 2013, Louis C.K. brought the necessity for solitude, especially for children, to a late-night television audience. He began by telling Conan O'Brien how he explains to his two daughters why they can't have cell phones. He set the stage by making clear that when it comes to his children, he takes the long view: "I'm not raising the children. I'm raising the grown-ups that they're going to be." For him, phones are "toxic, especially for kids."

They don't look at people when they talk to them. And they don't build the empathy. You know, kids are mean. And it's because they're trying it out. They look at a kid and they go, "You're fat." And then they see the kid's face scrunch up and they go, "Ooh, that doesn't feel good to make a person do that."... But when they write "You're fat," then they just go, "Mmm, that was fun. I like that."...

You need to build an ability to just be yourself and not be doing something. That's what the phones are taking away. The ability to just sit there. That's just being a person.... Because underneath everything in your life there is that thing, that empty, forever empty. That knowl-edge that it's all for nothing and you're alone. It's down there. And sometimes when things clear away and you're not watching and you're in your car and you start going, Ooh, here it comes that I'm alone, like it starts to visit on you just like this sadness. Life is tremendously sad. . . . That's why we text and drive. Pretty much 100 percent of people driving are texting. And they're killing and murdering each other with their cars. But people are willing to risk taking their life and ruin-ing another because they don't want to be alone for a second. . . . I was alone in my car and a Bruce Springsteen song came on . . . and I heard it and it gave me a kind of fall, back-to-school-depression feeling and it made me feel really sad and so I went, "Okay, I'm getting really sad," so I had to get the phone and write "Hi" to, like, fifty people. . . . Anyway, I started to get that sad feeling and reached for the phone and then I said, "You know what: Don't. Just be sad. Just stand in the way of it and let it hit you like a truck."

So I pulled over and I just cried like a bitch. I cried so much and it was beautiful. . . . Sadness is poetic. . . . You are lucky to live sad mo-ments. And then I had happy feelings because when you let yourself have sad feelings your body has like antibodies that come rushing in to meet the sad feelings. But because we don't want that first feeling of sad, we push it away with our phones. So you never feel completely happy or completely sad. You just feel kind of satisfied with your products. And then . . . you die.

So that's why I don't want to get a phone for my kids.

The Virtues of Solitude

Solitude doesn't necessarily mean a lack of activity. You know you are experiencing solitude when what you are doing brings you back to yourself. The writer Susan Cain has persuasively argued that solitude is important for introverts and that introverts are a significant number among us. Louis C.K. provides poetic support for an even broader argument. Solitude is important for everyone, including the most extroverted people. It's the time you become familiar and comfortable with yourself. And developing the capacity for solitude is one of the most important tasks of childhood, every childhood.

It's the capacity for solitude that allows you to reach out to others and see them as separate and independent. You don't need them to be anything other than who they are. This means you can listen to them and hear what they have to say. This makes the capacity for solitude essential to the development of empathy. And this is why solitude marks the beginning of conversation's virtuous circle. If you are comfortable with yourself, you can put yourself in someone else's place.

In his soliloquy on solitude, Louis C.K. raises a concern that lies beneath the surface of so many anxious conversations about children and technology. What if children are so absorbed in their phones that the alchemy of solitude and the capacity for empathy doesn't take place? Without empathy, the comedian points out, we don't understand the impact we have when we bully others because we don't see them as people like ourselves.

Developmental psychology has long made the case for the importance of solitude. And now so does neuroscience. It is only when we are alone with our thoughts—not reacting to external stimuli—that we engage that part of the brain's basic infrastructure devoted to building up a sense of our stable autobiographical past. This is the "default mode network." So, without solitude, we can't construct a stable sense of self. Yet children who grow up digital have always had something external to respond to. When they go online, their minds are not wandering but rather are captured and divided.

These days, we may mistake time on the net for solitude. It isn't. In fact, solitude is challenged by our habit of turning to our screens rather than inward. And it is challenged by our culture of continual sharing. People who grew up with social media will often say that they don't feel like themselves; indeed, they sometimes can't *feel* themselves, unless they are posting, messaging, or texting. Sometimes people say that they need to share a thought or feeling in order to think it, feel it. This is the sensibility of "I share, therefore I am." Or otherwise put: "I want to have a feeling; I need to send a text."

With this sensibility we risk building a false self, based on performances we think others will enjoy. In Thoreau's terms, we live too "thickly," responding to the world around rather than first learning to know ourselves.

In recent years, psychologists have learned more about how creative ideas come from the reveries of solitude. When we let our minds wander, we set our brains free. Our brains are most productive when there is no demand that they be reactive. For some, this goes against cultural expectations. American culture tends to worship sociality. We have *wanted* to believe that we are our most creative during "brainstorming" and "group-think" sessions. But this turns out not to be the case. New ideas are more likely to emerge from people thinking on their own. Solitude is where we learn to trust our imaginations.

When children grow up with time alone with their thoughts, they feel a certain ground under their feet. Their imaginations bring them comfort. If children always have something outside of themselves to respond to, they don't build up this resource. So it is not surprising that today young people become anxious if they are alone without a device. They are likely to say they are bored. From the youngest ages they have been diverted by structured play and the shiny objects of digital culture.

Shiny Objects

We have embarked on a giant experiment in which our children are the human subjects.

Breast-feeding mothers, fathers pushing strollers—their phones are rarely out of sight. New studies correlate the growing number of cell phones and the rise of playground accidents because at the park, parents and caretakers are paying attention to phones.

In every culture, young children want the objects of grown-up desire. So our children tell us they want phones and tablets, and, if they can afford it, very few parents say no. In parental slang, giving a smartphone to quiet your toddler in the rear seat of the car is known as the "pass-back."

In a moment of quiet, children have an alternative to turning within. And they are taken away from human faces and voices, because we let screens do jobs that people used to do—for example, reading to children and playing games with them. Checkers with your grandparents is an occasion to talk; checkers with a computer program is an occasion to strategize and perhaps be allowed to win. Screens serve up all kinds of educational, emotional, artistic, and erotic experiences, but they don't encourage solitude and they don't teach the richness of face-to-face conversation.

A fourteen-year-old girl sums up her feelings about spending an hour on Facebook: "Even if it is just seeing the 'likes' on things I posted, I feel that I've accomplished something." What has she accomplished? Time on Facebook makes a predictable outcome (if you post a likable photograph you will get "likes") feel like an achievement. Online, we become accustomed to the idea of nearly guaranteed results, something that the ups and downs of solitude can't promise. And, of course, time with people can't promise it either.

When children have experience in conversation, they learn that practice never leads to perfect but that perfect isn't the point. But perfect can be the goal in a simulation—in a computer game, for example. If you are tutored by simulation, you may become fearful of not being in control even when control is not the point.

An eight-year-old boy is in a park, his back against a large tree. He is engrossed in his shiny object—a small tablet computer, a recent present. He plays a treasure-hunt game that connects him with a network of players all over the world. The boy bites his lip in concentration as his fingers do their work. From the point of view of the other children in the park, the boy is carrying a Do Not Disturb sign. His focus marks him as unavailable to join in a round of Frisbee, maybe, or a race to climb the monkey bars. This is not a day he will accept such an invitation, or make one himself. This is not a day he will learn to ask questions of other children or listen to their answers. And most of the adults at the park are staring at screens; the eight-year-old is connected in the game, but in the park, he is very much alone.

Yet unlike time in nature or with a book, where his mind might wander, the experience of his online game drives him back to the task at hand. He masters the rules of a virtual treasure hunt but doesn't get to hang by his knees on a jungle gym, contemplating the patterns in an upside-down winter sky.

Whereas screen activity tends to rev kids up, the concrete worlds of modeling clay, finger paints, and building blocks slow them down. The physicality of these materials—the sticky thickness of clay, the hard solidity of blocks—offers a very real resistance that gives children time to think, to use their imaginations, to make up their own worlds.

The psychoanalyst Erik Erikson, a specialist in adolescent development, wrote that children thrive when they are given time and stillness. The shiny objects of today's childhood demand time and interrupt stillness.

Of course, there are many ways to use the computer that encourage children to work creatively. One example is when children don't simply play computer games but learn to program so that they can build their own games. But when we expect to see children at screens, that becomes the new normal and we stop noticing the details. We stop noticing exactly what is on our children's screens. What we need to do is stop seeing child and screen as natural partners. Then, we can step back and notice what exactly is on those screens. Then, we can talk about what we want childhood to accomplish.

"Alone With"

How can the capacity for solitude be cultivated? With attention and respectful conversation.

Children develop the capacity for solitude in the presence of an attentive other. Consider the silences that fall when you take a young boy on a quiet walk in nature. The child comes to feel increasingly aware of what it is to be alone in nature, supported by being "with" someone who is introducing him to this experience. Gradually, the child takes walks alone. Or imagine a mother giving her two-year-old daughter a bath, allowing the girl's reverie with her bath toys as she makes up stories and learns to be alone with her thoughts, all the while knowing her mother is present and available to her. Gradually, the bath, taken alone, is a time when the child is comfortable with her imagination. Attachment enables solitude.

So we practice being "alone with"—and, if successful, end up with a self peopled by those who have mattered most. Hannah Arendt talks about the solitary person as free to keep himself company. He is not lonely, but always accompanied, "together with himself." For Arendt, "All thinking, strictly speaking, is done in solitude and is a dialogue between me and myself; but this dialogue of the two-in-one does not lose contact with the world of my fellow-men because they are represented in the self with whom I lead the dialogue of thought."

Paul Tillich has a beautiful formulation: "Language . . . has created the word 'loneliness' to express the pain of being alone. And it has created the word 'solitude' to express the glory of being alone." Loneliness is painful, emotionally and even physically, born from a "want of intimacy" when we need it most, in early childhood. Solitude—the capacity to be contentedly and constructively alone—is built from successful human connection at just that time. But if we don't have experience with solitude—and this is often the case today—we start to equate loneliness and solitude. This reflects the impoverishment of our experience. If we don't know the satisfactions of solitude, we only know the panic of loneliness.

Recently, I was working on my computer during a train ride from Boston to New York, passing through a snowy Connecticut landscape. I wouldn't have known this but for the fact that I looked up when I walked to the dining car to get a coffee. As I did, I noted that every other adult on the train was staring at a screen. We deny ourselves the benefits of solitude because we see the time it requires as a resource to exploit. Instead of using time alone to think (or not think), we think of filling it with digital connection.

And we get our children to live the same way. The children on the Boston–New York train had their own devices—tablets and phones. I said that we use digital "passbacks" to placate young children who say they are bored. We are not teaching them that boredom can be recognized as your imagination calling you.

Of course, any too-poetic picture of solitude needs correction. Solitude may be a touchstone for empathy and creativity, but it certainly does not always feel good. For the poet Rainer Maria Rilke, "Openness, patience, receptivity, solitude is everything." And yet, in a way that Louis C.K. would have understood, Rilke confronted its difficulty: "And you should not let yourself be confused in your solitude by the fact that there is something in you that wants to move out of it." Indeed, research shows that adolescents experience solitude as downtime that can feel bad in the short run. But in the long run it facilitates healthy development. Without solitude, in days and nights of continual connection, we may experience those "moments of more" but lives of less.

When I ask children and teens about quiet time alone with their thoughts, most tell me that it is not something they seek. As soon as they are alone, they reach for their phones. No matter where they are. Most are already sleeping with their phones. So, if they wake up in the middle of the night, they check their messages. They never take a walk without their phones. Time alone is not, most say, something their parents taught them to value. If we care about solitude, we have to communicate this to our children. They are not going to pick it up on their own. And more than telling our children that we value solitude, we have to show them that we think it is important by finding some for ourselves.

Disconnection Anxiety

We have testimony about solitude from the most creative among us. For Mozart, "When I am, as it were, completely myself, entirely alone, and of good cheer—say, traveling in a carriage or walking after a good meal or during the night when I cannot sleep—it is on such occasions that my ideas flow best and most abundantly." For Kafka, "You need not leave your room. Remain sitting at your table and listen. You need not even listen, simply wait, just learn to become quiet, and still, and solitary. The world will freely offer itself to you to be unmasked." For Thomas Mann, "Solitude gives birth to the original in us, to beauty unfamiliar and perilous—to poetry." For Picasso, "Without great solitude, no serious work is possible."

Answering these warm poetic voices are the cool results of social science. Susan Cain, writing about the importance of privacy for creative work, cites a study known as "The Coding War Games." Here, researchers compared the work of more than six hundred programmers at ninety-two companies. Within companies, programmers performed at about the same level, but among different organizations, the performance gaps were striking. One thing characterized the programmers in the high-performing organizations: They had more privacy. The top performers "overwhelmingly worked for companies that gave their workers the most privacy, personal space, control over their physical environments, and freedom from interruption."

It is not surprising that privacy allows for greater creativity. When we let our focus shift away from the people and things around us, we are better able to think critically about our own thoughts, a process psychologists call meta-cognition. Everyone has this potential. The important thing is to nurture it. The danger is that in a life of constant connection, we lose the capacity to do so.

A vice-president of a Fortune 500 company tells me that he recently had to write an important presentation and asked his secretary to "protect" him from all interruptions for three hours.

I wanted my email disabled. I asked her to take my cell phone away from me. I told her to let no calls through except for family emergencies. She did exactly as I wished. But three hours without connection were intolerable. I could barely concentrate on the presentation, I felt so anxious. I know this sounds crazy but I felt panicky. I felt that no one cared about me, loved me.

His experience illustrates disconnection anxiety. Now that connection is always on offer, people don't know what to do with time alone, even time they asked for. They can't concentrate; they say they are bored, and boredom becomes a reason to turn to their phones for a game or a text or a Facebook update. But mostly, it is anxiety that leads them back to their phones. They want to feel a part of things. That is the message of our messages: We are on someone's radar.

I've talked so much about virtuous circles; here is a vicious cycle. Knowing we have someplace "else" to go in a moment of boredom leaves us less experienced at exploring our inner lives and therefore more likely to want the stimulation of what is on our phones. To reclaim solitude we have to learn to experience a moment of boredom as a reason to turn inward, to defer going "elsewhere" at least some of the time.

Where Empathy Begins

I've spoken about Holbrooke, a middle school in upstate New York. It is small, with about a hundred and fifty students, boys and girls in grades six to eight. For several years, the teachers have felt that something is amiss. This year, they have called me in as a consultant. The main thing on their minds: Their students are not showing empathy toward each other. The teachers themselves make the connection between this lack of empathy and the difficulty children have with solitude. As the teachers see it, if students can't take time for themselves, how will they take time for others?

The teachers say they are trying to slow things down for their students. They want each student to have an experience of "breathing room." Right now, students struggle to sit quietly and concentrate. They have very little patience. In the past, there were always some students who would balk at lengthy assignments. But now, even academically ambitious students rebel when they see a reading list that includes more than one long book.

While our brains are wired for talk, we can also train them to do deep reading, the kind that demands concentration on a sustained narrative thread with complex characters. It is the kind of reading the Holbrooke students say they don't want to do. Generations of English teachers told their charges that reading this kind of fiction was "good for them." It sounded like something teachers would say; no one really believed them in a literal sense. But now we know that literary fiction significantly improves empathic capacity, as measured by the ability to infer emotional states from people's facial expressions. The English teachers were right, literally. First one identifies with the characters in a complex novel and then the effect generalizes.

Jane Austen endures because readers identify with the mix of pride and prejudice in her most famous hero and heroine. Readers groan at the mountain of complications that character and circumstance throw in their path and celebrate when Elizabeth and Darcy can find each other despite. Literary fiction exercises a reader's imagination in matters of character and emotional nuance. The parallels to conversation are clear. Conversation, like literary fiction, asks for imagination and engagement. And conversation, like literary fiction, demands quiet time.

It's time that today's students don't seem to have. An English teacher at Holbrooke says of her seventh graders: "They don't want to be assigned projects that will claim their attention over time. They don't want to see things through." One teacher tries to sum up a new distractedness: "My students say things like, 'I misplaced my journal. I looked for it for ten minutes.' And then they look at me. The understanding is that now, it is my job to organize the search."

At Holbrooke, my mind jumps to conversations with businesspeople who talk about the "special needs" of recent college graduates who come to them seeking employment. One advertising executive, with thirty-five years of experience, describes the sensibility of her recent hires. As she talks about them, she is arguably describing the kinds of workers the Holbrooke students will become:

> *These young people are not used to working on their own on a project. In the past, if you think of employees . . . who are now in their forties, fifties, sixties . . . if you gave them a project, they thought it was their job to do it. Alone. Now, people can't be alone. They need continual contact and support and reinforcement. They want to know they are doing well. Left on their own to do their work, they feel truly bereft. They are always connected to each other online, but as I listen to their supervisors, they also need more support than before. They need a different kind of management.*

An art director at an advertising agency says of her new hires, all from elite colleges: "They are incredibly talented, but they grew up in a world of Facebook 'thumbs-ups.' They are accustomed to a lot of encouragement. So, you don't know if you should indulge that or if the management challenge is to teach them how to be alone and give themselves a 'thumbs-up.'"

Negotiating Boredom

The concerns of the Holbrooke teachers are shared by those who teach older children. At one high school in Maine, teachers from all academic departments worry that students lack downtime. They say that high school students need it to learn how to think with autonomy.

But the teachers don't think that parents are on their side. As the teachers see it, "Parents don't want their kids to have downtime. There can always be more piano lessons or soccer practice. . . . The kids in our school are shuttled from activity to activity; they eat dinner in their cars. . . . If parents think their children have any free time, they say to us and to the child: 'You're not doing enough to succeed.'" Or parents worry that downtime is the same as boredom and see it as a waste of time.

But childhood boredom is a driver. It sparks imagination. It builds up inner emotional resources. For the child psychoanalyst Donald W. Winnicott, a child's capacity to be bored—closely linked to the child's capacity to play contentedly alone while in the quiet presence of a parent—is a critical sign of psychological health. Negotiating boredom is a signal developmental achievement.

The high school teachers say that most of their students don't have this achievement behind them. Even short periods of time alone make their students uncomfortable. If there is an open space in the day, students expect an adult to come in with an activity. If not, they expect to turn to their phones for distraction, a new connection, or a new game. What they don't allow themselves is stillness. A high school math teacher tries to sum up the costs: "Seeing things takes time. Seeing yourself takes time. Having a friend takes time. And it takes time to do things well. . . . These kids don't have time."

Back at Holbrooke, an art teacher describes her most recent attempt to get a class of twelve-year-olds to slow down. She asked students to take five minutes to draw an object of their choice. "Several," she says, "told me that this was the longest they had ever concentrated on one thing, uninterrupted." And then she says, "They got upset when they couldn't do it well. They asked for help. So, what happened is that I went over to help. But then, as soon as I stepped away, they lost interest. Some turned to their phones."

A drama teacher says she had similar problems during rehearsals for a recent school play: "I tell them that acting is not about the verbal performance. The actor is really doing 'deep listening.' That is, the actor is responding to the other actors." But the students could not sit still long enough to listen to each other. In the end, the drama teacher presented them with an ultimatum: Listen to each other or leave the play. The ultimatum had its effects: A group of students dropped out.

The Holbrooke teachers worry that they are making some problems worse. At Holbrooke, each student is given an iPad for reading textbooks, organizing assignments, and keeping up with the school schedule. The school is asking students to work from the very devices that distract them.

One fifteen-year-old says that once he's on his iPad, "I am lost. I go on to check the time for a team practice, but it pulls me in. So I check my Facebook." Life, for him, "would be simpler with a printed schedule." A fourteen-year-old girl describes the strain of having to do all her class reading online. "Once I'm on the iPad for assignments, I'm messaging my friends and playing a game. It's hard to stay on school things. I don't see why they got rid of books."

Right now, the Holbrooke teachers are in no position to take the iPads away. They tell me that as a school they have made a commitment to the platform's "efficiency" and to the "content available online." But it's hard to keep students from jumping online whenever they have a free moment. And once students are online, it's hard to keep them from the path of least resistance. That path leads to texting, games, and shopping. That path leads to Facebook.

The Facebook Zone

How does technology hold us close, so close that we turn to it instead of turning within? It keeps us in a "machine zone." When she considered gamblers' connection to their slot machines, the anthropologist Natasha Dow Schüll wrote about the machine zone as a state of mind in which people don't know where they begin and the machine ends. One of the gamblers Schüll interviewed said, "I'm almost hypnotized into *being* that machine." For gamblers in the machine zone, money doesn't matter. Neither does winning or losing. What matters is remaining at the machine and in the zone. Technology critic Alexis Madrigal thinks of the "Facebook zone" as a softer version of the numbed state of Schüll's gamblers. When you're on social media, you don't leave, but you are not sure if you are making a conscious decision to stay.

Here is how Maggie, a college junior, describes that place: "When I check my Facebook and Twitter and email on my cell phone, I feel like I am forgetting to check something and I'll continue to look through those three things because I feel like I am missing something." The process of checking draws her into the process of checking. Judy, another junior, speaks about Facebook on her phone as a "lucky charm" that will protect her from boredom. But when she describes her time with her phone, it seems as if it is training her to be bored with anything other than her phone:

> *If you're on some app and looking through stuff because you're bored, you can click your little round button and go through a circuit of apps. Even if nothing is happening you probably have an email. Sometimes when you're just sitting and talking to someone or in class it's boring. So you check your phone even if you know nothing has happened. That switching makes it so that when you're just sitting or engaged in one thing, it feels weird.*

As Judy would put it, in the Facebook zone, you are never available for "just sitting" or "being engaged in one thing." That's a problem: These are the building blocks of solitude.

It is helpful to compare the Facebook zone with what the psychologist Mihaly Csikszentmihalyi calls "flow." In flow, you are asked to do a task that isn't so easy as to be mindless but isn't so hard as to be out of your grasp. If, when skiing, you are challenged but your skills are sufficient to give you a feeling of connection with the mountain, you are experiencing flow. For Csikszentmihalyi, experiences in the flow state always lead to new learning and a stronger sense of self. Schüll's gamblers don't experience growth but entrapment and repetition. Madrigal calls the machine zone the "dark side of flow."

Between flow and its dark side, where are we when we enter the Facebook zone? Maggie and Judy both say that cycling through apps takes them away from other—and they think more important—things they used to do, like going for a walk, drawing, and reading. They no longer make time for these activities, but they can't break away from their phones and are not sure they want to. In their stories, we see the "success" of devices whose goal, ultimately, is to keep their users connected.

A humorous moment made this point during a Boston visit of Eric Schmidt, the executive chairman of Google. Schmidt was in town to speak about his recently published book. When he walked into the hall, he asked the audience, "How many of you are going to be on your phones during the lecture?" When a roomful of hands shot up he said, "Good! That's what we want you to be doing." Apps are designed to keep you on apps. And the more of your downtime you spend cycling through apps, the less time you have to be alone with yourself.

Surfing as Solitude

College students are clear: What they count as solitude involves being online. One college junior tells me that she doesn't daydream but does something she calls "chilling." It involves "aimlessly searching the web." Think of it as daydreaming 2.0. But it doesn't do the work of daydreaming. In fact, she calls the web her "safety mechanism" against daydreaming. Time wandering the web protects her from the "danger" of having her mind wander. Another, in a similar spirit, calls her phone an "insurance policy" against boredom. Like the Fortune 500 vice-president alone at his desk, these young women understand that time alone without a phone creates anxiety.

I ask Carmen, twenty, if she ever has time to just sit and think. Her answer: "I would never do that." If she has a quiet moment she goes to Facebook. She says she doesn't want to think about the past without it. "To think about your past experiences instead of looking at pictures or messages, it takes more effort to do that."

Effort she would rather not put in. "The problem," she explains, is that "if you think about the past without Facebook, you would have to consciously say, 'Okay, now I am going to think. . . .' You would have to prepare to go sit by yourself." To her, this is an unlikely idea. Carmen has reached a point where solitude means being alone with her laptop and the people she reaches through it, a new definition of solitude as crowd management.

Anya, twenty, describes an evening when she accompanied her college roommate to the hospital. A triage nurse decided that the roommate's stomach pain was not an emergency and so the two women had to wait for over five hours to see a doctor. They both went to their phones. When her phone began to lose its charge, Anya panicked.

> *My phone gets to the red mark and I started freaking out, like, "Oh no, it's about to die." That anxious feeling. I really get anxious when my phone is about to die. And then it dies. I am not even joking when I tell you that I went around the entire hospital. I asked every worker, every nurse, every random person I could find if they had an iPhone charger. I finally found a random security guard. He took me to a back room so I could charge my phone. I will go to that length—even invade people's privacy.*

This is disconnection anxiety in the presence of your best friend. Anya explains that she and her roommate didn't want to sit quietly with their thoughts. And in a related development, conversation felt like too much work. "We just wanted to be quiet and look at our phones and keep our minds preoccupied."

Lightbulb Moments and the
Value of Your Inner World

People like the image of a creative idea coming to someone as though a lightbulb turned on. But usually these "lightbulb" ideas have been long prepared.

Writing about his own experience, the French mathematician and philosopher Henri Poincaré explored the slow unfolding of what seem like "lightbulb" ideas. "Sudden illumination," says Poincaré, is only "a manifest sign of long, unconscious prior work," work usually done alone.

> *Often when one works at a hard question, nothing good is accomplished at the first attack. Then one takes a rest, longer or shorter, and sits down anew to the work. During the first half-hour, as before, nothing is found, and then all of a sudden the decisive idea presents itself to the mind.*

It was the dream of early computer scientists to have machines do the fast and routine work so that the slow and creative work could be done by people. In 1945, the inventor and engineer Vannevar Bush dreamed of a device he called a Memex (an idea often considered a precursor to the web) that would take care of logical processes in order to leave more time for the slow unfolding of human creativity. Ironically, as we move closer to the world Bush imagined, the opposite may have happened. Machines present us with information at a volume and velocity that we try, unsuccessfully, to keep up with. But we try. And the effort means that we are often so busy communicating that we don't have time to think. K–12 teachers and college professors use the same words to describe their students: rushed, impatient, not interested in process, unable to be alone with their thoughts. It's as though we are waiting for the lightbulb without taking the time or the time alone for the "long, unconscious prior work."

The psychologist Jonathan Schooler demonstrated that "mind wan-

dering" is a stepping-stone to creativity. "The mind is inherently restless," says Schooler. "It's always looking to attend to the most interesting
thing in its environment." If children grow up expecting that the most
interesting thing in their environment is going to be on their phones, we
have to teach them to give their inner worlds a chance. Indeed, in a quiet
moment, all of us, child and adult, have to fight the impulse to turn first
to our devices.

Our devices compel us because we respond to every search and every
new piece of information (and every new text) as though it had the urgency of a threat in the wild. So stimulation by what is new (and social)
draws us toward some immediate goal. But daydreaming moves us toward the longer term. It helps us develop the base for a stable self and
helps us come up with new solutions. To mentor for innovation we need
to convince people to slow things down, let their minds wander, and
take time alone.

Reclaiming conversation begins with reclaiming our capacity for solitude. When we reach for a phone to push reverie away, we should get
into the habit of asking why. Perhaps we are not moving toward our
phones but away from something else. Are we hiding from anxiety? Are
we hiding from a good idea that will demand difficult work? Are we hiding from a question that will take time to sort through?

In our world of "I share, therefore I am" we are not primed to give
solitude a chance. We can cultivate a different attitude, beginning with
our children. We can give them time without electronic devices. And we
can give them more time alone. The teachers who complain that parents
see free time as their children's enemy are pointing to something real.
Children can't develop the capacity for solitude if they don't have the
experience of being "bored" and then turning within rather than to a
screen.

When young children go to their bedrooms at night, they should go
without their phones or tablets. Recall Erikson's thought that children
need "stillness" to find their identity. The social critic William Deresiewicz argues that these days, online, we rob ourselves of the conditions to
think independently. Leadership, he says, "means gathering yourself

together into a single point rather than letting yourself be dispersed everywhere into a cloud of electronic and social input." You don't have to move to a cabin in the woods to get these benefits, but even a short amount of solitude lets people hear their own thoughts. It opens up the space for self-reflection.

Self-Reflection

I Tweet, Therefore I Am

As long as I have my phone, I would never just sit alone and think. . . . When I have a quiet moment, I never just think. My phone is my safety mechanism from having to talk to new people or letting my mind wander. I know that this is very bad . . . but texting to pass the time is my way of life.

—VANESSA, A COLLEGE JUNIOR

One of the rewards of solitude is an increased capacity for self-reflection—the conversations we have with ourselves in the hope of greater insight about who we are and want to be. Professionally, what is our vocation? Personally, what gives us purpose and meaning? Can we forgive our transgressions and those of others? In self-reflection, we come to understand ourselves better and we nurture our capacity for relationship.

Different traditions—philosophical, religious, spiritual, and psychological—have made claims on these high-stakes conversations. In the West, since the early twentieth century, the psychoanalytic tradition made its own claim. At its core, psychoanalysis is a therapeutic technique, but it proposed itself as a sensibility for thinking about the self that went beyond the professional boundaries of psychoanalysts and their patients. The psychoanalytic movement became a psychoanalytic culture whose core assumptions were popularized in novels, films, and the press.

So, whether or not you had ever been in treatment with an analyst or read a word of Freud, a certain set of ideas became familiar to you as you thought about your past, your present, and your possibilities for change. This tradition of self-reflection stresses history, the meaning of language, and the power of the unconscious. It teaches that our lives are "peopled" by those who have mattered most to us. They live within us for better and worse. We learn to recognize their influence in our strengths and vulnerabilities. If your parents were aggressive, you may be on the defensive whether or not it is warranted. If your parents were withdrawn, you may feel orphaned even if surrounded by loved ones.

The psychoanalytic tradition makes us aware of our human tendency to see the world through the prism of what our most significant relationships have told us about ourselves. It teaches that self-reflection can help us make our way past this cacophony of internalized voices to a place that feels more authentically "ours." In that place, we can see how we are shaped by our histories but achieve a certain distance from them.

Understanding our capacity for projection helps us see what is around us rather than use our present to work out unresolved conflicts from our past. So, the psychoanalytic tradition sees self-reflection as a path toward realism. If jealousy and danger threaten, you don't paper it over. If love is offered, you can see it.

These rewards of self-reflection take time to achieve—and of course, we don't give ourselves much time these days. And they take discipline. In every case, they depend on developing the capacity to pause and think through the knotty thought, the tangled relationship. *If I am afraid, is there danger or inhibition? If I feel bold, am I well prepared or reckless? If I want to leave a relationship, have I been treated badly or am I afraid of commitment?*

And Then: The Algorithmic Self

The psychoanalytic tradition asks us to cultivate both the capacity for solitude and the capacity for disciplined self-reflection. There are many things that discourage us. Sometimes it is just the hope for a simpler way to understand ourselves. It would be nice if troubles could be cured by the right pill or the right mantra or the right behavioral adjustment.

And now, there is the hope that self-reflection could perhaps be made more efficient by technological intervention. The list of candidate technologies is already long: a computer programmed to behave in the manner of a therapist; devices that help you track your physiology for patterns that will help you understand your psychology; programs that analyze the words in your diary and come up with a diagnosis of your mental state. These last are certified as the "real you" because they are based on what is measurable about your behavior, your "output." They are served up as your quantified or algorithmic self.

Never underestimate the power of a new evocative object. The story of how we use technologies of self-report and quantified self-report to think about ourselves is just beginning. Used with intention, they may provoke reflection that brings us closer to ourselves. But they can't do it alone. Apps can give you a number; only people can provide a narrative. Technology can expose mechanism; people have to find meaning.

It is striking that some of our most-used applications—such as Facebook—seem set up to inspire narration. After all, on Facebook, the basic protocol is to record and illustrate the events of one's life. Of course, we've seen that the story is not so simple. Social media can also inhibit inner dialogue, shifting our focus from reflection to self-presentation.

From a Journal to a Newsfeed

M elissa's home life is turbulent. She's a high school senior and for years, her parents, threatening divorce, have turned every meal into a quarrel. In the past, Melissa found refuge in modern dance, photography, and, most of all, in her handwritten journal. She says that sometimes she rereads it just to see the changes in her penmanship, entry by entry. They offer clues to her state of mind.

> *I wrote in it every night. In a book. I like writing. And it's funny to go back and see—you can tell if I'm angry. Sometimes, the letters look angry. That means I'm angry and I'm writing angry. And . . . then— if something was really bothering me—I can go back and read what I wrote down, how I felt, how I dealt with it.*

These days, Melissa's journaling is hasty; she usually skips it and turns instead to social media. I meet her just as Facebook is becoming the emotional center of her life. She has been rejected from the four colleges that were her "first choice" schools. She is leaving home to attend a small rural college in upstate New York. She says that her increased involvement with Facebook began when she found a Facebook page that perfectly suits her situation. It's called "I GOT REJECTED FROM MY FIRST CHOICE SCHOOL." There, Melissa corresponds with other people who share her disappointments about college. Among them are people who survived going to their "fourth choice school" and had successful careers afterward. Now, Melissa says, she spends almost all her free time on Facebook. And then she adds, softly, "I wish I wasn't but I am."

Why the conflict? Melissa needs social support. Her college plans disappoint her; her home life offers no comfort. Life on Facebook (with its tailor-made "I GOT REJECTED" page) is a place to tell her story. But Melissa says that even with all of these positive things, it's "hard to find balance" when she goes on Facebook, because once she gets there, it's "consuming" and very hard to put away. More disturbing, Melissa says that she now finds it "almost impossible to do the things I actually think I need to do—to sit by myself, write in my journal, talk to my brother, call my best friend." Instead she feels "stuck" on Facebook, posting about food, reading profiles, and "stalking" people in her class. "I get lost in reading other people's messages or profiles or talking to them. And it's always stuff that is so pointless and it's just a waste of time, and I hate wasting time, but I get lost in it. I'll look at the clock and it'll say 7:14, and I'll look back and it'll seem like a minute later and it'll be 8:30 p.m." Facebook wasn't designed to stall self-reflection. But it often does.

Melissa thinks that part of what keeps her stuck on Facebook is anxiety about being left out. In middle school, she felt excluded, and "that fear just creeps up. Yeah. So wanting to be in the know, always online, is a way of saying, 'OK, if it's happening, I want to be on top of it.'" So, she checks Facebook. "I always *have* to check it. . . . One of my fears is being left out or missing something." Facebook assuages that fear.

Although Melissa uses Facebook as a substitute for her journal (she says, "It's easier"), she is less honest on the digital page. She says that when she wrote in her journal, she felt as if she was writing for herself. When she switched to Facebook, she went into "performance" mode. She shares her thoughts, but she also thinks about how they will "play." Melissa says that sometimes when she wrote in her journal, she had fantasies of other people finding or reading it someday, but her fantasies put that day far in the future—they really didn't influence what she wrote. What she writes on Facebook, however, is designed to make her popular *now*.

So Melissa wrote a pleasing profile for Facebook, one that reflected the person she *wanted* to be, her aspirational self. She said things that would draw people toward her. And when she does her daily sharing, she is selective. For example, she doesn't write about the arguments in her family. All of this had made it onto the pages of her journal, but now, on Facebook, Melissa only wants to publish good news.

I have found that when people use the aspirational self as an object for self-reflection, it can make them feel curiously envious—of themselves. It can be helpful, of course, to know your aspirations. That's useful information for reflecting on who you want to become. But on Facebook, you can get busy performing that self, pretending it is who you already are.

Our performances of self on Facebook are very different from how people use game avatars for self-reflection. I have long studied how digital objects inform how we think about ourselves, including many years of work on the psychology of role-playing games. The avatars we create for online gaming (in most games we choose their bodies, their faces, and their personality traits) were not designed to facilitate self-reflection. And yet they can do just that. When people construct an avatar, they often give it qualities that allow them to express aspects of themselves they would like to explore. This means that a game world can become a place to experiment with identity. In his mid-thirties, a software engineer found himself frustrated by his difficulties being assertive. In his mind, assertive men came across as bullies while assertive women seemed like attractive "Katharine Hepburn types." He decided to experiment with being more assertive by playing strong women in online games. His virtual practice served him well. After years online as a strong woman, he became comfortable as a more assertive man.

I've found that, surprisingly, using avatars to experiment with identity can be more straightforward than using a Facebook profile for this purpose. In the case of the avatar, you begin with clarity that you are "playing" a character that is someone other than you. That's the game. On Facebook, you are, ostensibly, representing yourself and talking about your own life. That's why people friend you. They want to know what *you* are doing and thinking.

In theory, you know the difference between yourself and your Facebook self. But lines blur and it can be hard to keep them straight. It's like telling very small lies over time. You forget the truth because it is so close to the lies.

And these days, using the web for self-reflection poses the very real question of how truthful to be. For we know that it is not a private space, not a journal or a diary locked away. It is a new thing: a public space that we may nevertheless experience as the most private place in the world.

The Only Two People in the World

Self-reflection makes us vulnerable. That's why its traditions so often include ways of protecting one's privacy (we lock and hide our diaries) and confidentiality (as in relationships with a therapist or a clergyman). Social media encourage us to play by another set of rules. You share as you reflect; you reflect as you share. And the companies that provide the platforms for all of this get to see and keep it all. Privacy, loosely defined as freedom from being observed, is gone. At what cost?

In the mid-1990s, when the web was new, I spoke to Alan, a history graduate student, twenty-seven, about Netscape, one of the first web browsers. He said, "I search what interests me and I learn what interests me by what I search." Alan did those early searches believing that they left no trace. He talked about the freedom to "look at things I would be embarrassed to take out of the library. Somebody might see the book." This kind of exploration is compromised if we don't feel in a private space. And now we know that online, we are *not* in a private space. Yet people still tell me they behave as Alan did, *as though* their activities were private.

So now consider David, forty-seven, a television producer who shares Alan's sensibility. He, too, discovers his interests as he searches the web. But I meet David in 2013, two decades after I spoke with Alan. David is eager to elaborate on the "giant upside" of the time he spends online: "Putting on my earbuds and getting into my iPhone world is my Zen. That's my retreat." David says that cycling through his apps is his time for self-reflection: "You flip between your music, your news, your entertainment, *your people*. You control it. You own it. That's my zone." Here, the definition of self-reflection has narrowed: It means control over your connections. We've seen this before, solitude defined as time with a managed crowd.

Like Alan, David says that he likes to look back on his online history. David has email, Tweets, Facebook, and texts. He calls them his "tracks." Like Alan, he knows himself through where he's been. He says that for him, wandering the web "is like thinking aloud." But unlike Alan, the way he uses the net to explore his interests is starting to make him anxious. He knows that when he "thinks aloud" online, other people are in a position to listen.

For David, being plugged in provides a sense of identity, but he knows that it also creates him as a data product to be bought and sold. And as an object for potential government surveillance. So as David follows his "tracks," he is in a setting for self-reflection where if he does not self-censor, he feels he is being foolish, naive, or even transgressive. And yet this potential transgression has become such an everyday thing that he chooses to forget it might be transgression at all.

The gap between the reality of online life and how we experience it stalls our discussion of Internet privacy. Consider email. People "know" email is not private. And yet many will use email, at least sometimes, for intimate correspondence. Over decades, I have asked why. The answer is always the same: When you stare at a screen, you feel completely alone. That sense of being alone with the person to whom you are writing—as though you were the only two people in the world—often as not blocks out what you know to be true. Email can be seen; it will be stored; and then it can be seen again. The seeming ephemerality of what is on the screen masks the truth: What you write is indelible. More generally, the experience of the net undermines the reality of the net. So David continues to wander online, reflect on his tracks, and think of what he does as a kind of meditation. Until he thinks of it as a more public disclosure—and chides himself for doing something he can't quite condone.

When people are in conflict, they don't do what they advise. The wise begin to say such things as, "Only say online what you wouldn't mind having posted on a company bulletin board." But then, the wise go on Facebook and Instagram and don't follow their own rules.

This conflict limits the possibilities of digital space as a place for self-reflection. Over time and with more knowledge of who sees it, you may want to say less on it. At the same time, every time you try a new app, you put more of yourself into it. And onto a system you no longer control. And in a new twist, your apps start to talk back to you, telling you who you are based on what you have told and shown them.

It's Never Bad to Have a New Evocative Object

To celebrate its tenth birthday, Facebook used an algorithm to create a "highlights collage" that organized its members' "biggest moments" since they joined Facebook. The algorithm that created the collage took account of which posts and photos had received the most "likes" and comments. In this instance, self-reflection by algorithm struck most people as harmless fun. The author of one article about the collage notes that according to Facebook, one of his past year's "top moments" came when he posted: "Who wants to watch the football?"

But there was a more serious side to Facebook's curation: It got some people thinking about what was really important to them. The highlights collage became a scaffolding for a narrative and they didn't mind that Facebook had authored the first draft. Then they had a chance to revise it. One father of three printed out the "highlights reel" and talked about it with his family at breakfast. He tells me how happy he is to have that printout: "I would never have made a scrapbook that elegant! It was awesome!"

Shortly after the publication of that highlights collage, I received a letter from Sid, a man in his forties, who suffers from ALS, Lou Gehrig's disease. He told me of his complicated reaction to being offered a "highlights reel" of 2013. That was the year of his diagnosis.

I sat there and stared for I don't know how long. Last year at this time I had an appointment scheduled with an orthopedist to sort out the weird things going on with my hands. Maybe I should have had a sense of what was to come but I didn't. Months later my family's life was changed. I was diagnosed with ALS. No treatment. No cure. Good luck. At the start of 2013 I had no idea.

Sid did press the button to see Facebook's version of 2013. Not surprisingly, it did not capture what the year had meant to him. There was no helping it: The timeline "had to treat some things a bit too matter-of-factly. A picture of my son's first birthday and then a post sharing my ALS diagnosis with a nice musical transition in between."

Sid begins his letter to me by suggesting that no automatic system could ever understand a life with ALS—the way that event changes the meaning of everything that came before and everything that comes after. But then, in his letter, Sid backtracks. Perhaps what Facebook offered "did capture 2013 for me." That year had been about intolerably fast cuts. It had been about moving too quickly from the normalcy of birthday cake to a doctor's office and a death sentence. Facebook had captured this, "but it is too stark a contrast to comfortably watch. . . . I couldn't watch the video knowing that the next post in the montage might be too big of a change in gears."

Sid's experience illustrates the complexity of using the products of algorithms to think about the self. To understand what might be really important to Sid, you needed a person who could imagine living with a terminal illness. A person might understand that too-stark contrasts would be painful. But the machine-curated images did get Sid to think about his year in a new way. Facing death is about the surreal contrast between buying balloons for a birthday party and the certainty of nonexistence. The fast cuts of the Facebook postings got Sid thinking about that. The Facebook algorithm wasn't written to have this effect. This is what a human being did with its results.

Reading Sid's email, I thought: It is never bad to have a new evocative object. What matters is how we use it. But the objects of our lives do constrain how we tell our stories. On Facebook and Twitter, we want to tell stories that others will like, ones that will be followed. I am often told that "Twitter is my memoir; Facebook is my way of keeping a diary," but as Melissa's case made so clear, shared journaling, like all publishing, leaves us vulnerable to the natural desire to gratify our readers. And when we use devices that track our physical state to provide clues for self-understanding, we work with another constraint: We try to find a narrative that fits our numbers.

In one common way of doing things, wearable technology collects data that track such things as our heart rate, respiration, perspiration, body temperature, movement, and sleep routines. These data can go right to a display on our phones where we can use them to work toward physical self-improvement. A readout of how many steps we've taken can encourage better exercise habits. In another kind of tracking app, physiological signs are used as windows onto our psychological state.

Here, the desire to wear a tracking device responds to the same impulse that had nearly everyone in my generation buying a mood ring. The difference is that even though the ring was fun, it had no authority. The new tracking devices come with substantial authority. We develop a view of ourselves (body and mind) that is tied to what measurement tells us.

While some tracking applications use sensors to read your body *for* you, others ask *you* to report your mood or degree of focus or the fights you are having with your partner. Over time, there is a subtle shift. In some sense, "you" become the number of steps you walked this week compared to last. "You" become a lowered resting heart rate over the span of two months. You move to a view of self as the sum, bit by bit, of its measurable elements. Self-tracking does not logically imply a machine view of self, or the reduction of self-worth to a number, but it gets people in the habit of thinking of themselves as made up of measurable units and achievements. It makes it natural to ask, "What is my score?"

In the 1980s, I wrote of the movement from the psychoanalytic to the computer culture as a shift from meaning to mechanism—from depth to surface. At that time, as computation gained ground as the dominant metaphor for describing the mind, there was a shift from thinking about the self as constituted by human language and history to seeing it as something that could be modeled in machine code.

Today's "quantified" or "algorithmic" self is certainly part of that larger story but adds something new. Instead of taking the computer as the model for a person, the quantified self goes directly to people and asks each of us to treat ourselves as though we were computational objects, subject to a printout of our ever more knowable states. The psychoanalytic self looks to history as it leaves traces in language; the algorithmic self to what it can track as data points in a time series.

Numbers and Narration

Numbers are seductive. People like thinking about themselves in terms of readouts and scores. This is not new. We have always been drawn to horoscopes, personality tests, and quizzes in magazines. Benjamin Franklin famously included a self-tracker in his autobiography, measuring himself on thirteen personal virtues every day. The difference now is that there is, as we say, "an app for that"—indeed, for all of that and more. More and more of our lives—body and soul—can be captured as data and fed back to us, analyzed by algorithm. And in the process, we are usually asked to treat ourselves and the algorithm as a black box.

We see the frustration of having a number without a narrative in Trish, twenty-one, who uses an online journaling program called 750 Words. Every day, Trish writes 750 words and the program analyzes what she has written. It compares her daily writing to what she has written before and to the universe of all the other people writing. It rates her words—or as she sees it, it rates "her"—on maturity, sexual content, on the violence in her writing and how much she uses swear words. And it gives her a reading of her preoccupations. When I talk to Trish, she is confused. One day last week, 750 Words told her that her daily writing exercise had shown her to be preoccupied with death.

Trish is a study in contrasts. A competitive athlete and a philosophy student, she wants to go to drama school when she graduates from college. She became acquainted with feedback devices when she bought a

Fitbit, a popular commercial product that provides readings on daily steps taken, calories burned, and sleep quality. From there, she became curious about programs that would give her other kinds of feedback. When I met her, she had spent six months working with 750 Words.

On the day Trish was told that she was preoccupied with death, she had used her 750 words to describe a conversation with a friend that had left her feeling misunderstood. Trish said it felt good to write it down. But then, alone with the program's readout, she felt frustrated. She didn't understand what her misunderstanding with her friend had to do with death. She wanted to understand the algorithm.

> *It's shocking that I write about death more than others. Actually, I don't mind the comparisons to the rest of the world's writing. What's hard are the comparisons to myself. It's hard not to take it personally, so it gets me thinking. The death thing is really strange. It makes me wonder why it thinks that.*

What most frustrates Trish is that once the program gets her thinking, there is no place to take her thoughts or her objections. Trish says, "It's not like the program is my therapist. There isn't a relationship. I can't talk to it about why it feels that way. I don't feel that I'm thinking about death." And even if 750 Words could tell her which words had "triggered" the program's reactions, she is not sure that would help. Trish wants a conversation.

Technology critic Evgeny Morozov argues the limitations of the kinds of data that Trish has been left with. A narrative has been reduced to a number. And now the number seems like a result. Morozov fears that when you have your readout from the black box, you are tempted to stop there. You are pleased. Or you are upset.

But as we become more sophisticated about the kinds of data that self-monitoring devices return to us, that first impulse need not be our last impulse. We can construct narratives around our numbers. Indeed, in Trish we see the impulse to do that. ("It makes me wonder why it thinks that.") And in meetings of those who declare themselves to be part of the "quantified self movement," people do bring in data from sensors and programs and attempt to construct stories around them.

In this spirit, a recently divorced woman in her thirties posted a blog of self-reflection and called it "The Quantified Breakup." In the days and months after her divorce, she tracked the number of texts she wrote and calls she made (and to whom), songs she listened to (classified happy or sad), places she went, unnecessary purchases and their costs. She tracked her sleeping and waking hours, when and for how long she exercised, ate out, and went to the movies. When did she cry in public and post on social media?

Reading this material is arresting. Yet as I read her blog, it seems like raw data for another story about what the purchases and the tears and the songs mean. Does this experience bring her back to other times when she has felt alone? To other losses?

What strategies worked then? What potential stumbling blocks can be determined from her history? What kind of support does she need? On the blog, there isn't much of this kind of talk. But we do learn that when she tried online dating and met someone she liked, they exchanged "1,146 [texts] in the first four weeks alone, an average of 40.9 per day." And then it was over. What can we make of this? What can she? The numbers of "The Quantified Breakup" need their narrative.

I have a similar reaction to quantified self enthusiasts who have a death in the family and numerically track their period of grief with the expressed intent of not wanting to skip over any part of the mourning process. The impulse is admirable, moving. But one wonders if in tracking their grief, they keep themselves too busy to feel it. Does taking our emotional pulse and giving it a number keep us on the feeling or does it distract us because, once categorized, we have done something "constructive" with the feeling and don't have to attend to it anymore?

Does tracking mourning help us mourn or does it deflect us because if we feel we must start and end our story with a number, we limit the stories we tell?

Natasha Dow Schüll, the anthropologist, is doing an ethnographic study of the meetings of the quantitative self movement. At these meetings, members of the movement who have been "self-tracking" stand up to tell their stories. Schüll writes: "The defining activity of QS [the quantified self movement] is its Show and Tell events, in which individual self-trackers get onstage and tell a story about what they tracked, what they learned, etcetera." Schüll is impressed by the QS Show and Tell. She asks, "Aren't numbers just an element in a narrative process?"

The answer for me is not simple. Numbers are an element in a narrative process, but they are not *just* an element. When we have a number, it tends to take on special importance even as it leaves to us all the heavy lifting of narrative construction. Yet it constrains that construction because the story we tell has to justify the number. Your quantified data history can provide material for constructing a story. But here, our language betrays us. We talk about the "output" from our tracking programs as "results." But they are not results. They are first steps. But too often, they are first steps that don't suggest second steps.

For if the program's results make no sense to us, we have no place to go. So when 750 Words gave Trish a "result" that baffled her (she doesn't think she has morbidity on her mind), it provided no further guidance and no interlocutor. Trish is left puzzled and does not know how to further understand why her words are associated with death—by the numbers.

I talk about tracking and self-reflection with Margaret E. Morris, a psychologist at the Intel Corporation who for over a decade has worked on applications that help people record and visualize their emotional and physical health. When Morris considers her work over the years, she says that what strikes her about the feedback devices she has made is that "they are most powerful as a starting point, not an ending point," and that "every one of them started a conversation." In terms of making a difference to health and family dynamics, *it was the conversation that brought about change.*

Morris says that sometimes the conversation was begun by a family member or friend. In one of Morris's cases, a woman housebound by chronic illness was asked to report her moods to a mobile phone app. Several times a day, this program, called Mood Map, asked the woman to indicate her mood on a visual display. When she was sad, the program would suggest techniques drawn from cognitive behavioral therapy that might help her see things in a more positive light. In this case, it was the patient's son who used the Mood Map to start a conversation. The technology gave him an opening to talk about his mother's loneliness, something he had not been able to do on his own. Morris sums up: "To the extent that these technologies have an impact, it is because they spark conversations along the way."

Performing for and Deferring to the Algorithm

Linda, a thirty-three-year-old business student, is more enthusiastic than Trish about her experience with 750 Words because Linda sees the program as dispensing a kind of therapy. She began using the program when she was under stress, coping with academic pressure, life in a new city, and not having as much money as she did when she was working. As she tried to get her life in order, Linda wanted to know how she was doing, and 750 Words' algorithms promised that they would report on how affectionate, happy, upset, anxious, or sad she was. But after a few weeks with the program, Linda is disgruntled: "Who wants to pour out your heart and find out that you're a self-important introvert? Who wants to be told that you're sadder than most other users? And not only that, but you're not as happy as you were last week?"

But Linda also sees an upside. She says that after two weeks of the program's "constructive criticism," the program has begun to "train" her. *She now writes what she thinks the program would like to hear.* She makes an effort to be upbeat and to talk more about other people in her 750 words. Linda says that according to the program, she's not as self-important as she once was.

I'm in a group where Linda discusses her relationship with 750 Words. The question comes up as to whether Linda's approach is making her a better person. Sure, she is gaming the system, but maybe the system is gaming her—in a good way. Is this therapy? Is writing a positive version of your day every day a bad thing? Someone says, "I believe in the idea of 'fake it till you make it.'" Research shows that if you smile, smiling itself triggers the release of the chemicals associated with happiness. Linda believes that if she consciously talks more about other people, she may in fact *become* less self-absorbed. So what starts as an exercise in self-reflection ends up, at least for Linda, as behavioral therapy.

Trish and Linda face the same dilemma: What to do if your feelings don't match the readout. Cara, a college student who has been using an iPhone app called the Happiness Tracker, has a different problem. How much should you look to the "output" of a tracking program to clue you in on your feelings? Over several weeks, the Happiness Tracker has asked for Cara's level of happiness as well as information about where she is, what she is doing, and who she is with. Its report: Her happiness is declining. There is no clear link to any one factor.

When she gets this result, Cara finds herself feeling less happy with her boyfriend. The app did not link him to her declining happiness, but she begins to wonder if he is the cause of her discontent. Uncertain of her feelings, she ends up breaking up with her boyfriend, in partial deference to the app. She says what she got from the tracker was like "a tipping point." It felt like something external that "proved" she was not on the right path.

In "happiness tracking," a lot can get lost in translation. Everything depends on how you interpret what the app is telling you. If Cara had brought her "discontented" reading to a psychotherapist, she might have been asked if she and her boyfriend talked about difficult issues—not necessarily things to avoid, but things that upset her because they were painful to deal with. Perhaps it was with her boyfriend—because she felt safe—that she allowed stressful conversations to occur. That might be a good thing, not a bad thing. Perhaps the "discontented" reading was a sign that he was, on balance, a positive force even if his presence provoked feelings that the program registered as stress. All discontent is not equal. Some bring us toward new understandings.

As things played out, Cara's "happiness tracker" didn't lead to this kind of reflection. Indeed, she saw the number she got from the program as a "failing grade" and it sparked a desire to get a better one. It pushed her into action. But without a person with whom to discuss the meaning behind the number, without a methodology for looking at her current feelings in relation to her history, she was flying blind.

Insights and Practices: The Psychoanalytic Culture

As a psychologist, I was trained in a technology of talk, the conversational technology of the psychoanalytic tradition, which would suggest a different perspective to the unhappy Cara. These days, classical psychoanalysis has had many of its ideas taken up in non-classical treatments, usually referred to as "psychodynamic." Here I'll call them "talk therapy," with the understanding that this is the kind of therapeutic conversation I mean. In contrast with technologies that propose themselves as quantitative mirrors of self, talk therapy offers interpretive strategies to understand your life story. Here I mention two to give a flavor of the kind of conversations that talk therapy encourages.

A first strategy is not to take words literally but to have patience with them. Wait and see where words lead you if you let them take you anywhere. The therapist creates a space for a kind of conversation that encourages you to say what comes to mind without self-censorship. An algorithm asks for specifications. In talk therapy, one is encouraged to wander.

A second strategy is to pay special attention to how the legacy of past relationships persist in the present. To this end, talk therapy creates a space in which therapists do not offer themselves as standard conversational partners but remain more neutral. This makes it easier to see when we project feelings from the past onto them. These feelings can be of every sort, positive and negative—of abandonment, of love, dependency, or rage. Our projections are known as the transference: *The feelings we have for therapists not because of what they do but because of who we are, the legacies we bring to the consulting room.*

When these feelings can be identified and discussed, a great deal is gained, because these projections are most likely brought into other relationships as well, where they are harder to recognize and sort out.

In the safety of talk therapy you learn that you tell yourself small, unconscious lies—to large effect. And you learn to stop, reflect, and correct. You come to recognize moments when you accuse your therapist of inattention but are actually addressing someone in your past who ignored you. Similarly, you learn to recognize moments when you accuse an intimate of the qualities that you most dislike in yourself. If you see your husband as a profligate spender, it is worth taking the time to ask if you worry that you spend too much money yourself.

As the therapeutic conversation continues over time—for this is a conversation that is meant to take time—it models a particular kind of self-reflection. You pay attention but you let your mind wander. You focus on detail and discover the hidden dimensions of ordinary things. Talk therapy slows things down so that they can be opened out. Over time, consulting room strategies clarify the conversations of everyday life.

My goal here is not a primer on psychoanalysis. I want only to say enough to say this: The sensibility of psychodynamic therapy—its focus on meaning, its commitment to patience and developing a working therapeutic relationship, its belief that following an associative thread of ideas, even if they seem unrelated, will ultimately have a big payoff—has a lot to offer digital culture. In particular, the psychoanalytic tradition suggests ways to approach technologies that try to capture us through algorithms.

When a computer program told Cara she was discontent, she seized on her relationship with her boyfriend as a reason. Once she had "evidence" in hand, doing nothing became intolerable. In the psychoanalytic tradition, what Cara did is called "acting out." Conflicted about her feelings, she found relief in changing something. She took action that had no certain relationship to the "readout," but it was action that made her feel temporarily in control. Talk therapy encourages reflection when we are seized by the need to "fix" something—and now! The psychoanalytic tradition suggests that action before self-understanding is rarely a good way to improve one's situation. I've said that a therapist might have gotten Cara to talk about whether her boyfriend allowed her to explore unhappy feelings because she felt safe in his presence. That's not something to discard. It's discomfort worth having.

If you act out, you create change and perhaps crisis. All of the new noise you make can drown out the feelings you were originally trying to understand. Nevertheless, it is often what people try first. Central to the method in talk therapy is learning what you think by listening to yourself in conversation. You can't do this if you are caught up in crises of your own devising. To the adage "Stop and think," talk therapy adds "Stop and listen to yourself thinking."

The conversations of talk therapy do not follow any pre-set protocol. Therapeutic conversations work not because therapists pass down information but because they form relationships in conversation. The psychoanalyst Adam Phillips has called psychoanalysis "solitude for two." By the end of a successful treatment, the patient leaves with the voice of the therapist "brought within." Patients have learned to be their own dialogue partner. One learns to take first reactions and give them a second look. One learns to ask, "Who is really speaking here? Where are my feelings coming from? Before I accuse the world of neglecting me, am I neglecting the world?"

In talk therapy's model for active listening you learn to attend not only to the words but also to the music, to the silences, to how people *sound as they speak.* And you learn to listen to yourself with this kind of attention. You learn to avoid self-censorship and to take yourself seriously. You learn to see patterns in your behavior; you learn to respect history and how it tends to repeat itself unless you are vigilant.

The psychoanalytic tradition deepens the culture of conversation because it demonstrates how much we can get out of it. It teaches that the ways your conversations unfold are unique to your history and that of the person you are speaking with. Conversations have a particularity that matters. As I said at the start, psychoanalysis is more than a treatment; it contributes a vocabulary that suggests a set of core values: patience, meaning, the centrality of narrative.

The vocabulary has its critics, and there are things to criticize. But it provides a powerful approach, even in our most technological times: If you ever have a vexing number from a happiness tracker, you will know how to interrogate it. You'll know that the answer isn't in the readout but in the conversation it helps you begin and how prepared you are to have it. Our quantitative selves leave data trails that are the beginning of our stories, not the results, not the conclusions.

I have a fantasy that in the future, people will look at the output of their tracking apps with a computer scientist to explain how its algorithms work—and a therapist who will help them put the readout in the context of their individual lives. More realistically, people will develop a dual sensibility: The psychoanalytic and computer culture will find their necessary points of synergy.

Two Chairs

Family

"Daddy! Stop Googling! I Want to Talk to You!"

In my family we have our disagreements in Gchat conversations.
It makes things smoother. What would be the value
proposition of disagreeing with each other face-to-face?

—COLIN, A COLLEGE JUNIOR

A close friend invites me to a family dinner in Maine. I make the drive up from Boston. I see friends with whom I share a long history; there are conversations about politics, work, children, and local gossip. My attention goes to a girl in her late teens, Alexa, who is staring down at her phone. We exchange a few words. She is polite, but when her phone lights up, she looks at me with a half smile and I understand that our time together is over. She has received a Snapchat, an image that will disappear a few seconds after she opens it. She's anxious to begin. So I excuse myself and she goes to her phone. During the next few hours, Alexa puts down her phone and joins the other guests perhaps four or five times, each time for a few minutes. I look around for younger children and they, too, are on phones.

Stan, a friend in his mid-fifties, has also been watching Alexa. He and I begin to talk. We think back to the family gatherings of our own childhoods. We recall that sometimes we were put at a children's table and would strain to hear the grown-ups' conversations. When our parents spoke to other grown-ups, they seemed to express themselves in a different language. There was juicy gossip about neighbors. There were stories about relatives that you didn't even know you had. Stan says, "I remember how excited I was when I thought I might finally have something to say to the grown-ups. And if they were interested, I would think to myself, 'I know how to talk!'" I've found many nostalgics like us. But nostalgia does not reliably drive behavior. Just as people say it is wrong to break up a relationship by text message but do it anyway, those who wax poetic about the conversations during dinners of the past admit to being on their phones, texting, during family dinners today.

So children, from the earliest ages, complain about having to compete with smartphones for their parents' attention. At dinner, a five-year-old girl cajoles, "Mommy, please! You promised! You had five minutes before!" when her mother's phone vibrates for the third time. An eight-year-old boy gets up from the table and tugs at his mother's sleeve when she takes out her phone during the meal. "No. Not now. Not now!" he pleads. As she turns her back to her child, the mother says, "Mommy has to make a quick call." The boy returns to his chair, sullen.

In what for me is an iconic moment, fifteen-year-old Chelsea, who is on summer vacation at a device-free camp, describes her disappointment when her father interrupted their dinner during parents' weekend by looking things up on his phone.

> The other night I went out to dinner with my dad. And we were just having this conversation and I didn't know the answer to something, like the director of a movie we had seen. And he automatically wanted to look it up on his phone. And I was like, "Daddy, stop Googling. I want to talk to you. I don't care what the right answer is! I just want to talk to you."

Chelsea wants her father's full attention. His preoccupation with his phone upsets her. But when she is not at camp, she says that she treats her friends just as her father treated her, interrupting conversations to look things up or send a text or check her Instagram account. This is the complexity of our moment. These are its contradictions.

Families 2.0: The Work of Family Conversations

At first glance, family life today looks much as it always has; we have preserved the form of things—there are dinners, school trips, family meetings.

At second glance, we seem to live a family life squared: We can share so much more with our families—videos, photographs, games, the whole wide world. And we can be "with" our families in new ways—in some ways, never apart. I still remember my first night away from my daughter who was then a year old. I remember sitting alone in a hotel room in Washington, D.C., as I spoke to her in western Massachusetts. I gripped the telephone receiver as my husband held the phone to my daughter's ear and I pretended that she understood I was on the other end of the call. When we both hung up, I wept because I didn't think she had understood anything at all. Now she and I would have Skype. We would have FaceTime. If separated, I could watch her play for hours.

But with yet another glance, the role of technology in family life is more complicated. As in many other aspects of life, we are tempted to be with each other but also elsewhere. At dinner and in the park, parents and children turn to their phones and tablets. Conversations that used to take place face-to-face migrate online. Families tell me they like to have their arguments through text, email, and Gchat—that this helps them express themselves more precisely. Some call it "fighting by text."

In families, the flight from conversation adds up to a crisis in mentorship. We need family conversations because of the work they do—beginning with what they teach children about themselves and how to get along with other people. To join in conversation is to imagine another mind, to empathize, and to enjoy gesture, humor, and irony in the medium of talk. As with language, the capacity to learn these human subtleties is innate. But their development depends on the environment in which a child is placed. Of course, conversations at school and at play are crucial. But the family has the child first, over sustained time, and in the most highly charged emotional relationships. When adults listen during conversations, they show children how listening works. In family conversation, children learn that it is comforting and pleasurable to be heard and understood.

Family conversation is where children first learn to see other people as different from themselves and worthy of understanding. It is where children learn to put themselves in someone else's shoes, often the shoes of a sibling. If your child is angry at a classmate, you can suggest that it might help to try to understand the other child's point of view.

It is in family conversations that children have the greatest chance of learning that what other people are saying (and how they are saying it) is the key to what they are feeling. And that this matters. So family conversations are a training ground for empathy. When an adult asks an upset child, "How are you feeling?" the adult can make it clear that anger and frustration are acceptable emotions; they are part of being a person. Upset feelings don't have to be hidden or denied. What matters is what you do with them.

Family conversation is a place to learn that you can talk things out rather than act on your feelings, however strong. In this way, family conversation can work to inoculate children against bullying. Bullying is discouraged when children can put themselves in the place of others and reflect on the impact of their actions.

The privacy of family conversation teaches children that part of our lives can be lived in a closed, protected circle. This is always a bit of a fiction but the idea of a protected family space does a lot of work. It means that relationships have boundaries you can count on. This makes family conversation a place to let ideas grow without self-censorship. In the performative world of "I share, therefore I am," family conversation is a space to be authentic. Family conversation also teaches that some things take time to sort through—quite a bit of time. And that it is possible to find this time because there are people who will take the time. A phone at the dinner table can disrupt all of this. Once a phone is there, you are, like everyone else, in competition with everything else.

The privileged circle of family conversation is delicate. Roberta, twenty-one, complains that her mother has begun to post pictures of family dinners to Facebook. For Roberta, something has been broken. Now it never feels as though her family is alone: "I can't even relax and wear sweatpants when I chill with my family. My mom might post it." Roberta says this in a half-joking manner, but she is upset about more than losing an occasion to relax in sweatpants. She wants time when she can feel like "herself" and not worry about the impression she is making.

When you have a protected space, you don't need to watch every word. But these days, so much of what I hear from parents and children is about their desire to say the "right things" to each other. Ideally, the family circle is a place where you don't always have to worry about getting it right. What you can feel is that your family is committed to you. You can feel trust and a sense of security. To give children these rewards, adults have to show up, put their phones away, look at children, and listen. And then, repeat.

Yes, repeat. In family conversation, much of the work is done as children learn they are in a place they can come back to, tomorrow and tomorrow. When digital media encourage us to edit ourselves until we have said the "right thing," we can lose sight of the important thing: Relationships deepen not because we necessarily say anything in particular but because we are invested enough to show up for another conversation. In family conversations, children learn that what can matter most is not the information shared but the relationships sustained.

It is hard to sustain those relationships if you are on your phone.

Elsewhere: A Study of Distraction

In 2010, a young pediatrician, Jenny Radesky, began to notice that more and more parents and caregivers were using smartphones when they were with young children. "In restaurants, on mass transit, in playgrounds," she says, "the phones were always there." Radesky knew that attention to children during these kinds of moments was crucial: "the bread and butter of relationship building."

These are the times when we get to listen to our kids, respond to them verbally and nonverbally, help them problem-solve around new challenges or intense reactions, and help them understand themselves and their experiences. . . . This is how children learn to regulate strong emotions, how to read other people's social cues, and how to have a conversation—all skills that are much harder to learn later on, say at 10 or 15 years of age.

With caretakers on their phones, Radesky thought, those crucial early conversations are disrupted. How disrupted? And how much are caretakers really on their phones? Radesky did a study of fifty-five adults who were watching over children as they ate meals together in fast-food restaurants. The results: Across the board, the adults paid more attention to their phones than to the children. Some adults interacted with children intermittently; most withdrew completely into their devices. For their part, children became passive and detached or began to seek adult attention in futile bursts of bad behavior.

At such moments we see the new silences of family life. We see children learning that no matter what they do, they will not win adults away from technology. And we see children deprived not only of words but of adults who will look them in the eye. Children's inner wisdom is at work as they strain to make eye contact in the fast-food restaurants. From infancy, the foundations for emotional stability and social fluency are developed when children make eye contact and interact with active, engaged faces. Infants deprived of eye contact and facing a parent's "still face" become agitated, then withdrawn, then depressed. These days, neuroscientists speculate that when parents caring for children turn to their phones, they may "effectively simulate a still-face paradigm"—in their homes or out in a restaurant—with all of the attendant damage. It is not surprising if children deprived of words, eye contact, and expressive faces become stiff and unresponsive with others.

Parents wonder if cell phone use leads to Asperger's syndrome. It is not necessary to settle this debate to state the obvious. If we don't look at our children and engage them in conversation, it is not surprising if they grow up awkward and withdrawn. And anxious about talk.

The "Missing Chip" Hypothesis

A t Leslie's home, eyes are often down and mealtimes silent. Leslie, fifteen, says that the silences begin with her mother breaking her own rule that there are to be no phones at meals. Then, with her mother's phone out, there is a "chain reaction." Family conversations at dinner are fragile things.

> So my mom is always on her email, always on her phone, she always has it next to her at the dinner table. . . . And if there's the slightest little buzz or anything, she'll look at it. She always has some excuse. When we are out to dinner she'll pretend to put it away—she'll have it on her lap. She'll be looking down but it will be so obvious. Me and my dad and my sister will all tell her to get off her phone.
>
> If I were to even be on my phone at the table I would get grounded by her—but she has her phone out. . . . At dinner, my mom is doing her own thing on her phone, and it ends up my dad is sitting there, I am sitting there, my sister is sitting there, and no one is talking or anything.
>
> It's a chain reaction. Only one person has to start. Only one person has to stop talking.

Leslie lives in a world of missed opportunities. At home, she is not learning what conversation can teach: the worth of her feelings, how to talk them through, and how to understand and respect the feelings of others. She tells me that "right now," the place she feels "most important" is on social media. But social media is set up to teach different lessons. Instead of promoting the value of authenticity, it encourages performance. Instead of teaching the rewards of vulnerability, it suggests that you put on your best face. And instead of learning how to listen, you learn what goes into an effective broadcast. Leslie is not becoming better at "reading" other people; she is simply more adept at getting them to "like" her.

Recently, I see an encouraging sign: young people's discontent. Leslie is not alone in expressing her disappointment. Children, even very young children, say they are unhappy with how much attention their parents give to phones. Some are clear that they are going to bring up their own children in a very different way than how they have been raised.

And what is that different way? For Leslie, that would be in the kind of family where there are no phones at breakfast or dinner, not just rules against it that parents break. She wants a family where you have conversations at meals. But some children who have spent their early years eating at silent tables worry that they won't know how to be in that kind of family. Recall the young man who told me, "Someday, someday soon, but certainly not now, I'd like to learn how to have a conversation." He added the "certainly not now" because right then, at that moment, he preferred to text rather than talk. He is not confident that he can express himself without a chance to edit his messages. He knows he needs practice in conversation.

The notion of practice is key. Neuroscientists talk about the "use it or lose it" quality of our brains. Nicholas Carr, who introduced the notion of "the shallows" to help people think about how their brains adapt to life on the web, said: "We become, neurologically, what we think." If you don't use certain parts of the brain, they will fail to develop, or be connected more weakly. By extension, if young children do not use the parts of their brain activated by conversing with an attentive parent, they will fail to develop the appropriate circuitry. I think of this as the "missing chip" hypothesis. The name, of course, is a bit of levity, but my concern is serious: If young children are not engaged in conversation, they will start out a step behind in their development.

There is an analogy between children's relationship to conversation and to reading. Teachers complain that students—from middle school and beyond—are less able than their peers of only a decade ago to read books that require sustained attention. Cognitive neuroscientist Mary-anne Wolf studies this shift away from what she calls "deep reading." Today, adults who grew up reading serious literature can *force* themselves to focus on long texts and reactivate the neural circuits for deep reading that they may have lost after spending more time online than with books. But children need to develop these circuits in the first place. Wolf suggests that to get children back to reading, the first, crucial step is to read to children and with them.

The parallels with conversation are clear. To get children back to conversation—and learning the empathic skills that come from conversation—the first, crucial step is to talk with children. These days, it is often children who seem least afraid to point out that technology is too often getting in the way.

Missed Opportunities

Of course, the fear that technology can get in the way of family conversation is nothing new. Television prompted similar anxieties. Considering the case of television makes the point that we use technology in a context and that context counts. As a little girl in the 1950s, I watched *I Remember Mama* and *The Molly Goldberg Hour* with my family. Commercial breaks provided precious time to discuss the characters' problems and how our family would do things differently. More recently, as I wrote this book's chapter on solitude, I binge-watched *True Detective* with my daughter and we paused every ten minutes to argue fine details of the plot. As I wrote the chapter on friendship, we watched *Game of Thrones*, and in this case the conversation included a fair amount of talking back to the television. What was happening on the screen couldn't possibly be happening! Too many of the main characters were being killed off!

Technologies come with affordances. Television can be watched socially or alone in one's room. Television can isolate a family, but if you take advantage of the fact that it can be used socially, it can also bring families together.

I interview Alli, fifteen. The installation of a new flat screen television in her family's kitchen did not make it a family hearth. During meals, Alli eats silently, watching television, while her parents retreat to their phones. Alli misses her parents. When she needs advice, when she has questions about boy trouble, school trouble, friend trouble, she goes to her anonymous Instagram account, on which she has over two thousand followers.

Right now, Alli says, she is looking for advice about a "friend problem," so she recently posted a picture and a question on Instagram and got back hundreds of answers from all over the world. Alli says she uses Instagram "carefully" and knows how to keep safe. When someone asks if they can send her a personal message, she declines. In Alli's fluency with Instagram, we see a virtue of the online world: Teens now have a place to ask questions and have conversations that might not feel comfortable in their local surroundings. To take a classic example of how this works: Gay or transgender adolescents in a small, culturally conservative rural town can find a larger community online; a circumstance that once would have been isolating no longer needs to be. If your own values or aspirations deviate from those of your family or local community, it is easy to discover a world of peers beyond them.

But in this particular case, Alli *wants* to talk to her parents. She's going to the network because her parents are going to their phones.

The irony is that if Alli and her family were separated by distance, if her mother had to work in a different city, they might well be using apps on their phones and computers to bring them together. Dinner might be a time to Skype. Families use social media to keep everyone informed of big events and milestones. But living together, the members of Alli's family let their devices isolate them.

Like Alli, fifteen-year-old Hillary says that when it comes to personal matters, she would rather turn to her mother than the network, but "When my mother is texting, she can't be reached." And, like Alli, she doesn't know how to get her mother's attention. But on Instagram or Facebook, someone is always listening.

Hillary describes how her mother shuts down conversations. "When I am talking to my mom and she's emailing someone, she's like, 'Wait.' Or she's talking to me and she stops her sentence in the middle to finish her email and then keeps talking. And then stops and starts." Hillary says that the effect of these stops and starts is an erosion of trust. She says, "Trust . . . knowing that someone is not understanding you, not paying attention, makes it easy to lose trust. . . . If someone was on their phone and not really in the conversation, I don't feel like I can trust them as much."

For the psychoanalyst Erik Erikson, basic trust is the building block upon which all other development rests. For the infant, trust takes a primitive form: "When I am hungry, I shall be fed." Later in life, trust is built in other ways; beyond being fed, one wants to be heard. Hillary says she has never confronted her mother about how she uses her phone. In contrast, Austin, fifteen, says that he frequently calls out his parents for being on their smartphones when "house rules" forbid it. He says, "My mom will always be like, 'Stop using your phone, you're addicted to your phone.'" But moments later, his mother will be on *her* phone. Austin says, "Whenever I'm having a conversation at the dinner table or something, she'll have her phone out . . . you'll ask her a question and it'll be the shortest answer possible. Like, she'll say, 'Okay.' The shortest possible answer. Or sometimes she just won't even hear me. It's like a bubble around her head. [She's] in her phone, not noticing the people around."

So Austin challenges his mother: "I say to her, 'Why are *you* on *your* phone all the time?'" Usually his mother answers that she is using her phone for a work project. But Austin says that when he looks at his mother's phone, he is more likely to see text messages and games. Austin pauses. "If you're always on your phone, you just miss so many things in life." What he doesn't say is that his mother has "missed" him and he misses her.

Dreaming a Different Life

We cannot know if the parents we see ignoring children would be more attentive if they didn't have phones. What we do know is that our phones are seductive. When our phones are around, we are vulnerable to ignoring the people we love. Given this, it doesn't make sense to bring a phone to dinner with your children. Accept your vulnerability. Remove the temptation.

There is another story here. Parents have become preoccupied with technology just as our links to community have become more tenuous. Tod, fifteen, imagines, nostalgically, that his parents grew up in a world of greater community, but he doesn't see that world. He doesn't go to a neighborhood school. He lives in a run-down part of town and his parents don't want him out on the street or even out with friends who live close to his house. When Tod comes off the school bus, his parents want him to go straight home. He expresses his dependence on his family by saying he "doesn't really have a town." What he means by this is that he doesn't really know his neighbors. And his parents have disappeared into their phones. So now he's starting to feel that all he has is what social media can provide. Tod imagines the days before cell phones:

> In the olden days, people were friends with their neighbors. They weren't friends with people who lived ten miles away. So nowadays, people aren't so close with their neighbors. Their friends don't live close by. And there's more traveling, and you're associated with people everywhere, but in the olden days, you basically knew what you were familiar with. Your town, your people.
>
> Now, if you don't have your phone, you are alone. . . . People used to know their neighbors; now all you've got is your phone.

I meet Tod when I visit a device-free summer camp. The ten boys in his bunk describe a vicious circle. Parents give their children phones. Children can't get their parents' attention away from their phones, so children take refuge in their own devices. Then, parents use their children's absorption with phones as permission to have their own phones out as much as they wish.

Everyone thinks that everyone else is occupied and preoccupied. The most realistic way to disrupt this circle is to have parents step up to their responsibilities as mentors. They can't do this if they are texting or doing email while their children are trying to get their attention.

Of course, distracted parents are nothing new, but sharing parents with laptops and mobile phones is different than sharing parents with an open book or a television or a newspaper. Texting and email take people away to worlds of more intense and concentrated focus and engagement. This difference is something that children comment on. (One teenage boy says: "I could interrupt my father if he was reading the paper. We used to read it together while we watched Sunday sports and if I had something to talk about, I just had to ask. His laptop is different. He's gone.")

Here is a fifteen-year-old boy, disappointed and resigned: "When I come home from school, my mom is usually on her computer doing work. . . . Sometimes she doesn't look up from her screen when I am talking to her." One of his friends says that his mother, too, is usually unavailable. Once his family took a vacation where there was a bad Internet connection and his mother became so stressed that she almost cut the vacation short. "She said, 'I can't wait to get back from vacation because I feel like I am missing all the stuff I have to do.'" He sums up what he makes of his mother's stress: "Obviously, the Internet has helped us create a lot of jobs, but it can definitely be a hindrance to life."

Mitch, fifteen, who lives in rural Pennsylvania, feels he has lost his parents to their phones. His mother's rule is no phones at dinner, but she brings her phone to dinner all the time. He expresses a thought that I hear more and more: He is going to learn from his parents' mistakes. *He says, "I'm going to raise my children the way my parents think they are raising me. Not the way they really are raising me."*

We know how Mitch is being raised: with phones at dinner and no conversation. How do his parents think he is being raised? That would be closer to the way they themselves grew up, in a simpler and lower-tech way. Mitch thinks his parents have the right idea when they keep this idealized picture in mind. He says, "I think it is a good sign. It's a sign that they can see that technology is not leading to good things even if they can't help themselves from using it."

Mitch has worked out his own theory of why conversation is disappearing: People are getting out of practice.

I think my mom has forgotten how to talk. I kind of feel the reason why so many of us keep using our phones even though it takes away from meaningful conversations is that some people have kind of forgotten how to really have a good conversation because they've used their phones for so long that they don't really know what else to do but text. It gets awkward talking in front of real people—they haven't done that. I think really they just don't know what to do.

The young people I interview are in conflict. They talk about the Internet as a "hindrance to life." They say they want a different kind of life for themselves and the families they will build in the future than what their parents are providing for them. But for now, they lead the life their parents model. They carry their phones at all times. They sleep with their phones. Some post to their networks rather than talk to their parents when they need emotional support. They say it's easier, and besides, they are not confident they can command their parents' attention for the amounts of time it takes to really sort things out. And some doubt if their parents have the needed resources to help them. They are more confident that the right information will be available online, accessible from strangers or search.

Young people have grown up in a world of search, and information is the end point of search. They have been taught that information is the key to making things better—in fact, to making everything better. Family conversation teaches another message. Talking to your parents doesn't just offer up information. You experience the commitment of a lifelong relationship. A parent may have no immediate "solution" for you but may simply say, "No matter what, I will always love you." And "I'm staying around for another conversation; we'll keep talking this out." Even if a family is broken and a parent lives at a distance from a child, this last message is what a child wants to hear, no matter what the circumstances.

Left to Their Own Devices

It's easy, as Alli found, to post a picture with a question on Instagram and get hundreds of suggestions back. She says that doing this makes her feel good; it makes her feel less alone. But despite the pleasure of positive feedback from her followers, Alli knows that the "hearts" she gets on Instagram and the "likes" she gets on Facebook are not about affection. They are more like a rating system that tells her if her problem is interesting. Online, even the statement of a problem is a performance.

I have said that, in some measure, all of our behaviors are performances. But there are important differences among them. A tearful conversation with your mother and a sad blog post are both a kind of performance, but they ask and offer very different things. Ideally, the conversation with your mother can teach how empathy works. It is an opportunity to watch her attend to how you look and sound. It is an opportunity to notice that when she pays attention to you, her responses will begin to mirror your tone and body language. You can observe that when she says, "I don't understand," she leans forward, signaling that she is trying to put herself in your place. Children learn empathy by observing the efforts of others to be empathic toward them.

Why do parents turn to their phones and away from their children? They tell me that they simply become distracted by something they see online, often something that relates to work. And then one thing leads to another. And sometimes, more is in play: Parents want to "shut down" the stress of family life. We've met Melissa, eighteen, a high school senior whose parents are on the verge of divorce. There is constant bickering and dinner is often the place where things come to a head. Melissa's father will make small aggressive gestures—he'll put too much pepper in the spaghetti sauce even though he knows his wife dislikes pepper. When a fight blows up, as it does practically every night, Melissa's mother explodes in rage and Melissa follows, screaming.

Melissa says that when this happens she wants to talk to her mother, but in the chaos at dinner, with everyone yelling, cell phones come out. Her mother disappears to get support from her friends on her phone. And Melissa does her version of the same thing. She goes to her phone and to Facebook—her network.

It is hard for Melissa's mother to turn to her upset daughter and give her the quiet conversation she needs. Our phones are not the cause of the new silences in our families. But they make it easy for us to avoid difficult conversations. From the point of view of our children and their development, these difficult conversations are necessary conversations.

Left to her own devices, Melissa is not getting the help she needs. When someone is being empathic toward you, you learn that someone is listening to you, and that they have made a commitment to see things through. Melissa's mother is in a position to express this commitment to her daughter, to say to her, "This situation is bad. I'm sorry that as an adult I've put you into it. Tell me how you feel. I can't necessarily help right now, but we are in this together and I'm working to get us out of this." Instead, she goes to her phone.

Some parents tell me that (at least in some measure) they don't put down their phones because they are intimidated by their children, who seem to live in an online social world they don't understand. Parents say they are afraid of being "shown up" and so they try to keep up. They don't want to feel irrelevant. "My phone feels like an equalizer," says one mother in her early forties.

Parents should not be looking for an equalizer, because all things are not equal. If parents fear their children's technological expertise, it can lead parents to forget that they have a lifetime of experience to share—*that their children don't have.*

Your fifteen-year-old daughter who can set up your household network—printers, cable, and smart TV—is afraid to talk on the telephone because she has no confidence that she can find her words. She doesn't know what to do about a bully at school. She dreads a face-to-face meeting with her teachers. She needs you.

And we've seen that sometimes, parents will interrupt conversations to do online searches because they think it will make family conversations richer. From the parents' point of view, they are not turning away from their children at all. They think they are bringing more data into the conversation. But that is rarely how children see it.

Recall the fifteen-year-old who stopped her dad when he went online to "fact-check" a question that had come up at dinner. She said, "Daddy! Stop Googling! I want to talk to you!" She wants her simple presence to be enough. She doesn't want to be trumped, quizzed, edified, or in competition with the whole online world. A college junior whose father is in the habit of taking out his phone during dinner in order to make conversations more accurate describes its effect as putting conversations on a punishing "time-out." He says, "It's like pushing the reset button that takes things back to square one. Conversations aren't given a chance to develop."

Haley, a college junior, says that her parents "always placed a premium on talk and sitting down to dinner together as a family," but this "broke down when my parents both got iPhones." Now "they are hooked and they don't even know it."

Only two days into Haley's last visit home, there was a dinner table quarrel about the table settings at Thanksgiving the previous year. Both her parents took out their iPhones to call up photographic evidence.

Haley asks her parents to put away their phones during dinner but they cannot hear her: "They don't feel bad. They tell me they are looking at something quickly or checking the weather or writing a quick email and that they are sorry." According to Haley, even when her parents don't bring their phones to dinner, their phones are on their minds. All through the meal, she says, her parents are waiting for it to be over, and then, as soon as they possibly can, "they both stand up from dinner and get their phones."

Only a few weeks earlier, her parents took out their phones when the three of them were having dinner with her grandfather, her mother's father. Haley says that when the phones came out, her grandfather was "flustered," and as for her, she felt betrayed. When the four of them had been eating dinner and talking, she had felt she was in a special place, a closed circle that crossed generations. The phones broke the circle: "It felt like something stopped . . . and we had to start from square one." But they couldn't. The mood had shifted.

When Haley talks to her parents about her concerns, they accuse her of being a hypocrite. They see their daughter on *her* phone and don't think she has any standing to be the "technology police." But Haley thinks she does have standing. She is a child who wants to talk to her parents. That should be standing enough.

These days, Haley says that her strategy for talking to her parents is to save up things for when she thinks they are open to listening. "Sometimes this means waiting for the next day. Or maybe I will wait to talk to my mom the next time I see her." By adolescence, children have learned that they are not always on their parents' minds or the only things on their minds. But it makes them feel safe to know that they can always get their parents' attention when necessary. Haley has lost that confidence.

Asymmetry

Relationships between parents and children are not symmetrical. It is natural that children want parental attention but don't necessarily want to give attention back. In fact, children who say they want to talk to their distracted parents may make a show of shutting them out. Amelie, a graduate student, now twenty-seven, looks back on the "asymmetries" of her teenage years:

> *When I was a teenager I would be angry at my parents for their using their phones, but at the same time, when my mother would reach to hug*

me or get close, I turned away from her and looked down at my
phone. . . . That was just to frustrate her. I needed to separate from her.
To show her I didn't need her.

Yet Amelie admits that she appreciated her parents' phone-free dinner table conversations, often so engaging that they continued on past dinner. "Sometimes we would have people over—a neighbor or a relative—and they would continue talking after dinner. They would go into the living room and have coffee and cake. And my sister and I would follow and listen and sometimes say something. I would not have admitted it, but I really liked that."

I am reminded of Amelie when I talk with adolescents who grudgingly admit how much they appreciate conversations that family rules (such as no phones at the dinner table) make possible.

Marni, fifteen, keeps up a small rebellion against her family's "no phones at dinner" policy by keeping her phone tucked under her thigh so she can take quick looks. Nevertheless, she is happy with the "no phones" rule.

She wants the rule and she wants to break it, just a little. I think of my students who tell me that in class they like to be able to glance at their phones, but that they also like it when professors insist, as I do, on class discussions with no phones. One says, "It shows that the professor cares."

As Amelie put it, when young people hit adolescence they have to push away from parents. Gratitude for rules you want to break seems a developmental norm. These days, it can express itself by declaring fealty to the world on your phone while being grateful to your parents for insisting that sometimes you put your phone aside.

Thus Doreen, fourteen, expresses a grudging appreciation for her mother's insistence that all family matters be discussed in person, face-to-face. Sometimes, she says, if there is a family problem, "my mother will play Monopoly and Clue with us" and the conversation will happen over the board game. "And no electronics are allowed in our bedrooms. We have this thing called the dock. And it has all of the chargers and stuff. So, like, at the end of the day all of the phones and tablets and laptops, they all go there." Doreen is not happy to put her phone in the dock—she doesn't want to miss any messages—but she admires what her mother is doing: The ritual of the dock frees the family up for talk. And she can get to sleep at night—her phone is off-limits.

When Knowing Better Is Not Doing Better

Paradoxically, the technology that offers us so many new ways to connect to each other can also make it harder to find each other.

Jon, thirty-seven, wants a closer relationship with his seven-year-old daughter, Simone. A recently divorced management consultant in Los Angeles, Jon eagerly looks forward to time with Simone but he also finds it stressful. His time with his daughter is sporadic and out of their previous domestic routines. So, Jon explains, there are only so many times that it feels reasonable to take Simone to the museum or the American Girl store or the zoo. He finds it difficult to "just hang out" with her. That was easier when he lived at home with her mother. Then, his exchanges with Simone came easily. Now, things seem forced. So when Jon hears that Simone's second-grade class is going on a field trip, he welcomes the chance to be on the bus. He looks forward to a "natural" way for them to spend time together.

When I meet Jon, the field trip is fresh in his mind. He describes the time on the bus:

> *Naturally, I brought my phone. Without my phone, I can't work or read emails, or write to the women in my life. I can't write to Simone's nanny. I can't take pictures of my daughter. You can't do anything. The phone is you—a phone is your extension of your body. It's like, "What can you do if we take your hands away for the next four hours?" . . .*
>
> *So number one, I took eight hundred pictures and I was sending out every picture, sending out every picture while I'm on the field trip. And then I'm writing and texting and people are responding to pictures, "Oh! So cute. Where are you?" And I'm writing, writing, writing. And*

all of a sudden I'm realizing as I'm sitting there that Simone has been
sitting there for, like, an hour without me saying a word to her.

And then I was like, "I've got to put my phone down." Granted, it
was all revolving around pictures of Simone—and I'm telling everyone
I'm texting that I'm on a field trip. But then [on the bus] Simone said,
"Put your phone down."

Jon wants to be with Simone, but talking with her makes him anxious. He loses confidence when he isn't holding his phone. He tells me that recently his phone died when he was at a museum with Simone and he felt he had lost his inner world. "It was just like, 'I'm not even a person.'" And talking to a seven-year-old takes patience and knowing how. Instead of settling down and figuring out what to say to his daughter, it is easier for Jon to show love by taking pictures and posting them to the network.

I've said that a first step toward reclaiming necessary conversations can be to create device-free times and places for them to happen. For families, those places would be the kitchen, the dining room, the car (and in Jon's case, the bus). Sometimes people take exception to this approach and suggest that it makes more sense for families to focus on how to spark engaging conversations. If people find that their devices help them have better conversations, the devices should be welcomed.

When people make this argument, I ask them to illustrate with an example, a story. One mother of two teenagers talks about how her family, when discussing *Game of Thrones*, likes to pull up memorable gory scenes on their tablets. Another mother of three children in their twenties recalls a political conversation at a large holiday dinner. She wanted to make the point that politicians could start significant national conversations. She took out her phone and showed a few minutes of Barack Obama's speech on race during his first presidential campaign. "Taking out the phone to show that—it made the conversation richer."

If you apply this way of thinking to Jon's case, he could, if he is feeling shy with Simone, use his phone to find a photo of a trip they had taken together and begin a conversation about it. Or he could use his phone to play a scene from a recent movie they had seen together and start to talk about its characters.

But this is not what Jon does. When he brings out his phone in what he says is a high-stakes family situation (he hasn't been spending enough time with his daughter—the field trip is his chance), he ends up using it in a way that isn't good for his daughter or for his feelings about himself as a father.

We imagine (as when the mother of three describes "screening" a political speech at a family dinner) that bringing out a phone will enhance conversation. And sometimes it does. *Sometimes it does.* But more often, once a phone is out, it is hard to resist the temptation to also check our email. Or we notice that a text has come in. And we give it a quick response. When we have our phones in our hands, we are invited to stay in the world of our phones. *Our phones give the false sense of demanding little and giving a lot.* One of the most consistent lessons I have learned from studying families: We have to be more compassionate with ourselves. We are vulnerable. Our phones exert a strong holding power and we want to stay with them. But our families need us.

Jon never considered going on the school trip without his phone. The idea of time without his phone makes him feel less than himself, like "half a person," a man "without hands." Jon has to find a way to see himself as a whole person without his phone so he can bring that person to a conversation with Simone. She has to learn that she, too, can grow up to be a whole person without her phone. Right now, her father can't teach her that.

Jon's story illustrates how we have all learned to put our face-to-face relationships "on pause" when we send or receive a text, image, email, or call. And Jon did all of this without thinking. It was only, he says, after more than an hour on the road that he realized he hadn't said a word to his daughter.

When on late night television Louis C.K. discussed why he doesn't want to give cell phones to his daughters, he was led to a meditation on the importance of feeling the deep sadness of life. He said that when he senses this feeling coming on, his first impulse is not to let himself feel it, but to "get the phone and write 'Hi' to, like, fifty people." And then wait for the responses to come in. Louis C.K. was talking about using phones to block sadness, but we use them to block other feelings as well. Jon, feeling uncomfortable, disrupts the potential for quiet time with Simone by sending out a blizzard of messages to friends, relatives, and women he is dating.

So, Jon's frenetic sharing is part of a larger story. We become accustomed to seeing life as something we can pause in order to document it, get another thread running in it, or hook it up to another feed. We've seen that in all of this activity, we no longer experience interruptions as disruptions. We experience them as connection. We seek them out, and when they're not there, we create them. Interruptions enable us to avoid difficult feelings and awkward moments. They become a convenience. And over time we have trained our brains to crave them. Of course, all of this makes it hard to settle down into conversation.

When I speak with Jon, he makes it clear that, as he sees it, he began the field trip with the intention to spend the day with his daughter but his phone stood in his way. He admits that his phone also stands in the way of talking to Simone when they are at home. He says, "If I want to talk to somebody, whatever, I will put on a cartoon so she can watch. I don't usually acknowledge this, but I am right now. . . . You know, I don't think I'm so bad with her, but I am somewhat bad with her."

Here is how Jon describes Simone's objections when he plants her in front of a television cartoon: As on the bus, she puts up with it for a while and then objects. (Jon speaks in the second and third person—describing Simone as "she" and himself as "you"—when he talks about Simone's objections.) "She will tell you to put your phone away and stuff . . . and then you get sad. You are like, 'God! I've been on my phone a lot.' You know? . . . I think kids are probably suffering a lot."

Indeed, for many parents, knowing their children's unhappiness is not enough to make them put down their phones. There is a flight from responsibility. It can be addressed.

First, parents need a fuller understanding of what is at stake in con-versations with children—qualities like the development of trust and self-esteem, and the capacity for empathy, friendship, and intimacy.

Second, parents need to move beyond thinking of their own attach-ment to their phones with simple metaphors of addiction or, more usu-ally, a smiling reference to a "semi-addiction," as in "I'm semi-addicted to my phone and can't do anything about it." The fact is, we are all vul-nerable to the emotional gratifications that our phones offer—and we are neurochemically rewarded when we attend to their constant stimulation.

Once we recognize the affordances of a technology—what a technol-ogy makes easy or attractive—we are in a position to look at our vulner-ability with a clearer eye. If we feel "addicted to our phones," it is not a personal weakness. We are exhibiting a predictable response to a per-fectly executed design. Looking at things through this lens might put us halfway to making new choices, needed changes.

In our families, we can take responsibility for using technology in the same way as we take responsibility for the food we eat: Despite advertis-ing and marketing and the biochemical power of sugar, we recognize that healthy foods in healthy amounts serve our families' best interests. And over time, we have put pressure on food producers to change their offerings. Right now, the apps on our phones are designed to keep us at our phones. Their designers profit from our attention, not from how well the technology supports us in the lives we want to lead.

Exporting Conflict

In Colin's family, the three children are taking paths very different from those their parents anticipated. All were sent to New England prep schools in the hope that they would pursue traditional professions, but Colin, a college junior, is on his way to a career as a musician, and his older brother teaches skiing in Vail. His parents would like to get the family together for periodic trips; only his sister, who works as a pro-grammer for an Internet company in New York, feels she can structure her time sufficiently to make these kinds of reunions possible. Colin tells me that when his family has conflicts, usually about the children not meeting parental expectations, "we take our disagreements to Gchat conversations." He likes this because he says "it makes things smoother." He appreciates that this smoother operation gives him time to collect his thoughts. But when he pauses to ask if something might be lost, a question as much directed to himself as to me, Colin responds with a business metaphor: "What would be the value proposition of disagreeing with each other face-to-face?"

He can't think of an answer. His family takes care of conflict by cooling it down online. Colin thinks they are now more "productive" as a family. But what is a family's product? Should a successful family produce children who are comfortable with "hot" emotions?

Margot, a mother of two in her late forties, uses texting and messaging for difficult family conversations. Like Colin's family, she finds it an improvement on all other options. Her practice began with a failed face-to-face conversation with her son Toby, a high school senior. Toby was upset and told his parents that he wanted to have a conversation, but one in which he could present his case to them without being interrupted. He had a message and he wanted to be "heard out." In person. The message: He wanted his parents to accept that he was working as hard as he could in school even if he was not living up to their expectations.

The conversation took place in the family's kitchen. But Toby's father broke the rules. Instead of listening in silence, he made a comment and Toby stormed out and retreated to his bedroom. From there, he began furiously texting both his parents, inundating them with angry messages. Toby's father did not want to respond to these messages, but Margot began to reply. In response, Toby sent more texts saying that he wasn't going to read any of her texts, but Margot persevered. "I kept copying and pasting the same messages over and over until my son began to read them."

In the past, this situation might have called for a bit of time to cool off, and then for what some refer to as "a family meeting." A family would get together and commit to hearing each other out. Or, matters such as these could be discussed at dinner. Even if the atmosphere was tense, the fact of regular dinners meant that families knew that tomorrow there would be another dinner and another chance to sort things out. But in this case, Margot made a conscious effort not to bring this discussion into any "in person" space. Instead, conflict was explicitly exported to the world of online interactions. This is the "family meeting 2.0." Margot liked how it worked, so she and her family decided to keep it up.

Margot calls what her family does when they work out problems by texting each other "conversations." As she sees it, they are exchanges designed to minimize the risk that family members will say something they might regret. Margot says her family works better as a result. In their first set of exchanges, Toby was able to tell his parents that he felt his academic efforts were unappreciated because he wasn't always successful. And Margot was happy that she got to express her point of view: She feels that Toby does not use all the help he is offered.

For Margot, the key to successful family conversations is preparation and editing. Margot says she is able to have more successful interactions with Toby because she composes her thoughts before sending them. Without the "time delay" of texting, she says she could not find the right words to reach him. And in her view, the right words matter. And the right emotional tone, caring but cool, is also something she doesn't think she could consistently achieve in person.

Margot could, of course, take the time to think through what she wants to say to Toby, and then have a face-to-face conversation with him. Margot rejects this option. She says that if she had been face-to-face with her son in that first argument, her emotions would have taken over. And she would not have had the self-discipline to keep saying the same thing over and over. "It would have felt weird." But it did not seem weird to repeatedly copy and paste the same message in a text box. And Margot is certain that this is what the situation called for.

Now, Margot is a true believer. There is no need, in her view, to let emotional turmoil get in the way of solving important family differences. In fact, she and her husband began to use online exchanges to work out their own disagreements in the aftermath of their argument with Toby. Toby's spotty achievement in high school had a cost. He is not going to attend a prestigious college; instead he will attend the college he was able to get into. Margot became angry with her husband because she felt he was not at peace with how the college admissions process had ended. She felt her husband was undermining their family's chance to be fully accepting of each other.

This disagreement was not about something trivial. It began about a child's college plans but ended up about the meaning of family commitment. Yet Margot and her husband chose to have their entire argument over text. Margot says that this allowed them to do away with many of the "messy and irrational" parts of a fight. As when she discusses her texting marathon with her son, Margot stresses that in this medium, you have time to compose your thoughts. As Margot sees it, in the controlled world of the digital fight, there is less danger of doing "lasting damage."

In Margot's view, technology enables family fights to be what they always should have been: cleaner, calmer, and more considered. Therapists have been telling family members to calm down and slow down for years. The point of that advice is to help them better listen to each other, in each other's presence. Margot thinks that what she calls "fighting by text" is a method in that spirit. You don't get face-to-face contact, but family members get to hear each other out and have time to reflect on each other's point of view.

Certainly this tool opens new channels of family communication. But to say to a child, partner, or spouse, "I choose to absent myself from you in order to talk to you," suggests many things that may do their own damage. It suggests that in real time, it is too hard for you to put yourself in their place and listen with some equanimity to what they are thinking and feeling. Being able to be enough in control of our feelings to listen to another person is a requirement for empathy. If a parent doesn't model this—if you go directly to a text or email—a child isn't going to learn it, or see it as a value.

Telling a family member that you will get back to them when you have composed yourself is a time-honored way of handling a difficult turn in a relationship. What is different in "fighting by text" is that a moment becomes a method. It may send the message that you are so reactive that you can't even try to process your feelings in real time. Or perhaps that you don't think they can. And even if you don't mean to send this message, this may be what is understood.

And there is this: Since fighting by text puts the emphasis on your getting the "right" message *out*, it sets up the expectation that you require the "right" message *back*. This implies that you think there is a way for people to talk to each other in which each party will say the *right* thing. Relations within families are messy and untidy. If we clean them up with technology, we don't necessarily do them justice.

Colin and Margot are content in their technologically mediated conversations. Others feel that when it comes to emotional things, only face-to-face communication counts. So, for example, when Haley is home on college breaks, "house rules" require her to call or text her parents to tell them if she will be out all night. Haley says that she sometimes forgets and this produces a predictable response: alarmed text messages from her mother. Here is how Haley describes them: "There are texts saying that she is about to call the police, that she hasn't slept for the whole night, that I have to stop doing this. . . . And then I think 'Oh, shit!'" But Haley says that she shrugs off her mother's texts—she's gotten used to them.

But only a week ago, Haley stayed out all night without being in touch. There had been a technical problem with her phone ("I texted my parents but it didn't send"). This time her mother didn't send any texts. She came down to breakfast the following morning to talk to her daughter face-to-face. Haley says that she could see that her mother had been up all night and that she had been crying. Haley says, "This is the first time she got mad at me in person."

Somehow, the years of alarmed texts from her mother had become something like seasonal rituals, part of going home. For Haley, only when the argument went live did it become real. Haley says, "It is streamlined . . . clean to take care of things over text . . . [but] it did not spark the thoughts I had when my mom got mad at me in person."

I saw her face. My mom was almost crying. That can't be conveyed via
text. She could be bawling. . . . If she sent a text, I wouldn't know. So in
terms of sparking real reflection, there is something that is conveyed in
emotions and facial expressions. . . . The way it made me feel didn't
come from her words.

Recall Colin's question: What could be the "value proposition" of
face-to-face conflict in a family? Haley's story suggests an answer. Texting about conflict cooled things down to the point where she lost track
of her mother.

Since the early 1990s, as I have explored people's emotional investments in their online lives, I have suggested to psychotherapists that
when they meet with patients, they use their patients' lives on the screen
to spark conversations. Our profiles, avatars, websites—these are all
places where, as we represent ourselves, we have an opportunity to rethink our identity. Using therapy to talk about our online lives can open
up new conversations about the self. For many years, when I expressed
this idea, I met with considerable resistance. And now, with far less resistance. Now, therapists are more likely to appreciate the extent to
which online lives are evocative objects, tools for thinking about the self.
They are dream spaces for the digital age.

Indeed, these days, therapists often don't have to ask patients to show
them what they are doing online. Patients take the initiative themselves.
As one family therapist told me: "When patients want to tell me what is
going on in their lives, they read from their phones. A patient reads me
texts from his children, his wife, his boss. This is usual. They want me
to analyze what these texts 'really mean.'" So these days, in addition to
encouraging patients to share their lives on the screen, therapists often
find it necessary to ask patients to put away their phones in order to be
fully present in therapy.

But we know why patients want their therapists to see their screens:
That is where there is a record of the exchanges that make us most anxious or elated or confused.

My Problems with Punctuation

I have my own family confusions when my daughter, at around sixteen, asks me if I am angry with her.

It turns out that my text messages have no or insufficient punctuation. Without exclamation marks and extra question marks and emoticons, what I think of as practical and loving messages sound brusque.

In texting, punctuation is everything. Every period, every comma, every exclamation point in a text counts. Communities of practice form. It's not so different from learning the rules of body language when you go to a foreign culture. If you don't know the rules and you make the wrong assumptions, meaningful connection can stop. When it comes to texting, a lack of fluency with the rules can divide generations and families.

Why does my daughter think I am angry with her when I text? She explains: "Mom, your texts are always, like, 'Great.' And I know it's not great. What's happening? What are you really thinking?" There is no convincing her. When I texted her "Great," it was because that really was what I meant. If she were there with me in person, that is what I would have said. But "Great" as a text message is cold. At the very least, it needs a lot of exclamation points.

My first—and it turns out, clumsy—move was to include terms of endearment in my texting. To little avail. She said that a text from me ("May I speak with you tonight, sweetheart?") came off "like a death in the family." I learn from my research that "Call??? When good for you????" would have been better. I add emojis to my iPhone. Emojis are little pictures of cats, hearts, buildings, lightning bolts, many hundreds of little things, and I feel ridiculous when I use them. I use them anyway. I ask my daughter if they are helping. She makes it clear that she knows I am trying.

If we are making any progress, it is not because my texting is improving but because she understands that I don't know how to text. This means she less frequently allows herself to "hear" what my texts would communicate if you applied what she considers "standard texting rules." In other words, I alarm my daughter less frequently.

Once, my inability to parse my daughter's rules of texting truly frustrated me. I had uncertain results in a round of medical testing and was scheduled for a critical diagnostic test. I debated whether to tell my daughter in advance that the test was taking place. If nothing was wrong, why worry her before there was anything to worry about? In this case, talking with friends convinced me that if things did not go well, my daughter might be upset to learn that I had struggled with a serious problem without telling her. She was not a child. She was a twenty-one-year-old woman. She might not be happy that I had avoided a conversation.

There is no reliable way to reach my daughter without texting her, so I texted: "Darling, call me when you can." Within seconds, she texted back: "What's wrong?" I texted back: "Nothing is wrong. I just want to make a date to get together." She pressed: "What about?" My next text: "I'd rather talk in person, sweetheart." And again from her: "What about? What's wrong?" Now we were on the phone. "Becca, why are you so concerned? I just want to have coffee." At the time, my daughter was in college in Cambridge, Massachusetts. I live in Boston. We often had coffee.

She knew why she was concerned. "It's your text. There is no punctuation. The whole way you are texting is weird. It says that something is the matter." There was no going back. The conversation I wanted to have in person would happen on the telephone. I told her about my test. I told her that I thought she should know about it. She got it all out of me. And over time, I came to understand the hypothetical text message that *might* have gotten me to the coffee date I wanted. It would have had to be nonchalant, with another message or punctuation carrying the message that nothing much was at stake. I *should* have said something like, "Hey . . . am swinging by the Square tomorrow :) on my way to a meeting later!!!!! . . . do you have time for an early breakfast??? Henrietta's Table? Not dorm food???"

Something truthful emerges. The "right" punctuation might have gotten me to a face-to-face meeting by creating a pretense. My inability to follow the codes simply got us to the truth. In the end that was fine. But I didn't want to have that conversation over the telephone. Across the generations, there is a lot of learning to do.

Find My Friends

When Margot—the enthusiast of "fighting by text"—becomes frustrated that her son, Toby, the high school senior, won't commit to telling her where he and his friends are going (something she feels she has a right to know), she decides not to keep asking. Instead of working out his responsibility to her in a conversation, she goes to a technical workaround.

She asks Toby to install the application Find My Friends. With the application turned on, he will show up on a map on her iPhone as a dot.

Find My Friends began as Margot's way of dealing with an uncommunicative son, but now her entire family uses it. In Margot's family, there is a new compact. If your phone is on, your family knows where you are. You don't need to check in.

This new compact makes certain conversations easy to sidestep. For example, you can avoid the conversation that Haley's mother finally insisted on when she tearfully confronted her surprised daughter and made clear that there will be no more staying out all night without checking in to say she is safe. With Find My Friends, Margot can check the location of any family member. But is it progress to be able to avoid that parent-child conversation—in this case a conversation that would have been with Toby? The conversation would have been about good judgment and understanding the concern of those who love you. It would also have been about what we owe each other.

Even awkward, unpleasant conversations can do a lot of work. A face-to-face conversation about Toby's whereabouts could teach how to set boundaries and how to stand up for yourself without diminishing the feelings of the person you address. It could also teach about legal things: Margot is responsible for her underage son. It could teach about separation: Toby may want to assert himself—to have secrets. That may not be a bad thing. Even if he can't get precisely what he wants, it might do his parents good to know that he wants more privacy. Maybe they can find some other way to give it to him.

Margot is getting what she wants without conversation. But she is giving up a lot. In her family, location dots are calming. There is now no need—and no obvious opportunity—to have difficult conversations about responsibility and trust. Instead of talking, you agree to surveillance.

Future Talk

There is no reason to idealize family conversations of the past. They could be stilted. They could be dominated by parents who proclaimed opinions or who demanded idealized accounts of the day from obedient children.

But you don't need to idealize the past to cast a steady eye on the present. Digital culture offers us new possibilities for talk and new possibilities for silence.

We are vulnerable to our new technologies in ways we did not anticipate.

We sense that new social rules allow us to check our phones almost all the time, but we also sense that on some human level these rules don't feel right. One woman tells me of a long hospitalization. Her husband can be with her almost all the time because Wi-Fi at the hospital enables him to work from her bedside. But she also says that during her long weeks of hospitalization, she and her husband have barely spoken because he hardly looks up from his laptop and smartphone.

Another talks about her experience during the period of mourning after her mother's death, known in the Jewish tradition as "sitting Shiva." During the Shiva, the immediate family of the deceased stays at home and receives guests. Traditionally, they bring food. The Wi-Fi network in her house has been disabled for the mourning period, but the cellular network, over which individuals have no control, is on. During this woman's Shiva, her guests sit and talk to her. But after a bit, they retreat to quiet corners of her house to text and do email on their phones. She tells me that she finds herself upset by these guests although she understands that being able to "hop on their email" may be what allows them to make lengthier visits.

Both women—the hospitalized woman and the woman describing her period of mourning—ask me what I think is the "right attitude" for someone in their situation. They want attention. They find themselves taken aback that they have to compete for it. They are hurt, even resentful. But they are insecure in their feelings.

Each woman expects a certain kind of conversation and finds an unexpected silence. But neither woman is confident that she has a case to make because now it is normal to bring a phone wherever you go. We almost forget we are carrying our phones, so much do they seem a part of us. Each woman presents her story as though it poses questions of etiquette. Each muses aloud about "What is the correct way to view this situation?" But the stories are about more than etiquette. They are about the challenges to close ties when technology enters our most intimate circles. In each case, their questions about the "right attitude" are about more than what to do. They are about what to *feel*.

We are vulnerable: Going to technology starts to feel easier, if not better, than going to each other. Simply keeping this in mind may help us make more deliberate choices for our families.

Whether a family chooses to create device-free "sacred spaces" at home or chooses to cultivate daily habits of family conversation—devices or no devices—children recognize a commitment to conversation. And they see it as a commitment to family and to them. I think this can make the difference between children who struggle to express themselves and those who are fluent, between children who can reach out and form friendships and those who may find it hard to Find Their Friends.

Friendship

The Quality of Empathy (Is Strained)

With my friends, it's either no conversation or conversation
about what's going on, on your phone.

—A FIFTEEN-YEAR-OLD BOY

You can put so little effort in when you text and then you
get instant gratification. I can connect with fifteen people with
no effort and it feels so good to just extend the feelers and get
a positive response. I would rather have that than a
conversation a lot of the time.

—A TWENTY-ONE-YEAR-OLD WOMAN

Trevor, twenty-six, is a master of phubbing—the art of talking to other people but with your eyes on your phone. And Trevor is never far from his phone. When I tell him I'm working on a book on conversation, his reaction is close to a snort: "Conversation? It died in 2009."

That was the year he was a college senior, majoring in history.

That's the year we shared things on Facebook instead of talking to each other. We put our energy into our profiles. We talked about what we had put online. The focus of friendship became what you found online and how you would share that with your friends. These days, you do it with Instagram or Snapchat. People are less into their profiles. But the idea is the same. Don't talk it. Post it. Share it.

Trevor says that when he was in college, social media changed his "face-to-face world." He recalls a farewell party for graduating seniors:

People barely spoke. They ordered drinks and food. Sat with their dates. Looked at their phones. They didn't even try. Everyone knew that when they got home they would see the pictures of the party. They could save the comments until then. We weren't really saying good-bye. It was just good-bye until we got to our rooms and logged onto Facebook.

And, says Trevor, "even our style of talking in class was different." There was less give-and-take during class time. Students got into a style that was less conversational but resembled the composed "postings" you would do on Facebook. In class,

You would try to say something brilliant . . . something prepared in advance . . . and then you'd sit back and wait for your responses. You didn't have to really engage. The idea of saying something as it occurred to you and getting a conversation going, that was gone. . . . And you didn't just do this new thing in classes, you did it with your friends. Now, you'd say what you [had planned] to say. And then, you'd get your responses.

Using this style of participation was a balm for academic anxiety. And Trevor says that his friends used it to relieve social anxiety as well. "By composing your thoughts in advance the social anxieties of friendship could go away." His comment reminds me of the Stanford freshman who told Clifford Nass that "technology makes emotions easy."

The March of Generations with
Their Generations of Technology, 2008–2014

Trevor's report, as Mark Twain might have it, greatly exaggerates the death of conversation. But this much is true: These days, day to day, teenagers choose to use texting more than any other form of communication, including face-to-face communication. And styles of online talk can change in the time it takes for a new app to capture the collective imagination.

Since Trevor met Facebook, young people have moved from wanting to put their energy into managing a Facebook-style profile to being more interested in ephemeral ten-second communications on Snapchat. They seem less interested in being defined by what they say *about* themselves and would rather be known as they are in the everyday, by how they behave and what they share. Snapchats and Instagrams and the very short videos of Vine have become the media of the moment.

I see the rapidity of change in two conversations in early 2014. In the first I am with a college senior who talks to me about FaceTime. She dismisses it: "*We* don't do that. You have to hold it [the phone] in front of your face with your *arm*; you can't do anything else." Only a week later, a group of high school freshmen talk to me about the merits of FaceTime—they use it for after-school conversations with friends while running other apps on their iPads or phones. They *like* FaceTime because it allows them to multitask during conversations. Tired arms never come up.

Junior high school students use Snapchat video to record "sides" of conversation that they send back and forth—sort of like an asynchronous FaceTime. Recently, Snapchat introduced a new feature. Where users could previously only send pictures that would automatically disappear after the receiver viewed them for a preset time, now people can send self-destructing text messages. The ephemerality of conversation reborn—this time with a chance to edit before you hit send.

What is clear is that across generations, the profile, once the defining concept of social media, has come to seem almost onerous. Trevor describes it as too "heavy." But as he contemplates the "lightness" of posting a photo on Instagram, he points out that "what endures" across the apps—old and new—is "that going out for a drink often seems like too much work." He adds that "it still takes a lot to risk having to sit down with each other and just see what happens." A group of thirteen-year-old FaceTime enthusiasts tell me that they use the app to talk to friends who live in their neighborhood. Why not visit? They explain: Keeping the exchange online means "you can always leave" and "you can do other things on social media at the same time." Continual attention is what 2009 taught that friendship didn't require.

That year—and for several before—I was interviewing students in high schools in the Northeast and I heard the idea take hold that friendship always presents you with a choice. If you have something to say, you can wait to say it until you are together—online. Young people came to this at first slowly, then faster as their technology gave them new options. Flip phones, Sidekicks, instant messages. And then there were the game changers: MySpace, Facebook, and smartphones that gave messaging a new fluidity, turning it into something that seemed close to magic.

I've kept up with the cohort of students who graduated from high school in the years 2008–2010. As they have matured, certain things have remained constant. Friends want to be together, but when they get together, the point isn't necessarily to talk—what counts most is physical closeness. And when friends are physically together, they often layer their conversation so that part of it is online (with the same people who are in the room).

Bree, a college senior in 2014, says that when she is with her friends, "I'll jump online with the people I'm with, just briefly, to get a point across. . . . I never really learned how to do a good job with talking in person." James, a classmate, does the same thing: "Even when I'm with my friends, I'll go online to make a point. . . . I'm more at home. Online life makes the conversation work. . . . It's just so relaxing to have that texting channel open."

If you punctuate face-to-face conversation with text messages, have you opened up conversation or disrupted it? James thinks you have made it more "relaxing." Bree thinks she needs the extra channel because she is missing the skills for "in-person talk."

I think of Bree when I look back to the early years of the smartphone and how it presented an alternative to conversation. I recall a 2008 birthday party for a fifteen-year-old girl with very little talking, the guests in small groups, several looking at phones together. Some guests stood alone, immersed in their own phones, texting. Some took pictures of themselves and friends. There was clustering near the refreshments; people took pictures of the food. Fifteen is a difficult year for socializing across the sexes. Here, phones provided a welcome alternative to talk.

Before there were smartphones, an event such as the birthday party would have meant long silences, some stumbling around, and a few brief conversations with members of the opposite sex. These might have been awkward. But when they occurred, an important step would have been taken. Developmentally, the fifteen-year-olds would be closer to having sixteen-year-old confidence in their ability to connect. Eyes down at screens do not provide this groundwork.

The social preferences of Amy as a high school senior in 2008 help to explain the silences of a birthday party when the teenage guests have Facebook on their mind. Amy barely says a word to boys at school or a party, but she rushes home to talk to them online. There, Amy says, you can "take a breath," relax, and plan what you are going to say before sending your message. In person a conversation can get out of control, go flat, or stop dead. Online, Amy feels playful.

If you have a relationship with a person, you think they're cute and stuff, you can make more of a conversation online than you would be able to in person because when you're in person, you're intimidated by the person. You like them. You don't know if they like you back. Online, you can say "Hi," and they'll say "Hi" back, and you can start a full-blown conversation. In person, there are so many reasons why you don't want to talk to that person. Because you think, "Maybe they think I'm ugly" or something like that.

Given these anxieties, when she is having a face-to-face conversation with a boy, Amy tries to keep things short and then get him online as soon as she can.

When we talk online, we talk about a whole bunch of stuff, but when I'm on the phone with a boy or in person, it's like "Ahh, mad awkward!" . . . Let's say you are both together face-to-face. Unless you come up with some kind of question or something, like if you say, "How was school?" or whatever, you've got nothing. And let's say he says, "Good," or "Fine" . . . You've still got nothing.

By the time Amy was a high school senior, the culture had made her anxieties easier to live with. In fact, the social mores around cell phones had moved most friendships toward online exchanges, not just those with a promise of romance. Facebook friending and group texting— these were among the first steps in creating an online circle that felt like your own private community, a family of always-available friends.

Friends like Family

In 2008, I talk to Rona, a high school senior, who has just joined Facebook and says what this means to her: "Your friends become more like family and you want to talk to them in the most relaxed way." It turns out that what Rona means by "relaxed" is particular: She can reach her friends immediately and have them get back to her immediately. New habits take hold as children feel a responsibility to be on call for their friends. In 2008, high school homework means, as Rona puts it, "an open laptop, Sidekick, and an every-five-minute check to see if anyone sent me anything." She knows the rules: *"If someone sends me a message on Facebook, I have to . . . I feel the need to get it and get back to them when they're still online."*

In contrast, telephone calls don't have to be returned. Rona says that if she calls her best friend, her friend will respond by text. Rona understands. Telephone calls "put you on the spot." Texting gives more space to say things right and make things right. If "you do something wrong you can fix it right away." I ask Rona to go over this again because I want to make sure I understand. Isn't the telephone a way to have the person *right there* if you want to correct a misunderstanding?

"Not really," says Rona. The phone call is in real time and she sees real time as a place of awkwardness. Again, relaxation comes from fast response time with the possibility of editing. The phone is not a safe place to "just kind of put yourself together with somebody to see what your feelings are."

That's what Facebook and texting are for. That's where you share a self in process. But you share best if you can edit, because you want to share what your friends will find acceptable. And young people come to expect their friends to be there to receive their messages. They need them to be. Sharing is how you come to feel most real to yourself.

But now Rona, accustomed to her online social life, is afraid to "put herself out there," unedited, when she meets people face-to-face. In person, Rona says, "you could do something that the other person might not like . . . and you're scared that something is going to make you look stupid."

Looking back, Trevor's comment that conversation died during his senior year in college no longer seems so flip. In interviews I conducted from 2008 to 2010 with high school and college students, they make it clear that the back-and-forth of unrehearsed "real-time" conversation is something that makes you "unnecessarily" vulnerable. And it presents technical difficulties. When you are with your friends in person, you will also want to be on your phone, *texting them and other friends*. This parallel set of commitments doesn't leave much space for "real-time" conversation.

At the limit, you have to get your friends to pipe down in order to get down to the serious business of composing your notes to them. It may be at the limit, but it is common enough that there are collections of comic strips devoted to depicting friends and lovers sitting opposite each other, texting each other, trying to set up dates to be together.

Our Phones, Our Selves:
A Natural History of Texting

It is spring 2008 and eight seniors at an all-male day school in Connecticut are talking about their phones. Only a few months earlier, most of them had received smartphones as holiday gifts and texting has exploded.

Oliver begins by saying that "it's official"—texting is the "baseline" for his friendships. In fact, his friends would think that something was wrong if he didn't keep it up. He tells me that most of his conversations with friends start with a text and continue in person. He searches for a metaphor: "The text is an outline of what you're going to talk to a person about if they're your good friend." But then he corrects himself: That is not right. Most often, the in-person conversation doesn't happen, so you just "go with the text." So the "outline" actually ends up being the conversation itself, and Oliver says he has gotten used to this; it doesn't bother him.

Oliver's friend Jasper thinks they are all embarked on a future from which there is no turning back, but he nevertheless wants his friends to know that he sees a downside: Even when he is there *in person* with his close friends, he is having text conversations with other friends elsewhere.

Why? Because Jasper can do it silently "as soon as they [the friends who are not physically present] cross my mind." And because "when you are with your friends, other friends are texting you. . . . And the 'other friends' can make it sound like their problems are more urgent than what you are talking about with the friends who are with you."

Jasper tries to be tactful because he is telling his best friends that once he has his phone, they exist in an ecology of "all his friends." And once he is dealing with "all his friends," the ones who are with him (in person) lose a certain priority. He tries to make his point sound less personal by linking it to a larger question: When you have your phone, maybe it's not just the people in front of you who lose priority. Does the world in front of you lose priority? Does the place you are in lose priority? Your phone reminds you, all the time, that you could be in so many different places. Jasper says:

There are so many things you can do . . . so many connections that are at your fingertips. You can look through your phone book, and there's probably one hundred, two hundred people that you can call, you can text, you can find. You don't have to rely on other people to find a party and stuff, if you go hang out with your friends or if they come hang out with you. You find a party by texting around. . . . To find a party is five buttons away.

Jasper says that all this power makes him feel independent, but his description of finding a party with "five buttons" foreshadows what Kati, a college junior only six years later, will experience as a general anxiety about too many choices, any choices.

In spring 2014 Kati is interested in politics, the Italian Renaissance, and training for the Boston Marathon. When she goes to parties, she reports that there is a lot of texting. Here is what she tells me: At any party, her friends are texting friends at *other* parties to figure out "whether we are at the right party." Kati says, "Maybe we can find a better party. Maybe there are better people at a party just down the block." Kati is describing how smartphones and social media have infused friendship with the Fear of Missing Out—now a feeling so well known that most people just call it by its acronym, FOMO. In its narrow definition, the acronym stands for tensions that follow from knowing so much about the lives of others because of social media. You develop self-doubt from knowing that so many of your friends are having enviable fun. As the term caught on, it came to capture the widespread anxiety about what to do and where to go now that so many options are apparent to you.

The sociologist David Riesman spoke of an other-directed life, where you measure your worth by what friends and neighbors think of you and by whether you have what they have. He contrasted other-directedness with an inner-directed point of view, where your choices are measured against a personal standard. These days, as social media let us all track our friends' homes, jobs, lovers, children, spouses, divorces, and vacations, we are tempted to measure ourselves—every day—against what other people are doing. From middle school on, I have found evidence of Riesman's "other-direction."

And that is what Kati and her friends are living. Wherever she and her friends are, they strategize about where they *could* be. With so much choice, says Kati, it becomes harder to choose, because "you're afraid you won't make the right choice." And nothing seems like the right choice. Nothing Kati and her friends decide seems to measure up to their fantasy of what they might have done. With this state of mind, being at any party can turn into a research project to make sure it is the right party:

> *Instead of talking to who we are with, we are on our phones, checking out other parties, asking what's happening at other parties, trying to figure out if we should be there. You end up not talking to your friends because you're on your phone, getting information about whether you should be someplace else altogether.*

I ask Kati if, while this frantic foraging is happening, she and her friends feel warmly toward each other, part of a group. "Oh, definitely. We feel that we're there together. We came to the party together. But we end up not talking about anything other than the best places we could go. So you end up not even talking to your friends. We're focused on what our phones are saying about what our other options are. It's not much of a conversation."

Five Buttons, Then and Now

When texting was new and pressing five buttons was a novelty, Jasper felt independent and a master of his choices. Six years later, Kati sounds exhausted. By 2014, the fear of missing out has become a fear of missing anything.

In 2008, Jasper is not there yet. He is high-spirited about how on-line choice gives him independence, but even he warns his friends about the downside of infinite choice: They are all paying less attention to where they are and the people they are with. "People forget . . . that sitting here right now might be the best thing that you can get. That might be the best you have."

Jasper's comment is followed by a long silence in the group of young men. Finally, Oliver breaks the silence: "What if you're always looking for something better and then you die? You've searched all the way until you're dead. And you've never said, 'Maybe I've found it.'" The group gets quiet again.

And since all the members of the group admit that they are now having a hard time focusing their attention because their minds are always on their phones, it's not surprising that they begin to talk about how to keep their attention on each other. They decide that there should be a rule: *A good friend should keep you off your phone when you are together.*

But as they talk about what it is actually like when they go out together, it becomes clear that even in 2008, this "mission statement for friends" has already become aspirational. It's how they think friends should behave; it's not what they do. Staying off their phones is so hard that one of the boys, Aidan, has taken on the role of "monitor." The group tells Aidan that they want him to keep them in line, to call them out. If they take out their phones, he should shame them. They talk about how they don't want to be "that guy" who is hanging out, going to the beach with his friends, but also on his phone. "That guy" is not cool.

But they feel closer to that guy than they would like to be. One by one they admit that they need Aidan as a monitor because when they are together, they almost always want to go to their phones.

Jasper reminds the group of something they seem to have conveniently forgotten: When he first got his phone, he wanted to resist the pressure to make it the center of his life. After six months, he noticed that he was texting all day, right until he went to bed, and so he put his phone in a drawer and got off Facebook. It lasted seven weeks. As he tells it, he was "forced back online" by his friends: "People were just really annoyed that they couldn't keep in contact with me. They hated it. They needed constant contact."

The group is subdued as Jasper tells this story. They don't contradict him. They know they forced him back onto Facebook. Jasper was angry with them at first, but now he simply says of life with phones and social media: "This is where we are. Once you get used to it, heaven forbid someone takes it away."

My interviews with high school students in those early years, 2008–2010, most often began with their optimistic statement that they had texting and social media under control. And then, at some point, they recounted an incident that made it clear that things were not so simple. Often, it would be a story about how, when they went out together, each of them was on the phone with other friends.

Today that same cohort, now college graduates, is alert to the ways their friendships have been shaped by their phones. *Young people know this: If you want to get friendship right, you have to get right with your phone. But this will most probably not involve talking on the phone.*

Phone Phobia

It was in 2008–2009 that I first became aware of how averse a new generation was to talking on the phone. Jasper and his friends make elaborate plans to avoid it. They receive calls from college sports coaches who want to interview them. These are important calls. But the young men have their parents take the calls, and they, the college hopefuls, send a follow-up email. As soon as young people saw a real alternative to the telephone call, they found ways around it, usually email. Their problem with the telephone call is by now familiar: Recall how Rona said that she disliked the way telephone calls put her "on the spot." Voice calls unfold in "real time." I am told that "this is no longer necessary." Yet this is the pace at which life unfolds.

Not much has changed since 2008 in how young people talk about voice calls. In 2014, a high school senior sums up his feelings about phone calls: "Sending an email is so much easier because you get to think about everything, you get to write it down. . . . There are just so many variables on the phone or in an in-person conversation." When he avoids the phone, he gets more than the ability to self-edit. The fact that he can answer emails and texts when he wants gives him the feeling that the world is there for him, when he wants it. And a telephone call makes it hard to do more than one thing at a time. He is bound for an Ivy League university and is worried about the demands of "a fair amount of on-the-spot talking."

I've followed this generation's anxiety about voice calls through their college years and well into first jobs. In 2014, a group of junior and senior college women talk about the rigors of a phone call. One describes it as "the absolute worst. . . . I instantly become this awkward person. On the phone—I have to have little scripts in front of me." For a second woman, a call is stressful because it needs "a reason . . . so I have to plan what I'm going to say so it doesn't sound awkward." A third also needs to prepare with notes: "It all goes too fast on the phone. I can't imagine the person's face. I can't keep up. You have to be listening and responding in real time. . . . You have to be listening to the emotion in a person's voice." This is exhausting and, whenever possible, something to avoid.

A twenty-six-year-old takes a job at a trade publication and is asked to research a group of potential media consultants. Her supervisor makes it clear that their personal qualities are crucial to determining who will be chosen. The new hire completes the project based exclusively on web research. I speak to her supervisor, who had to insist that the project be started anew, this time with voice contact. She says of the young woman, "Talking on the phone had been such an onerous prospect, she didn't even want to consider it."

In another organization, a large non-profit that consults to the health-care industry, staff members are told to check when new hires say they have "talked" to clients. Have they *spoken* with clients on the phone? Out of college and graduate school, new recruits will use the word "talk" to refer to an email exchange. Very few will use the phone unless specifically instructed to do so.

Never a Dull Moment: Friends Talk About What Is on Their Phones

While young people today don't want to talk on their phones, they can't stop talking about what is on their phones. Here is Devon, fifteen, assessing lunchtime talk: "With my friends, it's either no conversation, or conversation about what's on your phone." And as phones have more and more on them, their role as the touchstone of conversation grows for all generations.

Maureen, thirty-two, recently received a master's degree in social work. She describes a monthly brunch with her friends as getting together, with phone in hand. Maureen spends some of brunch texting friends who are not present, but even if she didn't need her phone for these connections, she says it is hard to imagine socializing without its support. "The things I talk about now, I feel they come from my phone. I'm aware that if I don't have my phone to tell me what is going on, I would feel like a person without anything to say."

And here is Randall, twenty-four, a real estate broker, on how he and his friends spend their free time: He stresses that it is important that they get together, physically, but when together, at a bar or restaurant, "someone always has their phone out, showing something." I ask Randall what happens when there is a lull in the conversation. He looks at me, seeming not to understand. Later he explains that in his mind, he has just made it clear that there is never a lull in the conversation. Anything like that would be filled by showing something on your phone or doing something with your phone. But I haven't understood this yet, so I try again. I say, "Like, if things got quiet among your friends?" Randall says, "Oh, if the conversation was not providing information, I'd check out some YouTube stuff I'm behind on . . . or take a picture of us and post it."

Maureen and Randall talk about the value of getting together with friends in person. But they describe friendships in which they hold back from giving full attention to the people they are with. They both describe a hard time tolerating what Maureen calls "the boring bits" when friends get together. Or letting conversations go beyond sharing information. And, of course, they feel pressure to have information to share.

There is another way to think about conversation, one that is less about information and more about creating a space to be explored. You are interested in hearing about how another person approaches things—his or her opinions and associations. In this kind of conversation—I think of it as "whole person conversation"—if things go quiet for a while you look deeper, you don't look away or text another friend. You try to read your friends in a different way. Perhaps you look into their faces or attend to their body language. Or you allow for silence. Perhaps when we talk about conversations being "boring," such a frequent complaint, we are saying how uncomfortable we are with stillness. And how hard we find it to "read" the face and voice, changes in body language, and changes in tone.

Indeed, Randall says that when things get quiet with a friend, he finds it "hard to focus." That's when he is likely to take a photograph and upload it to social media. When he does this, he takes his attention off his friend. But in another way, the photograph is his effort to reach out. Randall is doing what he knows how to do. The conversation has stopped, but the photograph says "We are together." The photograph speaks when Randall doesn't have words or is not sure what his friend is trying to communicate. It is Randall's effort to navigate the conversation's quiet spaces. When he moves his friend's image to the screen, he is ready for Facebook and a conversation he can manage.

Posting often involves choosing among several similar photographs, cropping, or selecting a favorite filter—for example, one that turns the photograph sepia or into something that looks as though it was shot on a 1950s Brownie camera. There are moments, as one plays with all of this, when one has the occasion to attend to a friend in a different way, to notice a change in expression, a change in posture, to sense something new. Is this communion, but at a manageable distance?

In 1979 Susan Sontag wrote, "Today, everything exists to end in a photograph." Today, does everything exist to end online? One thing

seems clear: Time with friends becomes more comfortable when it produces images to be shared.

As this happens, our ideas about comfort change. For Randall, they
expand from what a friend can offer to what a phone can offer—among
other things, "comfortable" places to find your friends.

Right now: Facebook, texting, Instagram, Snapchat, and Vine. In the
pipeline: everything from glasses that transmit messages directly onto
the visual field of the person you are trying to reach to a bracelet you tap
to send a coded message to someone wearing a matching bracelet. What
all of these have in common: They are "friendship technologies" to make
you less vulnerable to ever feeling alone.

Security Blankets

Joelle, a senior at a large state university, talks about her phone as a
"security blanket." It's easy to feel isolated if you are not with your
closest friends; people won't talk to you. "You can't expect a lot from
your peers. Certainly not conversation." A phone always gives you a way
to look busy.

> So we never have to be truly alone in any situation. You get to a party
> and text your friend that you are at a party and don't know anyone.
> You ask them where they are. But you aren't necessarily being vulnerable
> at the party. Because you're removing yourself and showing that you
> are choosing to be on your phone. It isn't that no one wants to talk to
> you. It's that you're choosing not to talk to anyone else because you're on
> your phone.

Vanessa, a college junior, shares a similar story to illustrate how her
phone almost always makes her feel less vulnerable. If she arrives at an
exam room a few minutes early, or at a party where she doesn't know
anyone, she will take out her phone rather than turn to the person next

to her. I ask Vanessa if she is shy. She says she doesn't think so. It's more that in her group of friends, striking up a conversation with strangers would go against the norm. And besides, it takes so much work. The phone gives her an easy way to stay in touch with her private social world.

In these accounts, there are new silences. Classes where you don't talk to classmates because you pretend to be doing important things on your phone. Conversations you interrupt to "refresh" your phone, text a distant friend, or take a photo. Parties where you sit in a corner and text friends who are not with you.

What makes these new silences acceptable? Or appealing? We've met Haley, the college junior who was upset when her parents used their phones at dinner. She thinks she has part of the answer to why we are willing to put up with phones that cut off conversations. She calls it "the seven-minute rule."

Haley thinks that realistically, seven minutes is the amount of time you have to wait to see if something interesting is going to happen in a conversation. It's the amount of time you have to wait before you should give up and take out your phone. *If you want to be in real conversations, you have to be willing to put in those seven minutes.* She says that they are not necessarily interesting minutes. In those seven minutes, "you might be bored."

You know the seven-minute rule? It's that lull. That really uncomfort-able, shitty thing where you're, like, "Oh no, should I go? Should I leave? Is this over?" And you don't know how to end it. And just like the work you have to put in, you have to go through so much unpleasantness be-fore you actually hit something. In real conversation, sitting next to each other. And then it can be really good. But inevitably . . . you're, like, "Okay . . . What now?" It's an art.

As Haley describes her own practice, she makes it clear that she often doesn't put in her seven minutes. She skips a conversation and sends a text instead. Why? "It feels enclosed and self-contained. Whereas it's messy in a conversation and it's scary for that reason." She speaks for many. We don't put in our seven minutes and we don't let the conversation happen. We use our phones to take what we can get. And often, we make what we can get good enough.

The Friend Beside You and the Friend on the Phone

In 2008, you had to justify being inattentive to friends you were physically with. Oliver, Jasper, and their crew even asked a friend to "monitor" them in case they fell into bad habits. By 2014, there are no more "monitors." The mores of friendship include being "there" for a friend by providing physical presence while your friend is on the phone, texting other people.

Among college students, some rebel—not many—and make strenuous efforts to stay off their phones when they are with friends. Some say they don't like dividing their attention, but take it as a given of "life today." Others talk about a "natural evolution"—we will get better at multitasked conversation. We will become better at picking up where conversations left off. Others think that the evolution will be in social expectations. We will come to experience people in the room and "people on the phone" as equally present. The trick, hard now, but perhaps not so hard in ten years, is not to devalue yourself when the friend beside you turns to the "people on the phone."

Carl, twenty-three, a graduate student in computer science, sees physical and electronic presence as socially on par. And when you see these as equal, you aren't critical of your friend if he or she turns away from you to pay attention to someone on the phone. Turning to the person on the phone is like turning to another friend present in the room.

Carl's position seems pragmatic, but I see little evidence that it makes emotional sense. I remember the first time—sometime in the late 1990s—that a graduate student pointed out to me how hurt he felt when his friends took cell phone calls when he was with them. He told me it made him feel like a tape recorder that someone was putting "on pause." A friend turning away from him to attend to a "friend in the phone" made him feel like a machine. These days, we have learned to crave interruption—we like the buzz of the new—but emotionally, not much has changed. When Haley tried to console an unhappy friend who started to text other people in the middle of their conversation, she says she felt invisible, like smoke that had disappeared.

The story Haley tells is this: She was out for dinner with her best friend, Natalie, when Natalie received an upsetting text from an ex-boyfriend. Haley tried to console Natalie, but her friend was more interested in what other friends were saying who were leaving messages on the network. Here is how Haley describes Natalie's turn to the "people in the phone":

> I am not great at consoling people at all but I was hugging her and trying so hard. I decided that it was my chance to console her. She had been there for me. It had been an uneven break. I decided to go all out. I was trying all of these different methods. And five minutes into me trying to console her she sent out five texts to people describing the situation and then started reading their feedback while I was talking to her. We were walking down the street and she was just texting her "consolation network." So then I changed my approach and started asking her what people were saying over text. And I tried to engage with her on that strange and oblique access point. But it was so weird to not be the primary person even though I was the only real person there.
>
> Terrible. She was texting people that were hundreds of miles away instead of talking to me.

Why do we turn away from the people before us to go to the people on our phones? Haley gave one answer. In person, we have to wait seven minutes in order to see where a conversation is going. But if it is acceptable to answer a text during a conversation with a friend, we have an excuse to not even try to put in those seven minutes. And then, once we are on the phone, we can get more of what we have become accustomed to: the validation that texts can provide, along with the fact that they come in great numbers.

Haley talked about Natalie's consolation network and her consolation texts. Think of those online consolations as the first minutes of a conversation, the first things you might say to an unhappy friend. You provide support. You say you are sorry and how much you care for them. When you allow yourself to be consoled by a friend in person, you take the chance that things might go beyond this. There is more of a chance for the conversation to open out onto more delicate areas. If, as Natalie, you are talking about a relationship that has ended, you could find yourself talking details: how each party in the relationship might have contributed to its demise. How the *other* person might be feeling.

If you confine yourself to consolation texts, you don't really have to take that chance. You are in a position to get solace and safety in numbers. If you don't like where things are going in any exchange, it is relatively easy to end it. But sticking with the consolation texts means you lose out on what the conversations of friendship can provide—not only solace, but a deeper understanding of yourself. And of your friend.

Of course, just as some conversations disappear, new ones appear. Just as you can make a friend feel invisible by going to your phone, you can make that same friend feel more important by *not* going to your phone. So, the existence of mobile phones has invented a new kind of privileged conversation. These are conversations with friends that are elevated when both participants know they are getting text messages and both choose to ignore their phones. After she recounts her dispiriting experience with Natalie, Haley describes this heady experience: "So you know that you are both getting texts but you are ignoring them and thereby elevating the importance of the conversation that you are having. You show each other that you're into it because you are both blowing up with texts. . . . Ignoring a text for me means a lot to me."

Arjun, a college senior, gave me another way to view why people turn away from a friend and to a phone. For him, the phone not only serves up comforting friends; it is a new kind of friend in itself. The phone itself is a source of solace.

Intellectually, I know that it's the people on the phone who keep me company. So when I go to check my messages, I am technically going to check for which people reached out to me. But let's say I see there are no new messages. Then I just start to check things—Twitter, Instagram, Facebook, the familiar places to me. Now, it's just the phone that is a comfort. The phone that is the friend.

Disruptions

We let phones disrupt the conversations of friendship in several ways: By having our phones out, we keep conversations light and we are less connected to each other in the conversations we do have. And we rarely talk to friends about how we feel when they turn away from us to their phones. This behavior has become a new normal. But behavior declared "normal" can still sting.

This is Richard, forty-eight, on what he misses when he visits his college roommate Bob. This happens about twice a year, every time that his work takes him to Washington, D.C.

I keep remembering what it used to be like before [cell] phones. We used to talk. I don't know. One thing would lead to another. Sometimes we would get into pretty serious conversations about books we had read, people we knew, our marriages. Now, he has his phone and he just idly will look at it from time to time. If I said, "I have something really important to talk about," I know Bob would put down the phone.

But Richard doesn't say that. He doesn't challenge his friend. "It seems so basic to him, to hold his phone," he says. Richard has accepted the new way their visits will work.

Not everyone is resigned. I interview a group of good friends in their late twenties, most of whom are still working in their first jobs. When I tell them I am writing a book about conversation, their thoughts turn to the conversations they are *not* having. What follows is something I rarely hear: friends calling out friends because of the time they spend on their phones. I attribute this unusual conversation to their degree of intimacy. So Maria accuses her best friend, Rose, of "hiding behind her phone." Maria says that Rose and her boyfriend "are the worst two cell phone people I have ever met." Maria says that when you're with them, it's tough to have a conversation.

> *You two just text constantly, check your phones constantly, like you are always on it. Sometimes I'll just go crazy because I can't stand how long your boyfriend stares at the phone. And sometimes I feel that way when I'm with you—because you're, like, text, text, text. And I'm, like, "Are you listening to me? I'm trying to talk to you!"*

The tone of sharp disappointment in this conversation helps me understand why friends don't often ask other friends to put down their phones. Raising the topic is a minefield.

On Call

Phones have become woven into a fraught sense of obligation in friendship. For the same young people who complain of inattention from their friends "in person," being a friend means being "on call"— tethered to your phone, ready to be attentive, online. From middle school on, children describe this as a responsibility. They sleep with their phones for many reasons—one of which, they say, is to be available to friends in case of what many refer to as "emergencies."

This sense of urgency extends from bad news to good. You always want to know who is reaching out to you. Your phone is your view onto that. When a friend sends a text and says it is urgent, you will stop whatever you are doing and attend to your friend on the phone.

Here, a fifteen-year-old explains why she worries about forgetting her phone. She sees herself as family to her friends.

During the school year if I forget my phone anywhere—going out anywhere—it really puts me on edge. Because a lot of my friends trust me for helping them feel better if they are upset. And so I worry when I am going out: What if someone is really upset and they need someone to talk to but I can't because I don't have my phone?

Another fifteen-year-old says she sleeps with her phone because only its constant presence allows her to meet her responsibilities to her friends. But then again, only her phone could create such demands. She explicitly refers to what she owes her friends as being "on call." And indeed, she describes her responsibilities as close to those of a small dispensary.

I've had to be on call for a friend during the school year. She was out using questionable substances and I messaged her—"Hey what's up?"—and I could tell by the text she sent back that she was quite obviously out of balance, like, completely. And so I talked to her—I got her to go to bed. The next morning I knew to bring aspirin to school and saltines and a water bottle. And I still—I'm always worried I'll miss something like that. And that someone might get hurt because of it.

A fourteen-year-old says she "is never completely relaxed," even when she sleeps with her phone by her side. Any bad news will show up first on her phone.

I feel like there's always something nagging me. There's always drama or something stressing me out—that I am always worried about. Most of it starts because of phones; the expectation is that when something big happens, you'll tell, like, your best friends right away. Because you can.

Even at night, she worries that she might be left out of some big development in her circle of friends. To miss that "would become a big deal." In large measure, she determines her worth by how much she knows about what is going on with her friends. And by how rapidly she is there to support them. In her circle, it is expected that you respond to a text from a friend within a few minutes.

And then consider Kristen, a junior majoring in economics who follows the rule of three during meals and then, after meals, continues to keep the conversation light if she is with people who have phones with them. Although I meet her during finals week, she is not under much stress. Her own classes are for the most part graduate economics seminars. She has a close relationship with her professors. After our interview, she will be off to proctor a freshman calculus exam. We talk about texting in classes. She shrugs. "It's a problem." Texting is a commitment. When you text, you are promising your friends that you will be there for them. She thinks that when you get a text from a close friend, it should be responded to within "about five minutes."

So, Kristen checks her phone periodically during classes. If she gets a text from a friend that in some way signals an emergency, "I leave class and go to the bathroom in order to respond to the text." I ask Kristen what would count as an emergency, and I learn that, in her world, the bar for emergencies is set fairly low. "My friends need me. I'm the one they see as the stable one. They'll text for boyfriend things. For when they feel a crisis. I need to get back to them." And so, a few times a week, this young economist walks out of her advanced seminars to go to the bathroom, sit in a stall, and text her friends.

"That's what friends do, respond to a crisis," says Kristen. That is why she is often in the bathroom, missing class.

When friends are together, they fall into inattention and feel comfortable retreating into their own worlds. Apart, they are alert for emergencies. It is striking that this often reflects how they describe the behavior of their parents: When their children are not at home, they become hovering "helicopters"; when their children are in plain sight, parents give themselves permission to turn to their phones. *This is our paradox. When we are apart: hypervigilance. When we are together: inattention.*

Perhaps on-call friendship, primed for "emergencies," begins as children's way to deal with parents who are less available than children want them to be—and indeed, than parents themselves might wish to be.

Middle School: The Feeling of Empathy

Recall Holbrooke, the middle school in upstate New York, where I have been called in to consult with a faculty worried about students' lack of empathy.

At a meeting, we go around the table and over twenty teachers voice their concerns: Students don't seem to form anything but superficial friendships. In the past few years, faculty conversations with students have become increasingly strained. And students don't seem much interested in one another. Teachers eavesdrop on student conversations: "Among themselves, they talk about what is on their phones." And the teachers worry whether students are learning the rudiments of conversation: listening and turn taking.

At the first break, teachers say over coffee what they were not ready to admit around the table:

Students don't make eye contact.

They don't respond to body language.

They have trouble listening. I have to rephrase a question many times before a child will answer a question in class.

I'm not convinced they are interested in each other. It is as though they all have some signs of being on an Asperger's spectrum. But that's impossible. We are talking about a schoolwide problem.

Holbrooke is not a school for emotionally or cognitively challenged students. It is a private school with competitive admissions that finds that the academically promising students it admits are not developing as expected. Ava Reade, the school's dean, puts her concern in the strongest possible terms: "Even as ninth graders, they can't see things from another person's point of view." Many students don't seem to have the patience to wait and hear what someone else has to say. Three teachers back her up; students have trouble with the empathy that conversation both teaches and requires.

> *They are talking at each other with local comments, minutiae really, short bursts, as though they were speaking texts. They are communicating immediate social needs. They aren't listening to each other.*

> *The most painful thing to watch is that they don't know when they have hurt each other's feelings. They hurt each other, but then you sit down with them and try to get them to see what has happened and they can't imagine things from the other side.*

> *My students can build websites, but they can't talk to teachers. And students don't want to talk to other students. They don't want the pressure of conversation.*

Because Holbrooke is a small private school, its teachers are given the time to be both emotional and intellectual mentors to their students. This is why they enjoy teaching at Holbrooke. But now they say they are unable to do their jobs as before. For the first time, they feel they must explicitly teach empathy and even turn-taking in conversation. One says, "Emotional intelligence has to become an explicit part of our curriculum."

The teachers have theories about what stands behind the changes they observe. Perhaps their students grew up playing video games instead of reading and didn't develop their imaginations. Perhaps video games kept them from the playground, where they would have developed their social skills. Perhaps students are overscheduled. Or perhaps they don't get enough practice with conversation when they go home.

Their parents may be preoccupied with work—on their own phones and computers. The teachers' talk circles back many times to technology. A history teacher sums up how powerful he feels it to be: "My students are so caught up in their phones that they don't know how to pay attention to class or to themselves or to another person or to look in each other's eyes and see what is going on."

One Holbrooke teacher is distressed that, at least in her view, student friendships have moved from an emotional to an instrumental register. Friendships seem based on what students think someone else can do for them. She calls these "Who has my back?" friendships. In these kinds of connections, she says, "[Friendship] serves you and then you move on." A friendship based on "Who has my back?" is the shadow of friendship, just as time alone with a phone is the shadow of solitude. Both provide substitutions that make you think you have what you don't. Perhaps the substitutions make you forget what you have lost.

Reade, the dean, comes to the group meeting with the results of a small exercise, a small experiment, really. One of Reade's jobs is to run advisory groups of about twenty students each. She asked members of her groups to list three things they want in a friend. In the more than sixty responses she received, only three students mentioned trust, caring, kindness, or compassion. Most of the students say they are interested in someone who could make them laugh, who could make them happy. One student writes, "As long as I'm with somebody, I'm happy." Reade says that she has to conclude that these students don't understand or value what a "best friend" can be. Best friends are more than amusements or insurance that you won't be alone. Best friends are people you care about. They are people to whom you reveal yourself. You learn about yourself as you learn about them. But Reade notes that these lessons are hard to learn online.

Reade sums up her "What do you want in a friend?" exercise: "I feel that these kids have a sense that friendships are one-sided. It is a place for them to broadcast. It is not a place for them to listen. And there isn't an emotional level. You just have to have someone there. There is no investment in another person. It's like they can turn the friendship off." She doesn't say so, but the implied end to this thought is "the way you can turn off an online exchange." After Reade's exercise, she came to fear that children are treating other children as "apps," as means to an end. She observes that her students are quick to say to each other, "Can you do this for me?" and then, she says, "they just 'toggle' to another friend once the job is done or if they don't get satisfaction, either way."

Reade worries that the habits developed with online "friending" have become the habits of friendships in face-to-face, everyday life. She says:

> *When they hurt each other, they don't realize it and show no remorse. When you try to help them, you have to go over it over and over with them, to try to role-play why they might have hurt another person. And even then, they don't seem sorry. They exclude each other from social events, parties, school functions, and seem surprised when others are hurt. One time, everyone was talking about a concert that one student hadn't gone to, right in front of this girl—she didn't have the money for the tickets—but they went on and on. She had tears in her eyes.*
>
> *They are not developing that way of relating where they listen and learn how to look at each other and hear each other.*

By middle school, the Holbrooke teachers hope to see children content to quietly work on projects—in art, science, or writing. Teachers talk about becoming teachers for the thrill of watching children discover a gift and the capacity to concentrate on it, both during school hours and in their spare time. But at this meeting, teachers mourn that they no longer have this pleasure. Their students can't concentrate, don't have any downtime, and actually can't tolerate it when they do. As early as sixth grade, students come to school with smartphones and tablets, caught up in a constant stream of messages to which they feel the need to instantly respond. Teachers know the student culture. At Holbrooke, a text from a friend requires a response within minutes.

What children are sharing, of course, are tokens that they belong—a funny video, a joke, a photograph, the things that happen to be circulating that day. "It's all about affiliation," says one teacher. Another reflects: "It's as though they spend their day in a circle exchanging charms for their charm bracelets. But it takes place in a circle where they never get time off."

The teachers know that students text under their desks and take bathroom breaks to respond to messages on their phones, and now the phones are even making their way onto the playing fields. The teachers want to make school a time when students can take a step away from the pressure to be sending and receiving. But more and more course content is delivered electronically, so students are never away from the medium that distracts them.

At a meeting with another group of middle school teachers, I hear similar concerns: Students have long, heart-to-heart text conversations online and then meet in school the next day without acknowledging the person with whom they have been sharing intimacies. It seems more important for students to get reinforcement from a large number of online "likes" than to have in-person conversations. But teachers worry that without face-to-face conversation, students aren't developing empathic capacity or listening skills.

A middle school teacher says, "One girl told me: 'I always keep thirteen unanswered texts on my phone. I have thirteen people who are trying to reach me.'" The teacher found this exchange disturbing. The phone was not there to communicate but to make this girl feel good about herself. The teacher asked the girl about how the people who had left the unanswered texts might feel. The girl seemed puzzled. She said she had never really thought about their feelings.

Two years after I visit Holbrooke, the issues I met there seem as pressing as ever. In winter 2015, I visit with Greg Adams, the headmaster of Radway, a middle school in New York City, who tells me about a sixth grader, Luis, whose father committed suicide the year before. Ever since, Luis has been fragile and dependent on his sister, Juanita, a year ahead of him at school.

One day, Anna, a classmate of Luis's, becomes irritated that he interrupted her in the lunchroom when she was trying to talk to Juanita. The next day, Radway is in an uproar. Anna has posted on Facebook: "I hope Luis ends up just the way his father did." Adams calls Anna into his office. He says he was "steaming, trying to stay in control. Smoke was coming out of my ears." He asks Anna, "Why? Why would you do this?" Anna has an answer ready: "It was just on Facebook." It is clear to Adams that Anna doesn't see what she did as altogether real.

The headmaster sets himself to "making Anna put herself in Luis's place." In his office, Adams tells Anna, "We are not leaving until I have made you cry. We are not leaving my office until you are melted in tears." He says that this takes him about fifteen minutes. "And then," he says, "of course, I have to call Anna's mother about why I made her daughter cry." But Adams is not reassured by Anna's tears. Somehow, Facebook gave her a way to think about other people as objects that can't be hurt. And a way to think about a kind of cruelty that doesn't count.

We have learned that people who would never allow themselves to be bullies in person feel free to be aggressive and vulgar online. The presence of a face and a voice reminds us that we are talking to a person. Rules of civility usually apply. But when we communicate on screens, we experience a kind of disinhibition. Research tells us that social media decrease self-control just as they cause a momentary spike in self-confidence. This means that online we are tempted to behave in ways that part of us knows will hurt others, but we seem to stop caring.

It is as though a signal is being jammed. For Adams, what is not getting through is a model of other people in which you see them as like you. Without this, his students can't feel empathy or form secure attachments. It is an environment that fosters bullying and casual cruelty. He does not find it surprising that a recent study concluded that the percentage of college students who feel safe and trusting in their attachments has decreased and the percentage who feel insecure in their attachments has increased.

Hoarders

The last time we saw Haley she was trying to console Natalie, a friend by her side who in a moment of loss had turned to "the people on the phone." Haley was disappointed, but she says she understands what drove Natalie to her phone. At the time of that encounter, Haley's own social life centered around texting and messaging. She's not altogether happy about this, but this is what her life is about. Constant connectivity makes her feel that she belongs. "You can put so little effort in when you text and then you get instant gratification. I can connect with fifteen people with no effort and it feels so good to just extend the feelers and get a positive response. I would rather have that than a conversation a lot of the time."

Haley has a cool eye on her numbers. Those "fifteen people," and indeed her many hundreds of contacts on Facebook, are not so much friends as "people who will text me if I text them." These relationships are close to contractual. Yet she says, "It's really hard for me to turn down a new friend on the network. It's hard for me not to try to accumulate as big a network as I can." But she knows that not all of these "friends on the network" are friends. "In a weird way we treat friends like capital market items. You keep hangers-on, just to have more. . . . I do hoard friends." Haley uses the "hangers-on" to keep up her numbers. She says it enables "that weird hoarding impulse."

Is this kind of hoarding abundance or the sense of abundance? Haley's description of her pleasures helps us understand life in a gray zone, where the accumulation of friends who are not friends is at the same time both gratifying and alienating.

Haley insists that she likes the feeling of abundance that online friendships provide. But she also describes a half-formulated plan for getting back to basics. She says that next year, when she takes a semester abroad, she might delete her Facebook account. She worries that she will want to "show people what I'm doing and will miss having Facebook."

But she's getting uncomfortable seeing friends as "capital market items" and with "that weird hoarding feeling."

By the end of senior year, Haley has taken action. She has discarded her smartphone. She decided that her smartphone—she'd had one for five years—was overwhelming her friendships. For Haley, it wasn't just the phone "but the history on the phone. . . . When I texted someone I was so aware of the history the phone held. Every relationship was documented. And I carried the documentation—the texts and the email—with me all the time."

Haley shows me her current phone, a flip phone, a "retro" phone. It makes calls. It sends texts but doesn't have enough memory to store more than a hundred of them. And of course it has no apps. This means it's not a way to access Facebook. Haley says she feels lighter. She says her friendships feel "unencumbered by past history. I am able to be more forgiving."

Empathy Machines

We are at a choice point. Some feel liberated by the prospect of giving up their personal archives (to Haley, even the history of her texts feels like a burden), but some feel comforted by the prospect of developing an ever more sophisticated archive of every aspect of their life. This is the case for a group of people who experimented with a technology called Google Glass. Glass is a pair of spectacles that let you carry the web—along with all of its apps—wherever you go.

Andi, twenty-seven, is a graphic designer who applied to be in the first group of "explorers" who were issued Google Glass when it was ready for real-world trials. Andi joined the explorers because she wanted to experiment with ways to have a more reflective life. Glass can take photographs or video from the wearer's point of view. Andi programs her Glass to take a picture and record a minute of video every ten minutes. She tries to review and annotate her photographs every evening. So far, she finds her project comforting: "I don't know now what will be important in my life. I will only know this later. I won't have to rely on memory to retrieve the important conversations. I'll have some record of them, even if I didn't think they were important at the time." But at home, she usually takes off the glasses because her husband objects to the project. He thinks their conversations change when she is recording. And he doesn't like the idea that if he says something off-putting, it won't be enough to simply see the reaction in Andi's face and say he is sorry. His wife will have the record forever. Perhaps she will never be able to forgive because she will never be able to forget.

Andi has a strong reaction to her husband's concerns: "I think this is about inequality. I think he would feel different if he had Glass. It doesn't seem fair if only one person has a record. What you need is both partners keeping a record. I hope that when Glass is more widely available, he'll get it as well."

Haley and Andi have opposite intuitions about what is important about memory. Haley is betting that everyone will want to power down. "I want people to live in the moment for friendship. Don't come with your history or expectations. You should be able to start your relationship from where you are now." Andi has the opposite feeling. She believes that having a record of her past will allow her to live more fully in the present.

I speak to several users of Google Glass who go further than Andi. They hope that Glass (or something like it), by recording your life, will evolve into a kind of empathy machine. If you record your life from your point of view, you can then show it to others in the hope that they will understand you better. And if they, too, are recording their lives, you can see the world through their eyes. Conversation, in this case, may be a supplement to understanding. But they say it will often be unnecessary and that could be a good thing because not everyone is good at it. Glass reassures. If you fear you cannot adequately express your point of view, Glass will be a way to share it more effectively. If you fear you lack empathy, you look forward to being able to take on the visual perspective of others.

Ronald, twenty-six, a programmer at a renewable energy start-up, has had Glass for six months. He says, "If you are bad at conversation, like me, Glass is important. You don't have to be good at describing what is happening with you, how you feel. Someone you care about can [look at a Glass video and] experience it directly."

We've seen families who hoped to export conflict by having their disagreements by text message and email. Here is another idea that involves export—this time the wholesale export of your experience. Behind technological fantasies there is so often a deep sadness that human beings have simply not gotten it right and technology will help us do better.

I'm not optimistic about the empathy machine as a shortcut, or what one enthusiast describes to me as "training wheels for empathy." Perhaps for some it makes sense as a supplement. But of course, with technology, we have a tendency to take what begins as a supplement and turn it into a way of life. Text messages weren't meant to disrupt dinner table conversations, but this supplement to talk became a substitution.

But it is a substitution that doesn't provide the essential. George Eliot referred to what the mother gives a child with her gaze as "the meeting eyes of love." Research supports what literature and philosophy have told us for a long time. The development of empathy needs face-to-face conversation. And it needs eye contact.

The work of psychiatrist Daniel Siegel has taught us that children need eye contact to develop parts of the brain that are involved with attachment. Without eye contact, there is a persistent sense of disconnection and problems with empathy. Siegel sums up what a moment of eye contact accomplishes: "Repeated tens of thousands of times in the child's life, these small moments of mutual rapport [serve to] transmit the best part of our humanity—our capacity for love—from one generation to the next." Atsushi Senju, a cognitive neuroscientist, studies this mechanism through adulthood, showing that the parts of the brain that allow us to process another person's feelings and intentions are activated by eye contact. Emoticons on texts and emails, Senju found, don't have the same effect. He says, "A richer mode of communication is possible right after making eye contact. It amplifies your ability to compute all the signals so you are able to read the other person's brain."

With all of this to consider, what are we to make of the fact that when we have our phones out, our eyes are downward? (And of course, with Glass, our eyes are often busy reading what is on our screen display.) We've seen more and more research suggest that the always-on life erodes our capacity for empathy. Most dramatic to me is the study that found a 40 percent drop in empathy among college students in the past twenty years, as measured by standard psychological tests, a decline its authors suggested was due to students having less direct face-to-face contact with each other. We pay a price when we live our lives at a remove.

Some believe that children cope with the challenges of today's technology just as young people have coped with the new technologies that have come before. They are changing their styles of communication and will find their own balance. If adults worry, it is because we do not fully appreciate the resourcefulness of the young. I do think the young are resourceful, but there is also this: Phones, tablets, and the always-on-us wearables of our futures—all of these technologies of partial attention and downturned eyes—touch the most intimate moments in human development. They are poised to accompany children as they try to develop the capacity for attachment, solitude, and empathy. What looks like coping can take its toll.

I've said that to keep what we cherish about conversation, we have to design for our vulnerability. This has at least two aspects. A first is technical. If we don't want to be captured by our phones, we can, for example, design phones that intentionally "release" us after each transaction. And we can construct social environments that support our intentions. If we want to lose weight, we don't take for granted that the desire to go on a diet will lead to weight loss. It helps to diet with a friend. It helps to stock the right foods in the kitchen and to schedule regular meals. We'll go further in reclaiming conversation if we create environments that support conversation.

Since Socrates lamented the movement from speech to writing, observers have warned against each new mode of communication as destructive to a cherished mode of thought. I see mobile phones as having a distinctive quality that makes them stand out in this long historical conversation. When we write instead of speak, we are aware that we are making a choice, writing instead of speaking. In contrast, when we have our phones with us, we don't consider that by this fact we have compromised our face-to-face conversations. On the contrary, we defend the idea that we can text loving exchanges and catch-ups with friends as we have (parallel) conversations with the people around us. We find it hard to give up the idea that our phones are an accessory, a harmless, helpful supplement. But our technologies have not only changed what we do; they have changed who we are. And nowhere as profoundly as in our capacity for empathy.

In a series of 2014 lectures, Rowan Williams, the former archbishop of Canterbury, took empathy out of its accustomed place in a discussion of how to treat others and focused instead on what it does to the development of the individual who offers it.

For Williams, the empathic relationship does not begin with "I know how you feel." It begins with the realization that you *don't* know how another feels. In that ignorance, you begin with an offer of conversation: "Tell me how you feel." Empathy, for Williams, is an offer of accompaniment and commitment. And making the offer changes you. When you have a growing awareness of how much you don't know about someone else, you begin to understand how much you don't know about yourself. You learn, says Williams, "a more demanding kind of attention. You learn patience and a new skill and habit of perspective."

When you give someone a thumbs-up or respond to a question posed on Instagram, these can be first steps in an empathic process. In the online exchange, you might be saying to someone else, "I want to hear you. I'm with you." Like the consolation texts that Natalie receives, they are a beginning. Everything depends on what happens next.

The Sense of Empathy

So many of us have friendships with people we could, with planning, see face-to-face but choose instead to "see" online. We become accustomed to experiencing this "convenience" as the normal way to spend time together.

Across generations, we get used to rerouting conversations—from sharing birthday wishes to sending condolences—to our screens. We no longer expect friends to show up and may not want them to. It starts to feel like too much emotional work.

There is so much positive in what online relationships can bring us. Someone like Alli, socially isolated, distant from her parents, can use the Internet to reach out—to try to find someone who speaks directly to her problem. But perhaps not to her. Empathy is not merely about giving someone information or helping them find a support group. It's about convincing another person that you are there for the duration. Empathy means staying long enough for someone to believe that you want to know how they feel, not that you want to tell them what you would do in their circumstance. Empathy requires time and emotional discipline.

The essayist William Deresiewicz said that as our communities have atrophied, we have moved from living in actual communities to making efforts to feel as though we are living in them. So, when we talk about communities now, we have moved "from a relationship to a feeling." We have moved from *being* in a community to having a *sense* of community. Have we moved from empathy to a *sense* of empathy? From friendship to a *sense* of friendship? We need to pay close attention here. Artificial intelligences are being offered to us as sociable companions. They are being called a new kind of friend. If we are settling for a "sense of friendship" from people, the idea of machine companionship does not seem like much of a fall. But what is at stake is precious, the most precious things that people know how to offer each other.

Next Generations

A s I write this chapter, my computer develops a glitch and I make my way to the Apple Store. My problem is so minor that I don't even need the Genius Bar—an Apple salesperson knows how to help. I sit alongside a twenty-six-year-old graduate student in design who teaches me how to make my computer hum. He asks what I do and when I tell him I'm writing a book about conversation, he says, speaking of his clients at the store, "I worry about the young kids. Some seem so desensitized. It's like they have never had a conversation without their phones out. But some—well, some—give me hope. Like they're over it."

I know what he means. I also see a next generation that shows some evidence of pulling back from where momentum would take them. A few fourteen-year-old girls share their reservations about texting and the bonds of friendship. Liz says that "memories don't happen when you get a text. It's the stories you can tell." Ginger appreciates that "when you text and message, you don't mess up." But then she adds that the important moments with her friends, "the funny moments," come precisely from messing up and making mistakes. "The best stuff," she says, "is friends making mistakes together. . . . If you're talking you can mess up and it turns into something really funny. That's how people bond. . . . It's not like everything is made to be perfect. It's like you should make mistakes and you should—well, with friends, it's good to see their faces." For Ginger's classmate Sabrina, the "perfect" exchanges of texting aren't "conversations that mean anything real."

The psychologist Mihaly Csikszentmihalyi has studied the "real" conversations of friendship. Some friendships, he says, are built around conversations that provide validation. He calls these "reinforcement friendships": They accomplish "what everyone likes . . . reciprocal attention paid to one another's ideas and idiosyncrasies." These are perhaps Haley's "hoarded" friends, who will text her if she texts them first. These are perhaps her Facebook friends: If you "like" what is on their wall, they will "like" what is on yours. Csikszentmihalyi says that what these friendships do best is support a self that needs to use other people as a mirror, a self that has not found itself.

But Thoreau spoke of more ("My friend is one . . . who takes me for what I am"), and Csikszentmihalyi writes about the possibility of more. There are friends who question each other's dreams and desires, who encourage each other to try out the new. "A true friend is someone we can occasionally be crazy with, someone who does not expect us to be always true to form. It is someone who shares our goal of self-realization, and therefore is willing to share the risks that any increase in complexity entails."

Tellingly, Csikszentmihalyi describes a "true friend" by describing friendship in action—among other things, in conversation. He is describing intimacy.

Again, I think of the "young kids" who gave hope to my Apple consultant. I think they take their devices for granted and for that are perhaps less enamored with them than their parents and many of their only slightly older peers.

One fifteen-year-old reflects on how hard it is to talk to the kids at school. Right now, he is at summer camp. There will be no phones for the six weeks he'll be there. He's okay with that.

When I am at home and in the car with a friend or on the bus and I am trying to make conversation [with other kids] . . . they could be on their phones. And the conversation could be kind of spotty. They're drifting in and out of what they're talking about. They aren't really focusing, so the conversation kind of breaks down. But when you're here, you have each other to focus on . . . and not just your electronics. So I think you can really focus on what people say and then add on more to the conversation— you have more thoughts shared than in those conversations where you have your phones out and you are taking the fullness out of the conversation.

His bunkmates support his point by bringing up a recent wilderness hike, a three-day trek where they had each other's company without any hope of phones. One of them remarks on how much, at home, he talks with his friends about what is on their phones. On the hike, he says, "What I noticed was that we were only focusing on ourselves and what was right in front of us and in the moment." Another remarks that while he was on the hike, the people he was with were not competing with the people he could potentially reach on his phone. "When I am at home, I don't really get to sit down next to someone . . . and just talk with them. There are always other things going on, their phone is always out, they're talking to other people." For this young man, conversation itself seemed a revelation—a large, new space. He says, "It was a stream, very ongoing. It wouldn't break apart."

Romance

Where Are You? Who Are You?
Wait, What Just Happened?

I only ask, "How's the conversation?"
—OPERA SINGER LUCIANO PAVAROTTI, WHEN ASKED
ABOUT RAISING ONLY DAUGHTERS

True love is a lack of desire to check one's
smartphone in another's presence.

—ALAIN DE BOTTON

For adults as for teenagers, it comes down to this: You always expect other people to have their phones with them. You expect that no matter what else they are doing, they will see a message you sent. So, if they care about you, you should be getting a text back. If they care. But in romantic texting, responding to a communication with silence happens all the time. It's the NOTHING gambit. It appeared early. As soon as texting had established itself in flirting, there was talk about how to handle the strategy of silence. Even in high school.

The NOTHING Gambit

In 2008, eighteen-year-old Hannah tells me that in online flirting, "the hardest thing" is that the person you text has the option of simply not responding—that is, of responding with NOTHING, a conversational choice not really available in face-to-face talk. Her assessment of its effects: "It is a way of driving someone crazy. . . . You don't exist."

Hannah explains that after a no-response, she feels a strong temptation to make things worse for herself by following the online activities of the boy who ignored her—on Facebook she can see if he's been out to dinner or a party. In the past, you could console yourself that a person ignoring you was perhaps busy with a family emergency. You could tell yourself all manner of improbable stories. Now, as one of Hannah's friends puts it, "You have to cope with the reality: they are busy with everything but you." Hannah says that this makes rejection on social media "five times as great as regular rejection."

The NOTHING gambit is not a resolved conversation or a conversation that has trailed off. It is not, Hannah insists, like "someone telling you a few times that they are busy and then you get the picture." It is more like a conversation with someone who simply looks away as if they don't understand that human beings need to be responded to when they speak. Online, we give ourselves permission to behave this way.

And when it happens to you, the only way to react with dignity is to pretend it didn't happen. Hannah describes the rules: If people don't respond to you online, your job is to pretend to not notice. "I'm *not* going to be that person who goes off on people saying, 'Why don't you get back to me, blah, blah, blah.' . . . Not cool. I'm *not* going to be, like, 'Hello, are you still there? If you don't want to talk, just tell me.'"

Hannah and I are talking in a circle of seven high school seniors, boys and girls. When she says, "Why don't you get back to me, blah, blah, blah," everyone breaks out laughing. Hannah is doing a perfect imitation of a pathetic loser. The behavior she describes is what no one would ever do. When someone hits you with a no-response, you meet silence with silence. Hannah is explicit: "If people want to disappear, I'll be, like, 'Okay, I'm fine with it.'" In fact, in Hannah's circle, the socially correct response to the NOTHING gambit is to get aggressively busy on social media—busy enough that your activity will be noticed by the person who has gone silent on you.

In the early days of texting, 2008–2010, I spoke with more than three hundred teens and young adults about their online lives. I saw a generation settle into a new way of dealing with silence from other people: namely, deny that it hurts and put aside your understanding that if you do it to others, it will hurt them as well. We tolerate that we are not being shown empathy. And then we tolerate that we don't show it to others.

This style of relating is part of a larger pattern. You learn to give your parents a pass when they turn to their phones instead of responding to you. You learn to give your friends a pass when they drop in and out of conversations to talk with friends on their phones. And in flirtation, you learn to treat NOTHING as something to put out of your mind.

You could say that in romance, being ignored is a staple and that this is old wine in new bottles. But in the past, the silent treatment was a moment. It could be the beginning of a chase or what led a suitor to abandon hope. But it was a moment. Now, as we've seen before, a moment has turned into a method.

Friction-Free

Even the apps we use to find love are in formats that make it easy to ignore being ignored. On Tinder, a mobile dating app, rejection is no longer rejection, it is "swiping left," and when it happens to you, you don't even know it happened. Tinder asks, "Who is available, right now, near you, to go out for a coffee or a drink, to maybe be your lover?" People who want to be considered sign up, and their photograph and a brief bio appear on the system.

Once you have the app open, if you like the looks of someone, you swipe right on your phone. If you're not interested, you swipe left. If

I swipe right on you and you swipe right on me, then we are notified that we have been "matched" and can begin to communicate. But if I choose you with a right swipe and you don't do the same for me, you simply don't appear in my visual field again.

This is what people mean by "friction-free," the buzzword for what a life of apps can bring us. Without an app, it would not be possible to reject hundreds, even thousands of potential mates with no awkwardness. It has never been easier to think of potential romantic partners as commodities in abundance.

In this social environment, studies show a decline in the ability to form secure attachments—the kind where you trust and share your life. Ironically, our new efficient quests for romance are tied up in behavior that discourages empathy and intimacy. The preliminaries of traditional courtship, the dinner dates that emphasized patience and deference, did not necessarily lead to intimacy but provided practice in what intimacy requires. The new preliminaries—the presentation of candidates as if in a game—don't offer that opportunity.

This chapter is primarily about love talk during the chase. It involves new skills. You'll want a fluidity with apps that will become part of your romantic game—apps for meeting, apps for texting and messaging, apps for video chat. All of these bring the promise of businesslike crispness to falling in love. They bring efficiency into the realm of our intimacies. In a world where people live far away from parents and neighborhood ties, apps bring hope that they will smooth out the hard job of finding a partner without the community connections enjoyed by previous generations. And so, the first story that young people tell about technology and romance is that their phones have made things more efficient. But the first story is not the whole story.

In fact, technology brings significant complications to the conversations of modern romance. We feel we have permission to simply drop out. It encourages us to feel that we have infinite choice in romantic partners, a prospect that turns out to be as stressful as it is helpful in finding a mate. It offers a dialogue that is often not a dialogue at all because it is not unusual for people to come to online conversations with a team of writers. You want a team because you feel you are working in an unforgiving medium. Timing matters and punctuation counts!

Finally, although technology offers so much to the chase—new ways to meet, new ways to express interest and passion—it also makes a false promise. It is easy to think that if you feel close to someone because of their words on a screen, you understand the person behind them. In fact, you may be overwhelmed with data but have little of the wisdom that comes with face-to-face encounters.

Our new ways of communicating have an effect on every stage of romance, from searching for love to presenting ourselves when we are hopeful of finding it to the new complexities we encounter as we try to make it work. In this environment, we move from "Where are you?" (the technology-enhanced encounter) to "Who are you?" and then to "Wait, what just happened? Did I make you disappear?"

Where Are You? The Game Changers

Liam, a twenty-four-year-old graduate student in New York, is trying to right-swipe his way to love on Tinder. Liam tells me, "I use Tinder when I'm bored." Liam is good-looking, stylishly dressed. He says of Tinder, with a modest grin, "It's a game changer." What he likes most is that he doesn't have to worry about witty pickup lines, because with Tinder, every encounter has already been put in a potentially romantic context. "For me," he says, "the awkward part . . . is trying to convert a friendly conversation into a more romantic one. That job is done by the app." He finds this almost magical.

For Liam, experiments with Tinder are only the beginning of how technology increases his romantic possibilities. Texting is at the heart of things. He tells me that on a Friday night in Manhattan, there is no need to have made firm plans. He'll text a few friends to find out where the parties are.

And then, you are, potentially, in several games. You know a few places to go, a few bars to go to, where to meet . . . and once you're at a party, you can avoid embarrassment by texting your interest to a girl with something flirty.

So I use that first text to get some signal of interest, and you should know whether this thing is worth being pursued. Or drop it. Remember . . . wherever you are, you always have Tinder and you can see all the other available people. . . . So you always know you have a lot of choices.

Technology encourages Liam to see his romantic life in terms of product placement. He is the product and he is direct marketing. You pass your photo through Photoshop and then others go photo shopping. But despite this ease of first contact, Liam does not have a girlfriend and is not optimistic about his prospects.

For a start, complications follow from the first thing Liam mentions as a *positive* aspect of dating technology: the feeling of *infinite choice*.

The psychologist Barry Schwartz popularized the notion of the "paradox of choice." While we think we would be happiest if we had more choices, constrained choice often leads to a more satisfied life. In the 1950s, the Nobel Prize–winning economist and psychologist Herbert A. Simon made a distinction between people who try to *maximize* and those who *satisfice*, a word he invented. A *maximizer* is like a perfectionist, someone who needs to be assured that every purchase or personal decision (including the decision about a mate) is the best that could be made. The only way maximizers can know this for certain is to consider all the alternatives they can imagine. This creates a psychologically daunting task that only becomes more daunting as the number of options increases.

The alternative is to be a *satisficer*. You can still have standards, but you are not haunted by the universe of possible choices. You are happy to take what is before you and make the most of it. Satisficers are, in general, happier because their life tasks are simpler. You are not obsessed about finding the best house—you might take a house that is comfortable and available and make it into a home. You don't think about the *best* mate. You are attracted to someone and allow yourself to attach.

Enter social media. Enter Facebook. Enter Tinder. Enter the world where one can fantasize infinite and *knowable* choices. *We are all encouraged to develop the psychology of maximizers.* In the domain of dating, maximizing can make you very unhappy indeed. Of course, people were always able, in theory, to enter into this psychological state. But the Internet makes it seem a logical state of mind. As one college senior puts it: "When people are just a click away, it is tempting to never settle."

The psychologists David Myers and Robert Lane independently concluded that in American society today, abundance of choice (and this would apply to choices in products, career paths, or people) often leads to depression and feelings of loneliness. Lane points out that Americans used to make their choices in communities, surrounded by the "givens" of family, neighborhood, and workplace. Now, if individuals achieve a sense of community, it is because they have actively cultivated and maintained these connections over a lifetime. It is something they have committed to.

In a classic study of the effects of choice, people were given either a small or large array of chocolates and then asked to rate how pleased they were with their selection. Those who had selected from a smaller array were more satisfied with how the chocolates tasted. So, the problem with infinite choice is that it makes us unhappy because we can't bring ourselves to make any choice, and no choice feels definitive.

Danny, thirty-two, lives in Chicago. He is a real estate investor, with money and appealing looks. He is convinced that technology has made it harder to commit. Here is how Danny states his choice problem, although of course he is talking about women, not chocolates.

I broke up with a girl, let's call her "Lakeshore Drive Girl" because we used to go for long walks by the water. I broke up just because I thought there was something better online and these other women were start-

*ing to text me back and forth. . . . Lakeshore Drive Girl got on to me
and dumped me. I don't know if going out with others, being tempted
by those girls in the phone . . . I don't know if that was the right
thing to do.*

Danny says he was ready to commit to "Lakeshore Drive Girl." He
doesn't seem happy when he looks down at his phone and says, "I thought
there was something better online." He speaks with a certain nostalgia
for the arranged marriage of his grandparents.

*I hate to say it, but there must have been something to it. Their fami-
lies knew they came from a similar background, with similar taste.
Their families wanted the best for both of them. And they were both
committed to making it work, so they took the time to get to know each
other. . . . And then, they were all in and supported by their families.
Everyone was going to help them if there was any problem. Now, you
are on your own. And if someone finds a fault in you, you're off the
list. Next.*

Where Are You? In the Machine Zone

As Danny says "Next," he makes a gesture with his finger; it looks as
though he is swiping his phone. It's the swipe gesture from Tinder.
I first met the gesture on Chatroulette, a website which lets you cycle
through video sessions with people all over the world. Danny wasn't
talking about Chatroulette when he shared his romantic ennui (and
Chatroulette was never intended for dating), but its aesthetic of moving
on with a swipe or a click has become part of our conversation about
romance. "Nexting" has become part of our emotional ecology.

Danny says that for him the combination of infinite choice and anonymity on dating sites is "toxic." He spends hours in front of the computer, on a daily routine: He checks his social media sites and looks at

the relationship status of friends. Does he have friends who can be converted into lovers? Then he moves on to checking the relationship status of friends of friends. And then he moves on to Tinder. He tells himself that he is looking for a "real relationship," indeed, for a wife, but he admits that his daily routine often feels "unreal." He says, "Even when I am talking to someone I know, it can feel like a game." A twenty-five-year-old woman makes a similar comment about how she is never "off the game." She remarks that "if you have your phone, and you always have your phone, you are always looking for a date . . . or you can be."

Terry, a twenty-six-year-old graduate student in mathematics, says that when he uses apps to meet people, "I feel that I am processing people. . . . And if I start to text them . . . these are interviews. Like recruitment interviews. I sometimes look at twenty girls in an evening, just to look, and I text with five. . . . It's a game you want to win. You get people to want to talk to you. You refine those skills."

Terry tells me that this round of what starts to feel "like recruitment interviews" rarely leads to something more intimate. But he also says that sometimes he almost stops caring. Sometimes he just tries to beat his previous score on how many girls will talk to him. When his dating game becomes more salient than its ostensible goal, he is in a loop that brings to mind the compulsions of the "machine zone." In the Facebook zone, you don't want to leave but you don't know why you want to stay. On the dating app, you can't break away, but you're not so sure you want a date. For the math student, the game becomes getting women to respond to him. The high comes from the feeling that anything is possible.

We last saw Liam at a bar in the West Village, armed with a technology that seems to offer infinite possibility—gleaming profiles of women within a ten-block radius. But technology, says Liam, has made it almost impossible for a "normal guy" like him to get a woman's attention. He says that one girl he had been pursuing, Rachel, is attractive, so her time at any party is usually spent monitoring her phone for "best offers."

A lot of guys are texting, getting in touch. So, there is a lot of pressure on me to get her out of that party. To get her away from her phone. A lot of times, girls think that a guy is trying to make sexual moves on them, but really it isn't. I'm just trying to think of a way to get them away from their phones.

When I talk with women, I learn that Liam does not have it so wrong. Women talk about being on dates with men and going to the bathroom to check their phones to see who else has contacted them. They say they feel a little guilty, but over time, acting on the impulse to check your phone—to check your options—comes to feel normal. Consider Madeleine, thirty-two, a financial analyst in New York. She's out to drinks with a group of friends, including a man who seems interested in her. But, phone-enabled, she is clear that "drinks do not imply the entire evening." Messages on her phone mean "things could go anywhere." In this world, she says, "if I get a message from a guy who interests me and I want to leave the group of friends I'm with, I do. I usually go to the ladies' room to set things up so I'm not sitting at the table where people can look over my shoulder as I get too specific about my next plan."

In settings such as this, the conversations that could keep someone's attention need to happen quickly.

Where Are You Now? A Question of Timing

It is cliché to say that love is all about timing. In the past, this usually referred to the timing of when lovers met. Were they ready for commitment? Were they on the rebound? Now, when people talk about timing, they are more likely to be talking about the micromanagement of messages. A small group of high school senior men discusses "timing rules."

Darren explains that if a girl tries to contact you by writing on your Facebook wall, "It's almost common etiquette to wait a day to get back." Why? "You don't want her to think that you are checking Facebook to see if you have messages." Answering too soon could be interpreted that way.

Say you get a post from a girl on a Monday night at nine-thirty. You don't want to respond for maybe a day, maybe two days, because . . . of the creep factor. You don't want them to think . . . you are always on Facebook. So, if they said, "Hey, haven't seen you in a while. How're you doing?" you want to make them wait, maybe wonder. . . . Maybe if it's a girl you like, you want to have her think about you. That type of thing. Having them look forward to your response even more.

Darren continues. The rules of projecting nonchalance are similar if you are texting. "If you get a text message from someone, the ball's in your court, so you can make them sweat it out . . . for a half hour at least." His friends agree. Luke offers: "You can't respond to a text too soon. You want people to think you have a life." But waiting before responding to a text is what you do both to look good to a girl and to feel good about yourself. Jonas adds this: "You don't want to feel like a loser sitting at home. You don't want to feel 'on call.' Of course, it's hard to stay cool when a girl is making you wait. . . . If you text a girl midday, and if she doesn't get back to you, you're kind of worried."

Still, these young men see texting as a far better option than having to talk to a girl to ask her out. Talking is a commitment. Texting is low risk. In texting, says Jonas, if you don't like the outcome of the conversation, *you can pretend it didn't happen.*

Let's say you wanted to talk to a girl and hang out with her: If you just texted, "Hey, what are you doing tonight?" that's so much different than calling her up and being, like, "Hey, what are you doing tonight?" She'll look and respond, like, "Oh, I don't know." "Oh, maybe we can hang out later." And it's a lot less pressure on you. . . . It's almost like you leave it out there, and if she's, like, "No, I don't want to hang out," it's almost like you're not there to experience her shutting you down.

It's a paradox of the medium: Online exchanges exist forever, but you imagine the ones that didn't work out as not having happened at all.

After hearing these young men describe how they feel protected by texting, I speak to a young woman their age who confirms that the boys she knows like to keep things online for a long time before they make any plan to get together in person. She says, "It gives them cover. If things don't work out, they don't have to feel rejected. It's as though they weren't there to feel the embarrassment."

Her formulation "It's as though they weren't there to feel the embarrassment" is close to Jonas's "It's almost like you're not there to experience her shutting you down." Texting allows for romantic conversations where rejection can't happen, because if it does, you never had the conversation.

Yet these young men make it clear that online flirting comes with its own unique problems. Unlike in "regular conversation," if you make a mistake when texting, "it will never go away." Messages are stamped and everything you say can be reviewed. So texting has you poised between feeling that your words are of no consequence (the conversation never happened) and feeling that any one word could do permanent damage.

And practice does not seem to make perfect. Eight college juniors, all of whom have been texting since they were thirteen, tell me they are still working on their timing. The men begin by talking about how careful they are to let just the right amount of time pass between receiving a text from a woman and responding to it. For Cameron, the magic number is twenty minutes. Ryan points out that it's hard to know the magic number, because if a woman responds to him immediately, he sometimes takes it as a good sign, but he sometimes thinks, "She's psycho, man."

When Ryan throws out the idea that he might consider a woman "psycho" if she texted too soon, his tone is light. But the girls in the group know better than to take it as a joke. They've had experiences where men turned off if they were seen as too available online. And men recoil if a woman responds to a text with an actual telephone call. Elaine says, "As soon as a woman calls, it's like, 'She's crazy.'" No one disagrees with her. The intrusion of a telephone call, at least in the early stages of dating, crosses a line.

This point is reinforced by an older woman, Candice, thirty, who says that falling in love has silenced her. She's met someone she likes and is afraid to do anything but text him: "I'm dating a guy. I like him so much. I think I could fall in love with him. I don't want him to see how much I like him. If we speak on the phone, I will blow it." So she arranges to have as few telephone calls as possible. She mentions that it was easier to navigate all of this when she was in college, with roommates. A group of them worked on her texts together. They helped her send "good messages."

Who Are You? An Army of Cyranos

These days, men and women find it natural to collaborate on romantic texts, particularly during the early days of a relationship. Dorian, twenty, describes his process of composition: "First, I can spend, like, ten minutes to write the message. And then I can ask my friend, 'Dude, what do you think of that? Is that cool?' . . . And he'll say, 'Yeah, that's good. Say it that way.'" Both men and women say collaboration in romantic texting is acceptable because the stakes are so high. Gregory, thirty, puts it tersely: "One strike and you're out."

In face-to-face conversation, we see facial expressions and body language; we hear tone of voice. In texting, you don't have these rich clues, so small details of punctuation can mean the difference between being understood or not. And without context, small details easily lead to a rush to judgment.

Vanessa, one of the New Hampshire college juniors, talks about a text exchange where she may have misunderstood a small detail. She was texting with a visiting Spanish exchange student. In one of the Spaniard's first texts to her, he winked, using an emoticon—the combinations of keyboard punctuation that can resemble smiling faces, sad faces, and indeed, winking faces. Vanessa says that she interpreted the wink as flirting. She says that she doesn't mind online flirting in general, but the emoticon wink seemed odd, sexual in an uncomfortable way. In her circle, you wouldn't do that. She never got back to him. As she finishes the story, Cameron laughs. He, too, has an emoticon story.

It is pretty much the same story. When an Italian exchange student sent him a wink the first time they texted, Cameron assumed he was being hit on and cut off the friendship. Vanessa and Cameron had both applied the "one strike and you're out" rule. But do foreigners perhaps use winks in a different spirit? The two friends laugh uneasily.

Vanessa says the story makes it clear that although her "whole life is texts," she has a problem because texts are "not a good tool for flirting . . . because there is this amazing game theory tree of 'What did that mean? Oh, he put in an exclamation point! Now what did that mean?'"

Vanessa says that when she texts, she relies heavily on emoticons because texts are read as angry unless you soften them with emoticons and punctuation, a lot of punctuation. "I always assume that when I send a text it will be read as my being two times as angry as if I were speaking the same words." So she tries to correct. "I will do something like put two exclamation points and a smiley face just to be, like, 'I am not mad.'" Cameron agrees: "You're right. My main thing when I get a text is that I can't tell if this person is mad." Elaine says that this is the aspect of texting that makes her most nervous: "My fear that people are angry is the worst thing about texting. 'Cause a text will end with a period and you're, like . . . 'Oh, you're furious with me.'" Ryan laughs. To him, when a girl adds an ellipsis, that is a very bad sign. "Or copious ellipses. The dreaded ellipses."

This is a world where it is easy to get things wrong; that's why consultation is so frequent. And the sense of being on a tightrope is not something that people seem to grow out of. It was, after all, the thirty-year-old Gregory who said, "One strike and you're out."

Who Are You? Technical Difficulties

The new love talk depends on technology, but technology is not designed with love talk in mind. Vanessa explains that for the past year she has been dating Julian, who attends a university in London. They use WhatsApp to communicate because it makes it easy to text internationally. Vanessa says that she sometimes likes to check WhatsApp to see if Julian has texted her even when she doesn't have the time to text him back. Just seeing a message from Julian puts Vanessa in a good mood and she doesn't want to deny herself that. But WhatsApp shows when a user is or has been online. So when Vanessa goes online to read Julian's message but does not immediately compose her reply, Julian can see that she's online and feels hurt, ignored. "That causes a lot of issues," says Vanessa. "Huge issues."

The texts she was sending to her other friends were logistical: where to meet up, whether to go out for Chinese food or Italian. But Julian could not see that. All he sees is that she is online but not responding to him. She may not be doing anything wrong, but her relationship suffers.

Cameron minimizes Vanessa's problem. He says that after all, the transparency of WhatsApp "keeps you honest," but Ryan sees her point. The program is just transparent enough to do damage. And he would be annoyed if a girl was texting other friends if she hadn't gotten back to him. More than that, WhatsApp makes it impossible to time your texts for maximum seductive impact. Ryan wants to wait twenty minutes before getting back to a girl so she will fantasize about what he might be up to. But she won't be getting jealous if she can see that he is on his phone texting. The transparency of WhatsApp, he says, "erases the *entire point* of texting because it dictates when you have to respond."

For Ryan, the advantage of texting in a romantic context is that it allows you to hide in a sexy way. Now, as he considers WhatsApp, it is as though the designers of the technology didn't understand its human purpose. At this point the conversation among the friends turns technical: This is a bad feature. Which phones and which apps have it?

Which don't? How can this feature be disabled? How can you work around it?

It turns out that there is much expertise to go around once these clever twenty-two-year-old minds are concentrated on the problem. They end up concluding that to keep romantic texting alive, the best solution is to go "retro" in your technology. They want some version of "I didn't get your mail" or "I was out when your call came in." These kinds of lies have always been staples of romantic exchange. And these young people want technology to make space for them. Elaine thinks she has her worst problems solved by turning off her iPhone's "read receipt" feature. This means that she can at least pretend not to have seen a text. "If I want to take my time responding, I can still say, 'Oh, I put my phone down for a second—so sorry.'"

Who Are You? Can Our Romance Be Efficient?

Ryan worries that too much information takes the romance out of texting. I have dinner with nine San Francisco professionals in their late twenties who hold texting up to a different standard: Does it increase the efficiency of their romantic lives?

Our dinner and the two-hour conversation that follows take place in a downtown conference room so that the participants can join as their workday ends. Most hold their phones during our meeting. A few put their phones on the table. One young woman begins dinner with her phone in her pocketbook, but when it vibrates she takes it out and announces that she will leave it on the table because she is more relaxed when she can see it.

And phones are at the center of our conversation. At this meeting, the men complain that their girlfriends are always on their phones. The women complain that their boyfriends won't take their eyes off their screens. They are certainly not alone. A recent survey reports that nearly half of cell-owning young people in serious relationships say that their partners have been distracted by their mobile phones while they were together. Callie, twenty-six, who works in sales for a large insurance company, has a boyfriend in the financial industry. Even at intimate moments, she says, screens are close at hand.

My boyfriend drives me nuts. . . . He has four computer screens. So he is used to looking at everything going on all the time. . . . So he can actually listen to me and text other people at the same time. But because I can't do that, I think he's not listening and I'll get so mad and be, like, "You're not paying attention to anything I'm saying to you!"

I ask Callie about the effects of these always-present screens on her relationship. She says it forces her to concentrate when she approaches her boyfriend. "I definitely don't talk to him about nonsense because I need to make the best use of my time with him. Because if he is actually spending time listening, I'm making sure that I'm saying things that are actually worth saying."

What about the role of small talk in love? Talk about nothing at all? Callie makes it clear that her relationship does not have a lot of room for that. When she has face-to-face time, there is "just no nonsense."

Callie offers that sometimes she and her boyfriend find a place for "nonsense" on Gchat. Generally, her boyfriend has Gchat in one window on his screen while he keeps an eye on business in other windows. But sometimes, Callie says, she will just put her hand over his screen and fondly say, "Enough." As she makes this gesture in the group, pantomiming her hand on his screen, her phone rings. Everyone laughs.

Ray, twenty-eight, comments on what it's like to have a relationship when you compete with screens: "I think the way we're going, a lot of people are getting the feeling that even though the person they're with is there, you don't get the feeling of real connection. You just have information."

Kim is a college junior from New Jersey. Like Callie, she is frustrated by a boyfriend who is always on his phone. And she shares Ray's concern that conversations in her relationship are mostly about information. It's hard to make them about more because they are usually being interrupted by an incoming text. Her patience is wearing thin. These days, she says, "If me and my boyfriend fight and we are talking and he stops to text someone back, even if it is for two seconds, I'm, like, 'What are you doing? I'm not good enough for you?' I freak out."

Recently Kim's boyfriend broke his phone:

And these past couple [of] weeks, because he hasn't had a phone, the interactions we have—even if it is a date night or lying in bed doing nothing, it's so much better. I'm not trying to compete with a phone. It's so much easier. It's a lot more relaxing. It puts my mind at ease.

Kim reflects on her conversations with her boyfriend before the broken phone: "He owns his own business . . . so that means he is constantly on his phone. So our conversation would be really small. It would be about nothing important. At dinnertime, it would be me saying, 'Who are you texting?' or 'How's your iPhone?'" Kim got used to a conversational regimen so restricted that for her, now, a "larger" conversation with her boyfriend means things as simple as talking about their day.

Who Are You? Imposing Order

The San Francisco twenty-somethings are always pressed for time. They work so many hours a week that they barely see their partners. It seems natural that when they talk about love and texting, they stress its efficiency. For others, what messaging, email, and texting can do is bring order and cool into the untidiness of relationships.

In *Taipei*, a 2013 novel heralded as depicting the post-net sensibility, the lovers at the center of the story use technology to avoid the risks of real-time arguments. When they're angry they agree to type to each other.

Erin sat at the foot of the bed, facing away from Paul, who lay on his back with his MacBook against his thighs, and they communicated by email (they'd agreed to type, not talk, whenever one of them, currently Paul, felt unable to speak in a friendly tone) for around fifty minutes.

Life tracks art. Some couples tell me they have their arguments online (usually on Gchat or instant messenger) so they can keep a record. One desired goal is to make the fights more "fair." Some use "fight tracking" apps. Here, the idea is that gathering more data about the pattern of quarrels will help couples improve their relationships.

Talia, in her early thirties, talks about how she and her partner used to work out their differences in online chat sessions. "What I like about chat for fighting is that I'm getting my case out and I'm sure I will be heard. When we argue face-to-face, I get so upset that I don't remember what I said. . . . We were having these fights and it was destructive." In online talk, she can collect her thoughts and leave a record. But after a while, she and her partner had second thoughts about the online quarrels. The method began to feel awkward and they wanted to return to what Talia calls a more "spontaneous" style of arguing. But they could not go back to how they had done things before. They knew they would miss the "accountability" of online chat with its data trail. They found a compromise. As soon as a conversation gets heated, they begin to videotape it. So now they have an archive of their "fights."

And our promise to each other is that when we feel we are in that destructive space, we stop, take a break, and continue that face-to-face conversation on tape. We take the value of what we used to get out of fighting by text and chat—that we had the record—and use it for face-to-face.

Leaving a record makes both Talia and her partner feel safer. They won't be misheard. They are trying to use technology to make their relationship—untidy as all relationships are—more tidy. In the language that I hear so much, their goal is to make the conversations of romance more efficient and controlled.

But getting to know other people, appreciating them, is not necessarily a task enhanced by efficiency. This is because people don't reveal themselves, deeply, in efficient ways. Things take time to unfold. There is need for backtracking and repetition. There is a deepening of understanding when you have gone through the same thing twice, or more.

Where Did You Go?

In a stand-up routine on modern romance, Aziz Ansari asks people to raise their hands if they have ever just stopped texting someone when they were not "into" the relationship. A theater of hands goes up. Then he asks people to raise their hands if that is how they'd like someone to convey to them a lack of continuing interest. There are no hands. There is a lot we accept as the new normal that we don't like at all.

Sloane, a college junior, went on only four dates with Evan, but each one lasted more than five hours. Sloane felt they had that all-elusive "chemistry." On their fourth date, Evan initiated a serious conversation, a discussion of what each of them wanted from the relationship. Sloane says, "I told him that I was happy to be with him as long as we both enjoyed each other's company. He seemed relieved and pleased with my response . . . but he made it clear that he didn't want to use 'labels,' which was an unusually cliché thing for him to say."

Sloane left the conversation about "no labels" feeling excited. She thought that she and Evan were at the beginning of something important. But then, she didn't hear from Evan for a few days. Usually he would have sent her a text or several, just to check in. Finally, on a Saturday morning, as she was just home from a run, Sloane looked at her phone to check the time and saw the green message bubble containing an excerpt of a text she had missed. Scanning the message, she registered the phrases "amazing woman," "wish you all the best," and "not the best time."

I put the phone down as though it were some terrible thing and walked to the kitchen, where I sat on the floor with my back against the refrigerator. My heart was still pounding rapidly, but it was no longer from the exercise. I was upset to receive this message because it was such bad news, because he had chosen to text me this bad news, and because it contradicted the understanding I thought we had between us.

Sloane responds to Evan's text with a simple text accepting his decision. ("thanks for letting me know," "best of luck," etc.) But Sloane wants closure and there is none in this transaction.

What just happened? Sloane is left with questions that won't go away about Evan's unavailability to have a conversation. She feels devalued. "If he actually cared for me, why didn't he make the effort to have a conversation with me so that I could address his concerns?" From this follow other painful possibilities. Her mind races round and round: "Because he did not want to have such a conversation, he must have decided that he did not care for me, after all."

Beyond the rejection, Sloane cannot let go of the idea that Evan misunderstood her point of view in the "funny conversation" that ended in the discussion of "labels." Sloane worries that she gave Evan the impression that any relationship with her would require commitment. In fact, she would have been happy to take their relationship slowly. "If we had actually had a breakup conversation, I would have had fewer—if any— questions like these." Despite all of this, Sloane feels silenced by the breakup text. She wishes she could be certain that Evan did not misunderstand her. But she comes to this conclusion: You don't answer a breakup text with a call saying, "I want to talk."

What Just Happened?

I am in Seattle at a three-day conference on social media, and one of the other speakers, a thirty-six-year-old architect named Adam tells me he would like to share his story about love enabled by online communication. Specifically, he wants to show me the electronic archive of his now broken-off relationship with Tessa, then an art student, with whom he had spent three joyful, if turbulent, years.

Adam says that it was with Tessa that he was his best self. Now, even three years after the relationship ended, he is still sorting through the question "Who am I outside of this relationship?" After every failed relationship, lovers try to hold on to the "better self" they felt themselves to be in the presence of their beloved. So Adam is asking a very old question.

But since so much of Adam's relationship with Tessa took place online, this old question has a new twist. Online, Adam was able to "edit" himself. Now, he wonders if he needs editing delays to be his best self. And how does the fact that he has an archive of his relationship with Tessa—the two were electronically in touch from thirty to fifty times a day—change how he looks back and how he moves forward?

When Adam and I first meet, he begins by quoting the comedian Chris Rock, who said that to marry a woman, you have only two questions you need to ask yourself: "Do you like to fuck her? Do you like to have dinner with her?" Adam says that Tessa more than met the Chris Rock standard: Talking with Tessa, including and especially over text and email, could feel like sex. "In talking to Tessa, I would find myself crying literally tears of joy, I felt so understood and so, like, pushed and challenged in a loving way. And I felt empathized with, and she knew just how to mock me in the way that I mock myself and vice versa." But Chris Rock also said that on first dates, we don't send ourselves but we send our "representatives"; we send our best selves. Over time, our representatives can't do the job and "we" start to show up. And that is where a relationship either works or doesn't. In digital connections, the danger is that we can keep sending in our representatives. So, it's harder to know what is working, if it is working.

Adam says, "The most important thing for Tessa was to feel empathy, that I was with her, sharing, on the same page." Every couple has a contract, usually implicit, about what will make the relationship work. In this relationship, Adam was to provide empathy and Tessa would appreciate his efforts, tutoring him along the way.

In the end, Tessa accused Adam of being insufficiently empathic and broke things off. Three years later, Adam sees their split as inevitable. He was held to an unrealistic standard: "If every conversation has to fulfill these deep needs, then occasionally a conversation isn't going to." And with Tessa, every conversation was put to a test.

Adam says he wanted to be the more "open" man that Tessa needed. He consoles himself that he gave it his best shot because electronic messaging allowed him to "pause and get it right" in his exchanges with Tessa. "If Tessa and I [had been a couple] at a time when emails and text messages were unavailable, I don't think we would have stayed together."

Old Phones

Adam and I have several meetings. At our first, he shows me the phone he used when he first met Tessa. It has long since been replaced, but his first exchanges with Tessa are "trapped" on it. After the breakup, Adam didn't know how to connect this phone to his computer and this propelled him into a frenzy of activity: "So my first step was to crazily transcribe our text messages onto paper. . . . I would painstakingly note what I said and what she said and I would have to jerk between the sent messages folder on this crappy phone to the received messages and then, from the notes I took on paper, I typed things into a computer file."

There are still over a thousand messages left to transcribe, so in our interviews, Adam and I switch our attention from his old phone to computer files of transcribed conversations and then back again to the phone.

Adam considers his general texting strategy: "I try for the Twitter effect. . . . I want them short and explosive. Like little bon-bons. . . . Like gifts." Even before he met Tessa, he says, his texts were "crafted." But once he was writing to Tessa, things moved beyond craft. Now Adam was compelled by something deeper. He was trying to be what Tessa needed: "a better self, a more empathic person, someone more able to share himself." Adam says that Tessa used texting to help him be that person.

I ask for examples. By this point in my research I'm not surprised that the first one I get involves punctuation. In texting, we've seen that punctuation is one of the main ways to express all of the information that tone of voice and body posture would convey in face-to-face conversation. And we've seen that putting so much interpretive weight on punctuation means that a lot of attention is paid to seemingly little things—say, using a period instead of ellipses, elements in a code both partners understand. So to show me how Tessa helped him be a "better self," Adam looks through a group of texts and finds a message with a well-placed exclamation point. He is jubilant: "Here! Something as small as the word 'Sure!' with an exclamation point. . . . She's recognizing my need to feel acknowledged."

In another text, Tessa writes, "Just parked, will call!" Adam explains why this message is just right, punctuation-wise: "There's that kind of, like—there's a kind of joy that we're going to see one another soon." Adam acknowledges that the codes can change and what matters is keeping up with them: "I mean, who knows? Five years from now, maybe it would have been, 'Just parked, will call you.' Maybe that exclamation point would be gone."

Adam remembers the day he received the "just parked" text. It was during one of the happiest times of his life. He was in love. He was getting things right with Tessa. And then he explains how, for him, getting things right depended on editing.

The Better, Edited, Self

Adam says that early in their relationship, Tessa would sometimes present him with a problem, and his first instinct was often to suggest a solution. For example, she told him about a misunderstanding with her thesis supervisor and Adam was ready with some advice. Adam tells me that giving Tessa advice was always a mistake. It made her feel that he was not listening to her but trying to fix things. "The right thing is usually to say it is hard to imagine her pain but that I am there for her." But Adam admits that if Tessa brought up a problem during a face-to-face conversation, he often forgot himself and presented her with advice. He says that he did better online, where he had time to reflect and revise.

Adam looks for other examples that show how editing made him a better self. He pulls up a text he sent Tessa after a fight. Adam says that after this quarrel he was frightened, afraid of what would happen next. But in his text he lessened the tension by sending a photo of his feet, beneath which he wrote, "Try to control your sexual passion in seeing me in Crocs and socks." In person, Adam says that his anxiety would have led him to try to corner Tessa into forgiving him. His panic would have made things worse. Online, he used humor to signal confidence in their enduring connection. So what the text communicated is not the "real" Adam; it's the Adam he wants to be.

Adam is troubled by the gap between his in-person self and the self he can summon in online exchanges. But the Adam I have before me is a reflective, caring man. Online, we do not become different selves. Our online identities are facets of ourselves that usually are harder for us to express in the physical realm. This is why the online world can be a place for personal growth. People work on desired qualities in the virtual and gradually bring them into their lives "off the screen." Adam is in the process of recognizing that, in person, he is closer to the online Adam than he sometimes thinks.

In retrospect, Adam is aware that the intensity and frequency of their digital communications encouraged Tessa's fantasy that their relationship could take "total empathy" as its goal. This made their relationship sure to fail. But Adam admits that during the relationship, he did not discourage Tessa's fantasy. He tried to live it out. He sums up how online life made his effort easier: "That Gchat box, it's delicious."

There is always a fine line that separates romantic love from a complicity in which the boundaries between partners become blurred. Romantically, each becomes "lost" in the other. This kind of love can sound like a sought-after state. But when it happens, communication is blocked because each partner can only hear what he or she needs to hear to keep the fantasy alive. Continual texting does not cause this kind of relationship to develop, but it makes it easier to fall into. Adam talks about having Tessa "in his phone," "in his pocket."

So, in the end, Adam thinks his relationship with Tessa was made possible and then undone by texting. It supported an unrealistic fantasy of "total empathic understanding." And even though Adam made a continual effort to present himself as he wanted to be, he shared so much and over such a long period that he revealed himself. And that self wasn't who Tessa wanted.

People feel that digital media put them in a comfort zone where they can share "just the right amount" of themselves. This is the Goldilocks effect. Texting and email make people feel in control, but when they talk in detail about their online exchanges, the stories are usually about misunderstandings and crossed signals. The feelings of control are just that: feelings.

In theory, digital media can keep you at the "just right" distance, but in practice, at least in romantic relationships, they rarely do that job. When two people are continually connected, over time, it is almost impossible to maintain any "just right" distance. So the Goldilocks effect is really the Goldilocks fallacy. And when Adam makes what he considers a "mistake," it is on the record. Online, he reminds me, "once things are in black and white, every mistake is there to see and review and there is no forgetting."

What We Really Need to Know

Beyond the Goldilocks fallacy about emotional distance, there is another misunderstanding about what online communication offers. This is the data fallacy. This is the feeling that online exchanges give us so much data that we now know all that we need to know about our partners. Certainly enough to get it "just right." Adam was reassured by the amount of information he had about Tessa, but too often, he had Tessa's words but no way to sense her body language, facial expression, or the cadence of her speech. So he often missed what he really needed to know, what her presence would have provided.

One such lapse occurred in a Gchat exchange that took place toward the end of their relationship. Adam presents it to me as a "good conversation" even though it upset Tessa. As he describes it, it seems clear that he couldn't see how the more he wrote, the worse things were becoming. Why is this? Although he and Tessa were at cross purposes on Gchat, Adam felt reassured by the volume and animation of their repartee. There was so much going on! The absence of intimacy was disguised by frenetic rounds of connection.

The context: Adam is staying in Tessa's apartment while she is on a business trip. They had an argument and now, the following day, they use Gchat to reconcile. When Adam shows me the transcript of their conversation, he points out how comforting it was to him that his "voice" overlapped with Tessa's.

Most reassuring of all is when Tessa explicitly draws him close:

TESSA: *It must be weird being in my apartment without me, and wearing my tank tops.*

ADAM: *I didn't see your name on them. I have purchased a gift for you at the clothing store on Copp Street. Very hip.*

TESSA: *Personalized shirts went out of style just as I got *some* bit of breast that would have sexily shown my moniker. A gift! Which store? Copp's Closet? . . .*

ADAM: *Did you mean to bold the word "some"?*

TESSA: *Yes.*

ADAM: *I want to kiss you.*

TESSA: *Me too.*

ADAM: *So kiss you.*

TESSA: *I did.*

ADAM: *Hot. . . . Yes weird to be in your place without you. I love it though. It truly reflects your spirit, taste. I am awed and obsessed by your books. Mind.*

Adam explains that in this last line he is trying to equate Tessa's books and mind because she worries that she is "not as smart as the people writing the books she owns." But at his words, Tessa becomes defensive: "Mind and books are sadly not equated." Adam reassures her: "Allegedly. I want to type/talk forever love." This time, at his attempt to reassure, Tessa moves to cut the conversation off. She replies: "I'll let you go."

In this exchange, when Tessa feels insecure in the face of Adam's overabundance of praise, she ends the conversation and then adds a thought to reassure herself. After cutting Adam off to say good-bye, Tessa tells him that she is going to "sit outside to read for a bit. I really miss reading for a couple of hours, or um, half-hour stretches." He has made her anxious about her reading. So she makes sure to say that she is going to go read, but qualifies her statement, defensively. It's been hard to read. Her work makes it difficult. She has to do it in short bits.

Adam says that this exchange shows him and Tessa "at their best." He says that they are "sharing," "supporting each other," and "aware of each other's needs." What Adam doesn't mention is that the conversation also shows Tessa turning away from him when he touches on a subject that threatens her. And when this happens, Adam doesn't retreat, but doubles down and says something Tessa probably does not believe: that he equates her mind with the brilliance of her books. If Adam had Tessa before him, in person, would he have seen her pull away, in retreat, her gaze withdrawn?

Closure and the Archive

The relationship ends when even the "better Adam"—with his crafted email and texting—cannot be empathic enough to meet Tessa's standard. In a final telephone call, Tessa tells Adam that she needs more.

The call leaves Adam feeling bereft and then angry. He writes Tessa an email to tell her that what she is asking for would destroy any relationship. "I said that when she doesn't get what she wants she's petulant and childlike. Which is damn true. . . . But I didn't call her and say, 'Hey, I want to talk to you about this.' Why didn't I level that charge face-to-face?"

Adam begins to answer his own question. He says that when he wrote his angry email, he could imagine Tessa receiving it instantly but had some protection from her response. When she did respond, by text, she told him he was wrong and laid into him. Adam cannot bear to look at that text. He only says, "She responded with something pretty brutal." He faced those cutting words on the screen but had not been willing to see her in person, perhaps saying such things.

Adam stays on the subject of why he sent that final email to Tessa.

When Tessa broke up with him he was plagued with self-doubt. Perhaps Tessa was right. Perhaps he was insufficiently empathic. "So, when I wanted to express my feelings to her and I thought I might be inadequate if I talked, I just went ahead and expressed my feelings in a way where I knew I would not fail: an email." But the email failed miserably. All it provoked were more words designed to most hurt the other.

What have new media done to the communications of love? They have deepened them and given them new immediacy. But online, with an archive of messages on hand, we feel we know more than we really do about our partners. Online, we are more likely to say cruel things. Digital exchanges disinhibit when love might be better served by tact. Adam says that online messaging "allows you to be slightly warmer than in real life." And then he adds that it also allows you to be "slightly crueler" as well.

Lovers have left each other insecure since the beginning of love. What I am struck with as I watch Adam juggling his phones and laptop is that when he wants to think about who he is and can be, he looks to his archive, beginning with the rapturous early messages "trapped" on his old phone. Indeed, Adam thinks the idea of a record was part of his relationship with Tessa from the very beginning.

> *Even when we were doing this, we knew we had a record. A record of our conversations. I think it is powerful. I reread the conversations all the time. . . . There's a permanence to it. We loved to talk on the phone, but sometimes . . . I wonder if one of the reasons that at some times we gravitated to this medium of conversation was . . . to be able to remember. . . . I treasure that permanence. . . . When she writes . . . "you are great," she is saying "I have a need and you met it." How central that is to have that written evidence, for the rest of my life in my Gmail . . . or to print it out if I want, whenever.*

The archive affirms Adam—he sees the self he wants to be—but of course, he is aware that having the archive also "cuts the other way." Adam says, "When she says in this medium 'You are insufficient,' it's devastating to read. . . . It wasn't just something she said at the height of a fight. It was, like, measured. There's a level of deliberation that's baked in."

Adam thinks electronic communication helped him in this relationship because it allowed him time to craft his writing. But this means that Tessa's texts and messages were also crafted. This seems fairly straightforward, but Adam admits that this is not something he has thought much about. He has always liked to think of Tessa's messages as "straight from the heart"—more spontaneous than his own. But now, he says, "My mind is racing. I'm thinking, 'Oh shit. . . . Maybe I shouldn't value [the emails] as much as I do. Maybe there is something more deliberate and insincere than I give credit for.'" Adam wonders if he is a prisoner of his archive and is moved to ask, "How do you know someone in a true way?"

Three Chairs

Education

Attentional Disarray

*I need to see who wants me. We are not
as strong as technology's pull.*

—A JUNIOR AT MIT, EXPLAINING WHY SHE
CHECKS HER TEXTS DURING CLASS

*From what I hear, really good actors can
actually teach really well.*

—ANANT AGARWAL, CEO OF EDX, THE HARVARD/MIT
CONSORTIUM ON ONLINE EDUCATION, CONTEMPLATING
THE SUBSTITUTION OF ACTORS FOR PROFESSORS
IN ONLINE COURSES

At MIT, I teach a seminar on science, technology, and memoir. Enrollment is capped at twenty students. The atmosphere is intimate. We read memoirs by scientists, engineers, and designers (one student favorite is Oliver Sacks's *Uncle Tungsten*) and then the students tell their own stories.

MIT students come from diverse backgrounds. Some have lived hardscrabble lives. During a recent fall semester, their stories were particularly poignant. One had escaped with his family from what was then the Soviet Union. Another had overcome deep poverty; there were many nights when he had no choice but to sleep in his car. And yet, through all of this, these students had found their way to science or engineering or design. Sometimes the inspiration had come from a teacher, parent, or friend. Sometimes it came from fascination with an object—a broken-down car, an old computer, a grandfather clock. The students seemed to understand each other, to find a rhythm. I thought the class was working.

And then, halfway through the semester, a group of students asks to see me. They want to say that they have been texting during class and feel bad because of the very personal material being discussed. They say that they text in all their classes, but here, well, it somehow seems wrong. We decide that this is something the class should discuss as a group.

In that discussion, more students admit that they, too, text in class. A small group says they are upset to hear this. They have been talking about the roughest times of their childhoods, about abuse and abandonment. But even they admit that they see checking for texts during class as the norm and have since high school. But why in *this* class? It's a small seminar. *They are talking about their lives.*

In the conversation that follows, my students portray constant connection as a necessity. These students don't feel they can be present unless they are also, in a way, absent. For some, three minutes is too long to go without checking their phones. Some say two minutes is their rule. Those who bring tablets to class point out that a "social check" is as simple as touching a Facebook icon on their screen. They want to see who is in touch with them, a comfort in itself.

We decide to try a device-free class with a short break to check phones. For me, something shifts. Conversations become more relaxed and cohesive. Students finish their thoughts, unrushed. What the students tell me is that they feel relief: When they are not tempted by their phones, they feel more in control of their attention. An irony emerges. For of course, on one level, we all see our phones as instruments for giving us greater control, not less.

My students became upset because, in this class, their usual split attention (looking at their phones; listening to their classmates) felt wrong. It devalued their classmates' life stories (and their own) and made them feel that they were crossing some moral line. They could imagine a day when people around you would be upset and you would still be pulled away to your phone.

A lot is at stake in attention. Where we put it is not only how we decide what we will learn; it is how we show what we value.

The Myth of Multitasking

These days, attention is in short supply—in college classrooms, its scarcity poses special problems because, after all, so much money, time, and effort has been spent to bring together these students, this professor, these educational resources. And yet here, like everywhere, if we have a device in our hands, we want to multitask.

But in this, we pursue an illusion. When we think we are multitasking, our brains are actually moving quickly from one thing to the next, and our performance degrades for each new task we add to the mix. Multitasking gives us a neurochemical high so we think we are doing better and better when actually we are doing worse and worse. We've seen that not only do multitaskers have trouble deciding how to organize their time, but over time, they "forget" how to read human emotions. Students—for example, my students—think that texting during class does not interrupt their understanding of class conversation, but they are wrong. The myth of multitasking is just that: a myth.

And yet, multitasking is the norm in classrooms. By 2012, nine in ten college students said that they text in class.

The widespread adoption of texting was a landmark in the unfolding of the multitasked life. We've met the group of high school seniors in Connecticut for whom getting a smartphone over the 2008 holiday break made the spring term that followed it a new kind of experience: When these students are at school, in class and out of class, they text continually. There is so much texting during school hours that their school put a "no texting in class" policy into effect, but the young men ignore it: Some claim to have never heard of it. Andrew says, "Most kids can text without looking, so . . . you'll just be looking at the teacher, and under the table you've got your thumbs going crazy."

One of the more studious boys in the group, Oliver, takes pains to insist that his teachers should not take it personally when he texts in class. Teachers put the notes online; he "gets" what is going on in class, so "I'm almost always bored and I want to be somewhere else and I'm almost always texting." He does admit that once he's texting, the possibilities for concentrating are pretty much gone: "You can't focus on the thing you are doing when you are sending the text . . . or waiting to receive a text . . . there is so much going on with other things you might want to receive on your phone."

Despite his new problem with focus, even in 2008, Oliver expects that what he has now is what he'll have in the future. He imagines that from now on, when he feels bored, he will immediately add a new layer of communication. So for him, "boredom is a thing of the past." Every generation, he says, had its own way of responding to being bored, especially during classes. Other generations passed notes, doodled, or zoned out. His generation can send texts and go to Facebook. He calls his generation "lucky": "We have the awesome new power to erase boredom."

His friend Aidan disagrees. He thinks that this "awesome new power" means they have all lost focus. Maybe Oliver isn't bored, but has he noticed that none of them are paying attention in class?

When they went on to college, this early smartphone generation did not grow more tolerant of what they are so quick to call boredom. We've met Judy, whom I interview when she is a college junior. A slow moment in class sends her immediately to her phone, where she goes through the "circuit" of all of her social apps, just to check them. She says that she likes the feeling of "rapid-fire switching" and thinks that no class could ever compete with it, no matter how engaging. Why? The class "is only one mode of stimulus."

So, dropping out of a classroom conversation can begin with a moment of boredom, because a friend reaches out to you, or because, as one student in my memoir class put it, "You just want to see who wants you." And once you are in that "circuit of apps," you want to stay with them.

In classrooms, the distracted are a distraction: Studies show that when students are in class multitasking on laptops, everyone around them learns less. One college senior says, "I'll be in a great lecture and look over and see someone shopping for shoes and think to myself, 'Are you kidding me?' So I get mad at them, but then I get mad at myself for being self-righteous. But after I've gone through my cycle of indignation to self-hate, I realize that I have missed a minute of the lecture, and then I'm really mad."

It's easy to see how concentration would be disrupted in this crucible of emotion. But even for those who don't get stirred up, when you see someone in your class on Facebook or checking their email, two things cross your mind: Maybe this class is boring, and maybe I, too, should attend to some online business. Yet despite research that shows that multitasking is bad for learning, the myth of the moment is still that multitasking is a good idea. A series of ads for AT&T show a young man chatting with a group of schoolchildren about the things children know. Or perhaps, the things children know that adults want to validate. One of the things that the children and the adult agree on is that faster is better. A second is that it is better to do more than one thing at a time. This is a myth that dies hard.

And we are not inclined to let it die because multitasking feels good. It is commonplace to talk about multitaskers as addicted. I don't like to talk about addiction in this context because I find that discussing the holding power of technology in these terms makes people feel helpless. It makes them feel they are facing something against which resistance seems almost futile. This is a fallacy. In this case, resistance is not futile but highly productive. Writers, artists, scientists, and literary scholars talk openly about disenabling the Wi-Fi on their computers in order to get creative work done. In the acknowledgments of her most recent book, the novelist Zadie Smith thanks Freedom and SelfControl, programs that shut off connectivity on her Mac.

The analogy between screens and drugs breaks down for other reasons. There is only one thing that you should do if you are on heroin: Get off the heroin. Your life is at stake. But laptops and smartphones are not things to remove. *They are facts of life and part of our creative lives. The goal is to use them with greater intention.*

Instead of thinking about addiction, it makes sense to confront this reality: We are faced with technologies to which we are extremely vulnerable and we don't always respect that fact. The path forward is to learn more about our vulnerabilities. Then, we can design technology and the environments in which we use them with these insights in mind. For example, since we know that multitasking is seductive but not helpful to learning, it's up to us to promote "unitasking."

It's encouraging that it is often children who recognize their vulnerabilities to technology and come up with ways to deal with them, even when adults are pulling them in another direction. In fact, the critique of multitasking is a good example of where I've seen children take the lead. Reyna, fourteen, has been issued an iPad at school. The entire eighth-grade curriculum is on it. But so are her email and favorite games, including *Candy Crush*. In order to get work done, she prints out her reading assignments and puts aside the iPad. She learned to do this from her sister, who had experienced the same attention problems with a curriculum-on-a-tablet. Reyna describes the problem:

> *People really liked [the iPad] because . . . they could look things up really quickly in class, but also . . . people were getting really distracted. Like, my sister had an iPad and she said that her and her friends' texts were blocked but they had school emails. And they would sit in class and pretend to be researching but really they were emailing back and forth just because they were bored—or they would take screenshots of a test practice sheet and send it out to their friends that hadn't had the class yet.*
>
> *But my sister also said that even when she and her friends were just trying to study for a test, "they would go and print everything that they had on their iPads," because studying was made a lot more difficult*

because of all the other distractions on the iPad, all the other apps they could download.

This student knows that it is hard to concentrate in class when you are holding a device that you associate with games and messaging—a device built to encourage doing one thing and then another and another. Reyna came to her experience with the iPad at school with many advantages: She had experienced school without it. She remembered that she used to be less distracted. She had a point of comparison and she had her sister as a mentor. But increasingly, students like Reyna are the exception. Children who begin school with an iPad won't know that you can "force" a state of greater concentration by using media that allow you to do only one thing at a time. It's up to a more experienced generation to teach them.

Students who print out their assignments in order to have time away from screens should give educators pause when they, with the best of intentions, try to make things more efficient by closing the library and declaring books obsolete.

The Opposite of Unitasking: Hyper Attention

Many educators begin with an accommodation: They note that students text and search the web in class, and they say, "Fine"—in previous days, students would find other ways to zone out, and this is the twenty-first-century equivalent. But some educators do more than accommodate the distractions of digital media. They see a new sensibility of fractured attention and they want to use it as an opportunity to teach in a new way.

So, literary theorist Katherine Hayles argues that fractured attention is the sensibility of the twenty-first century and that to look back to "deep attention" in the classroom is to be unhelpfully nostalgic. (My skepticism begins here, as I think of Reyna and her sister, who print out their reading assignments so as not to be distracted on the iPad.) Students, says Hayles, think in a new mode, the mode of "hyper attention." Given the realities of the classroom, educators have a choice: "Change the students to fit the educational environment or change that environment to fit the students."

In other words, for Hayles, there is no real choice. Education must embrace the culture of hyper attention. As an example of a constructive way to do this, Hayles points to experiments at the University of Southern California in a classroom outfitted with screens.

One mode of interaction is "Google jockeying": While a speaker is making a presentation, participants search the web for appropriate content to display on the screens—for example, sites with examples, definitions, images, or opposing views. Another mode of interaction is "backchanneling," in which participants type in comments as the speaker talks, providing running commentary on the material being presented.

There is no doubt that Google jockeying speaks to our moment. Students say that they want to turn away from class when there is a lull. Google jockeying implicitly says, all right, we will get rid of those lulls. Even experienced faculty start to ramp up their PowerPoint presentations in a spirit (not always acknowledged) of competing with students' screens. Or we tell them, as Hayles suggests, to go to the web during class time for opposing views, images, and comments. Or to make a comment of their own.

But there is another way to respond to students who complain that they need more stimulation than class conversation provides. It is to tell them that a moment of boredom can be an opportunity to go inward to your imagination, an opportunity for new thinking.

If a moment of boredom happens in a classroom, rather than competing for student attention with ever more extravagant technological fireworks (*Google jockeying!*), we should encourage our students to stay with their moment of silence or distraction. We can try to build their confidence that such moments—when you stay with your thoughts—have a payoff. We can present classrooms as places where you can encounter a moment of boredom and "walk" toward its challenges. A chemistry professor puts it this way: "In my class I want students to daydream. They can go back to the text if they missed a key fact. But if they went off in thought . . . they might be making the private connection that pulls the course together for them."

When those who are fluent in both deep attention and hyper attention—and certainly Hayles is in this group—look at hyper attention, it is tempting to see something exciting because it is new. But they still have a choice. They can switch between ways of knowing. But children who grow up in an all-multitasking environment may not have a choice.

A life of multitasking limits your options so that you cannot simply "pick up" deep attention. What is most enriching is having fluency in both deep and hyper attention. This is attentional pluralism and it should be our educational goal. You can choose multitasking. You can also focus on one thing at a time. And you know when you should.

But attentional pluralism is hard to achieve. Hyper attention feels good. And without practice, we can lose the ability to summon deep attention.

Eric Schmidt, of Google, spoke to a college audience and expressed his own concern. He told the students that he used to read books on airplanes, the one place where there was no Wi-Fi. Now, with Wi-Fi on airplanes, things have changed: "Now I spend all my time being online, doing my emails, interacting and all that, and the book doesn't get read. I think we've got to work on that." Schmidt made this comment while promoting a book he authored that celebrates, even in its subtitle, how technology will "reshape" people. Schmidt isn't happy that he has exchanged books for email and messages, but he believes in the forward march of technology.

Elizabeth, a graduate student in economics, is not so sure about the forward march. She is convinced that the "natural multitasking" of her work life has left her with diminished cognitive capacity.

Before graduate school, Elizabeth worked as a consultant. It was a job that led her to make multitasking a way of life. "For instance, I could be fielding emails from clients, looking up industry data to insert into a PowerPoint presentation for an urgent meeting, researching which restaurant to take my best friend to that night, while writing the actual requirements document I was supposed to be working on that day. My routine practice of multitasking led to another behavior—skimming." It was only when Elizabeth returned to the university that she saw the full effect of years spent multitasking, a life lived in hyper attention. Now, as a graduate student, she has been assigned an excerpt of Plato's *Republic* for an ethics class.

> *I had skimmed the chapter, as was my habit, then, realizing that I hadn't retained much, reread it again and even made a few notes. Unfortunately, on the day of the class, I did not have that notebook with me, and while I remembered the overall gist of the chapter (moderation— good; desire for luxury—bad), I struggled to recall specific ideas expressed in it. Without access to my cell phone to refer to the article or read up on Plato on Wikipedia, I wasn't able to participate in the class discussion. Having access to information is always wonderful, but without having at least some information retained in my brain, I am not able to build on those ideas or connect them together to form new ones.*

As I speak with Elizabeth, it is clear that more is at stake than disappointment in her class performance. If she can't "build on ideas or connect them together to form new ones," she knows she won't be able to have certain kinds of conversations—in her view, probably the most important ones.

And attention is not a skill we learn for one domain. When you train your brain to multitask as your basic approach—when you embrace hyper attention—you won't be able to focus even when you want to. So, you're going to have trouble sitting and listening to your children tell you about their day at school. You're going to have trouble at work sitting in a meeting and listening to your colleagues. Their narrative will seem painfully slow. Just as middle school children don't acquire the skills for conversation because they lack practice, university students lose the capacity to sit in a class and follow a complex argument. Research shows that when college students watch online educational videos, they watch for six minutes no matter how long the video. So videos for online courses are being produced at six minutes. But if you become accustomed to getting your information in six-minute bites, you will grow impatient with more extended presentations. One college senior describes her friends' taste for the short and terse: "If they had their choice, conversations would begin with a tweet and end in a tweet."

Maryanne Wolf, a cognitive neuroscientist at Tufts University, had long observed students' fractured attention spans but did not feel personally implicated until one evening when she sat down to read *The Glass Bead Game* by Hermann Hesse, one of her favorite authors. Wolf found it impossible to focus on the book. She panicked and wondered if her life on the web had cost her this ability. When Eric Schmidt noted his difficulty with sustained reading, he remarked, "We've got to work on that." Wolf immediately got to work. She began to study what skimming, scanning, and scrolling do to our ability to read with deep attention—what she calls "deep reading." Her thesis is that a life lived online makes deep attention harder to summon. This happens because the brain is plastic—it is constantly in flux over a lifetime—so it "rewires" itself depending on how attention is allocated.

Wolf, Hayles, and Schmidt have all diagnosed a problem with deep attention. But they turn in different directions when it comes to what to do next. Hayles argues for a conscious pedagogical accommodation to the new sensibility. Schmidt shrugs and says that in the end, technology will lead us in the right direction. Wolf's focus on the plasticity of the brain gives her a different perspective. For if the brain is plastic, this means that at any age, it can be set to work on deep attention. Put otherwise, if we decide that deep attention is a value, we can cultivate it. Indeed, that is what Wolf discovered for herself. She had trouble with the Hesse but kept at it. And she says that after two weeks of effort, she was once again able to focus sufficiently to immerse herself in deep reading. Wolf's experience suggests a pedagogy that supports unitasking and deep reading. But if we value these, we have to actively choose them.

Grazing

H ayles is not alone in her enthusiasm for hyper attention. In *Born Digital*, John Palfrey and Urs Gasser describe in glowing terms a new style of learner who picks up things here and there, taking bits and pieces from a Wikipedia article, a clip from Comedy Central, a Twitter feed, the results of a Google search. In general, these new learners read headlines and gaze at images; they tinker and associate. They graze. When they need to go deep, they pause and dive. Palfrey and Gasser argue that there is no reason to think that an older generation, trained to gather information by focusing on several trusted sources read in depth, had a better learning style. It was just different.

But in practice, grazing makes it hard to develop a narrative to frame events, for example, to think about history or current events. The problem can sometimes begin with something as simple as not knowing the names of the actors in the drama. An eleventh grade teacher puts it this way: "My students are struggling. No dates, no geography, no sense of how to weigh the importance of things."

The problem isn't web surfing. It's turning to bits and pieces at times when a more sustained narrative, the kind you are more likely to meet in a book or long article, would be a better choice. *This teacher is saying that her students don't have the materials in mind to consider the whole and so they have trouble arguing a point of view.* But they continue to skip what this teacher calls "basic content," thinking that this is something the web will fill them in on—someday. The web is their "information prosthetic" and they see no cost to having one.

We have met Maureen, thirty-two, who feels that without her phone she "doesn't have anything to say." Maureen compares herself to her mother, who knew poetry by heart. Maureen knows no poetry; more than this, in school, she says, she was never asked to memorize anything, "no dates or places in history." When she needed a fact, she looked it up online. This leaves Maureen feeling empty without her phone. But when she has her phone, she has facts at her fingertips but no timeline or narrative to slide them into. For her, another fact about the United States in 1863 simply floats free in its own universe, somewhere out there in the cloud; it is not added to a story about the Civil War that Maureen already knows.

When I talk to high school and college students today, I see a lot of Maureens in the making, students confident they will always have their phones if they need to look something up, and who will perhaps someday regret their lack of "context." For now, teachers in middle and high school are left trying to make a case for why students should be asked to remember people, places, chronology—the story. And why they should slow down.

"They Want the Right Answer. Quickly!"

I run a focus group on technology in education for twenty teachers and administrators from independent high schools in the Northeast. They worry that their students are in a rush. Here are some of the thoughts around the table: "They don't think anything should take time." "They are not particularly interested in listening to each other. If they have a question, they want the right answer. Quickly!" They want that answer directly and "don't understand the idea of a process." Ideas should appear with the immediacy of search results: "They don't appreciate how an argument develops and sometimes needs to take side paths and turns."

And the teachers don't think that what they call "the cult of Power-Point" has served their students well. As early as elementary school, many of their students have been allowed to substitute PowerPoint presentations for writing assignments such as book reports. Bullet points help you organize your ideas, certainly, but the presentation carries its own way of thinking, one that values speed and simplicity.

By the end of the focus group, there is some consensus about next steps: These educators think their schools need more classroom time where students present opinions, hear the objections of others, and are asked to refine their ideas. They need practice making and defending an argument. In other words, their students need more time talking to each other, face-to-face.

And even if every one of their students will always have the web by their side, these educators insist that on-demand information does not make an education. You need to have a strong background of facts and concepts on board *before* you know you need them. We think with what we know; we use what we know to ask new questions. As they make this point, I think of Maureen. She wants more facts for "context." She wants more "things to think with." That's what her mother's poems represent to her. Her mother had ownership of more ideas.

A similar concern about using the web to provide just-in-time information shows up among physicians arguing the future of medical education. Increasingly, and particularly while making a first diagnosis, physicians rely on handheld databases, what one philosopher calls "E-memory." The physicians type in symptoms and the digital tool recommends a potential diagnosis and suggested course of treatment. Eighty-nine percent of medical residents regard one of these E-memory tools, UpToDate, as their first choice for answering clinical questions. But will this "just-in-time" and "just enough" information teach young doctors to organize their *own* ideas and draw their *own* conclusions?

Quick, accurate judgments depend on having internalized an extensive library of facts. If you come to rely on E-memory, you may not take the time to build up your own. More than this, you may stop feeling you have to.

Jerome P. Kassirer, a professor of medicine at Tufts University, notes that doctors used to build their own internal database by reading and organizing the contents of medical journals. For Kassirer, the undirectedness of that learning was a feature, not a bug—an asset, not a problem. Kassirer stresses that in medicine, "we don't always know what we need to know, and searches that are constrained to information we need at a given moment may not generate information that may be critically useful later." Searches return what we ask for—that's what they are made to do. When we depend on E-memory we lose that wide, unfiltered array of information that creates the conditions needed for creativity, for serendipity. Nicholas Carr broadens the concern about search and memory when he says, "To remain vital, culture must be renewed in the minds of the members of every generation. Outsource memory, and culture withers."

Seduced by Transcription: Putting Machines Aside

Carol Steiker, a professor at Harvard Law School, is committed to a particular form of unitasking: the unitasking that follows naturally when students take class notes *by hand*. Harvard, like so many other law schools, took great pride in having all classrooms "wired" over the past decade or so, and for many years, Steiker allowed her students to take notes on laptops.

I speak with Steiker and a group of other law professors. At one time they had all allowed their students to take class notes on laptops. It seemed natural. Coming out of college, students were accustomed to doing things this way. And the professors didn't want to be in the position of "thought police," checking if students were on Facebook during class time. The consensus: If a student couldn't pay attention in a law school class, that would soon become the student's problem. That student would fall behind.

Steiker explains why her position has changed, radically. She saw that students taking notes with computers suffered from more than inattention. They were losing the ability to take notes at all. She puts it this way: "Students taking notes on computers seemed compelled to type out the full record of what was said in class. They were trying to establish transcripts of the class." To put it too simply: Students were putting themselves in the role of court stenographers. For Steiker, this was a problem in itself. She wants note taking to help students integrate the themes of her class. For her, note taking trains students to organize a subject in a personal way. It cultivates an art of listening and thinking that will be important to the future lawyer.

And Steiker says that the urge to "transcribe" had a curious side effect: *Her law students didn't want to be interrupted in class.* Steiker says, "They sometimes seemed annoyed if you called on them because it broke up their work on their transcriptions. If your notes are meant to capture the themes of the class, you remember your own participation and you make it part of the story. If you are trying to write a transcript of a class, class participation takes you away from your job."

Here is how Steiker describes a turning point in her understanding of how note taking on computers stands in the way of what she wants to accomplish in her classroom:

> *One of the students in the first year had a serious illness that kept her out of class for several weeks. The students banded together into teams that would take notes for her in every course. After one class, the young woman who had been responsible for note taking in my class on that day came up to me, upset. Could she please have my class notes to send to her absent classmate? Her computer had run out of power and she had no power cord. She hadn't been able to take notes in class. I asked the obvious: Why hadn't she taken notes with pen and paper? The student looked at me blankly. This simply had not occurred as a possibility. This simply was something she no longer could do.*

There are at least two ironies here. First, behind our note taking on computers was a fantasy: When the machines made it possible for us to take notes faster, we would take notes better. Instead, we don't take notes at all but behave like transcribing machines. Second, when the day comes that machines are able to take notes for us, it will not serve our purposes, because note taking is part of how we learn to think.

So now, Steiker allows no technology in any of her classes. She says, laughingly, that she came to this position in steps. She first told her students that they couldn't use computers in class. So they put their laptops away but kept checking their phones in class. "I found this amazing," she says. In fact, her students were thinking like lawyers, following the letter but not the spirit of her instructions. "So, then, I had to be explicit that

I really meant no devices at all. This seemed surprising to them. They are so used to looking down at their phones—having a phone in class didn't seem to them like holding on to a technology." There is much talk about the advantage of our devices becoming so habitual and easy to use that they become invisible. It is usually assumed this is a good thing. But if we don't "see" our devices, we are less likely to register the effect they are having on us. We begin to think that the way we think when we have our devices in hand is the "natural" way to think.

Now, in a device-free class, Steiker says, "The students aren't annoyed when you call on them." She's optimistic, convinced that taking notes by hand is forcing her students to be better listeners. "They can't write fast enough to do a transcript, so they have to figure out what is most important." When she tells this story, I think back to a comment that an eleventh grader made to me a decade ago about why she likes to bring her laptop to class. "When I have my computer, I like it that I can write everything down." At the time, I didn't pursue the comment. Some costs take a while to become apparent.

MOOCs to Think With

If you tried to design an educational technology perfectly suited to the sensibilities of hyper attention, you might come up with MOOCs, or massive open online courses. Typically, when you take a MOOC as they were initially imagined, you—and potentially hundreds of thousands of classmates—watch short online videos and take tests on their content. This completed, you move on to the next course unit. There are usually readings, a discussion board to share ideas, and supplementary exercises. If you turn away from the screen to check your messages or send a quick text, no one is insulted. You just watch the video again. If you have several windows open at once, no professor or fellow students feel slighted— the issue that came up in my memoir class. One teacher in a large Harvard MOOC says appreciatively of them, "You can walk away at any time. You can take a ten-minute break, a fifteen-minute break every minute, every ten minutes, every thirty minutes. I think that is a huge advantage to online learning right now."

And indeed, 2012, the year that my students confessed they couldn't sit through a class without texting, was called the year of the MOOC by the *New York Times*. MOOCs fit the times beyond how they dovetail with our new attentional style. College and university administrators under financial pressure see online education as a way to cut costs. If you take success in MOOCs as a yardstick, you have a new way to measure faculty productivity. And MOOCs inspire faculty because they are a way to experiment with new ideas. And, of course, to reach a much larger audience. Since you can record every action a student takes on a MOOC— every keystroke, how long any exercise takes to complete—you can easily test the result of any change in pedagogy. And there is the thrilling prospect of using online education to reach underserved populations, whether in remote villages, disadvantaged neighborhoods, or retirement homes.

Some MOOCs are envisaged for distance learning. When a MOOC is proposed for a residential campus, students come to class after the online work is done to discuss ideas, work on projects, and go over homework. The classroom is no longer the place for "content," as traditionally conceived. The classroom is considered "flipped." Some call it "blended," referring to the combination of online and off-line elements. The hope is to make the classroom a space for project-based learning and a new kind of conversation, more dynamic than what students had before. Many of my university colleagues hope that blended classrooms will end the "passive" technology of the traditional lecture.

So as I was working on this project—immersed in thinking about conversation today—my professional world buzzed about a revolution (some called it a tsunami) that some hoped would completely change the nature of conversation in education. The educational innovator Seymour Papert once said, "You can't think about thinking without thinking about thinking about something." That insight, generalized, is key to understanding the idea of evocative objects—objects to think with that provoke thinking about other things. As I thought about conversation in education, I often had MOOCs on my mind.

So, for example, it was exciting to consider how students taking MOOCs from remote locations were creating new communities of learners and new conversations that would have been impossible to imagine before.

In Professor Gregory Nagy's "The Ancient Greek Hero," a flagship project in Harvard's MOOC offerings, participants have used the online discussion board to share recordings of themselves reading Homer in their own languages. They talk about parallels between their personal lives and Homer's stories. One student from Mani in Greece, a region that still has a traditional village-based culture, posts a video of her grandmother's lament for a recently deceased family member. The student makes a connection between her grandmother's lament and the heroic form. So, just as the course faculty put up videos and readings and notes, the students respond with their own. A new kind of conversation evolves. Indeed, the teaching staff of "Hero" says that for them the *C* in MOOC stands for content, conversation, and community.

For one staff member whose main responsibility is facilitating conversation on the discussion boards, the MOOC is a way—imperfect, but a way—to return to a community you feel has been lost to you. It seems to her an improbable thing, but some of her childhood friends are taking the course and she is getting to share what she most loves about classics with people for whom she never thought this possible. She imagines that students all over the world who have no one to share Homer with are having a similar experience and finding unexpected companionship. She says, "This could be the community we all crave." Indeed, "graduates" of the Ancient Greek Hero MOOC, now called "The Greek Hero in 24 Hours," can go on to participate in a community known as "Hour 25." It has regular virtual meetings and guest speakers, a blog site, and ongoing discussions.

So MOOCs are an object to think with for thinking about what is possible with new educational technologies. And they also help us take the true measure of what we already have. Despite the power of what can take place in MOOCs, only a few years after the experiment with them began in earnest, even their most enthusiastic supporters were working hard to introduce more in-person conversation into MOOC design, certainly for MOOCs in residential settings. For it soon became clear that online learning works better if you also increase the amount of face-to-face contact between students and faculty.

An irony emerges. Research on MOOCs, the pedagogical form that was hailed because it offers so much to measure, shows that they work best when they are combined with the least measurable element of a traditional classroom: presence. Even in the most technical subjects, such as an introduction to calculus, students in online classes do better when the curriculum includes face-to-face encounters. The director of a Columbia University study that compared online and face-to-face learning sums up its findings: "The most important thing that helps students succeed in an online course is interpersonal interaction and support."

Andrew Ng, co-founder of Coursera, a MOOC initiative that began at Stanford, is humble about what the university classroom can offer that MOOCs cannot: "non-cognitive skills." Online, you can't learn "teamwork, ethics, the ability to regulate anxiety." This, says Ng, is what classrooms teach. Udacity, another Stanford online initiative, found that students did better in face-to-face courses than online courses and refocused its efforts on vocational training.

These days, students struggle with conversation. What makes sense is to engage them in it. The more you think about educational technology, with all its bells and whistles, the more you circle back to the simple power of conversation. When Lawrence Summers, former president of Harvard, was asked about the biggest challenge facing higher education, he said, "What's striking is how similar college experiences are to what they were a generation ago." Summers implied that this was reason to change a slow-to-change field. Perhaps it is also a sign that in the American college experience, something is going right.

With No One There, Everyone Can Be Heard

Many who were behind the early MOOC initiatives took the traditional classroom as a problem that technology could solve. Daphne Koller, the co-founder of Stanford's Coursera, saw traditional "live" classrooms as places that silence students. Why? Because for Koller, any live environment implies an imperfect system for being heard. "When a question is asked in a 'live' course," says Koller, "some students are online, shopping for shoes on Amazon, some are not paying attention, some smarty-pants in the front row answers the question before the rest of the class even has had a chance to know a question has been asked." In an online course, on the other hand, everyone has a chance to ask a question and get feedback. Your question will never be preempted. For Koller, the lack of "live" presence creates a new equality. With no one there, everyone can be "heard." There is no one in the front row who will upstage you.

As Koller sees it, flipped classrooms should mean that students spend more time with professors in a setting of real interaction. They would have learned the basic content online before the class even meets. Now, together, they are free for a deeper interaction. Unfortunately, it doesn't always work out that way. The "discussion sections" in blended classrooms are often, as they have always been, with teaching fellows. One student in an MIT class being taught with a large online component says that the discussion sections when her class gets together are times to go over homework. All the teaching fellows take sections and the professor moves from group to group. She gets to listen to the professor speak only in an online video. She wishes she could hear the professor lecture in person. He is an international figure and has a reputation for being charismatic. She feels she is missing out.

Her reaction is not surprising. If you ask people who are lifelong learners where their love for learning comes from, they usually talk about an inspiring teacher. The most powerful learning takes place in relationship. What kind of relationship can you form with a professor who is lecturing in the little square on the screen that is the MOOC delivery system? Will you want to be like him or her?

Administrators look at the dwindling numbers of students who show up to lectures and draw the reasonable conclusion that if the class were offered online, students would prefer to take it there. Students report more complex attitudes: Even if they skip classes, they are not so eager to trade in their classrooms.

So, for example, a student at the University of California at Santa Cruz waves the flag of "dialogue" to object to his university's decision to substitute MOOCs for a set of classes on his residential campus. Teaching, for him, isn't about "information." In classrooms, "we learn from each other. This is what is lost in the online experience, confined to a computer screen and digitized feedback."

Some student objections are more personal. They come from what students know of their own human natures, natures that I don't believe should be recast as human frailties. They tell me they want company. They are afraid that they already spend too much time alone and online. They say they need structure. A senior in Connecticut says, "I am going to listen to the lecture anyway. I have to. I don't want to do it all lonely and maybe sad. I'd rather go with my friends. I'm in college!" A junior in New Jersey says, "To motivate myself to sit alone and sit in front of the computer? No matter how motivated I am, to block out an hour, it would be so hard. I like the idea that I have to show up. You're showing up to something alive."

When this student talks about the value of "showing up to something alive," he is not denying the value of what you can learn online or what can be measured online, but he is suggesting that there is another kind of learning not so easily measured. If you go to class, you might see something unexpected.

Why do we forget something as simple as this? Again, *technology makes us forget what we know about life.* We become enchanted by technology's promises because we have so many problems we would like technology to solve. In the case of education, once MOOCs were declared a benign revolution that would solve many problems—from lack of student attention to our problems in measuring educational "productivity"— its imperatives had to be presented in a positive light. So, the imperative to learn from an online video *had* to be a good thing. It surely is, sometimes. In some courses. For some students. But not all the time. For all students. In all courses.

When we want technology to provide a simple fix for the problems of higher education, we necessarily idealize the online experience. So, for example, participating in an online forum is glamorized as always-available discussion. But in practice, thousands of people flow through such groups. Sometimes you make a comment that is noticed, but more often it is not picked up. Not by anyone. Professor Louis Bucciarelli of MIT wrote about his experiences participating as "Butch" in the Harvard Divinity School MOOC "The Letters of the Apostle Paul." Bucciarelli says he was a diligent student and wrote faithfully on the MOOC discussion board but that as far as he can tell, nothing he wrote on the discussion board was read by anyone except himself.

Even in the Harvard flagship MOOC "Hero," with its large, dedicated team—Nagy was able to recruit fifteen former teaching fellows and ninety-four former students to help moderate online discussions—satisfying exchanges can prove elusive. The "Hero" discussion board is sometimes thrilling but often chaotic and difficult to follow. Sometimes it calls forth personal material that seems too intense for the medium. Even the teaching fellows note that there were contributions to the discussion board that were so personal that they, when working together, "needed to look away."

In face-to-face settings, faculty become experienced in handling difficult conversations. For example, they can gently stop students who begin to share too much. Or help students deal with emotionally charged material that may be hard to process but is nonetheless relevant to the central themes of the class. In an online discussion, this is harder to do.

Some say that better discussion board software will make a difference. Some say that over time, we will learn how to better relate in this medium. We will invent new mores, a new etiquette, new boundaries. Others look forward to artificial intelligences moderating discussion. Others want to bring in people—for small talk.

When Udacity was having trouble in its partnership with San Jose State University, with dropout rates over 90 percent, they tried to improve matters by giving students conversation partners: real people who would check up on them and be available for online chat. The provost of San Jose State described these real people as "mentors" but made it clear that the mentors had no knowledge of the subjects they were mentoring. Their job was simply to be encouraging. He said that the mentors were like "moms." The idea was to use talk, but not talk on the topic, as a tactic to keep people in the game.

When gamblers begin to lose too much at a slot machine, they will sometimes get a visit from a casino "goodwill" ambassador, perhaps with a treat. MOOC designers have considered spicing up MOOC content with "real people" conversation just at the moments when students in online classes are most likely to tune out, as determined by AI programs monitoring their level of attention. As with the "moms" of Udacity, the idea is to use "real people talking" as incentive to keep people in their seats. Over time, revising online education to include conversation will need more than "mentor moms" or computer programs to monitor discussions. A student needs to talk to someone who knows what they are talking about.

"Showing Up to Something Alive"

The college junior who spoke about appreciating the in-person classroom as "showing up to something alive" brings me back to an earlier experience studying technology for educational innovation. Over twenty-five years ago MIT launched Project Athena, an educational initiative that used computer software to substitute for traditional classroom teaching. There, too, educational reformers had the lecture in their sights. But in the 1980s, the idea for reforming the lecture wasn't an online course but computer simulations that would substitute for demonstrations in lectures. The world of natural sciences—as well as social sciences and the humanities—could come alive, it was argued, if students felt in control of these simulations. MIT faculty were challenged to write the software themselves. Much of what they came up with gave students an experience of being able to manipulate data in a more direct way than had ever been possible before.

But there were also objections, and back then, most of them came from faculty who insisted that the lecture and live demonstration was a sacred space. Faculty talked about the importance of debating with students, responding to questions, and presenting a model for how to argue a point and respect differences. They talked about the sanctity of live demonstrations—the importance of doing science in real time. They wanted students to watch live, imperfect lectures and demonstrations and feel part of an in-person community. They saw the classroom as a place where you learned to love the "as-is" of nature as much as you love the "as-if" of the virtual. They fought hard for their lectures and live demonstrations and kept giving them. Now, a new generation, tutored in simulation, is moving toward putting those lectures and demonstrations on MOOCs.

More than years stand between us and those defenders of the live lecture and the flawed real. These are the decades in which most of our dreams have been centered on what the Internet might bring us. It is not surprising that when MOOCs arrived, we were so willing to imagine an educational revolution that looked to the perfection of virtual possibilities.

The professors who objected to Athena's incursions into the lecture hall were also defending what Thoreau might have called a "one-chair conversation." As teachers, they saw themselves thinking aloud, declaring openly. They wanted to lecture because they wanted their students to learn that there is not only something to know but that there are ways, and more ways, to know it and tell it. And questions after the lecture, for them, made the lecture hall also a place of friendship, collaboration, and community. For them, it was at the lecture that one-, two-, and three-chair conversations all came together.

The lecture is the easiest form of in-person pedagogy to criticize. It is the oldest form of instruction. It is the one most likely to have a passive student and an active teacher. It is the one most easily caricatured as having a teacher who might be passive as well, perhaps reading notes that were written many years ago. Daphne Koller saw the lecture and thought technology could make it right. But when I think back to the Athena story, I am reminded that for all its flaws, the lecture has a lot going for it.

It is a place where students come together, on good days and bad, and form a relatively small community. As in any live performance, anything can happen. An audience is present; the room is engaged. It nourishes a certain kind of inspiration. You see a professor several times a week. What makes the greatest impression in a college education is learning how to think like someone else, appreciating an intellectual personality, and thinking about what it might mean to have one of your own. When we hear someone speak, we imagine things about them that we wish for ourselves.

Students watch a professor thinking on his or her feet, thinking aloud, and in the best cases the student can say, "Someday, I could *do that*. Someday, I could *be that*." So, what the young man meant by showing up to "something alive" was really showing up to *someone* alive, to a teacher, present and thinking in front of him.

There are some lectures you never forget. In spring 1971, I heard Bruno Bettelheim ask a simple question during his large lecture course at the University of Chicago: "What is the best reason for a mother to breast-feed a child?" We were in the early days of the women's movement. Bettelheim went around the room and the answers came back with that era's version of political correctness: "Breast-feeding is natural." "The nutrition in milk is better for the child." "Breast-feeding takes corporations out of the intimate connections of the family."

Bettelheim, sitting on a chair placed at center stage, seemed almost impassive. He barely moved as he shook his head "no" to these answers.

And from up and down the aisles, it was these answers that came forth, in different variations. Finally, Bettelheim said softly, "It feels good." And then loudly, emphatically: "It feels good." He elaborated. The mother when she offers her breast does something that is pleasurable, satisfying. The child has a bodily sensation that he or she is satisfying the mother, giving pleasure by receiving pleasure, because the breast feels good to the child as well. And from this template, argued Bettelheim, all successful relationships are built. You give pleasure to another through something that gives you pleasure.

When Bettelheim offered this interpretation, the class exploded with talk. Not everyone agreed, but everyone agreed that we had not allowed ourselves to say this, to think this. It was a simple answer, but it referred to the body. Did that stop us? When the class ended, it reconvened informally outside the lecture hall. Bettelheim had created a space for a kind of talking we had not done before.

At the time, someone said that in other classes we brought only a part of ourselves. We presented what we had read in books. We did not try to include what we knew from our everyday experience. We saw all of that as something apart from what we should bring to our academic life. Bettelheim is a controversial figure, accused of fabricating academic degrees and plagiarizing other people's work. But on that day, in that lecture course, he did something remarkable. Bettelheim gave us permission to bring all of the resources at our disposal to our work in the academy. Common sense should not be devalued nor should simplicity be discarded. We need to build our answers up from our very human ground. And the experience of being there left a lifelong impression.

Being There

And even these days, when students talk about large, introductory lecture classes, they mention the importance of being there. A college junior: "I took an introduction to psychology class; it was big and I could see it might have been a MOOC, but there was something about being there with all those people. You are part of a group. That's where you make your friends. You talk about the class." And of course, you are there with the professor.

The lecture has other virtues. It disciplines a teacher to integrate content and its critique. It teaches students that no information should be partitioned from an opportunity to discuss and challenge it "live." When good faculty lecture many times a week, they improvise some new parts every time. They write new sections the week or night or month before. They make lectures relevant to what is in the news. Once you have written the script for an online class, filmed it, edited it, and put it online, such changes can happen but they are harder to envisage. It is natural to have the feeling that your "best performance" has been captured on video.

When the CEO of MIT's online educational initiative floated the idea that good actors might make good teachers, the idea was not dismissed out of hand but set the Internet buzzing. Students complain of boredom. Why not have presentations by professional presenters? Matt Damon, perhaps? If you want compelling delivery of content, actors can do that. Actors could not lead a conversation on the topic, but in online learning, conversations are deferred to another time and place. The actor could be the filmed "talking head" for the content before students are tested on it. Since the online classroom is not a place for conversation, why not an actor indeed?

Recently, a member of a university panel on online tools, fresh from developing a new MOOC, owned up to the temptation to "freeze" her elegant online presentations and use them in place of lecturing "live." The way things are now, she said, "fear" makes her go over her class readings the evening before every in-person class. "My children ask me, 'Mommy, haven't you read that already?'" Hers was an honest admission that anxiety helps to keep her materials fresh.

Students, too, get anxious about speaking in class. Some supporters of online education see as one of its virtues that it gives "voice" to students who are shy and don't participate in discussion when it is held in physical classrooms. Shy students, they argue, gladly participate in online forums, particularly if they can be anonymous. And even in "live" classrooms, professors can use digital tools to get feedback from shy students, using clickers, for example. Clickers attach to software that allows students to express an opinion without revealing a name. Student opinion shows up as "poll" projections on a screen. Similarly, "comment" software for classroom discussion masks identity, another boon for the shy.

The virtues of anonymous classroom polling were presented at MIT's 2013 MacVicar Day—an annual gathering set aside for reflections on teaching. In 2013, the focus was technology and education. From the audience came an objection. The speaker was Daniel Jackson, an MIT professor of electrical engineering and computer science. He argued that wearing a mask—what he thinks anonymous polling accomplishes— may free people up to express themselves, but face-to-face encounters encourage civility and a sense of accountability. When people know who you are, you take responsibility for what you say. For Jackson, the class-room is a place to learn how to participate in the conversations that make democracy work. Anonymous polling and comments don't teach you to stand up for your beliefs. Neither does anonymous posting on the online discussion board of a MOOC.

As Jackson spoke, I thought of old traditions: standing on Hyde Park's speaker's corner and being unafraid to say whatever you wished; the signed article in the newspaper that was protected speech. Where would students learn that they had the right to express their opinions if class opinions were registered through anonymous clicks?

Jackson acknowledged that the use of clickers in class to get anony-mous feedback provides "useful information." You learn what the group is thinking, but there is a cost:

> It seems to be reinforcing exactly the habits I'm trying to undo in class. I'm trying to get my students to engage more; I'm trying to get them to overcome their need to be anonymous. So everything I do to allow them to be more anonymous, to get more immediate feedback, to reduce their length of attention . . . in the long run is not good for the culture.

In this debate, professors worry that students are too embarrassed to talk. But in a classroom, one should "walk" toward embarrassment. Students should feel safe enough to take the risk of saying something that might not be worked through or popular. Students will get over feeling embarrassed. It may be easier to contribute anonymously, but it is better for all of us to learn how to take responsibility for what we believe.

At the MIT panel, no one wanted to discuss Jackson's critique of online materials as pandering to rather than challenging students' short attention spans. And no one wanted to discuss the idea that anonymous polling might reinforce bad habits learned on the Internet. These are difficult issues. Talking about them doesn't rule out the idea that technology solves certain educational problems. But they frame a conversation that assumes that technology won't solve all educational problems and might cause some of its own.

Real Time

During a panel discussion about the ethics of pedagogy, English professor and literary theorist Lee Edelman said that his biggest challenge as a professor "is not teaching his students to think intelligently, but getting them to actually respond to each other thoughtfully in the classroom." Like so many others, he finds that students are having a hard time with the give-and-take of face-to-face conversation.

Human resources officers tell me that their new hires have a hard time talking in business meetings. College graduates say the same thing about themselves. One graduate student in European history talks about his struggles with conversation in "real time." He has just returned, dejected, from his first academic conference. He is very happy with the paper he read (his department had been so happy with the paper that it paid his expenses to go to the conference), but he says, "I was rambling and scatterbrained in the question-and-answer session. While I thrive at writing, my conversation falls flat."

Why would we want to put at the center of our educational agenda a kind of learning in which we don't teach the skill of raising hands and entering a conversation? If doing this makes our students nervous, our job as educators should be to help them get over it.

In the best of cases, the college classroom has been a place where students stand up and defend their ideas in real time. They learn from speaking and they learn from listening to each other. "I've learned things from how people make mistakes when they ask questions in lectures," says a college junior. "Some kids will just ramble on and you shouldn't do that. You watch people. You learn not to say, 'I've read every book.'" None of this learning happens if you take your class alone in your room.

The value of attending a live lecture in college is a bit like the value of doing fieldwork. In fieldwork, there can be dry spells, but you learn to read people in real time. You share a bit of road with those around you and you come to understand how a group thinks. And you learn the rewards of patience: You have followed arguments as they unfold. If you are lucky, you learn that life repays close, focused attention.

Clickers Versus Conversation

In the political theorist Michael Sandel's classes, students have to pay very close attention. Sandel faces hundreds of students with a brief presentation and an interactive conversational format. Students speak up—there is no anonymity. Sandel calls only on students who raise their hands, but once they have made a comment, Sandel engages them. In one of his recent classes, "Ethics, Biotechnology, and the Future of Human Nature," he asks the question: "If you're a vegan, would you eat a 'hamburger' that has been bioengineered from cow muscle that did no harm to the cow and was cultured in such a way that it used no fossil fuels?"

A vegan student says, "No, it still uses animal tissues, it's still from an animal." Sandel nods. "But what about if we now have a technology that grows the hamburger from skin tissue that has sloughed off the cow. . . . We're solving the world food shortage and helping global warming by eating derivatives of a single cow. Are you okay with it now?" Now, the vegan is unsure, but holds firm: "No. No. It still comes from an animal." The student is embarrassed, but she has stood her ground. And in standing her ground, she's had to reconsider her position.

Only the vegetarians had reason to rethink things when Sandel brought up the example of the cow. Now Sandel expands the challenge. Would you eat biologically engineered *human* meat—meat made from taking a sample of human skin? Is it worth it? One student is impressed. It is as though we could solve world hunger by taking fingernail shavings. The class, animated, picks up the discussion.

Imagine how different the conversation would be if Sandel presented the case (food products made from cow tissue; food products made from fingernail shavings) and asked his class to hold clickers and register anonymous preferences. You would learn what the class thought, which is certainly interesting. But members of the class would not learn how to summon the bravery to voice and defend their opinions. One Harvard senior in Sandel's class says, "You do get embarrassed, but you get over it and get used to hearing yourself say things aloud. You say to yourself, 'Did I say that? I can't believe I think that, but I do think that. I've thought about this; I just never thought I could get myself to say it.'"

This is teaching by conversation: It is a delicate thing, a walk toward boredom and embarrassment. (Sandel allows awkward moments. Some of the students cannot follow through on their thoughts even as he asks them to find their courage.) These days, teaching by conversation is talked about as crucial (after all, the stated goal of putting content online in the flipped classroom is to have more dynamic in-class conversations). But at the same time, there is pressure to use technology in classrooms in ways that make conversation nearly impossible. Interestingly, this technology is often presented as supporting student "engagement."

An MIT colleague has just returned from a demonstration of high-technology classroom tools. Lecture slides were streamed to a front screen. Twitter comments from students were streamed to a back screen, fielded by a moderator. The professor asked questions and the class responded by electronic polling. In contrast to the extended examples and responses in the Sandel lecture, my colleague reports that here, terseness was all. Twitter limits comments to 140 characters, so, she says, "We were asked to keep our responses short, no more than two sentences."

But the students objected to the professor's original plan to have both his content and their commentary displayed at the same time, each on a different screen. The students said that the two screens made it hard to focus.

In this environment, my colleague found student comments disappointing. It was not just, she said, that remarks were short. It was also that for her, anonymity flattened out the discussion. It was her response to being asked to separate the dancer from the dance. "Real people," she said, "have real concerns and interests. . . . But once the questions are turned into a flat stream of questions and comments without faces . . . you end up not caring about them. You care about a question when you know whose question it is. A question that doesn't come from a person— it's only half a question."

For technical reasons, a final class poll was not taken, but no one suggested canvassing the class by asking for raised hands. My colleague shrugs and says she was not surprised: "After the blizzard of apps and demos, taking a poll by simply speaking with the people around you, or with a quick show of hands, frankly didn't come to mind. That kind of low-tech solution had lost its status. In this atmosphere, it seemed almost ephemeral, no longer worth it."

The high-tech class seemed to keep students too busy for Facebook, but when students wanted a break, they did some texting to get away from the buzz.

But in Sandel's class, it is, for the most part, tools down. A senior assesses the scene: So far, in his three and a half years at Harvard, he has seen texting in every class, even in small seminars where students take advantage of the brief moments when professors turn to the blackboard. In Sandel's class he isn't sure. He thinks there must be some, but he doesn't want to assume it: "I *think* people text but less so than in other courses because this class is very conversation-based!"

We want technology put in the service of our educational purposes.

But this can happen only if we are clear about them. If not, we may be tolerant of classroom technologies that distract teachers and students from focusing on each other.

A Love Letter to Collaboration

In a recent course, I required students to collaborate on a midterm project. I imagined my students in conversation, working together at long tables in a dining hall. I imagined late nights and cold coffee in Styrofoam cups. But there had been no late nights or long tables. All the collaboration had happened on Gchat and Google Docs, a program that allows several people to work on the same document at once. When my students handed in their projects, their work was good.

But when I gave out the assignment I was interested in more than the final product. I know that the alchemy of students sitting around a table can sometimes spark conversations that lead to a new idea. Instead, my students found an app that made presence unnecessary. They had a task; they accomplished it with efficiency. My experience in that course is a case study of why measurements of productivity in higher education are dicey. Gchat and Google Docs got the job done by classical "productivity" measures. But the value of what you produce, what you "make," in college is not just the final paper; it's the process of making it.

My students are unapologetic about not meeting in person. Jason, a sophomore, says, "The majority of my studying in the past year has been that someone makes a Google Doc with the terms that need definitions, you fill in the ones you know, and then you work on it together. You have a chat session and you do that to collaborate." This joyless description made me rethink my fantasy of long tables, cold coffee, and late nights. My fantasy, from his point of view, asks for the unnecessary. But his reality allows little space to talk about a new idea.

Sometimes, students who collaborate with online chat and electronically shared documents work in the same building. They simply choose not to study in the same room at the same table. They go into online chat sessions rather than chat in person. Why? For one thing, they tell me, roles can be made clear and it is clear when someone falls behind. More important, when you collaborate online, everyone stays on point. People may drop out to text or do some online shopping, but when they are on the chat, they are on topic.

In a face-to-face meeting, you can see people's attention wander off to their phones. On Gchat, the inattention of your peers is invisible to you. Once you make the assumption that when people work, they will want to text and shop as well, it helps to collaborate on a medium that hides what Jason calls their "true absences." Gchat lets the simulation of focused attention seem like attention enough. Whenever you see them, your colleagues are working on the problem at hand. So, Jason says, "We take the route of technology whenever possible."

Gchat makes Jason's group seem "on topic" even as their minds wander. But it doesn't leave room for what I've said I want when my students collaborate. I'll call it intellectual serendipity. It may happen when someone tells a joke. Or daydreams and comes back with an idea that goes in a new direction. None of this is necessarily efficient. But so many of our best ideas are born this way, in conversations that take a turn. I want my students to have this experience.

But given an opportunity to collaborate, my students glide toward the virtual. Some tell me that anything else, regardless of the merits, is totally impractical in today's college environment. Everyone is too "busy." I can't help but think that talking in person is one of the things they should be busy with.

In my interviews with college students, most insist that they will *know* when they have to schedule a face-to-face meeting. They will *know* if something comes up that they can't take care of over Gchat. But my experience is that you really don't know when you are going to have an important conversation. You have to show up for many conversations that feel inefficient or boring to be there for the conversation that changes your mind.

When the economist Daniel Kahneman won the Nobel Prize, he was, like every winner of the prize, asked to write an official Nobel biographical statement. One section of his biography is a tribute to his late colleague Amos Tversky. Kahneman explained that the ideas for which he won the prize grew out of their time spent working together. In the end, his Nobel biography amounted to a love letter to conversation.

> *We spent hours each day, just talking. When Amos's first son, Oren, then fifteen months old, was told that his father was at work, he volunteered the comment "Aba talk Danny." We were not only working, of course—we talked of everything under the sun, and got to know each other's mind almost as well as our own. We could (and often did) finish each other's sentences and complete the joke that the other had wanted to tell, but somehow we also kept surprising each other.*

Here we see conversation as not only an intellectual engine but the means by which colleagues were able to cross boundaries that are usually only dissolved by love. Conversation led to intellectual communion. When I explain my current project, people often say, "You're so right to study conversation. For communication, it has the broadest bandwidth— it's the best way to exchange information." Kahneman and Tversky teach us that while this may be true, it is far from the whole story. Conversation is a kind of intimacy. You don't just get more information. You get different information. The bandwidth argument leaves out this essential.

What also is striking in Kahneman's Nobel address is his description of the pace of his work with Tversky. In 1974, Kahneman and Tversky wrote an article for *Science* that went on to be one of the founding documents of behavioral economics. It took them a year, working four to six hours a day. Kahneman writes, "On a good day we would mark a net advance of a sentence or two." So the people who support conversation because they think it will make things go faster ("Don't email me, it's faster just to come to my desk and ask me!") are seeing only a small part of what makes face-to-face conversation powerful. For Kahneman and Tversky, conversation wasn't there to go faster, but to go deeper.

College should be a time to invest in teaching students about the long-term value of open-ended conversations, but in today's environment, it is hard to argue the value of conversation for learning because it is hard to measure its value with productivity metrics, especially in the short term.

Adam Falk, president of Williams College, has given it a try. He argued that what really matters in a college education is learning "to write effectively, argue persuasively, solve problems creatively," and "adapt and learn independently." He and his colleagues investigated where these skills blossom. It turns out that they correlate with the amount of time students spend with professors—not virtual contact, but live contact. Given Falk's findings, it is painful to hear faculty complain that students don't show up for office hours.

Office Hours

The year after MacVicar Day was dedicated to educational technology, it turned its attention to mentoring. Instead of a packed auditorium, the hall was half full. Considering student-faculty relationships is less flashy than presenting new tools. In the mentoring discussion, faculty talked about students standing them up at office hours and not coming to events designed to bring faculty and students together. The year before, everyone was excited to talk about apps that might fix everything. It's tougher to confront problems for which there is no clear solution. And mentoring is one of them. Students avoid faculty in large part because students are anxious about the give-and-take of face-to-face conversation.

Zvi, a college junior from New York City, explains why he prefers email to a live visit with his professors. He is not comfortable with conversation and he doesn't see office hours as a time to practice. Here is Zvi on his policy of strategically hiding from the people who might have the most to teach him: "I'm much better emailing professors than [seeing them] in person. I find that I don't represent myself well. . . . I am not natural with serious conversation [in person] yet. I'd prefer to be able to do that in email." He says that in email, he can edit and the editing will be invisible.

When asked when he might learn to have serious, in-person conversations, Zvi admits, "That's a good question." He feels it's a skill he'll need to develop soon, not just to talk to professors, "but also for people I'm hoping to work for." He thinks that he might try to talk with professors in his final year of college. But then he considers the reality of actually sitting down with a professor and despairs: "It's too late for that. I don't know—when do you grow up? It is a question."

When students tell me that they want to email me rather than see me in person, they usually say that it is only in email that they can best explain their ideas. And so, they explain, an email from them will put me in the best position to improve their ideas. They cast our meeting in transactional terms and make a judgment that the online transaction will be of a higher quality. Zvi, too, uses a transactional language to describe what he might get out of office hours. He has ideas; the professors have information that will improve them. But there's more to gain from a visit to a professor than improving your ideas, although this is certainly to be desired. You get to be with someone who is making an effort to understand you. You form an intellectual friendship. You may feel the support of an adult and of your institution.

When students are afraid to talk, they prefer to think that office hours are for a transfer of information that can happen by email. And with little or no experience of face-to-face conversation with faculty members, students don't have the data that might convince them that conversation offers more than information.

Zvi admits that he stays away from professors because he doesn't feel grown-up enough to talk to them. His professors might be able to help him with this, but not because they'll give him information. Studies of mentoring show that what makes a difference, what can change the life of a student, is the presence of one strong figure who shows an interest, who, the student would say, "gets me." You need a conversation for that.

Work

Is This a Meeting?

*My younger colleagues at the firm, the young associates, are pilots
in their cockpits. They assemble their multiple technologies—a
laptop, two iPhones, an iPad. And then they put their earphones
on. Big ones. Like pilots. They turn their desks into cockpits.
And then they are isolated. You wouldn't want to disturb
the pilot in his cockpit. You wouldn't want to disturb this lawyer
in his bubble. It's not how it used to be. . . . It used to be that
associates were available to be interrupted . . . but in a good
way. You could talk to them. They were there to be worked,
very hard, to be engaged and mentored. Now, the feeling
is that you are only getting the most you can out of them
if you leave them alone in their cockpits.*

—A SENIOR PARTNER AT A BOSTON LAW FIRM

Audrey Lister, a partner at Alan Johnson Miller and Associates,
has worked at this large Chicago law firm for more than twenty
years. She joined the firm straight out of law school. Lister talks
about her early days at AJM, when she and her colleague Sam Berger
were just starting out together. The two young associates would knock
on each other's office doors and visit all the time. Lister says that this
kind of close relationship made "work feel like family." But the meetings
with Berger were not purely social: "Business was done in those meet-

ings, exciting ideas were hatched, ideas for clients." Together, she says, "we discovered the nuances of the law."

These days, informal meetings are not as frequent. Lister says, "Young lawyers feel they can accomplish more if they sit and work in front of their screens." People get together for catch-up meetings that are prearranged by text or email. But Lister doesn't think that these scheduled meetings are doing the work of her impromptu chats with Berger. Once you have an agenda, she thinks, you are not as likely to play with ideas. For that, she says, "You need a conversation that is truly open-ended."

A Day in the Life

Her early days at AJM, Lister recalls, were marked by many conversations without an agenda. There was the time with Berger, of course, but there were also long lunches and late nights in the cafeteria. The young lawyers would call out for food as they worked on cases. Lister remembers their conversations as wide-ranging. Now, she observes that junior associates tend to work alone in their offices even when they are all working late. Everyone is at a screen. Lister isn't even sure they are working. "They may just be taking some personal catch-up time, some quiet downtime alone with their email." These days, when we think of downtime and reducing stress, we don't usually think of relaxing with peers but of getting some control over the crowd that the net brings to us.

Lister remarks that the new office practices (fewer informal meetings, less time in the cafeteria, more time alone at screens) impact her firm's sense of community. Speaking of the lawyers she began with, Lister says, "We helped each other. We were competing but we became devoted to this firm. That doesn't happen anymore. You never used to see partners being hired away from our firm. You see that now."

She is right in her intuitions about the business impact of time spent in conversation. Studies show a clear link between sociability and employee productivity. But these days at AJM, screens are getting in the way of sociability—and courtesy. It is common practice for lawyers, even at the most senior level, to keep phones and tablets out during meetings. Lister comments that she was recently asked to give a presentation on intrafirm communications, and "I gave my presentation to a room of people who on and off were texting and emailing." The irony did not escape her. She had been asked to talk about better communication and few were listening. "It made me think," she says, "'Why did I bother?'"

Lister does all she can to encourage her firm's young associates to meet face-to-face. For example, she asks them to join her in her office when she has important calls with clients. She wants them to hear her negotiate, to learn how to shape a conversation. Lister says she will often put a client call on mute so that she can talk to her junior associates and explain her strategy. For her junior colleagues, sitting in on one of these calls is a master class as well as an opportunity to build closer relationships with her and each other. But increasingly, the junior associates tell her they would rather listen to the call in their offices. Lister knows why: If they are alone, they can listen to the call and continue to work at their screens. They will miss the face-to-face conversations but they'll be able to multitask.

No longer surprised when her invitations are turned down, Lister recognizes that young lawyers believe that what maximizes their value is multitasking at their computers. This means that they set aside far less time to talk.

At AJM, the tendency to avoid face-to-face meetings now cuts across generations. Many partners no longer entertain clients by taking them out to meals or sporting events. At the holiday season, instead of having dinner with a client to celebrate a good year, a chance for a conversation, the lawyers are in a last-minute rush to buy a gift, something expensive. Younger associates (of course, with fewer funds available to them) also hold back from entertaining. Lister notes that to be fair, clients hold back as well. She says, "Everyone—including clients—prefers to send emails rather than be on the phone, prefers to send emails rather than go out to lunch."

For a time, the partners at AJM were divided as to whether all of this online activity was the future of legal practice or simply bad practice. Finally, the firm got curious about the relationship of face-to-face meetings and money. It turned out that the lawyers who spent more time with clients face-to-face brought in the most business. Now, how much lawyers socialize is part of their performance review. And now, Lister says, "people think twice when they put off having lunch with clients so they can work alone at their screens."

Lister's firm is not alone in recognizing the power of face-to-face conversation. Ben Waber, a graduate of the MIT Media Lab, designs technology to study collaboration. With MIT Media Lab professor Alex Pentland, Waber developed a tool he calls a "sociometric badge." The badge allows researchers to track employees' movements through an office as well as a range of measures about their conversations: who they talk to, for how long, on what topic, with what pace of speech, with what tone of voice, and how often they interrupt each other. The badges can analyze intimate aspects of conversation such as body language, interest and excitement, and the amount of influence people have on each other.

Waber quantified the previously unquantifiable, and his results were stunning. To sum up a large number of studies, face-to-face conversation leads to higher productivity and is also associated with reduced stress. Call centers are more productive when people take breaks together; software teams produce programs with fewer bugs when they talk more. And Waber's studies had disappointing news for those who equate email and talk: The "conversation effect" doesn't work the same way for online encounters. What matters is being together face-to-face.

Waber stresses that it is hard for people to really believe that for productive work, conversation counts, or at least as much as it does: "We think of productivity as . . . sitting in front of the computer and banging out emails, scheduling things; and that's what makes us productive. But it's not." What makes you productive is "your interactions with other people—you know, you give them new ideas, you get new ideas from them; and . . . if you even make five people a little bit more productive every day, those conversations are worth it."

I visit Waber when I learn of his work, and he explains that his findings are not always received as good news. They complicate the lives of businesses that have tried to cut costs by breaking up their "brick-and-mortar" operations and whose employees work mostly from home. And they complicate the lives of individuals who feel most productive when they sit alone in front of their screens or who find this the best way to feel in control of their time and information overload. Supported by the impression that this is when they are doing their "real work," many employees feel justified in avoiding face-to-face conversation. And because they avoid it, they don't understand what it can accomplish. Leadership can break this cycle. Fortunately, those who would lead a culture of conversation in the workplace now have research on their side.

There is a business case for conversation. But there are significant roadblocks to reclaiming it. For one thing, we are all tempted by meetings that are not quite meetings because we can be both at the meeting and on our phones. In response, sophisticated organizations design physical and social environments that support face-to-face conversation. But the most artful design will be subverted if a work culture, at its heart, does not understand the unique value of conversation.

Meetings That Aren't:
The Hansel and Gretel Experience

At ReadyLearn, a large international consulting company, face-to-face meetings are increasingly rare. Over the past ten years, in an effort to streamline operations, ReadyLearn has reduced office space wherever it could and asked employees to work from home whenever possible.

Caroline Tennant, a vice-president at ReadyLearn, reports to a physical office three days a week. The other two days, she has Skype meetings from her home. Whether she is at home or at the office, she participates in eight to ten meetings a day. Sometimes, on "home" days, Tennant wakes up at four in the morning for a Skype call that involves an international team. She notes drily that men are always at an advantage at these meetings because she feels the need to put on makeup before she takes her position in front of her computer. Technology makes it possible for Tennant to schedule a full day of international meetings. But the pace doesn't leave her time to think. She says, "The technology makes me more productive, but I know the quality of my thinking suffers." It's a telling formulation. What she is saying is that technology makes her *feel* more productive despite a lower quality of thought.

Eight to ten meetings take up Tennant's entire workday. So, to meet the demands of her job, every day Tennant has to pick two or three meetings where she will do other work. The question simply becomes which meetings. The obvious contenders are conference calls. At these, Tennant explains, she tries to say something from time to time, but her mind is on her email. She is not alone in this practice; at ReadyLearn, it is assumed that when you are on a conference call, you are available for email and messaging on the side. Increasingly, the assumption of divided attention is also made for in-person meetings, particularly status meetings where people catch up with ongoing projects. There, Tennant says, team members show up, greet each other, and soon turn to their email. At ReadyLearn, there are a lot of meetings that are not quite meetings.

Tennant describes her behavior at a status meeting. It is a workplace variation on the college students' "rule of three," where friends try to keep conversations going by making sure that some small quorum is participating at all times in a kind of round robin. Tennant says, "The meeting leader knows that she is speaking to a roomful of people doing email. . . . As for me, I try to do my part . . . to look around and make sure that the meeting leader is speaking to someone." In other words, no head down for her unless she sees some heads are up.

The situation at ReadyLearn is not unusual. The world's largest conference call provider, used by 85 percent of Fortune 100 firms, studied what people are doing during meetings: 65 percent do other work, 63 percent send email, 55 percent eat or make food, 47 percent go to the bathroom, and 6 percent take another phone call.

Darius Lehrer, a thirty-six-year-old manager at ReadyLearn, sums up meeting etiquette: "You come in, get some coffee, work on your laptop, listen for your name to be called, make your contribution, and then go back to your computer. A good meeting leader will give you a 'heads-up' signal about five minutes before she calls on you so that you can close out your email and get ready to speak."

At AJM, Audrey Lister asked herself why she was bothering to present to colleagues who were doing their email. At ReadyLearn, Lehrer has come to the same question: "The system is demoralizing for the meeting leader. And if you are presenting, there is little motivation to do a good job. You're saying to yourself, 'What's the point of my even doing anything? No one is listening.' People are speaking 'for the record.'" When people speak for the record, they usually don't listen to what comes before or after. Meetings are performances of what meetings used to be.

Nelson Rabinow, a forty-four-year-old manager at ReadyLearn, talks about how he handles the "falling away" of attention that characterizes most meetings. "At a meeting, I know that other people are dropping in and out, not just me, so when I speak, I make sure to summarize the little that I've heard and I encourage other people to do the same." In other words, Rabinow suggests that a group of people not paying full attention try, in effect, to collaborate on a project in collective intelligence. If all the people at the meeting contribute a summary of what they have picked up, hopefully, some "meeting markers" will rise to the surface and become the group's shared memory. Like Hansel and Gretel, you drop bread crumbs and hope they will be found.

Rabinow says the meeting markers can be "summary slogans." Or people can create markers by sending around photographs or other images that stand in for ideas. A trail of images—a meme track—can help communicate the high points of a meeting during which people have slipped in and out of attention. Sometimes the meme track can serve as more than simple bread crumbs. Sometimes, they are how people expect to contribute to the conversation.

At HeartTech, a large Silicon Valley software company, employees I meet in focus groups complain about overprogrammed meetings. So much is on the agenda that it is hard to get a chance to speak. I discuss this with a group of HeartTech managers, and they point out that alongside what is *said aloud* at any meeting, there is almost always a meme track, that parallel online visual conversation. The meme track allows people who have no way to participate in a conversation to keep up with it and make their presence felt. It gives them a way to critique the proceedings and other participants, even those senior to them. They can use humor, expressed in funny photos and cartoons.

The meme track begins as a compensation for not being in a conversation, but some at this meeting describe it as being just as important to them as the conversation itself. Or more important: "Perhaps it's even more expressive than talking." "It's good for those who might not be comfortable speaking up." "It's incredibly on point and provocative. . . . When you consider memes and traditional conversation, I wouldn't want to choose one exclusively over another."

The conversation about memes—at HeartTech as elsewhere—follows a familiar pattern. A technological possibility—such as using memes to create a communications sidebar—is first offered as a substitution, something better than nothing. In this case, it responds to a problem: Meeting time is short and not everyone gets a chance to talk. But then, this accommodation is given new status. In this case, I hear that employees who might not be comfortable with the give-and-take of conversation now have a chance to participate. And then people fall back on the adage. Pictures are said to be more powerful than words. The meme track is deeply pertinent. "Perhaps it's even more expressive than talking." Better than nothing is perhaps simply better.

I recall the enthusiasm about memes among the students at the Boston focus group who asked me to share their WhatsApp channel so that I could "see" what they were thinking. Like the HeartTech managers, they claimed that the images they shared were as important as the words they said. But this was among a group of young people who admitted that they weren't comfortable with telephone conversations or face-to-face talk. Do the memes do the job—or do they do a job we can't do?

In any organization, there are some kinds of ideas that only words can convey. There are some kinds of conflicts that only words can parse and resolve. We have to think about preparing our students and employees to participate in these conversations. No matter how rich and even subversive, the meme track can take them only so far.

Attendance: Who Is Present?

The president of a New York cultural foundation tells me that at a recent board meeting one of her members had spent the time consumed with a stream of images on his iPad. The board member seated next to him had been mesmerized, watching him shop online for a new car.

We all attend meetings during which we multitask and our minds are elsewhere. It turns out to be a stressful elsewhere. The multitasking life puts us into a state similar to vigilance, one of continual alert. In that condition, we can follow only the most rudimentary arguments. So multitasking encourages brevity and simplicity, even when more is called for. And the harm that multitasking does is contagious. We've seen that someone multitasking on a laptop distracts everyone around the machine, not just the person using it.

And we still call them meetings, after all. I get together with the director and production staff of the Seahorse, a small mid-Atlantic theater company. As we begin, with seven of us at the table, Claire Messing, the director, realizes that her phone is vibrating. She blushes but says, "I'm not sure I can continue until I deal with this." We had gathered to discuss how technology affects the work of the theater. It has taken us months to coordinate our schedules. And now, we are finally together, all staring at Messing's phone.

At the Seahorse, it is standard practice to bring phones and laptops to staff meetings. Messing encourages this in the hope that technology will allow her staff "to stretch their time together." So, during a staff meeting, one person might be online to review budget numbers and another might scan job applications from lighting designers. Messing's idea is that if something important comes up online, the group can discuss it "live" while they are all in the room together.

But the strategy does not work. Once laptops are open, there is the temptation to look at email and attend to urgent messages. The director of education says that the meetings-with-devices make it almost impossible for her not to "cheat," by which she means that she reads her email while others are talking. "So at a meeting, I'm not as present because I'm always cheating a little bit." These are meetings that give the illusion of collaboration with all the drawbacks of distraction.

Messing describes the irony: "Even though we're in the business of creating live performance, we don't take advantage of our time with each other to have a conversation with each other." She imagined that technology-enhanced meetings would multiply productivity, but everyone goes off in a different direction.

Messing had another idea for how to use technology to multiply productivity: The staff would prepare for meetings by reading materials in Dropbox, a file-sharing application. Messing leaves them scripts, biographies of potential actors, and financial reports. To begin with, her staff thought this was a good idea, but soon they were all leaving materials in Dropbox. Everyone agrees that Dropbox has encouraged magical thinking: If it is in Dropbox, it has been read. "Dropbox," says the publicity director, "creates the fantasy that some of the work of a meeting has already been done." But it hasn't been done. The publicity director says that she herself comes to meetings exhausted from trying and failing to read what's in her Dropbox. It's come to the point where she resents being asked to brainstorm at meetings. "I can't brainstorm . . . I'm too exhausted to brainstorm."

Another Meeting That Is Not Quite a Meeting

Alice Rattan, a manager at ReadyLearn, is teaching the business value of unitasking. She is no longer surprised that her young consultants want to multitask during meetings. They grew up on it; they have to learn better ways. But she is always surprised that her *clients* want to multitask when *their* accounts are being discussed. And they want her to multitask as well. Rattan explains that clients expect quick turn-around on matters that she should take time to think through. She has to teach them that she intends to work for them with the attention that their problems deserve.

Rattan sees a disconnect. Her new hires, young consultants, are coming out of the best colleges and business schools. They have done amazing things both academically and in their extracurricular lives. But they are struggling with the simplest workplace conventions and conversations. She marvels: "They've designed their own apps, but they are socially inept." They have a hard time showing empathy in the workplace. They don't seem to understand the perspectives of their colleagues or clients. In today's workplace, the first training often needs to be training in conversation. But it usually isn't given its rightful place as a business priority because we tend to assume that employees know how to listen and respond.

When a junior-level consultant went on Facebook during a client meeting, Rattan was at pains to explain to her why she had done something wrong. From the young woman's point of view, she had done her "part" of the client presentation. In college, she explained to Rattan, after making a comment, she "always" went online. Rattan's frustration shows: "I'm, like, 'Okay, but you can't do that in a professional work setting.'" In this case, for Rattan, changing the consultant's behavior did not feel like enough. Rattan felt she had to work on her expectations, her approach to being in a conversation. As the consultant sees it: When people get together, they do their "part" and then check out. For Rattan, multitasking has left this young woman with work habits that make collaboration impossible.

After a few years of taking younger colleagues aside individually, Rattan decided she could not work in these conditions. She began to make new rules for everyone. Her first was a strict no-phones policy for all meetings. Now, she says, "there is a parking lot for smartphones at the door." For each hour of meeting time, she gives her consultants two ten-minute breaks. "That's when people can check their phones." Rattan fondly remembers the first meeting on her new regime: "It was the most productive. We got so much done. And from that point on, that was the rule. And if you couldn't commit to that you could not attend."

One of Rattan's colleagues, listening to her describe the young consultants' trouble with attention at meetings, is brought back to the days of her first BlackBerry and how its red light went off when she had a message. No matter where she was or what she was doing, she could not will herself to ignore that blinking red light. In order to keep her mind on her work, she says, "I had to put stickies over the light."

Rattan has compassion for her young consultants. It is clear to her that they do their work assignments while doing other things on the web. That's how they worked in college and graduate school. They don't know any other way. But the impact of that work style is apparent to her. Their work is inconsistent; Rattan says that she can see the traces of their multitasking in the assignments they turn in.

> So you'll see great thought, then you'll see crap, then you'll see great thought. . . . It starts out well, because they're concentrating. Then they get an interruption, an email, a call, a text. So then, just illogical comments. I can see the interruptions in their work product. And so I'll go back and I'll say, "Hey, I like where you're going with this, but it didn't finish up too strong." And they just say, "Oh well, I got distracted."

Rattan tries to teach her team to do one thing at a time. When she is on a conference call with one or several of them, she tells them that her attention is only on them. She is not doing email; she is not on her phone. Rattan makes it explicit. "On a call, I'll say, 'Now I am looking away from my computer.' I tell them that the volume is down on my phone or computer so I can't hear that messages are coming in. . . . I sign off the company server." At first, the young consultants are shocked, but then they get the message.

Rattan has had her own problems with focus. A few years ago, at forty, she found that her life of always-on connection left her always distracted. She was unhappy and unproductive. She decided to take action. When she got to work, Rattan began to turn off the Wi-Fi and work in an empty office. She segmented her workday into times online and off. This helped her to unitask because she had long blocks of time when email and the web were no longer a temptation.

She suggests this strategy to others: Begin by admitting vulnerability and then design new behaviors around it.

This realism about vulnerability is a business "best practice." Technologies have affordances—for example, a networked computer can put you on a continual, stimulating feed of information. Designing for vulnerability means avoiding what undermines your attention. That can mean a "parking lot" for smartphones and tablets before you start a meeting; it can mean a "one task only" rule when you have to write something important. It helps to come to the design process with compassion for yourself and others. For you may have to say the seemingly obvious to young colleagues: You can't update your Facebook during client meetings. This may be something they do not know.

The notion of unitasking was picked up when the magazine *The Atlantic* produced a video on the problems associated with multitasking and suggested one remedy: a "Tabless Thursday." One day a week, you can work only on one thing instead of keeping multiple browser tabs open. It's a gimmick, certainly, but the basic idea is gaining traction.

"Breathing the Same Air Matters"

The director of technology for a large financial services company, Victor Tripp, tries to get his New York team—around fifteen people—to attend a meeting. Only three show up. And it's hard to convince them to have in-person meetings with clients. Like the lawyers at AJM and like the staff at the Seahorse, they prefer to use email whenever they can. Tripp says that "typically, things get into trouble when too much has been done by email." One of his team will come in to him to complain about a client. "It's up to me to say, 'Have a conversation, spend some face time, repair that relationship.' That isn't something they would come to themselves." Tripp tells me that when he has to suggest an in-person meeting, "I'm usually facing someone who wants to send twenty-nine emails to fix a problem. And I just have to say, 'Go talk to them.'"

Tripp explains that his younger colleagues have grown up thinking that electronic communication is a universal language. So when they think about choosing a communication tool, they consider such things as messaging, texts, Skype, email, videoconferencing, and memes. That's a lot of choices, and each carries its own "atmosphere." But they don't really consider a sit-down meeting. It's not on their menu. That idea has to come from the "outside." It is part of mentoring. Tripp sees this as his role.

For Tripp, the shared experience of people at a sit-down is like nothing else. It is the best way to learn how your colleagues think, how your clients think. And, he says, "When people are comfortable talking to each other, little disagreements don't grow into big problems."

The stage director Liana Hareet, who has more than thirty years of theatrical experience, has a similar experience in a very different kind of meeting. For Hareet, all the in-person meetings that lead up to the production of a play matter in the same way that live theater matters. "You get the unexpected; you get chemistry." She says, "I love design meetings . . . when we all sit in a room and we go, 'How the hell do we get Hermione's statue to come to life at the end of *Winter's Tale*? Let's all talk about this. Here is my idea. Let's all brainstorm.'"

Yet, Hareet explains, in regional theater, in-person design meetings happen with less and less frequency. Electronic communication makes it possible for the design and technical staff (those who do costumes, sets, and lighting) to work on many productions at the same time. So it has become standard practice for a director to meet individually with each design director and share decisions through email. Hareet mourns the loss. Even the most dedicated email exchange is not the same as a face-to-face conversation:

I send you an idea and you comment on it and send it back is a different process than us talking about an idea together. You lose the better idea that comes out of the exchange. . . . We underestimate how much we learn and read and take in of each other's breathing and body language and presence in a space. . . . Technology filters things out. . . . Breathing the same air matters.

Hareet says that even when she gets her actors together, breathing the same air, she has to work to keep them present to each other. Only a few years earlier, she explains, actors came to rehearsals with the expectation that they would be listening to the other actors as they did their scenes. This helped all the actors develop a shared language about the play. Now, this attention to the community is something she has to enforce.

You look around and actors aren't paying attention to the rehearsal. Before their entrance, they'll be sitting around checking their texts and mail. . . . If things don't seem relevant to them, people claim "boredom" and go to their phones. . . . They don't allow themselves to see the things that don't connect to them as relevant to them. But a play is an organic whole.

It is striking that similar comments come from a group of appellate court justices. Traditionally, they say, when listening to cases on appeal, a group of three judges met together, heard arguments about a case, and rendered a verdict. The process unfolded with a lot of meetings and telephone calls. Now, they say, they rely heavily on email before the case gets to its formal appeal. These judges are nostalgic for the rhythms of past practice, the time spent with colleagues that sparked new ideas. The judges are also concerned that generations of young lawyers don't fully understand the value of presence. The lawyers who appear before them are less and less accustomed to making their points in person. As the judges see it, the young lawyers are eloquent in email but don't have enough practice in oral argument. This means that they don't stand up as well to being challenged on the spot.

The judges, the director of technology, and the theater directors are circling the same issues. New ideas emerge from in-person meetings. Email conversations, no matter how efficient, trend toward the transactional. Emails pose questions and get answers—most of the time, emails boil down to an exchange of information. In acting, in law, in business, the loss of a face-to-face meeting means a loss of complexity and depth. A younger generation may be getting accustomed to this flattening of things. But Hareet believes that those who have experienced the change miss feeling part of an "organic whole. And they miss what the voice and the body communicate."

Mentoring for conversation requires that you address two questions. You will be asked, outright, "Why focus on one thing, as you must in a face-to-face conversation, when you can get greater 'value' from spreading around your attention?" The answer: Multitasking will not bring greater value. You will *feel* you are achieving more and more as you accomplish less and less. You will be asked, outright, "Why go through the anxiety of separating from all of your connections to focus on the small group you are with?" The answer: The more you talk to your colleagues, the greater your productivity.

But behind these questions, these objections, there is something else not so easy to answer with research results. The demands of the workplace come to everyone on screens, and these demands can seem overwhelming. Screens provide a way to organize these demands, to take them at a pace that seems tolerable. Sticking to your screen allows you to experience some measure of control. When people resist moving away from their screens and toward conversation, they are often afraid of giving up this feeling of mastery.

The View from the Cockpit: Seeking a Measure of Control

Raven Hassoun, thirty-five, works in the financial industry. She avoids conversations with her colleagues. She confines herself to texting, messaging, and email whenever she can. For her, it's about "maintaining sanity." She describes her job as "a pressure cooker." Sticking to her screen is a way of feeling in control of her life: "So many people put demands on my time. So many people want me to do things for them. If I read my email, I can hear all of these demands, but at a distance. I feel more in control. On the computer I can get up, or look away, or play some music." Or, says Hassoun, she can check in with friends in a way that feels safe because it is time-limited. I've called this the Goldilocks effect—we want our connections not too close, not too far, just right. If Hassoun checks Facebook and sends a few texts and emails, she can stay in contact with other people but not risk too much time away from her job. What she calls her quick "social checks" make the demands of work manageable. And keeping her social life online makes its demands manageable as well.

Hassoun craves control more than sociability. She will email a "Sorry" instead of delivering a face-to-face apology; at work, as in her personal life, when she faces a difficult conversation, she makes every effort to sidestep it with an email. The difficult, even if necessary, conversations take time she says she doesn't have. And they demand emotional exposure. Hassoun sees emotional exposure as stress she doesn't have to subject herself to.

Hassoun's protocols for self-protection leave her with a lot of work problems that email can't quite fix. And they leave her feeling lonely. So lonely, in fact, that when her manager comes by to talk, Hassoun says that she will sometimes imagine that her manager gives her a friendly hug. And sometimes Hassoun says that she imagines her manager putting a reassuring hand on her shoulder. Hassoun understands that she is not permitting herself a conversation so she fantasizes a hug. But she is not about to take these fantasies as a signal that she should spend more time with her work colleagues. Her final judgment: "I don't have the time."

"Get Together. Have a Conversation."

Stan Hammond is the CEO of a consulting practice that helps put together complex financial deals. He says that he understands people like Hassoun and their need to put some "white space" in their lives—the phrase I keep hearing to indicate "time out" to collect oneself. But he is also adamant that people who do not make time for conversation don't learn how to have conversations. And that this is ultimately bad for business. He says that his job is made harder because so many people are most comfortable alone in front of their screens, in what the Boston lawyer called their "cockpit." Hammond says, "Email—these guys are emailing all the time. I finally will go to their office and almost force a face-to-face meeting. But it's not what they want." He's talking about people who, like Hassoun, want to hide behind their email but get to a point where that simply doesn't work. The deal gets too big or something goes amiss. Moving things forward requires a conversation.

Hammond makes it clear that email is an essential business tool when you have a clear, instrumental purpose. The problems, he says, come up when you fall back on email for every purpose, just because it's there. In his experience, when it comes to negotiation, email will create a string of misunderstandings.

He describes a recent board meeting where an important deal was being discussed. His client, one of the key actors, sent Hammond an angry email during the meeting. Immediately after the meeting, Hammond called his client to make a date to talk out their differences. When Hammond made that call, he and his client were still in the same building. But in response, Hammond only got another email, referring him to the first. A series of miscommunications followed.

Hammond says that the incident is typical. People want to use email to avoid conversation. In a recent disagreement with a colleague, Hammond kept asking to see her and she kept sending him emails. Hammond says, "I finally was able to get a meeting, just to say, 'Sorry, let's clear the air; it's five minutes, move on. No stress. Five minutes; it's just a pinch, done.'" But he had to work hard to get that meeting. Too hard. She was acting against their common business interests.

Hammond sees a generational issue in play. "People who are over forty-five or fifty are more comfortable with face-to-face meetings." And those under that age "have a tendency to use email to avoid dealing with each other." And also, to use email to apologize. For Hammond, the ability to apologize face-to-face is a basic business skill. Not having it seems to him like "driving a car but not knowing how to go in reverse. This is what it must be for these people who can't say these words. But email encourages this; on email, you never learn to say 'I'm sorry.'"

Hammond says he is not surprised by the difficulties people are having with conversation. He has two young boys who, at dinnertime, need to be pried away from their devices and then "sit silent at the table instead of talking to each other." He is not content: "The more people hide in their devices, the more they lose practice in the skills they will need for success in the business world. They are getting faster with their gadgets but they are not learning the essence." That essence, for Hammond, is conversation.

This sentiment is echoed by the CEO of a large clothing company who tells me that his employees argue over email and then come to him as misunderstandings multiply. "At least once a day someone is in my office complaining about email exchanges with a fellow employee. And sometimes the person they are complaining about has also come in to complain. My message is always the same: 'Get together. Have a conversation.'"

But sometimes that is not as easy as it sounds. As we saw in Caroline Tennant's day of Skype meetings, other forces are at work. In most companies, the workforce is dispersed all over the world.

Dispersing the Workforce

At ReadyLearn, everyone works in far-flung international teams. And cost cutting has meant that money for travel and training has become harder to come by. So, I meet managers who have never had a face-to-face encounter with the people they supervise. I meet consultants who say they have spoken with their supervisors only on phone calls and teleconferences. In this situation, people improvise.

One global team celebrates the New Year by sending every member a hat, a bottle of champagne, and a noisemaker. Thus outfitted, the team holds a teleconference and comes together for a toast. Getting the treats and having an online party is charming and unexpected if it is not the norm. But when it becomes the norm, it isn't clear what it is.

I was told about the online New Year's party as a funny story, an example of creative camaraderie. About halfway through, the person telling the story realized that he didn't think it was funny, he thought it was sad, and he didn't know how to wind the story down. My question, "Was it successful?" was met with hesitation. These things are as successful as they can be. Everyone is doing the best they can.

When companies make the decision to decentralize in this way, employees are asked to buy into a narrative that represents all of this as "progress," or certainly what is needed for the company to succeed. But the day-to-day experience of this new way of work can make it easy to lose faith.

Victor Tripp used to have his technical team around him in New York, but his company's long-range plan is to use less office space in Manhattan and save on salaries by not hiring American workers. So now his team is dispersed around the world. Tripp is nostalgic for the old New York days. When he worked on the same floor as his team, he says, "We were talking all the time. I could stand up and see every person in the group. Shout out to them." Now, with an international team, they schedule calls and teleconferences.

Recently, Tripp's team had to address an international system failure. The global network had to be shut down and restarted. Tripp is sure that if he had "his guys in New York," he could have handled the system failure with dispatch. But "with everybody all over the world, it took a lot longer." Tripp thinks that the new, dispersed team brings his firm less value than the centralized New York team. He is convinced that there is a bottom-line business case for returning to the old system. But he adds, "Even making the case would cause all hell to break loose. Nobody wants to do a study to show that this [dispersing local teams] was a bad decision. When the decision to break up local teams was made, everybody said, 'This is ridiculous. Why are we doing this?' But then, it was done."

When Tripp looks ten years down the road, he imagines there will be even fewer people around him, and as for the few people on his team, "They won't even be in an office; they'll be at home." And "if they want to come to the 'office,'" he says, "they will be assigned a place to work . . . like a room in a hotel." The notion of a team that sits together and talks together will be a thing of the past.

> *I know one firm where you go up the elevator. You punch your code into an iPad. And it says, "Okay, this is your neighborhood, where your group normally sits. And here are three empty desks over there. Go sit over there." And away you go.*
>
> *You go in, sit down, work. Some people are, like, you know, "I just feel like a commodity. I have no ties to this business." I feel like I'm going to the library, because I don't have a picture of my family. I don't have— you know, nothing is mine anymore.*

As Tripp and I talk about the disadvantages of regularly working at home, with stints at the "hotel," the story of Marissa Mayer, the CEO of Yahoo, calling employees back to the firm by radically reducing the amount of telecommuting is in the news. Mayer says she wants people together in order to increase their productivity and creativity. Tripp says, "I think that's a great story. I like that story." But he doesn't think it will apply to him. Yahoo is calling its people back "home to work," but he sees a future without a desk.

Bringing People "Home to Work"

In 2004, the new CEO of Radnor Partners, a large high-tech consulting company, also became frustrated with the limitations of telecommuting, something that had been in the Radnor culture since the 1990s. As in so many firms, telecommuting cut costs and was widely seen as improving employee satisfaction. But now, this CEO decided to bring his far-flung workforce together.

When Radnor made its decision, the economy was in a downturn and companies were not typically making new investments in physical infrastructure. But the new CEO went against the conventional wisdom of the time. He invested in new, more welcoming office spaces and called people back to work in them.

At first, there was a lot of grumbling—the Radnor management and employees had gotten used to their flexible work arrangements. Also, there was genuine concern among senior management that this new policy would make recruiting difficult and cause talented people to leave Radnor. And there was something else: Radnor was making money. The CEO wanted to change its culture at a time when what it was doing was successful in the marketplace.

But the CEO stood firm. He communicated his vision to an unconvinced management team. Here is how Shelly Browning, the vice-president in charge of human resources, describes what she heard:

> He said, "We're a growing company. Change only happens when people collaborate. You can't collaborate as effectively at home, where you don't run into someone in the cafeteria. You don't bring them up to speed on that thing, you forget to tell them the nine other things. It slows down the rate of change. . . ." So, he said, "All of our leaders are going to be in offices. And to the extent that's possible, we're going to hire people to work in offices. . . . Your job is in an office because that's where we collaborate."

Grudgingly, people came back to work. Grudgingly. Browning describes the process as turbulent:

We wagged our fingers. We told him the world had changed. That he had an archaic view—that in management, people needed to work from home. But over eight years, he has changed every one of our minds. . . . And we have all become believers. We're growing. We work as a team.

Ben Waber's studies demonstrate that workers across different fields are more productive when they talk more. So it's not surprising that the positive effects of people brushing shoulders play out at every level of an organization. And that's what happened at Radnor. Physical proximity sparked new conversations. Those who had been skeptical, says Browning, saw for themselves that "face-to-face meetings are what good collaboration looks like." And the CEO's decision paid off in financial terms: When analysts, salespeople, and consultants worked in the same space, Radnor began to grow at five times its former rate.

Not only did the Radnor CEO bring employees back to local offices, he encouraged more communication among managers in different parts of the company. A group of managers were identified as crucial to the company's future and brought together for a three-day workshop. They weren't there to learn new skills but to be persuaded by a new idea: Radnor would now have a face-to-face leadership culture. They were being asked to be the company-wide advocates for this change in all their different departments.

Browning was given the job of designing the workshop. It was a tough assignment. The assembled managers were happy with the old system. They were able to work from home and had flexible hours. Browning describes the downbeat atmosphere when things began. "They came with their arms crossed and their BlackBerrys at the ready." But the workshop challenged their set ideas. "Nobody went to their laptop. Nobody went to their BlackBerry, even at night."

A crucial moment in the workshop came when the managers were asked how much they knew about the people they supervised. In particular, did they know how those they supervised would answer the question "What is your sense of purpose?" Even managers who had supervised the same employees for over a decade could not talk confidentially about their motivations. These are things that you don't learn without a conversation. That's what was missing and that's what the CEO wanted to change.

Since 2011, Radnor has put "sense of purpose" conversations at the heart of all performance reviews. Managers are directly asked, "Did you have the sense-of-purpose conversation?" It's a box that has to be checked. Knowledge about your colleagues that depends on face-to-face conversations has become part of the company's DNA.

As for the face-to-face intensive leadership development program, it is now a regular part of the Radnor system. It has been carefully evaluated and found to exceed expectations. It forged new bonds across the company. Indeed, that first, reticent group of managers continues to meet on monthly conference calls. Their in-person experience built trust that has paid off throughout the organization.

Conversation Dates

The Radnor story illustrates two simple lessons: *Getting together for face-to-face conversation is good for the bottom line, and proactive leaders can do things to make it happen.*

In 2008, the CEO of Stoddard, an international design firm, tried to schedule a meeting with a group of vice-presidents and found that it would take over two weeks to get it on his calendar. The senior leadership had 90 percent of its time booked in advance. The CEO realized that in this environment, with people moving from one scheduled meeting to another, there was little room for informal conversation. And not much room for meetings that needed to be scheduled because a problem was looming. Or because someone had a good idea and wanted to quickly share it with colleagues. So the CEO started a new program: breakfast.

One day a week at corporate headquarters, a senior management group would begin their day forty-five minutes earlier than usual. They would all come to a breakfast that had no agenda. People would simply be there, available to each other. Within months, scheduled meetings dropped by 20 percent. That meant that senior management had 20 percent more time for spontaneous conversations or for scheduling last-minute meetings. The breakfast group is uniformly enthusiastic about the program. At breakfast, problems are solved on the spot. And new ideas get a hearing.

Informal conversation counts. The stage director Liana Hareet recalls that in the theater, it used to happen naturally because of the technology of the "classical" rehearsal room. The actors' union required either a ten-minute break every eighty minutes or a five-minute break every hour. The group of actors rehearsing on any given day would decide how they would take their breaks and everyone took a break at the same time.

At the break, there would be a long line for the one or two pay phones outside the rehearsal room door. Everyone had to call his or her agent and/or answering machine.

You never knew when work was coming in, a last-minute audition. There would be a line at the phone. And on that line, there would be conversation. You would be with the other actors, all the time. There was a lot of kibitz in it. Now, the minute you say, "Take ten," everybody just takes out their cell and goes to a private space. Everyone goes to a different corner. And then they come back to work, but it's a different energy than everyone having been on the pay phone line, all returning.

The line around a pay phone brought people together. Now, the screens on our phones and laptops keep us apart, or at best, alone together, physically in the same space but isolated, with our minds on our devices. *Unless we act with intention.* The Stoddard breakfasts illustrate, once again, that if you want to spark conversation, you need the commitment of senior leadership. And you have to design for it.

Designing for Conversation: Culture Counts

Designing for conversation can be as simple as planning a pre-work breakfast or it can involve elaborate environmental engineering. Google has been a leader in this kind of engineering. It asked Ben Waber to determine whether there is an optimal amount of time for employees to stand in a cafeteria line to maximize conversation. Waber found out that there is: It's three to four minutes—short enough so that people don't feel that they are wasting time, but long enough to meet new people. Similarly, Waber determined the optimal size for a cafeteria table so that strangers wouldn't feel shy about sitting down to join an ongoing conversation. It's a large table, for ten to twelve people.

But in every case, design has to be reinforced by culture.

Stan Hammond, the financial consultant, was serious about designing his office space for conversation and personally committed himself to making the design work. Hammond's design constrains his employees so that they are "forced" to talk, much as the theater staff and actors once were trapped on the rehearsal studio's pay phone line. Everyone in Hammond's company begins the workday at the same place, with coffee and treats laid out for them.

Hammond's office space extends from the fourteenth to the sixteenth floor of a large Manhattan building. He insists that employees get off the elevator on the fifteenth floor even if they work on the fourteenth or sixteenth floor. That's where there is always food, drink, and comfortable seating. He wants his employees to bump into people they don't know at all or don't know very well. He wants to continually create new opportunities for conversation. When he catches an employee getting off on the fourteenth or sixteenth floor, Hammond firmly guides them back to the elevator.

Vincent Castell, who heads a venture capital firm in San Francisco, is equally committed to designing for conversation. He says that only a few years ago, the atmosphere at his company, Castell Advisors, was at "near-crisis levels." Meetings, he says, were "dead." Everyone was texting. Including Castell himself.

For Castell, the dead meetings were symptoms. He had allowed technology to shape a culture that taught its members that conversation didn't matter. "People emailed me from the office next door. There was no sense of inspiration or community." He felt his company slipping away from him: "In all of this silence, as you are emailing the people you work with, you lose the nuance of conversation and you lose the ability to see how someone thinks on their feet."

Castell made a commitment to reclaim conversation. He began modestly, with a "phones off" rule for meetings—but then he decided on radical change. He bought new office space. He met with several firms that specialize in innovative furniture design and with academics who study office interaction. He studied Ben Waber's work on collaboration. In his redesigned office, there are places where people can claim total privacy and there are casual, quiet areas for people to gather. Twenty percent of the office space is devoted to food, with bar-stool seating designed for conversation.

Now, each day begins with a short, device-free stand-up meeting that brings everyone up to date on company news. Anyone can speak; anyone can ask a question of any member of the firm.

Stand-up meetings were Castell's response to the kind of meetings where he himself gave in to the temptation to text and do his email. The stand-ups have become a staple of contemporary business culture because they force attention, if only for a while. They are not a panacea. Because they are designed to move quickly, they are not the place to work through complex problems. But Castell says that they have had a tonic effect on his organization. "There was a big change in the amount and types of conversation. There are now a huge number of thirty-second conversations and impromptu conversations that were not happening before. Now, people seem to want to go to work."

Castell feels that what he did to improve his company "responds to a basic human truth: People do business with people they like and trust." The reason to come to an office is to spur the conversations that will lead to that sense of community. Office design is a big part of the equation. For Castell, it should "stir the senses, promote intellectual curiosity."

Castell says that clients now choose to work with his firm because they like the work environment. "This is the kind of firm they want to work with; this is the kind of firm they can be excited about." His profits are up.

On a personal level, conversation is the path back to a capacity for empathy. At work, that capacity paves a path forward to greater productivity. Castell and Hammond see it working in their companies as it worked at Radnor and Stoddard.

HeartTech: Build It, but They May Not Come

When collaboration is key to productivity, companies do well if they design for conversation. At HeartTech, the large software company, there are all-day cafeterias, micro-kitchens, and company outings. And there is more, including a weekly all-company meeting that anyone can attend and where anyone can speak. Officially, at HeartTech, communication and transparency are core values.

But it is at HeartTech that I learn the limitations of "build it and they will come." Despite the right architecture and vision statement, at HeartTech, no one has time for much open-ended conversation—or people don't believe they have permission to take the time. In a micro-kitchen, marveling at how the healthy snacks are placed at eye level and the less healthy ones require a bit more effort to find, I say hello to a young man and get a laugh in return. "You must be new here." In this micro-kitchen, he tells me, most of the time you choose a snack and take it back to your desk. People aren't unfriendly. They just don't have time to talk.

HeartTech sees itself as the best in the world and those who work there as superheroes. This means that employees are preoccupied with trying to prove that they are equal to every challenge. The easiest way to demonstrate that you are a master of the universe is to show that, unlike mere mortals, you don't need to take time away from the network.

The early history of software was written by teams of hackers who had a night culture—they worked on time-sharing computers that had fewer users, and thus ran faster, during the night. Long after the technical imperative to work at night was gone, the cultural imperative stayed. Great software guys (and gradually, but only gradually, great software girls) showed their love of computers and code through devotion. Day and night devotion. At HeartTech that old ethos is reflected in a shared understanding that the best employees are always ready to work. They are "on" the company messaging system, with a glowing green heart next to their names.

In focus groups with HeartTech employees, I hear variations of the same story. Managers mean well. They don't want employees to be stressed. But everyone at this company is trying to prove that they are worthy of being there. Being always available, online, is the simplest way to show this. And since the company code of showing devotion through presence runs up the chain of command, your boss, too, is also likely to be always "on," a glowing green heart.

So employees complain that their managers will send emails at ten at night and give no sign if they expect that email to be answered that evening or if ten o'clock is simply when they got to their email because they have young children and are busy until their kids are down at nine. With no clear signal, those who report to these managers are afraid to assume that a late email doesn't call for an instant reply. One programmer says, "My manager talks the right talk, all about 'centering' and 'pausing' and 'taking time for you.' But she is like Twitter: reactive, always on—her mind responds like a feed. It's hard to know whether to follow what she says or what she does." This kind of confusion keeps people on a treadmill. It cuts down on face-to-face conversations because people are either in scheduled meetings or on their computers trying to keep up. And making sure to "show up" on the messaging system.

One programmer says she treasures her time in the office after six in the evening. During the day, she is in back-to-back meetings, so at night she feels more relaxed. She gets some food, she finds an unscheduled conference room, and she works quietly and sometimes talks with colleagues. She says, "People have real conversations after six." But even her after-hours schedule comes with the conflict she feels all day. Even at night she thinks it would be a mistake to appear on the messaging system as "away." And once she is on the system, she says, "There are always messages."

At HeartTech, there is conflict between what you are told and what you believe. I sit down at a cafeteria lunch table and a young engineer strikes up a conversation. Then he apologizes for bothering me and explains that he is new. His supervisor wants him to talk to strangers at lunch. But despite the kitchens, the food, and the explicit instructions to chat, he knows that what HeartTech most wants from him is to be available online: "My manager wants to see that green heart." Of course, once you are on the network, you can't easily get away for face-to-face talk. And solitude is interrupted by incoming messages.

The tensions in the HeartTech culture teach a lesson. If you think conversation is important for your organization, you can't just say so or design beautiful kitchens and cafeterias to facilitate it. You have to leave time and space. Most of all, senior management has to model it, leading by daily example. If not, the beautiful spaces simply become amenities. And new employees who start conversations will wonder if they should apologize.

Here is how Kristina Roberts, in her mid-thirties, looks back at what it has been like to "grow up" in the HeartTech culture, where she reads the key values to be responsibility, being the best, and devotion. She came to HeartTech determined to make a success of it:

From the beginning, I did not want to be seen as irresponsible. So being available on email was a great way to be shown as responsible.

I focused on having my little heart on the messaging system always being green. Engineers would focus on their little heart being green even when they are on the ski lift. And in that environment, my stress level and level of depression went higher and higher. The mountain just got taller. There was this desire and urge to keep climbing that mountain and I'm sitting with you at dinner and you can go to the bathroom and I can check my mail. So, I began to stay on the messaging system all the time.

As Roberts sees it, the company identified "strong performers" as those who were always online. But she couldn't think if she was responding to email every few minutes. Over time, her sense of what made her valuable as an employee (devotion as shown by availability) came to be at odds with what she personally needed to do her best work. It took a long time, many years, to get that clarity. For all those years, staying on the system was her highest priority. She was rewarded for it in the company. And personally, it became a requirement. She came to see her phone and the HeartTech messaging system as a kind of drug.

As Roberts sees it, the HeartTech culture undermined infrastructure that had been explicitly designed for conversation (the cafeterias, the micro-kitchens). The level of stress, particularly from the unstated demand to be always on the system, got in the way of collaboration. And spilled over to the rest of life.

Being "always on" for HeartTech meant that Roberts was always on for everything else as well. Her phone began to be everything to her—the way she connected to the rest of her life: her friends, her family, her romances. Roberts's efforts to show devotion at HeartTech put her in the machine zone: Communication came in a relentless stream; she felt reactive and scattered and *dependent*. Speaking of herself, she says, "You need to have your phone with you always. . . . Because if you imagine what happens if you drop below your baseline of stimulation, part of you is saying, 'I need to go back to the phone.'"

HeartTech is a large, diverse company, and I found best practices within it—places, for example, where managers make specific efforts to get people out of the expectation that one should always be online. I hear about one manager who sends out emails through the night but is explicit that she does this because she has young children and late at night is her best time to work. So, the emails she sends out at one in the morning are not emails to which she expects an immediate response. Everyone on her team is grateful for her clarity. Another HeartTech manager says she finds it even better to take the next step. She drafts her late-night emails but then she doesn't send them. She says, "Write it, get your work done in the hours that are convenient for you, but keep it in your draft folder. At 7:00 a.m., when you think that people may be up and starting to do early-morning emails, then hit send."

And indeed, some of the most admired managers at HeartTech are the ones who send emails out in bursts, not throughout the day, but at times that will be convenient for their employees. They model a relationship with the network that leaves time and space.

HeartTech knows its employees are stressed. To help them, the company has put in place mindfulness and meditation programs, designed to encourage a state of calm awareness. There is a regular company-wide "pause" during which employees are asked to relax and breathe during the workday. HeartTech employees see value in these programs; many see great value. But they harbor no illusions. To many, the message of the mindfulness programs seems at odds with the feel of their job. In focus groups of HeartTech employees, I hear that they are, after all, not being paid to be calm. And as one puts it, "We are not being paid to have conversations."

Yet, at HeartTech, the respect for mindfulness, like the many efforts to build spaces that are conversation-friendly, are significant. The more the business world appreciates the importance of composure, attention, and face-to-face communication to its own financial interests, the more distance it will take from technologies that disrupt them. Over time (but in this industry, time moves swiftly) this will give business common cause with consumers who are trying to reclaim all these things for themselves. One software developer has suggested that his industry redefine what it means for an app to be successful. It shouldn't be how much time a consumer has spent with it but whether it was time well spent. In the long run, consumers and industry together could reframe the design principles for our world of devices and apps.

Dialogue in Medicine

Here I have concentrated on the conversations that take place in offices because so many of us work in them. But other kinds of workplaces have equally vexed relationships with conversation. Perhaps medicine is the most dramatic case.

The medical exam is one of the most highly charged contexts for communication. There, it would seem, almost by definition, that the patient has the physician's full attention. Yet senior physicians are concerned that young doctors come into medicine expecting that the answers to problems will be found not so much in the examining room but "elsewhere"—in diagnostic tests the physician will see later. Because they believe in the scientific data they will get about the patient, they don't focus on the patient. The belief in data that will come in later becomes a way to justify an only cursory conversation with the patient now. A sixty-year-old faculty member at a major teaching hospital says of the residents he currently trains: "They want to use tests to rationalize not talking to patients because talking to patients is difficult and usually takes skills young doctors don't have."

In his view, in the new "rely on the test" culture, the standard physical exam seems strangely intimate to young doctors. You touch the body; you investigate the past; you ask odd questions. Some of this touching and talking starts to seem unnecessary if you believe the tests are going to tell you everything you need to know. You become comfortable with being a doctor who touches and talks less. Your skills for doing a physical exam degrade and you need the tests even more. This senior physician is sad as he considers his students' discomfort:

They don't want to take responsibility for the things that might come up in a conversation, things that would come out during a full patient history. They don't want to hear that their patients are anxious, depressed, or frightened. Doctors used to want to hear these things. They knew that the whole person got sick. The whole person needed to be treated. Today, young physicians don't want to have that conversation. My students welcome the fact that the new medical records system almost forces them to turn away from the patient and keep the interchange about relevant details. They don't want to step into a more complicated role.

The physician and author Abraham Verghese writes about how medicine has moved away from treating the patient to treating the "iPatient," the sum of the data we have collected about a person. In the process, Verghese argues, physicians lose more than an empathic connection with the human being in their care. They lose the ability to cure.

Yet medicine is also a place of hope in the story of how a professional culture can reclaim conversation. For one thing, it is a field that is talking about its flight from conversation. The dangers of physicians looking at screens rather than patients, the over-reliance on tests, the need to return to the extended conversations of the traditional medical history—all of these are being discussed. And acted upon. I meet a senior physician who is struggling with the intrusions of a new electronic record-keeping system in her hospital. She explains that if she uses the system as intended, she will not be able to make eye contact during patient visits. She will be too busy entering data into the program. Her accommodation to the system has been to take notes during patient meetings and enter the records into the system at night, after her children are asleep. Her system strains her, but she is trying to organize the other doctors on her service to change hospital rules to make room for conversation.

She belongs to a generation of senior physicians committed to teaching medical students how to have rich conversations with patients. An oncologist in his late fifties regularly participates in courses for first- and second-year medical students that focus on the physical examination and patient interview. He talks to me about all the pressures in the medical system that work to silence doctors—the expectations that they see so many patients during a day, the allure of running a high-tech diagnostic exam, the pressures of paperwork and forms—but he is proud that at least in his medical school, so much stress is placed on conversation. His students are learning how to form a trusting relationship, how to deliver bad news, and how to use good news to build a stronger bond. He worries how much his students will be able to "hold on to ten years out." But while they are in medical school, they are encouraged to see communication as central to practice.

And medicine has responded to the pressures that cut off conversation with a spirit of invention. A new profession—of medical scribes—has grown up, designed to separate the doctor from the many screens that demand his attention. The scribes are trained assistants who follow physicians around, filling in the reports required by insurance companies and computer record-keeping systems. With those responsibilities lifted from their shoulders, doctors can more easily engage with patients. The introduction of the scribes into medical practice illustrates how a profession can invent its way into necessary conversations.

We saw that spirit of invention in Alice Rattan's introduction of a "parking lot" for phones during meetings, in Stan Hammond's elevator to the fifteenth floor, and in the breakfasts without agenda at Stoddard. Like the scribes, all of these are inventions and interventions to reclaim conversation. We can invent more. They inspire next steps for the workplace that have resonance for what we can accomplish in education and in our families as well.

Next Steps: Inventions and Interventions

The next steps explore the special role of business leaders in reclaiming conversation. A business culture reaches far beyond the life of a firm. It can determine whether we feel we can put down our phones at family dinner or need to be on call all night. In a world where everyone "knows" that multitasking is bad for you but doesn't do anything about it, things change if your employer tells you that you are going to be given the time, space, and privacy to begin and complete important tasks one by one.

We are all the products of the conversations we have not had at home, the conversations we have sidestepped with family, friends, and intimates. When young people join the workforce, there is a new opportunity to show compassion and an understanding of their histories. If a young employee seems like a deer caught in the headlights during a job interview, this is an opportunity to mentor a person who might not know much about conversation.

So, at work, we are called to be more intentional about the use of technology and the value of conversation. We are called to be more explicit about where we are, how conversation can help, and what is likely to get in the way.

Champion conversation in the day-to-day. The moment needs mentors with humility, acknowledging that just as parents model the behavior (texting during dinner) they then criticize in their children, managers often model the behavior they criticize in their employees. Managers drop out of meetings to do email or play games. They take out their phones during lunch and coffee breaks with the professionals they supervise. I think of my own professional environment—if faculty members do email during faculty meetings, and we do, the fact that students text during class seems less shocking; we are all part of the same culture.

In the day-to-day, managers need to make conversation the norm. Showing up to a face-to-face mentoring session should not feel that it requires an act of courage. It should feel like business as usual.

In conversation, people build trust, get information, and build the connections that help them get their work done. Because we know this "by heart," we too often take it for granted and give ourselves permission to put it out of mind. To reclaim conversation, we have to be explicit and make conversation a value at every level of an organization. And in organizations of every size.

When Starbucks got into financial trouble, it rebuilt its brand with seemingly small changes, some of which highlighted the importance of conversations between customers and baristas. Every employee wore a name badge and counters were lowered so that it was easier to strike up a conversation.

At a small technology-support company in the American South, the leadership found that there was a greater chance of a first contact with a potential client turning into an ongoing account if that first contact was a telephone call rather than an email. This information was immediately translated into a business protocol: If you get a query by email, return it with a phone call, even if that email asks for a return email. The CEO put it this way: "An engineer buying support services is price sensitive, certainly. But what he really wants to buy is the assurance that in an emergency, day or night, if something goes wrong—and in technology, something will always go wrong—you will be there. You don't get that feeling of security from an email, you get it from a conversation."

Sometimes making conversation an explicit value means recognizing when our best interests conflict with our desire to stay on our phones. When Castell couldn't control his *own* texting at company meetings, he declared those meetings device-free and made himself live by his own rules.

Encouraging conversation gives you permission to encourage solitude. Give yourself and others permission to think—sometimes alone—and provide time and space to do so. A thirty-two-year-old talks about his first job out of business school, working at the financial services company for which he had interned for several summers:

> *Finally, after months of work, it was up to me to get things ready for my boss. It was actually a pretty complex analysis of an acquisition. . . . I really needed to think. But there was no way. The pressures of the phone did not go down, not even a little. It was constant. The messages, constant. Email. I told everyone I was sick. That I had the flu and was contagious. I stayed at home for four days. I just worked. The analysis turned out great. But I couldn't ever have done this job at my job.*

His situation is not unusual. A HeartTech engineer says, "If you just go to a conference room, that usually isn't enough privacy because they have glass walls—sometimes people will knock and come in." Other employees agree that it is hard to find a place for quiet reflection. At HeartTech, most people work in an open floor plan that allows for little privacy. They say that to do their "real" work they have to stay at home, take sick days, stay late at night, or "hide out" on the job. At HeartTech, "hiding" means finding out-of-the-way places in company headquarters where people feel they won't be found. One engineer explains to me that when she needs to think, she works under a desk.

I talk about the under-the-desk hideaway with one of HeartTech's architectural staff who knows all about it and is designing hiding spaces as part of the basic office plan. For now, employees are inventive. "In my group," says one thirty-two-year-old engineer, "we put on headphones not just to keep noise out, but to signal when it is acceptable to talk to us." When I visit with his team, they describe different ways of wearing earphones that signal how much privacy one desires. Earphones fully in ears: do not disturb. Earphones in one ear: can be disturbed but only for work. Earphones partly in ears: can be disturbed because I'm working on routine matters. But the group admits that even fully engaged earphones will not reliably get you undisturbed time. When you really need to concentrate, everyone agrees, you should probably stay home. There is an alternative: We can create environments where we expect that people will work uninterrupted, a "quiet car" for productivity.

Address the anxiety of disconnection. We work better together when we can also work alone. And we work best alone when we are undistracted. But studies show that on average, an office worker is distracted (electronically) every three minutes and that it takes an average of twenty-three minutes to get back on track. It's hard to break this cycle because when we get used to interruptions, we learn to interrupt ourselves as well. It's what has become most comfortable. The Fortune 500 vice-president became anxious at a quiet desk. It's more familiar to be in a state of agitated calm: distracted and unproductive.

I have said that if we don't teach our children to be alone, they will only know how to be lonely. If we don't teach our employees to be alone, they will only know how to be isolated. And frantic. The most successful managers know how to model an approach to business that includes disconnecting. When an employee says, "My manager . . . is like Twitter: reactive, always on—her mind responds like a feed," that manager is not demonstrating that she understands the importance of solitude for creativity and productivity. She herself may not have the capacity to be still.

We need to encourage the capacity for a solitude that is not isolating.

The Boston Consulting Group, a large international firm, tried an experiment in disconnection. It started small. One case team was given what the experimenters called predictable time off (PTO)—"afternoons or evenings totally disconnected from work and wireless devices, agreed-upon email blackout times, or uninterrupted work blocks that allow for greater focus." But the time off was coupled with weekly face-to-face meetings. There, the case team discussed its progress toward its business goals as well as any personal or professional effects of the time-off program. They had a place, a sociable place, to address the anxiety of disconnection. Sociability increases productivity and creativity. But so does the ability to have privacy when you need it.

Those involved in the PTO experiment reported more job satisfaction, were happier with their work-life balance, and were more excited to go to work in the morning than other employees. BCG turned the experiment into a global initiative that after four years involved more than nine hundred teams in thirty countries.

Support the first steps toward solitude. Recall that the "pilot in the cockpit" did not retreat from the sociability of the law office to be alone. He withdrew to his network. Managers can make it clear that they consider solitude the partner to creativity and collaboration, the place where new thinking begins. But if you have grown up always connected, developing the capacity for solitude requires support. If you grew up in the world of "I share, therefore I am," you may not have confidence that you have a thought unless you are sharing it.

Good management in the twenty-first century asks us to help our employees learn to tolerate the anxiety of being left alone long enough to think their own thoughts. If people always look to others for validation, they don't develop the confidence to develop creatively. This is one reason why meditation has become so popular in business settings. It encourages people to sit with themselves. It is a path—but not the only path—to becoming comfortable with yourself in a hyperconnected world.

A Drink and a Handshake

As I've researched this book, I've spoken to hundreds of business-people and I always ask this question: "When, in your business, do you need to have a face-to-face conversation? When will electronic conversation not do?"

Answers are forthcoming and with very little hesitation: You need face-to-face conversation to establish trust, to sell something, and to close the deal. One executive says that you need it when you have to get to the "root cause of the problem." You need to talk face-to-face when someone has lied to you. Sometimes people answer by telling a story of using an email in one of these situations and things not going well.

Professionals in service industries are particularly interested in this question. The success of lawyers, accountants, consultants, and bankers depends on being able to say that they do something different than all the other practitioners in their field. They don't want their services turned into commodities. The best way to avoid being seen as a commodity is to offer a relationship. And that takes conversation.

Janeen Hilmar, a forty-year-old manager at ReadyLearn, expresses this anxiety about commodification by using an analogy to a Disney film. "In *The Incredibles*," she says, "the evil guy wants to get rid of all the superheroes because if everyone is special then no one will be. And that, to me, is the crux. . . . If you can't differentiate yourself, then all this technology just makes us go faster, but it kind of makes us anonymous; it makes us all the same."

The fear of being commoditized is one of Audrey Lister's anxieties about the future of her law firm. She fears that if young associates don't form relationships, their product will be indistinguishable from the lawyers across the street. "And the lawyers across the street are very, very good," Lister says. "You keep clients because of the trust you build over years of face-to-face meetings, not because you write them emails."

This is the philosophy around which John Borning, the CEO of a large Los Angeles security firm, built his business. When business advisers urged him to expand his successful company across the country, he decided that being able to meet with and personally understand the needs of his clients was what gave him a competitive advantage in a crowded marketplace. But it is Borning who reminds me that sometimes, no matter what you do, you can feel like a commodity because all of a sudden someone treats you like one—for example, by turning down a conversation. During our meeting, he says that he needs to step away for a few minutes to take a call. When he returns, perhaps ten minutes later, he apologizes. He has just closed a big deal and that was his new partner on the line. But Borning looks upset rather than celebratory.

He tries to explain what's bothering him: His new partner works only a few blocks away. Borning had suggested that they meet for drinks or dinner after work that day or later in the week. He wants to toast their success and plan first steps. His colleague declined and didn't suggest another meeting. Borning reports their exchange: "He said to me, 'Let's just paper this.'"

Borning says something about the complexity of the business relationship they are about to launch. He is not content. He is already imagining endless emails from a partner who doesn't want to begin their collaboration with a drink and a handshake.

The Path Forward

The Public Square

What Do We Forget When
We Talk Through Machines?

You go on a website, you send in your money—that satisfied your requirement for being in the conversation.

—A PARTICIPANT IN THE ONLINE MOVEMENT #STOPKONY

L ife on our new digital landscape challenges us as citizens. Although the web provides incomparable tools to inform ourselves and mobilize for action, when we are faced with a social problem that troubles us, we are tempted to retreat to what I would call the online real. There, we can choose to see only the people with whom we agree. And to share only the ideas we think our followers want to hear.

There, things are simpler. Or rather, we can make them appear to be. And in that world we have called friction-free, we are used to the feeling of getting things done—generations have now grown up with the pleasures of mastering a game or a "level" and getting to a new screen. This history of easy dispatch is only one way that digital life shapes a new public self. It conditions us to see the world as a collection of crises calling for immediate action. In this context, it is easy to skip necessary conversations. What led to the problem? Who are the stakeholders? What is the situation on the ground? For on the ground there is never a simple fix, only friction, complexity, and history.

When the world of the computer was new, I used the metaphor of a second self to describe what was on our screens, because I observed how people defined themselves in the mirror of the machine. They looked at their computer desktops and felt ownership. The desktop was itself a new way to confirm their identities through the applications they had chosen, the content they had created and curated. This continues, of course. But now there is a parallel and less transparent movement. Now we know that our life online creates a digital double because we took actions (we don't know which) that are acted on by algorithms (we don't know how). Our life has been "mined" for clues to our desires. But when our screens suggest our desires back to us, they often seem like broken mirrors.

A State of Emergency

E lizabeth, the economics graduate student who struggled with multitasking, tells the story of her involvement in online politics. In 2012, online activists—a group called Invisible Children, Inc.—publicized the atrocities of Joseph Kony, head of a militant group with operations in Uganda, South Sudan, the Democratic Republic of Congo, and the Central African Republic. Invisible Children made a thirty-minute video that highlighted Kony's use of child soldiers. The video instructed people to send money in return for signs that had Kony's face on them. On April 20, in a program called "Cover the Night," the signs were to be placed on lawns and in community buildings. The organizers said that this would make Kony "famous" and would exert the moral pressure that would end his reign of terror.

Released on March 5, 2012, by July 2012 the video had over 91 million views on YouTube and over 18 million on Vimeo. In the days following its release, 58 percent of people aged eighteen through twenty-nine said that they had heard about it. Elizabeth was living in the United States when the video came out. She felt connected to the tragedy of the Kony story and became involved in the online movement.

Elizabeth's mother is a lawyer from Nairobi; her father, an American, met her when he was in the Peace Corps. Elizabeth has always felt both tied to Africa and at a distance from it—she always wanted to do more, but never saw an opportunity. The Kony action felt like a chance. She was optimistic about its promise and annoyed, almost uncomprehending, at the skepticism of her African friends, who did not believe that people really cared about what was going in Africa. They distinguished curiosity—enough curiosity to watch a video— from significant concern. And indeed, on the appointed day, few people stepped out into the physical world to put up their signs. Elizabeth sums up what she learned from this experience: "You go on a website, you send in your money—that satisfies your requirement for being in the conversation. You show solidarity with a movement by going online, and then, that's it."

The Kony video itself provides ways to understand the ultimate inaction. The video voice-over states as its premise that social media is a political idea that will change the world:

> *Right now there are more people on Facebook than there were on the planet two hundred years ago. Humanity's greatest desire is to belong and connect. And now we hear each other, we see each other . . . we share what we love, and it reminds us what we all have in common. . . . And this connection is changing the way the world works. Governments are trying to keep up . . . now we can taste the freedom.*

Freedom to what? The narrator of the video says, "Our goal is to change the conversation of our culture." It encouraged people to feel that they are doing just that when they post a video online, or "like" a cause, or buy a sign. Or go to a Twitter feed—here, it was #StopKony.

There is nothing wrong with doing these things. They build awareness for your cause. But the difference between online support and putting up a real sign on your real lawn is this: With the physical sign you might have had to confront a person in your neighborhood who might have asked, "What are we supposed to do next about Kony? What is your commitment? What is the plan?" (As of this writing, Kony's activities continue and the group that organized the website has dissolved.)

Friendship Politics: Things to Buy and Click On

The Kony 2012 video describes a "friendship model" for politics: "The people of the world see each other and can protect each other. . . . Arresting Joseph Kony will prove that the world we live in has new rules, that the technology that has brought our planet together is allowing us to respond to the problems of our *friends*." So, this is the new ideal scenario: In the Facebook world, we friend, we share, and those in political power ultimately surrender.

Why should power surrender? According to an artist interviewed in the Kony video, power will be shaken by the simple tools of friendship. He says, referring to the promotional materials and the very sharing of the video, "Here are really simple tools. Go out and rock it."

Elizabeth is chastened. As she sees it now, sharing warm feelings gave people the illusion that they were doing politics. The experience left her thinking that there are no "simple tools"—no things to buy, no links to click on—that can fix a problem as difficult as what Kony represents. The #StopKony action got people talking. But it did not begin to transfer their online "likes" to other actions. Expressions of interest in the physical world—for example, giving a few dollars to a cause when there is a neighborhood charity drive—can also lead to a dissipation of interest when the person who asked for money is no longer at your door. The difference, for Elizabeth, is that the scale of the online declarations (so many millions of likes!) was deceiving. It made her think that something important was happening.

For Elizabeth, the most important lesson of her Kony experience was that the connections you form with people you don't know have significant limitations. They are good for getting people talking but not effective in getting them to do much else. She was intoxicated by the feeling of being part of a vibrant and growing movement. But the website couldn't get people to put real signs on real lawns. It couldn't get people to declare themselves to their physical neighbors.

It was a lesson, although Elizabeth didn't put it in these terms, in what sociologists call the power of strong and weak ties. Weak ties are friends of friends or casual acquaintances. Strong ties are people you know and trust. They are people with whom you are likely to have a long history of face-to-face conversation. So Facebook connections, the kinds of conversations we have online, and in general what we mean by Internet "friending" all draw on the power of weak ties.

There are those who see the conversations of the Internet as a direct source of political change. Mark Pfeifle, a former U.S. national security adviser, wrote after the 2009 uprising in Iran, "Without Twitter, the people of Iran would not have felt empowered and confident to stand up for freedom and democracy," and called for Twitter to be nominated for the Nobel Peace Prize. When the demonstrations in Tehran began, the State Department asked Twitter not to perform scheduled maintenance operations so as not to take such a powerful political tool out of the hands of the protesters. We are, naturally, thrilled by the possibilities of a new, efficient activism.

But what do we forget when we talk through machines? We are tempted to forget the importance of face-to-face conversation, organization, and discipline in political action. We are tempted to forget that political change is often two steps forward and one step back. And that it usually takes a lot of time.

Malcolm Gladwell, writing about the strengths and limitations of social media in politics, contrasts online activism with what was needed during the American civil rights movement and comes to this formulation: If you are in a conversation with someone you don't know well—and these are most of your web contacts—the basic rule is to ask little. As in the Kony 2012 example, web activism works when you are asked to watch a video, give a thumbs-up, or buy a poster. Most recently, a fun gesture—dumping a bucket of ice on your head and asking a friend to do the same (and hopefully send a donation to the ALS Foundation)—has raised over a hundred million dollars for this cause. The power of weak ties is awesome. Quite literally, it inspires awe.

But if you want to take on political authority, says Gladwell, if you want to take those risks, you need ties of deeper trust, deeper history.

You will have moved beyond gestures and donations; you will need to reach consensus, set goals, think strategically, and have philosophical direction. Lives will depend on your deliberations. Perhaps your own life. You will need a lot of long conversations.

To make this point, Gladwell tells the story of the 1960 Woolworth's lunch counter sit-in that opened a new chapter in the civil rights movement. It was something that a group of friends had discussed for nearly a month. The first young black man who asked to be served a cup of coffee at the lunch counter "was flanked by his roommate and two good friends from high school." They had the strongest of ties. They needed these to organize against violent opposition, to change tactics, and to stay the course.

The discussions about what politics on the web can accomplish bring me back to a seemingly interminable political meeting during my college days in the late 1960s. A friend, trying to be witty, quoted George Orwell (and then was corrected on the spot by an English major, who said that it was really Oscar Wilde): "The trouble with socialism is that it takes too many evenings." Social networks enable a new fantasy: that online, even socialism can take a shortcut. But it is only that, a fantasy.

Politics still needs meetings that are meetings. It still needs conversations that require listening, conversations in which you are prepared to learn that a situation is more complex than you thought. You might want to change your mind. This is what our current political landscape discourages. There is a lot of conversation—both online and off—in which opponents broadcast prepared sound bites. There is a lot of staged conversation. You can avoid challenging conversations on and off the web. The web just makes it easier.

As Elizabeth sees it now, what she did with her friends during the heady days of #StopKony seems to have satisfied many people's requirements for political "action." Yet in her view, nothing got done. Hers is a story about activity at a frantic pace: a response to a crisis, followed by disillusion.

Catastrophe Culture

From the earliest days of mobile culture, it was understood—outside the context of flirting—that if you receive a call or a text, you are expected to respond. It might be an emergency. This was an etiquette that did not defer to considerations of what once would have been considered "politeness." For the new rules disrupt dinner, sleep, business meetings, and intimate conversations. We've seen college students leave classrooms to find quiet spaces in bathroom stalls to respond to text messages from friends. And we've seen how, among young people, the idea of immediate access to friends on a phone easily crosses over into a language of emergencies.

Children are quick to use the term *emergency* for everything they hope their phones will protect them from. So many of the young people I spoke with seem to be waiting for an emergency. It could be a personal emergency. But there could be another Katrina, another 9/11. The grid could crash. The story about life as emergencies is about how people, especially young people, develop a fretful self.

If you see life as a stream of emergencies, this frames your life narrative. Indeed, Twitter itself followed one of its co-founders' early enthusiasm for police scanners. You learn that framing things as emergencies gets attention, including attention from your friends. In a world where even middle schoolers say they can't handle the number of messages they receive, telling a friend "It's an emergency" bumps you to the top of the list.

The association of cell phones and emergencies began in earnest on September 11, 2001. On that day, schoolchildren were placed in basement shelters without public phones and their parents vowed that "never again" would they be so disconnected. Their children would have cell phones. When I talk with a circle of fourteen New England college students who remember being in grade school on that day, it is clear that for them, the world changed on 9/11, and in some sense, it hasn't changed back. These students talk about life in a "catastrophe culture." One senior, who says she has "always slept with her phone," comments, "Every channel, every day, the news is dominated by catastrophe."

The students in the circle of fourteen expand on this: As they see it, the media supports a view of the world as a series of emergencies that we can take on, one by one. Events that have a long social and political history are presented as special, unusual, "unthinkable" events: massive oil spills, gun violence against elementary school children and their teachers, extreme weather—for the most part, all are represented as catastrophes. You know you are thinking in terms of catastrophe if your attention is riveted on the short term. In catastrophe culture, everyone feels part of a state of emergency but our agitation is channeled to donating money and affiliating with a website.

When you have an emergency, problems are there to be dealt with on an ad hoc basis. Even problems that involve global climate change or disregard for critical infrastructure are covered by the media as disasters that need disaster relief. You turn something that has a politics and a pattern into something that needs an immediate response but not necessarily an analysis. A catastrophe doesn't seem to require legislation. It needs balm and prayers.

To the circle of fourteen, life in a catastrophe culture suggests that you cope through connecting. Faced with a situation that you experience as an emergency, you want to use social media to huddle with your friends.

A twenty-three-year-old who was in middle school during 9/11 says, "Most of the emergencies that are broadcast on the media, you can't do anything about. There's no action you know how to take that would improve the actual circumstances." This does much to explain how the fretful self navigates the media stream of bad news: We learn about something, get anxious, and connect online.

Catastrophes have the ring of an act of God. They happen to us and we can't see them coming. When terrorism is presented as a calamity, and it is, it is presented as separate from the history that created it, so that it comes to be more like a natural disaster, a state of evil, rather than something that can be addressed by politics or through a reconsideration of its historical roots. When terror is treated as a natural disaster, all we can do about it is kill terrorists.

When you name something a catastrophe, there is nothing much to say. If you confront a situation that you see as shaped by human actions, there is plenty to say. You are in a position to demand accountability. You need to understand causes. You are considering action. You need to have a conversation. Many.

It is easier to face an emergency than to have those difficult conversations. When we go into crisis mode, we give ourselves permission to defer the kinds of conversations that politics requires. And right now, our politics requires conversations, too long deferred, about being a self and a citizen in the world of big data.

Room to Think in a World of Big Data

On our new data landscape, conversations that we traditionally have thought of as private—talking on the phone, sending email and texts—are actually shared with corporations that claim ownership over our data because they have provided us with the tools to communicate. Wherever we let our gaze fall online, we leave a trace that is now someone else's data. Insofar as we soul-search when we search the web and let our minds wander as we wonder what to read, what to buy, what ideas intrigue us, these introspective activities, too, belong to the company that facilitates our search. It mines them for data it finds useful now and saves them for what it might find useful in the future. For all of this information exists independently of us and is in a state, in parts and slices, to be sold to third parties. And outside this world of commercial transactions, we've learned that our government, too, feels that it has a claim on listening in.

Over time, living with an electronic shadow begins to feel so natural that it seems to disappear. Mark Zuckerberg, founder and CEO of Facebook, has said, "Privacy is no longer a relevant social norm." Well, privacy may not be convenient for the social network, but what is intimacy without privacy? What is democracy without privacy? Is there free thought without privacy?

The World Without Privacy

My grandparents knew how to talk about this. At length. When I was ten, and my grandmother thought I was old enough to understand, she took me to the main public library in Brooklyn, a great, imposing structure at Grand Army Plaza. I already had a library card that I used at our local library, a few minutes' walk from our home. But now we were going to the big library.

My grandmother made a picnic lunch—chicken sandwiches on rye bread and lemonade—and we sat on the concrete-and-wood benches of the Prospect Park parade grounds. The conversation turned to the library "rules." My grandmother wanted me to understand that I could take out any book. But the books I chose would be a secret between me and the library. No one had a right to know the list of books I read. It was like the privacy of our mailbox. Both protected what I would call *mindspace*. It was crucial to why she was so glad to be raising her family in America.

My grandmother had explained to me that in the Europe of her parents, the government used the mail to spy on people. Here, it was a protected space. (Clearly, my grandmother was less than informed about the excesses of J. Edgar Hoover, but she had taken comfort from the demise of Senator Joseph McCarthy.) We had talked about the privacy of mailboxes from when I was very young; indeed, as I remember it, the morning ritual of going down to get the mail gave my grandmother a new chance—almost every day—to comment on the reassuring mailboxes.

But the secrecy of my book list was something we didn't talk about until later. She clearly saw it as a more subtle civics lesson: how to explain to a child that no one should ever be able to hold what I read against me. Indeed, no one had the right to know what I was reading.

My grandmother's reverence for the American mailbox and library was her deepest expression of patriotism. And mindspace was central to that patriotism. From my grandparents' perspective, as second-generation Americans in the Brooklyn working class, being able to think and communicate in private meant that you could disagree with your employer and make a private decision about whether you were going to join a union. When making this decision, you would be wise to read union literature in private. Otherwise you might be threatened or fired before you got to your decision. And you needed time to let your ideas jell. You needed privacy to change your mind about important matters.

During the televised confirmation hearings for Supreme Court justice Clarence Thomas, the question came up as to whether Anita Hill's testimony against Thomas would be supported if it could be shown that he was a regular viewer of pornography. Did he regularly check pornography out from his local video store? Hill's lawyers wanted those records to be entered as testimony. I believed Anita Hill; I wanted those video records to support her account of Thomas's vulgarity and harassment. But his advocates argued that video store records and the list of the books one withdraws from a public library should get the same protection. Clarence Thomas had a right to his mindspace. He won that round and I considered it a round that my grandmother would have wanted him to win.

We make our technologies and they make and shape us. I learned to be an American citizen at the mailboxes in an apartment lobby in Brooklyn. And my understanding of the mindspace that democracy requires was shaped by how things worked at the public library. I did not know where to take my daughter, now twenty-four, as she grew up with the Internet.

She had to learn that her email is not protected. And although her library books are still private, what she reads online is not. She shows me how she tries to protect her privacy—for example, on social media apps, she never uses her real name but rather multiple other names, a protective habit of a generation that learned to avoid predators on Facebook by not using real names. But she knows that anyone sophisticated and determined would be able to find her. And when it comes to her cell phone, she gives up all privacy for convenience. She wants to use maps, so the

GPS on her phone is turned on. This means that her phone leaves a trail of bread crumbs detailing her location. And the system knows her friends, what she searches for, what she reads.

When she was eighteen, my daughter showed me a program called Loopt. Like Find My Friends, it uses the GPS capability of the iPhone to show the location of friends. She thought it seemed creepy but told me that it would be hard to keep it off her phone if all her friends had it. "They would think I had something to hide."

And just recently, because I learned it just recently, I had to tell her that if she tries to protect her privacy by using browser settings designed to hide her identity, it may well activate greater surveillance of her online behavior. These days, the desire for privacy is considered suspicious and limits your ability to have it. This is distressing when I think of the lessons I learned at the public library. Wasn't the need for private mindspace why we protected the library books in the first place?

A generation grows up assuming nothing is private and offering faint resistance. Only a few years ago, a sixteen-year-old tried to reassure me that it somehow didn't matter that her email wasn't private by saying, "Who would care about my little life?" It was not an empowering mantra. And she turned out to be wrong. A lot of people care about her "little life."

Surveillance Creates the Digital Double

When the Internet was new, we thought of it as a frontier. Historian of technology Evgeny Morozov points out that the advertising tagline for Microsoft's Internet Explorer was "Where do you want to go today?" These days, our online practices put us in a world where the real question is "What do you have to *give* today?" What information about yourself will you offer up today? We exist alongside digital representations of ourselves—digital doubles—that are useful to different parties at different times, or for some, at a time to be determined. The digital self is archived forever.

Gradually, we have come to learn all of this. And in the post-Snowden years, we have learned more—that the calls, locations, and online searches of ordinary Americans are monitored. But almost everything about this process remains as secret as possible, shrouded under the mantle of national security or the claim of proprietary interests. Exactly what is taken? In what form? How long is it kept? What is it used for? What most people have come to understand is that this is out of their hands.

What happens to conversation in these circumstances? One thing I've already noted is that people tend to forget their circumstances. This is one of the great paradoxes of digital conversation: It feels private despite the fact that you are onstage. If you are on Gmail, your email is searched for clues for how to best sell to you, but for the individual, the experience of being on email remains intimate. You face a glowing screen and you feel alone. The experience of digital communication is out of sync with its reality. Online, you are under a kind of surveillance.

The Self of Self-Surveillance

Previously, when we thought about surveillance, we thought about the effects of being watched all the time. The English philosopher Jeremy Bentham had a model for it. He called it the panopticon. It is a way to construct a building: You put a guard at the hub of a spoked wheel. Since those who are living in the spokes don't know when the guard is looking at them, they act as if he always is, because he always could be. They put themselves on good behavior, conforming to what they think of as the norm.

It works for prisons; it works for asylums. The French sociologist Michel Foucault took Bentham's image of panopticon surveillance and made it relevant to thinking about being a citizen of the modern state. For Foucault, the task of the modern state is to reduce its need for surveillance by creating a citizenry that is always watching itself. With cameras on most corners, you don't misbehave even if you don't know if a camera is on any particular corner. It might be. This is the self of self-surveillance. And it operates on the digital landscape. If you know that your texts and email are not private, you watch out for what you write. You internalize the censor.

Now, participation in the life of the data-gathering web has given "self-surveillance" a new twist. We do more than actively give up information by reporting our preferences or by taking surveys or by filling out forms. *These days, the most important data to those who watch us are the data trails we leave as we go about the business of our daily lives.* We feed databases as we shop, chat, watch movies, and make travel plans. Tracking one's fitness, keeping in touch with friends on social media, using a smartphone—all of these make surveillance and social participation seem like the same thing. Every new service on our smartphone, every new app, potentially offers up a new "species" of data to our online representation. The goal for those who make the apps is to link surveillance with the feeling that we are cared for. If our apps take "care" of us, we are not focused on what they take from us.

In the world as Foucault analyzed it, when you put cameras on street corners, you want people to notice them and build a self that takes surveillance as a given. Knowing that the cameras are there makes you "be good" all by yourself. But in our new data regime, the goal is for everyone to be unaware, or at least to forget in the moment, that surveillance exists. The regime works best if people feel free to "be themselves." That way they can provide "natural data" to the system.

So these days, while I might have only a general sense of where I've spent my day shopping, my iPhone knows, and this means that Apple knows and Google knows—a development I was not thinking about when I was thrilled to discover that, with GPS, my phone could double as an interactive map and I would never have to get lost again.

Shaped by the System: Living in the Bubble

Each of us who "feeds" the system ends up being shaped by it, but in a very different way than the person caught in the panopticon. We don't so much conform because we fear the consequences of being caught out in deviant behavior; rather, we conform because what is shown to us online is shaped by our past interests. The system presents us with what it believes we will buy or read or vote for. It places us in a particular world that constrains our sense of what is out there and what is possible.

For any query, search engines curate results based on what they know about you, including your location and what kind of computer you are using. So, if you do a search about the Ukraine and opposition movements don't come up, this may be because an algorithm has decided that you don't want to see them. This means that you won't learn (at least not then) that they exist. Or, by the logic of the algorithm, you may be presented with only certain political advertisements. You may not learn that a candidate who seems "moderate" in national advertising sends anti–gun control advertising to other people, just not to you.

The web promises to make our world bigger. But as it works now, it also narrows our exposure to ideas. We can end up in a bubble in which we hear only the ideas we already know. Or already like. The philosopher Allan Bloom has suggested the cost: "Freedom of the mind requires not only, or not even especially, the absence of legal constraints but the presence of alternative thoughts. The most successful tyranny is not the one that uses force to assure uniformity, but the one that removes awareness of other possibilities."

Once you have a glimmer—and you only need a glimmer—of how this works, you have reason to believe that what the web shows you is a reflection of what you have shown it. So, if anti-abortion advertisements appear on your social media newsfeed, you may well ask what you did to put them there. What did you search or write or read? Little by little, as new things show up on the screen, you watch passively while the web actively constructs its version of you.

Karl Marx described how a simple wooden table, once turned into a commodity, danced to its own ghostlike tune. Marx's table, transcendent, "not only stands with its feet on the ground . . . it stands on its head, and evolves out of its wooden brain, grotesque ideas far more wonderful than 'table-turning' ever was." These days, it is our digital double that dances with a life of its own.

Advertising companies use it to build more targeted marketing campaigns. Insurance companies use it to apportion health benefits. From time to time, we are startled to get a view of who the algorithms that work over our data think we are. Technology writer Sara Watson describes such a moment. One day, Watson receives an invitation, a targeted advertisement, to participate in a study of anorexia in a Boston-area hospital. Watson says, "Ads *seem* trivial. But when they start to question whether I'm eating enough, a line has been crossed."

Watson finds the request to participate in the anorexia study personal and assaultive, because she is stuck with the idea that she made the invitation appear. But how? Is the study targeting women with small grocery bills? Women who buy diet supplements? We are talking through machines to algorithms whose rules we don't understand.

For Watson, what is most disorienting is that she doesn't understand how the algorithm reached its conclusion about her. And how can she challenge a black box? For the algorithms that build up your digital double are written across many different platforms. There is no place where you can "fix" your double. There is no place to make it conform more exactly to how you want to be represented. Watson ends up confused: "It's hard to tell whether the algorithm doesn't know us at all, or if it actually knows us better than we know ourselves." Does the black box know something she doesn't?

In conversations with others over a lifetime, you get to see yourself as others see you. You get to "meet yourself" in new ways. You get to object on the spot if somebody doesn't "get you." Now we are offered a new experience: *We are asked to see ourselves as the collection of things we are told we should want, as the collection of things we are told should interest us.* Is this a tidier version of identity?

Building narratives about oneself takes time, and you never know if they are done or if they are correct. It is easier to see yourself in the mirror of the machine. You have mail.

Thinking in Public

Thoreau went to Walden to try to think his own thoughts, to remove himself from living "too thickly"—how he referred to the constant chatter around him in society. These days, we live more "thickly" than Thoreau could ever have imagined, bombarded by the opinions, preferences, and "likes" of others. With the new sensibility of "I share, therefore I am," many are drawn to the premise that thinking together makes for better thinking.

Facebook's Zuckerberg thinks that thinking is a realm where together is always better. If you share what you are thinking and reading and watching, you will be richer for it. He says that he would always "rather go to a movie with [his] friends" because then they can share their experience and opinions. And if his friends can't be there physically, he can still have a richer experience of the movie through online sharing. Neil Richards, a lawyer, cross-examines this idea. Always sharing with friends has a cost.

> It means we'll always choose the movie they'd choose and won't choose the movie we want to see if they'd make fun of it. . . . If we're always with our friends, we're never alone, and we never get to explore ideas for ourselves. Of course, the stakes go beyond movies and extend to reading, to web-surfing, and even thinking.

And even thinking. Especially thinking. One student, who was used to blogging as a regular part of her academic program for her master's degree, changed styles when she changed universities and began her doctoral studies. In her new academic program blogging was discouraged. She comments that, looking back, the pressure to continually publish led to her thinking of herself as a brand. She wanted everything she wrote to conform to her confirmed identity. And blogging encouraged her to write about what she could write about best. It discouraged risk taking. Now, writing privately, she feels more curious. Research shows that people who use social media are less willing to share their opinions if they think their followers and friends might disagree with them. People need private space to develop their ideas.

Generations of Americans took as self-evident the idea that private space was essential to democratic life. My grandmother had a civics lesson ready when she talked about the privacy of my library books. In order to be open to the widest range of ideas, I had to feel protected when making my reading choices. "Crowdsourcing" your reading preferences, says Richards, drives you "to conformity and the mainstream by social pressures."

Objects-Not-to-Think-With

Cognitive science has taught us the several qualities that make it easy not to think about something you probably don't want to think about anyway. You don't know when it is going to "happen." You don't know exactly what it means for it to "happen." And there is no *immediate* cause and effect between actions you might take and consequences related to the problem.

So, for example, if you don't want to think about climate change, you are able to exploit the psychological distance between a family vacation in an SUV and danger to the planet. A similar sense of distance makes it easy to defer thinking about the hazards of "reading in public," the risks of living with a digital double, and threats to privacy on the digital landscape.

Here is Lana, a recent college graduate, thinking aloud about how she *doesn't think* about online privacy:

Cookies? I think that companies make it hard to understand what they are really doing. Even calling them cookies seems pretty brilliant. It makes it sound cute, like it's nothing. Just helpful to you. Sweet. And it is helpful to get better ads or better services for the things you want. But how do they work and what are they going to do with all that they know about you? I don't know and I don't like where this is going. But I'm not going to think about this until something really bad happens concretely.

Lana is uneasy that data are being collected about her, but she's decided that right now she's not going to worry about it. She says that when she was younger she was "creeped out" by Facebook having so much information about her, but now she deals with her distrust of Facebook by keeping her posts light, mostly about parties and social logistics. She doesn't want what she puts on Facebook "coming back to haunt me."

More than this, Lana says, she "is glad not to have anything controversial on my mind, because I can't think of any online place where it would be safe to have controversial conversations." And she would want to have any conversation online because that is where she is in touch with all her friends. Lana describes a circle that encourages silence: If she had controversial opinions she would express them online, so it's good that she has none, because what she would say would not be private in this medium. In fact, Lana's circle has one more reinforcing turn: She says it's good that she has nothing controversial to say because she would be saying it online and everything you say online is kept forever. And that is something she doesn't like at all.

I talk to Lana shortly after her graduation from college in June 2014. In the news are manifestations of disruptive climate change, escalating wars and terrorism, the limitations of the international response to the Ebola epidemic, and significant violence due to racial tensions. There is no lack of things to communicate about "controversially." Yet this very brilliant young woman, beginning a job in finance, is relieved not to have strong opinions on any of this because her medium for expressing them would be online and there is no way to talk "safely" there.

But Lana does not say that she finds any of this a problem. It would be inconvenient to label it that way. If you say something is a problem, that suggests you should be thinking about changing it and Lana is not sure that this is the direction she wants to take her feelings of discontent, at least not now. Right now, as for many others, her line is that "we all are willing to trade off privacy for convenience."

She treats this trade-off as arithmetic—as if, once it's calculated, it doesn't need to be revisited.

Vague on the Details

When I talk to young people, I learn that they are expert at keeping "local" privacy—privacy from each other when they want to keep things within their clique, privacy from parents or teachers who might be monitoring their online accounts; here they use code words, a blizzard of acronyms. But as for how to think about private mindspace on the net, most haven't thought much about it and don't seem to want to. They, like the larger society, are, for the most part, willing to defer thinking about this. We are all helped in this by staying vague on the details.

And the few details we know seem illogical or like half-truths. It is illegal to tap a phone, but it is not illegal to store a search. We are told that our searches are "anonymized," but then, experts tell us that this is not true. Large corporations take our data, which seems to be legal, and the government also wants our data—things such as what we search, whom we text, what we text, whom we call, what we buy.

And it's hard to even learn the rules. I am on the board of the Electronic Freedom Foundation, devoted to privacy rights in digital culture. But it was only in spring 2014 that an email circulated to board members that described how easy it is to provoke the government to put you on a list of those whose email and searches are "fully tracked." For example, you will get on that list if, from outside the United States, you try to use TOR, a method of browsing anonymously online. The same article explained that from within the United States, you will also activate "full tracking" if you try to use alternatives to standard operating systems—for example, if you go to the Linux home page. It would appear that the Linux forum has been declared an "extremist" site.

One of my graduate research assistants has been on that forum because she needed to use annotation software that ran only on Linux. When she reads the communiqué about Linux and full tracking, she is taken aback, but what she says is, "Theoretically I'm angry but I'm not having an emotional response." According to the source we both read, undisputed by the NSA, the content of her email and searches is surveilled. But still, she says, "Who knows what that means. Is it a person? Is it an algorithm? Is it tracking me by my name or my IP address?"

Confused by the details, she doesn't demand further details. Vague understandings support her sense that looking into this more closely can wait. So does the idea that she will be blocked or perhaps singled out for further surveillance if she tries to get more clarity.

One college senior tells me, with some satisfaction, that he has found a way around some of his concerns about online privacy. His strategy: He uses the "incognito" setting on his web browser. I decide that I'll do the same. I change the settings on my computer and go to bed thinking I have surely taken a step in the right direction. But what step have I taken? I learn that with an "incognito" setting I can protect my computer from recording my search history (so that family members, for example, can't check it), but I haven't slowed down Google or anyone else who might want access to it. And there is the irony that articles on how to protect your privacy online often recommend using TOR, but the NSA considers TOR users suspect and deserving of extra surveillance.

I come to understand that part of what sustains apathy is that people think they are being tracked by algorithms whose power will be checked by humans with good sense if the system finds anything that might actually get them into trouble. But we are in trouble together. Interest in Linux as probable cause for surveillance? We're starting not to take ourselves seriously.

My research assistant says she's not worried about her data trail because she sees the government as benign. They're interested in terrorists, not in her. But I persist. Now that my assistant knows she is subject to tracking because of her activity on the Linux forum, will it have a chilling effect on what she says online? Her answer is no, that she will say what she thinks and fight any attempt to use her thoughts against her "if it should ever come to that." But historically, the moments when "it came to that" have usually been moments when it has been hard or too late to take action.

I recall how Lana summed up her thoughts about online privacy: She said she would worry about it "if something bad happens." But we can turn this around and say that something bad *has* happened. We are challenged to draw the line, sometimes delicate, between "personalization" that seems banal (you buy shoes, so you see ads for shoes) and curation that poses larger questions.

In the 2012 presidential election, Facebook looked at random precincts and got people to go to the polls by telling them that their friends had voted. This political intervention was framed as a study, with the following research question: Can social media affect voter turnout? It can. Internet and law expert Jonathan Zittrain has called the manipulation of votes by social media "digital gerrymandering." It is an unregulated threat. Facebook also did a study, a mood experiment, in which some people were shown posts from happy friends and some people were shown posts from unhappy friends to see if this changed their moods. It did. Social media has the power to shape our political actions and emotional lives. We're accustomed to media manipulation—advertising has always tried to do this. But having unprecedented kinds of information about us—from what medications we take to what time we go to bed— allows for unprecedented interventions and intrusions. What is at stake is a sense of a self in control of itself. And a citizenry that can think for itself.

Snowden Changes the Game

I have been talking to high school and college students about online privacy for decades. For years, when young people saw the "results" of online data collection, chiefly through the advertisements that appeared on their screens, it was hard for them to see the problem. The fact that a desirable sneaker or the perfect dress popped up didn't seem like a big deal. But in the years since Edward Snowden's revelations about how the government tracks our data, young people are more able to talk about the problems of data mining, in some measure because it has become associated (at least in their minds) with something easier to think about: spying. What Snowden was talking about seemed enough like old-fashioned spying that it gave people a way into a conversation about the more elusive thing: the incursions of everyday tracking.

So, after the Snowden revelations, high school students would begin a conversation about Snowden and then pivot to "Facebook knowing too much." What did Facebook know? What did Facebook keep? And had they really given it permission to do all this?

Or they would begin a conversation by talking about how they were trying to stay away from Facebook, now a symbol of too much online data collection, and then pivot to Snowden. A different set of issues entirely, but Snowden gave them a handle on their general sense of worry. The worry, in essence: How much does the Internet "know" and what is the Internet going to do about it? After Snowden, the helpful ads on their screens had more of a backstory. Someone, many someones, knows a lot more about them than their sneaker preferences.

And yet it is easy for this conversation to slip away from us. Because just as we start to have it, we become infatuated with a new app that asks us to reveal more of ourselves: We could report our moods to see if there are concerns to address. We could track our resting heart rate or the amount of exercise we get each week. So we offer up data to improve ourselves and postpone the conversation about what happens to the data we share. If someday the fact that we were not careful about our diet in our forties is held against us—when it comes to giving us an insurance rate in our fifties—we will have offered up this data freely.

Instead of pursuing the political conversation, we sign up for another app.

Technology companies will say—and they do—that if you don't want to share your data, don't use their services. If you don't want Google to know what you are searching, don't search on Google. When asked to comment on all that Google knows, its executive chairman said, in essence, that "the way to deal is to just be good."

I have felt for a long time, as a mother and as a citizen, that in a democracy, we all need to begin with the assumption that everyone has something to "hide," a zone of private action and reflection, a zone that needs to be protected despite our techno-enthusiasms. You need space for real dissent. A mental space and a technical space (those mailboxes!). It's a private space where people are free to "not be good." To me, this conversation about technology, privacy, and democracy is not Luddite or too late.

The Nick of Time

In the end, we will be defined not only by what
we create but by what we refuse to destroy.

—JOHN SAWHILL, CONSERVATIONIST

horeau said that when the conversation in his cabin became loud and expansive, he pushed his chairs to its far corners. So to the idea that we might learn about ourselves through algorithms, the most ready answer is to embrace conversations that bring us back to ourselves, our friends, and our communities. As Thoreau would have it, the three chairs together, the room made large.

Thoreau's chairs capture a virtuous circle. We find our voice in solitude, and we bring it to public and private conversations that enrich our capacity for self-reflection. Now that circle has been disrupted; there is a crisis in our capacity to be alone and together. But we are in flight from those face-to-face conversations that enrich our imaginations and shepherd the imagined into the real. There is a crisis in our ability to understand others and be heard.

But we also demonstrate a striking resilience. I am not surprised that a study of children who put their devices away for five days at camp shows that they begin to recover their empathic capacity. In my own experiences observing children at such a camp, I saw how easy it was for them to appreciate—as though for the first time—the value of conversation, with themselves and others.

The campers I met spoke about solitude and empathy. Campers said they were more interested in their summer friends than in their friends at school. They thought the difference was that at home they talk with their friends about what's on their phones; at camp, they talk to each other about what's on their minds.

And as I participated in nightly cabin chats, campers remarked on their deepening relationships with counselors. The camp counselors were offering campers something close to exotic: undivided attention. While on duty, the counselors, too, had taken a break from their phones.

Many campers come back every year to this device-free camp. Several of the returning campers remark that each year they notice that they like themselves better at the end of the summer. They say that what they notice most is that they have become better friends and teammates. Also, they are nicer to their parents.

And they speak frankly about how hard it is to keep up their "camp selves" when they get home. There, family and friends are preoccupied with technology—and it is hard to resist following along.

At camp I learn many lessons. Among them: We don't have to give up our phones, but we have to use them more deliberately. And sometimes, just as deliberately, we need to take a break. I think of how Clifford Nass compared the parts of the brain that process emotion to muscles—they atrophy if not exercised but can be strengthened through face-to-face conversation. Time without our phones is restorative. It provides time to practice.

For most of us, our exercises in conversation will not be at device-free summer camps. Most of the time, we'll reclaim conversation by working to protect sacred spaces, spaces without technology, in our everyday lives. With more experience away from our devices, we'll develop a better sense of when we need solitude and when we need to give each other undivided attention.

As we become comfortable with our own need for "tools down" conversations, we'll learn to ask for them. And we'll take the petitions of others more seriously: when a child needs his parent to listen, when a teacher wants to reach a distracted class, when a business meeting is trying to rectify a serious misunderstanding, when a friend turns to a friend and says, "I want to talk."

Guideposts

People often say to me, "What next?"

Every technology asks us to confront our human values. This is a good thing, because it causes us to reaffirm what they are. From there it is easier to see next steps and guideposts. We are not looking for simple solutions. We are looking for beginnings.

Remember the power of your phone. It's not an accessory. It's a psychologically potent device that changes not just what you do but who you are. Don't automatically walk into every situation with a device in hand: When going to our phones is an option, we find it hard to turn back to each other, even when efficiency or politeness would suggest we do just that. The mere presence of a phone signals that your attention is divided, even if you don't intend it to be. It will limit the conversation in many ways: how you'll listen, what will be discussed, the degree of connection you'll feel. Rich conversations have difficulty competing with even a silent phone. To clear a path for conversation, set aside laptops and tablets. Put away your phone.

Slow down. Some of the most crucial conversations you will ever have will be with yourself. To have them, you have to learn to listen to your own voice. A first step is to slow down sufficiently to make this possible.

Online life has ramped up the volume of what everyone sees on any day and the velocity with which it whizzes by. We are often too busy communicating to think, create, or collaborate. We come to online life with the expectation that we can ask a question and get an almost immediate answer. In order to meet our expectations, we begin to ask simpler questions. We end up dumbing down our communications and this makes it harder to approach complex problems.

Protect your creativity. Take your time and take quiet time. Find your own agenda and keep your own pace. Tutored by technology, we become reactive and transactional in our exchanges because this is what technology makes easy. We all struggle with this. But many successful people I've talked with say that a key to their achievement is that they don't even try to empty their email inbox. They set aside specific times to deal with their most important messages but never let an inbox set their agenda.

So if as a parent or teacher or employer you receive an email request, respond by saying that you need time to *think* about it. This seems a small thing, but it is too rarely done. A thirty-year-old consultant tells me that in her world, this response would be "age-inappropriate." This makes me think that it is time to reconsider our sense of the appropriate in every domain. To respond to an email by saying "I'm thinking" says that you value reflection and you don't let yourself be rushed just because technology can rush you. Emails and texts make quick responses possible; they don't make them wise.

Again and again, I've seen people retreat to screens because only there do they feel they can "keep up" with the pace of machine life. I think of Vannevar Bush and his dream in 1945 that a mechanical "Memex" would free us for the kind of slow creative thinking that only people know how to do. Instead we too often try to speed up to a pace our machines suggest to us. It's time to return to the spirit of Bush's original idea.

We help children slow down by keeping them in touch with materials such as mud and modeling clay. The resistance of the physical fires their imaginations and keeps them grounded. This kind of creativity can be sparked beyond playrooms, classrooms, and parks. And it should happen all through life. At Google, employees come together to work with concrete materials in specially designed spaces known as "garages." The idea is simple: Adults need play as much as children do. Use space and materials to encourage thought, talk, and new ideas. It's an idea that can be brought from corporate spaces into family life.

Create sacred spaces for conversation. In the day-to-day, families carve them out—no devices at dinner, in the kitchen, or in the car. Introduce this idea to children when they are young so that it doesn't spring up as punitive but is set up as a baseline of family culture. It can be an ordinary thing for a mother of a four-year-old to say: "In our family we need time without any electronics to be alone, quietly. And we need time to talk to each other. I don't text in the car while I'm driving. So that makes it a perfect time for us to talk or just look out the window."

Remember that we teach the capacity for solitude by being quiet alongside children who have our attention. Design your environment to protect yourself against unnecessary interruptions. Take a neighborhood walk—alone or with family or friends—without devices. Experiment with an evening or a weekend off the net as a regular part of your routine. Be realistic about how you are going to signal a new attitude about committing focused attention to your children. What children need is to understand your intention and values. If you can't spend two hours with your children in the park without your phone, adjust your plan. Take your children to the park for one hour and give them your full attention.

And just as families need these protected spaces, so do schools and universities and workplaces. Increasingly, there is demand in universities for study and lounge space that is Wi-Fi-free. When we wired the universities, every last room of them, we didn't consider that we were making it harder for students to attend to their peers or their own thoughts. Yet these showed up as unintended consequences. In offices, we can make space for conversation without digital connection; we can trade casual Fridays for conversational Thursdays. Setting aside a space communicates that, in this place, people pay attention to each other. They take a breath.

Think of unitasking as the next big thing. In every domain of life, it will increase performance and decrease stress.

But doing one thing at a time is hard, because it means asserting ourselves over what technology makes easy and over what feels productive in the short term. Multitasking comes with its own high. Our brains crave the fast and unpredictable, the quick hit of the new. We know this is a human vulnerability. Unless we design our lives and technology to work around it, we resign ourselves to diminished performance.

When I talk to managers, parents, and educators, I realize that they are increasingly familiar with the studies that show how multitasking degrades performance. But in practice, I see multitasking everywhere. Unitasking is key to productivity and creativity. Conversation is a human way to practice unitasking.

Talk to people with whom you don't agree. Conversation is inhibited as much by our prejudices as by our distractions. A recent study characterizes the political conversations on social media as a "spiral of silence." People don't want to post opinions on social media that they fear their followers will disagree with. A technology that makes it possible to interact with everyone does not necessarily have everyone interacting. People use the Internet to limit their interactions to those with whom they agree. And social media users are less willing than non-users to discuss their views off-line.

Our reticence to talk to those with opposing opinions extends to the face-to-face world. A recent study shows that college students all across the United States who declare themselves to be committed Republicans or Democrats will not discuss political matters with students on their campus who do not share their views. This means that they will avoid political discussion with those who live down the hall, who share a bathroom. We turn the physical realm into an echo chamber of what we have so easily created online. It's a cozy life, but we risk not learning anything new.

We can do better. We can teach our children to talk to people who disagree with them by modeling these conversations ourselves. We can show them that it helps to begin by talking about how you see causes, reasons, values. Even a small amount of common ground can nurture a conversation.

Obey the seven-minute rule. This is the rule, suggested to me by a college junior, that grows out of the observation that it takes at least seven minutes to see how a conversation is going to unfold. The rule is that you have to let it unfold and not go to your phone before those seven minutes pass. If there is a lull in the conversation, let it be. The seven-minute rule suggests other strategies for a life enriched by solitude, self-reflection, and presence. Learn to see boredom as an opportunity to find something interesting within yourself. Let yourself go there, have your association, and then come back to your train of thought or to the conversation. Our minds work, and sometimes at their best, when we daydream. When you return from reverie, you may be bringing back something deeply pertinent.

Conversation, like life, has silences and boring bits. This bears repeating: It is often in the moments when we stumble and hesitate and fall silent that we reveal ourselves to each other. Digital communication can lead us to an edited life. We should not forget that an unedited life is also worth living.

Challenge a view of the world as apps. The "app generation" is what the psychologists Howard Gardner and Katie Davis called the generation that grew up with phones in hand and apps at the ready. It's a way to describe people who bring an engineering sensibility to everyday life and certainly to their educational experience. The app way of thinking starts with the idea that actions in the world will work like algorithms: Certain actions will lead to predictable results. By this logic, you go to certain schools, you get certain grades, you take certain summer enrichment courses and join certain extracurricular activities, and the app works: You get into an Ivy.

The app way of thinking can show up in friendship as a lack of empathy. Friendships become things to manage; you have a lot of them, and you come to them with a set of tools. At school and work, the app way of thinking can show up as a lack of creativity and innovation. Your options are laid out and you pick from the menu. We've seen middle school teachers facing students who had an instrumental view of friendship and parents who saw school as an app for getting their children into college. From the teachers' point of view, students had no time to dream. No occasion to structure their own time. Or learn about situations that had no certain outcomes.

In school, when the app generation has to deal with unpredictability, they become impatient, anxious, and disoriented. At work, the problems continue. One new manager at HeartTech, the large software company in Silicon Valley, moved there so he could leave engineering and try his hand at management. "I left my previous job because it was too predictable. I wanted to work with unpredictable systems [here he means people]." But he brings old habits with him: "I'm not really used to working with unpredictable systems. I'm not that good at thinking on my toes." He elaborates: "I'm not used to thinking fast with people in front of me . . . the back-and-forth of conversation."

His is a common plight. Engineers who move into management are asked to do a very different kind of work than that in which they were trained. They were groomed for today's scientific attitude toward management, one that encourages research and an instrumental and hard-edged view of the world. But in daily practice, what faces any manager is a life of hard calls, ambiguous situations, and difficult conversations. In the most concrete terms, there are performance reviews, negative feedback, firing people.

A human resources officer at a high-tech firm tells me: "The catchphrase among my peers is that 'engineers will not deliver difficult conversations.'" In the high-tech world, when I raise the topic of conversation, that's the phrase I often hear back.

Difficult conversations require empathic skills and, certainly, "thinking on your toes." Teaching engineers how to have these conversations requires significant coaching. Yet these days, as Gardner and Davis point out, a style of thinking that prefers the predictable extends beyond engineers.

It's not just the engineers who need coaching. As we all accept a more instrumental view of life, *we are all having trouble with difficult conversations.* In that sense, we are all engineers now. Our challenge is to deliver those difficult conversations, the ones that include others and the ones with ourselves.

Choose the right tool for the job. Sometimes we find a technology so amazing—and a smartphone, for example, is so amazing—that we can't stop ourselves from imagining it as a universal tool. One that should, because it is amazing, replace all the tools we had before. But when you replace a conversation with an email just because you can, there is a good chance that you have chosen the wrong tool. Not because email isn't a great tool for some jobs. Just not for all jobs.

There is nothing wrong with texting or email or videoconferencing.

And there is everything right with making them technically better, more intuitive, easier to use. But no matter how good they get, they have an intrinsic limitation: People require eye contact for emotional stability and social fluency. A lack of eye contact is associated with depression, isolation, and the development of antisocial traits such as exhibiting callousness. And the more we develop these psychological problems, the more we shy away from eye contact. Our slogan can be: If a tool gets in the way of our looking at each other, we should use it only when necessary. It shouldn't be the first thing we turn to.

One thing is certain: The tool that is handy is not always the right tool. So an email is often the simplest solution to a business problem, even as it makes the problem worse. A text has become the handy way to end a relationship, even as it upsets and diminishes all participants. As I write this, a new robot has been launched on the market as a companion for your child. It will teach a child to look for understanding from an object that has none to give.

Learn from moments of friction. We've met professionals who feel in conflict about the role technology plays in their lives. An enthusiast for remote work ends up taping the silence in his office and sending the audio file home to his wife. Architects build open workspaces even when they know that the people they design for crave more privacy. Young lawyers don't join their colleagues in the lunchroom even though they know that taking time for these meals would cement lifelong business relationships.

If you find yourself caught in this kind of conflict, pause and reconsider: Is your relationship to technology helping or hindering you? Can you recognize these moments as opportunities for new insight?

Remember what you know about life. We've seen that we learn the capacity for solitude by being "alone with" another. And I've found that if we distract ourselves with technology during these crucial moments, even the most passionate proponents of always-on connection admit to doubt. So, when parents email during a child's bath time or text during a beach walk, the parents may persist in their behavior but they admit they are not happy. They sense they have crossed some line. One father tells me that he takes his phone along when he and his ten-year-old son have a game of catch. The father says, "I can tell it's not as good as when I played catch with my dad." Early in my research I meet a mother who has gotten into the habit of texting while she breast-feeds. She tells me simply, "This is a habit I might want to break." It is a deeply human impulse to step back from these moments that endanger shared solitude.

Shared solitude grounds us. It can bring us back to ourselves and others. For Thoreau, walking was a kind of shared solitude, a way to "shake off the village" and find himself, sometimes in the company of others. In her writing about how people struggle to find their potential, Arianna Huffington notes the special resonance of Thoreau's phrase, for these days we have a new kind of village to shake off. It is most likely to be our digital village, with its demands for performance and speed and self-disclosure.

Huffington reminds us that if we find ourselves distracted, we should not judge ourselves too harshly. Even Thoreau became distracted. He got upset that when walking in the woods, he would sometimes find himself caught up in a work problem. He said, "But it sometimes happens that I cannot easily shake off the village. The thought of some work will run in my head and I am not where my body is—I am out of my senses. . . . What business have I in the woods, if I am thinking of something out of the woods?"

We know the answer to that question. Even if Thoreau's mind did sometimes travel to work or village, he accomplished a great deal on those walks. As in any meditative practice, the mind may wander, but then it comes back to the present, to the breath, to the moment. Even if he became distracted, Thoreau was making room for that. These days, we take so many walks in which we don't look at what is around us—not at the scenery, not at our companions. We are heads-down in our phones. But like Thoreau, we can come back to what is important. We can use our technology, all of our technology, with greater intention. We can practice getting closer to ourselves and other people. Practice may not make perfect. But this is a realm where perfect is not required. And practice always affirms our values, our true north.

Don't avoid difficult conversations. We've seen that beyond our personal and work lives, we are having trouble talking to one another in the public square. In particular, we are having trouble with new questions about privacy and self-ownership.

I've said that these matters are examples of objects-not-to-think-with. They are characterized by a lack of simple connections between actions and consequences. There is a danger, but it is hard to define the exact damage you fear. Moreover, it is hard to know if the damage has already been done. These questions vex us and we are tempted to turn our attention elsewhere. Remember Lana, who was happy she didn't have anything controversial to say so she wouldn't have to confront that online life gave her no place to say it. She didn't want to have the conversation.

To encourage these conversations, it helps to avoid generalities. We claim not to be interested in online privacy until we are asked about specifics—phone searches without warrants, or data collection by the National Security Agency. Then it turns out we are very interested indeed.

One reason we avoid conversations about online privacy is that we feel on shaky moral ground. If you complain that Google is keeping your data forever and this doesn't seem right, you are told that when you opened your Google account, you agreed to terms that gave Google the right to do just this. And to read the content of your mail. And to build a digital double. And to sell its contents. Since you didn't actually read the terms of agreement, you begin the conversation disempowered. It seems that by agreeing to be a consumer you gave away rights that you might want to claim as a citizen.

But then, if we feel that our digital doubles incorrectly represent us or block us from the information we want, we don't know how to object. Should we be talking with the companies that track and commodify us? Should our conversation be with the government, who might be in a position to regulate some of this activity? Yet the government, too, is claiming its right to our data. We are shut down by not knowing an appropriate interlocutor, just as we are shut down by not knowing exactly what they "have" on us, or how to define our rights.

But just because these conversations are difficult doesn't mean they are impossible. They are necessary and they have begun. One conversation is about how to develop a realistic notion of privacy today. It clearly can't be what it was before. But that doesn't mean that citizens can live in a world without privacy rights, which is where conversations end up when they begin with the overwhelmed stance, "This is too hard to think about."

One proposal from the legal community would shift the discussion from the language of privacy rights to the language of control over one's own data. In this approach, the companies that collect our data would have responsibilities to protect it—the way doctors and lawyers are bound to protect the information we share with them. In both cases, the person who provides the data retains control of how they are used.

And another conversation has grown up around transparency: How much do we have a right to know about the algorithms that reflect our data back to us? Being a smartphone user puts you in a new political class that has to learn to assert its rights.

An idea builds slowly. Those who take our data have one set of interests. We who give up our data have another. We have been led to believe that giving up our personal data is a fair trade for free services and helpful suggestions; this questionable notion of the fair trade has slowed down our ability to think critically.

It will take politicizing this conversation to get this conversation going. If it doesn't use a political language, a language of interests and conflicts, the conversation stalls—it moves to the language of cost-benefit analysis. Would you be willing to trade your privacy for the convenience of free email and word-processing programs? But the Constitution does not let us trade away certain freedoms. We don't get to "decide" if we want to give away freedom of speech.

And the conversation stalls if it moves too quickly to technical details. For example, I try to talk about the effect of knowing we are being tracked with a software engineer in his mid-sixties who has a special interest in public policy. I ask him, "Does tracking inhibit people's willingness to speak their minds online?" His response is dismissive: "Don't they [the public] know that these algorithms are stupid? They are so bad . . . they don't mean anything." This was meant as comfort to me. But it provided none. From his point of view, the discussion of individuals' rights to their personal data can be deferred because the algorithms that regularly invade individual privacy aren't "good enough." "Good enough" for what?

Try to avoid all-or-nothing thinking. The digital world is based on binary choice. Our thinking about it can't be. This is true whether we are talking about computers in classrooms, distance learning, or the use of teleconferencing in large organizations. But in all these arenas, when computational possibilities are introduced, camps form and the middle ground disappears.

The complexity of our circumstances calls for a flexibility of approach. But it is hard to summon. To return to the question of the Internet and privacy, one common reaction to how vulnerable we feel is to retreat to a position where any resistance is futile. When Internet companies are saving what you say, search, and share, you are offering up so much information that it begins to seem petty to object to any particular encroachment. It becomes like living in a city filled with security cameras and objecting to a particular camera on a particular street corner. So instead of talking about what should be our rights, we adapt to rules we actually object to.

Or, instead of talking about what our rights should be, we react with rigidity. When no one can think of a way to have *complete* online privacy, people start to say that no change will work unless it brings total openness. Technology critic Evgeny Morozov makes a pitch for a less binary view by considering the history of another by-product of technological progress: noise. An anti-noise movement in the early twentieth century insisted that noise was not just an individual problem but also a political one. And then the anti-noise campaigners compromised to achieve realistic goals that made a difference. Morozov says, "Not all of their reforms paid off, but the politicization of noise inspired a new generation of urban planners and architects to build differently, situating schools and hospitals in quieter zones, and using parks and gardens as buffers against traffic."

Just as industrialization "wanted" noise, the information society "wants" uncontrolled access to data. This doesn't mean they get to have everything they want.

The anti-noise campaigners didn't want to turn back industrialization. They didn't want silent cities, but cities that took the human need for rest, talk, and tranquillity into consideration. By analogy, in our current circumstance, we don't want to discard social media, but we may want to rewrite our social contract with it. If it operated more transparently, we might not feel so lost in our dialogue with it and about it. One way to begin this dialogue is to politicize our need for solitude, privacy, and mindspace.

Places

So, there are guideposts and ways to begin. But distractions too often override conversations. We've seen family dinner tables where children literally beg for the attention of parents who love them. We've seen classes where a teacher is present but students' faces are lowered to phones. And we've created a political culture in which contention rather than conversation is the rule. We show little interest in listening to good ideas if they come from political opponents. Indeed, we see politicians awkwardly rejecting their own good ideas if they are now put forth by members of an opposing party.

In this environment, it makes sense to recall what is hopeful: We can reclaim places for conversation, and we still know where to find each other. Parents can find children at the dinner table; teachers can find students in class and office hours. Colleagues at work can find each other in hallways, in mini-kitchens, and in meetings. In politics, we have institutions for debate and action. Looking at these, we've seen disruptions in the field: meetings that aren't meetings and classes that are waiting to be digitized. And of course, where this book began: family dinners that are silent because each member is taken away on a device.

But the importance of focusing on the places where conversation can happen, and reclaiming them—as opposed to just saying, "Put down your phone"—is that the places themselves propose a sustained conversation, week after week, year after year. Legislatures in democracies—these have been built over centuries. When they go through rough patches, we count on the idea that their existence means that there will be other days and other chances, because, in a democracy, certain conversations are a responsibility. The family dinner at your house is something created and built over time. As you build it, you teach your children that problems need not be catastrophes; they can be talked through today and again tomorrow. It is a place to develop a sense of proportion. It may seem innocuous when parents are too distracted to discuss the small ups and downs of childhood. But there is a cost. Parental attention helps children learn what is and is not an emergency and what children can handle on their own. Parental inattention can mean that, to a child, everything feels urgent.

A child alone with a problem has an emergency. A child in conversation with a grown-up is facing a moment in life and learning how to cope with it.

When we reclaim conversation and the places to have them, we are led to reconsider the importance of long-term thinking. Life is not a problem looking for a quick fix. Life is a conversation and you need places to have it. *The virtual provides us with more spaces for these conversations and these are enriching.* But what makes the physical so precious is that it supports continuity in a different way; it doesn't come and go, and it binds people to it. You can't just log off or drop out. You learn to live things through.

Students who resist coming to office hours speak in glowing terms of how, when they finally show up, they find mentors who have persisted in asking them to come in and talk. The phrase that sticks with me is a student quoting his teacher, who kept saying, "You're going to come tomorrow, right?"

I've said that our crisis in conversation can also be described as a crisis in mentorship. People step away from mentorship and use technology as an excuse. Employers delegate to email an evaluation that could be a mentoring conversation if done face-to-face. Teachers are encouraged to equate what they can offer their students in class with something that can be captured in a series of six-minute videos. Parents don't ask their children to put down their smartphones at dinner, as if the phones are a generational right; many parents seem prepared to accept robot babysitters if they can prove their safety. In all these cases, I see us turn away from what we know about love and work.

Public Conversations

We turn away because we feel helpless. And so many people tell me that they feel alone—that they have to figure things out by themselves, everything from their privacy on Facebook to their sense that their data are being used and they don't quite know how or why. But we can think through these things together.

Public conversations give us a way to reclaim private conversations by modeling them, including how to show tolerance and genuine interest in what other people are saying. They can teach how conversation unfolds, not in proclamations or bullet points but in turn taking, negotiation, and other rhythms of respect.

People have long sensed that this kind of public conversation is crucial to democracy. Historically, there have been markets and town squares and town meetings. There have been clubs and coffeehouses and salons. The sociologist Jürgen Habermas associates the seventeenth-century English coffeehouse with the rise of a "public sphere." That was a place where people of all classes could talk about politics without fear of arrest. "What a lesson," the Abbé Prévost said in 1728, "to see a lord, or two, a baronet, a shoemaker, a tailor, a wine merchant, and a few others of the same stamp poring over the same newspapers. Truly the coffeehouses . . . are the seats of English liberty."

Of course there was never any perfect public sphere. The coffeehouse required leisure and some money. It was not a place for women. Nevertheless, the coffeehouses were a place to talk about politics and *learn* how to talk about it. Joseph Addison, the essayist and politician, writing in 1714 as the voice of the newspaper *The Spectator*, makes the point that he enjoys coffeehouse debates because they are a place to learn. "Coffee houses have ever since been my chief Places of Resort, where I have made the greatest Improvements; in order to which I have taken a particular Care never to be of the same Opinion with the Man I conversed with."

When Addison went to the coffeehouse, he wanted to talk only to people he *disagreed* with. That is a long way from today's politically committed students who avoid talking about politics with those who disagree with them, even if they live just down the hall. But, long way or not, the image of Addison inspires: He uses a public conversation to keep him open to changing his mind.

A public conversation can model freedom of thought. It can model courage and compromise. It can help people think things through.

When Thoreau thought about our responsibility to occupy the present, he talked about improving his "nick of time." To capture this thought, Thoreau takes a moment to reflect, even to put a notch on his walking stick:

> *In any weather, at any hour of the day or night, I have been anxious to improve the nick of time, and notch it on my stick too; to stand on the meeting of two eternities, the past and the future, which is precisely the present moment; to toe that line.*

The "nick" raises the question of legacy. We represent a past that needs to be considered precisely, even as we create a new world. Whatever the weather, Thoreau chooses to improve his moment. He summons us to ours.

A Fourth Chair?

The End of Forgetting

What Do We Forget When We Talk to Machines?

*There are some people who have tried to make friends . . . but
they've fallen through so badly that they give up. So when they
hear this idea about robots being made to be companions, well,
it's not going to be like a human and have its own mind to
walk away or ever leave you or anything like that.*

—A SIXTEEN-YEAR-OLD GIRL, CONSIDERING THE
IDEA OF A MORE SOPHISTICATED SIRI

Thoreau talks of three chairs and I think about a fourth. Thoreau says that for the most expansive conversations, the deepest ones, he brought his guests out into nature—he calls it his withdrawing room, his "best room." For me, the fourth chair defines a philosophical space. Thoreau could go into nature, but now, we contemplate both nature and a second nature of our own making, the world of the artificial and virtual. There, we meet machines that present themselves as open for conversation. The fourth chair raises the question: Who do we become when we talk to machines?

Some talking machines have modest ambitions—such as putting you through the paces of a job interview. But others aspire to far more. Most of these are just now coming on the scene: "caring robots" that will tend to our children and elders if we ourselves don't have the time, patience, or resources; automated psychotherapy programs that will substitute for humans in conversation. These present us with something new.

It may not feel new. All day every day, we connect with witty apps, we type our information into dialogue programs, and we get information from personal digital assistants. We are comfortable talking at machines and through machines. Now we are asked to join a new kind of conversation, one that promises "empathic" connections.

Machines have none to offer, and yet we persist in the desire for companionship and even communion with the inanimate. Has the simulation of empathy become empathy enough? The simulation of communion, communion enough?

The fourth chair defines a space that Thoreau could not have seen. It is our nick of time.

What do we forget when we talk to machines—and what can we remember?

"A Computer Beautiful Enough That a Soul Would Want to Live in It"

In the early 1980s, I interviewed one of Marvin Minsky's young students who told me that, as he saw it, his hero, Minsky, one of the founders of artificial intelligence (AI), was "trying to create a computer beautiful enough that a soul would want to live in it."

That image has stayed with me for more than thirty years.

In the AI world, things have gone from mythic to prosaic. Today, children grow up with robotic pets and digital dolls. They think it natural to chat with their phones. We are at what I have called a "robotic moment," not because of the merits of the machines we've built but because of our eagerness for their company. Even before we make the robots, we remake ourselves as people ready to be their companions.

For a long time, putting hope in robots has expressed an enduring technological optimism, a belief that as things go wrong, science will go right. In a complicated world, what robots promise has always seemed like calling in the cavalry. Robots save lives in war zones; they can function in space and in the sea—indeed, anywhere that humans would be in danger. They perform medical procedures that humans cannot do; they have revolutionized design and manufacturing.

But robots get us to hope for more. Not only for the feats of the cavalry, but for simple salvations. What are the simple salvations? These are the hopes that robots will be our companions. That taking care of us will be their jobs. That we will take comfort in their company and conversation. This is a station on our voyage of forgetting.

What do we forget when we talk to machines? We forget what is special about being human. We forget what it means to have authentic conversation. Machines are programmed to have conversations "as if" they understood what the conversation is about. So when we talk to them, we, too, are reduced and confined to the "as if."

Simple Salvations

Over the decades, I have heard the hopes for robot companionship grow stronger, even though most people don't have experience with an embodied robot companion at all but rather with something like Siri, Apple's digital assistant, where the conversation is most likely to be "locate a restaurant" or "locate a friend."

But even telling Siri to "locate a friend" moves quickly to the fantasy of finding a friend in Siri. People tell me that they look forward to the time, not too far down the road, when Siri or one of her near cousins will be something like a best friend, but in some ways better: one you can always talk to, one that will never be angry, one you can never disappoint.

And, indeed, Apple's first television advertising campaign for Siri introduced "her" not as a feature, a convenient way of getting information, but as a companion. It featured a group of movie stars—Zooey Deschanel, Samuel L. Jackson, John Malkovich—who put Siri in the role of confidante. Deschanel, playing the ditzy ingénue, discusses the weather, and how she doesn't want to wear shoes or clean house on a rainy day. She just wants to dance and have tomato soup. Siri plays the role of the best friend who "gets her." Jackson has a conversation with Siri that is laced with double meanings about a hot date: A lady friend is coming over and Jackson is cooking gazpacho and risotto. It's fun to joke with his sidekick Siri about his plans for seduction. Malkovich, sitting in a deep leather chair in a room with heavy wall moldings and drapes—it might be an apartment in Paris or Barcelona—talks seriously with Siri about the meaning of life. He likes it that Siri has a sense of humor.

In all of this, we are being schooled in how to have conversations with a machine that may approximate banter but doesn't understand our meaning at all; in these conversations, we're doing all the work but we don't mind.

I was on a radio show about Siri with a panel of engineers and social scientists. The topic turned to how much people like to talk to Siri, part of the general phenomenon that people feel uninhibited when they talk to a machine. They like the feeling of no judgment. One of the social scientists on the program suggested that soon a souped-up and some-what smoothed-out Siri could serve as a psychiatrist.

It didn't seem to bother him that Siri, in the role of psychiatrist, would be counseling people about their lives without having lived one. If Siri could *behave* like a psychiatrist, he said, it could be a psychiatrist. If no one minded the difference between the as-if and the real thing, let the machine take the place of the person. This is the pragmatism of the robotic moment.

But the suggestions of a robotic friend or therapist—the simple salvations of the robotic moment—are not so simple at all.

Because for all that they are programmed to pretend, machines that talk to us as though they care about us don't know the arc of a human life. When we speak to them of our human problems of love and loss, or the pleasures of tomato soup and dancing barefoot on a rainy day, they can deliver only performances of empathy and connection.

What an artificial intelligence *can* know is your schedule, the literal content of your email, your preferences in film, TV, and food. If you wear body-sensing technologies, an AI can know what emotionally activates you because it may infer this from physiological markers. But it won't understand what any of these things *mean* to you.

But the meaning of things is just what we want our machines to understand. And we are willing to fuel the fantasy that they do.

Vulnerability Games

We have been playing vulnerability games with artificial intelligence for a very long time, since before programs were anywhere near as sophisticated as they are now. In the 1960s, a computer program called ELIZA, written by MIT's Joseph Weizenbaum, adopted the "mirroring" style of a Rogerian psychotherapist. So, if you typed, "Why do I hate my mother?" ELIZA might respond, "I hear you saying that you hate your mother." This program was effective—at least for a short while—in creating the illusion of intelligent listening. And there is this: *We want to talk to machines even when we know they do not deserve our confidences. I call this the "ELIZA effect."*

Weizenbaum was shocked that people (for example, his secretary and graduate students) who knew the limits of ELIZA's ability to know and understand nevertheless wanted to be alone with the program in order to confide in it. ELIZA demonstrated that almost universally, people project human attributes onto programs that present as humanlike, an effect that is magnified when they are with robots called "sociable" machines— machines that do such things as track your motion, make eye contact, and remember your name. Then people feel in the presence of a knowing other that cares about them. A young man, twenty-six, talks with a robot named Kismet that makes eye contact, reads facial expressions, and vocalizes with the cadences of human speech. The man finds Kismet so supportive that he speaks with it about the ups and downs of his day.

Machines with voices have particular power to make us feel understood. Children first learn to know their mothers by recognizing their voices, even while still in the womb. During our evolution, the only speech we heard was the speech of other humans. Now, with the development of sophisticated artificial speech, we are the first humans asked to distinguish human from non-human speech. Neurologically, we are not set up to do this job. Since human beings have for so long—say, 200,000 years—heard only human voices, it takes serious mental effort to distinguish human speech from the machine-generated kind. To our brains, speaking is something that people do.

And machines with humanlike faces have particular power as well.

In humans, the shape of a smile or a frown releases chemicals that affect our mental state. Our mirror neurons fire both when we act and when we observe others acting. *We feel what we see on the face of another.* An expressive robot face can have this impact on us. The philosopher Emmanuel Lévinas writes that the presence of a face initiates the human ethical compact. The face communicates, "Thou shalt not kill me." We are bound by the face even before we know what stands behind it, even before we might learn it is the face of a machine that cannot be killed. And the robot's face certainly announces, for Lévinas, "Thou shalt not abandon me"—again, an ethical and emotional compact that captures us but has no meaning when we feel it for a machine.

An expressive machine face—on a robot or on a screen-based computer program—puts us on a landscape where we seek recognition and feel we can get it. We are in fact triggered to seek empathy from an object that has none to give.

I worked at the MIT Artificial Intelligence Laboratory as people met the sociable, emotive robot Kismet for the first time. What Kismet actually said had no meaning, but the sound came out warm or inquiring or concerned.

Sometimes Kismet's visitors felt the robot had recognized them and had "heard" their story. When things worked perfectly from a technical standpoint, they experienced what felt like an empathic connection. This convincing imitation of understanding is impressive and can be a lot of fun if you think of these encounters as theater. But I saw children look to Kismet for a friend in the real. I saw children hope for the robot's recognition, and sometimes become bereft when there was nothing nourishing on offer.

Estelle, twelve, comes to Kismet wanting a conversation. She is lonely, her parents are divorced; her time with Kismet makes her feel special. Here is a robot who will listen just to her. On the day of Estelle's visit, she is engaged by Kismet's changing facial expressions, but Kismet is not at its vocal best. At the end of a disappointing session, Estelle and the small team of researchers who have been working with her go back to the room where we interview children before and after they meet the robots. Estelle begins to eat the juice, crackers, and cookies we have left out as snacks. And she does not stop, not until we ask her to please leave some food for the other children. Then she stops, but only briefly. She begins to eat again, hurriedly, as we wait for the car service that will take her back to her after-school program.

Estelle tells us why she is upset: Kismet does not like her. The robot began to talk with her and then turned away. We explain that this is not the case. The problem had been technical. Estelle is not convinced. From her point of view, she has failed on her most important day. As Estelle leaves, she takes four boxes of cookies from the supply closet and stuffs them into her backpack. We do not stop her. Exhausted, my team reconvenes at a nearby coffee shop to ask ourselves a hard question: Can a broken robot break a child?

We would not be concerned with the ethics of having a child play with a buggy copy of Microsoft Word or a torn Raggedy Ann doll. A word-processing program is there to do an instrumental thing. If it does worse than usual on a particular day, well, that leads to frustration but no more. But a program that encourages you to connect with it—this is a different matter.

How is a broken Kismet different from a broken doll? A doll encourages children to project their own stories and their own agendas onto a passive object. But children see sociable robots as "alive enough" to have their own agendas. Children attach to them not with the psychology of projection but with the psychology of relational engagement, more in the way they attach to people.

If a little girl is feeling guilty for breaking her mother's crystal, she may punish a row of Barbie dolls, putting the dolls into detention as a way of working through her own feelings. The dolls are material for what the child needs to accomplish emotionally. That is how the psychology of projection works: It enables the working through of the child's feelings. But the sociable robot presents itself as having a mind of its own. As the child sees it, if this robot turns away, it wanted to. That's why children consider winning the heart of a sociable robot to be a personal achievement. You've gotten something lovable to love you. Again, children interact with sociable robots not with the psychology of projection but with engagement. They react as though they face another person. There is room for new hurt.

Estelle responded to this emotionally charged situation with depression and a search for comfort food. Other children who faced a disappointing conversation with Kismet responded with aggression. When Kismet began an animated conversation that Edward, six, could not understand, he shoved objects into Kismet's mouth—a metal pin, a pencil, a toy caterpillar—things Edward found in the robotics laboratory. But at no point did Edward disengage from Kismet. He would not give up his chance for Kismet's recognition.

The important question here is not about the risks of broken robots. Rather, we should ask, "Emotionally, what positive thing would we have given to these children if the robots had been in top form?" Why do we propose machine companionship to children in the first place? For a lonely child, a conversational robot is a guarantee against rejection, a place to entrust confidences. But what children really need is not the guarantee that an inanimate object will simulate acceptance. They need relationships that will teach them real mutuality, caring, and empathy.

So, the problem doesn't start when the machine breaks down. Children are not well served even when the robots are working perfectly. In the case of a robot babysitter, you already have a problem when you have to explain to a child why there isn't a person available for the job.

Treating Machines as People;
Treating People as Machines

In all of this, an irony emerges: Even as we treat machines as if they were almost human, we develop habits that have us treating human beings as almost-machines. To take a simple example, we regularly put people "on pause" in the middle of a conversation in order to check our phones. And when we talk to people who are not paying attention to us, it is a kind of preparation for talking to uncomprehending machines. When people give us less, talking to machines doesn't seem as much of a downgrade.

At a panel on "cyberetiquette," I was onstage with a technology reporter and two "advice and manners" columnists. There was general agreement among the panelists on most matters: No texting at family dinners. No texting at restaurants. Don't bring your laptop to your children's sporting events, no matter how tempting.

And then came this question from the audience: A woman said that as a working mother she had very little time to talk to her friends, to email, to text, to keep up. "Actually," she confessed, "the only time I have is at night, after I'm off work and before I go home, when I go family shopping at Trader Joe's. But the cashier, the guy at the checkout counter, he wants to talk. I just want to be on my phone, into my texts and Facebook. Do I have the right to just ignore him?" The two manners experts went first. Each said a version of the same thing: The man who does the checkout has a job to do. The woman who asked the question has a right to privacy and to her texting as he provides his service.

I listened uncomfortably. I thought of all the years I went shopping with my grandmother as I grew up and all the relationships she had with tradespeople at every store: the baker, the fishmonger, the fruit man, the grocery man (for this is what we called them). These days, we all know that the job the man at the checkout counter does could be done by a machine. In fact, down the street at another supermarket, it is done by a machine that automatically scans your groceries. And so I shared this thought: Until a machine replaces the man, surely he summons in us the recognition and respect you show a person. Sharing a few words at the checkout may make this man feel that in his job, this job that *could* be done by a machine, he is still seen as a human being.

This was not what the audience and my fellow panelists wanted to hear. As I took stock of their cool reaction to what I said, I saw a new symmetry: We want more from technology and less from each other. What once would have seemed like "friendly service" at a community market had become an inconvenience that keeps us from our phones.

It used to be that we imagined our mobile phones were there so that we could talk to each other. Now we want our mobile phones to talk to us. That's what the new commercials for Siri are really about: fantasies of these new conversations and a kind of tutelage in what they might sound like. We are at a moment of temptation, ready to turn to machines for companionship even as we seem pained or inconvenienced to engage with each other in settings as simple as a grocery store. We want technology to step up as we ask people to step back.

People are lonely and fear intimacy, and robots seem ready to hand. *And we are ready for their company if we forget what intimacy is.* And having nothing to forget, our children learn new rules for when it is appropriate to talk to a machine.

Stephanie is forty, a real estate agent in Rhode Island. Her ten-year-old daughter, Tara, is a perfectionist, always the "good girl," sensitive to any suggestion of criticism. Recently, she has begun to talk to Siri. It is not surprising that children like to talk to Siri. There is just enough inventiveness in Siri's responses to make children feel that someone might be listening. And if children are afraid of judgment, Siri is safe. So Tara expresses anger to Siri that she doesn't show to her parents or friends—with them she plays the part of a "perfect child." Stephanie overhears her daughter yelling at Siri and says, "She vents to Siri. She starts to talk but then becomes enraged."

Stephanie wonders if this is "perhaps a good thing, certainly a more honest conversation" than Tara is having with others in her life. It's a thought worth looking at more closely. It is surely positive for Tara to discover feelings that she censors for other audiences. But talking to Siri leaves Tara vulnerable. She may get the idea that her feelings are something that people cannot handle. She may persist in her current idea that pretend perfection is all other people want from her or can accept from her. Instead of learning that people can value how she really feels, Tara is learning that it is easier not to deal with people at all.

If Tara can "be herself" only with a robot, she may grow up believing that only an object can tolerate her truth. What Tara is doing is not "training" for relating to people. For that, Tara needs to learn that you can attach to people with trust, make some mistakes, and risk open conversations. Her talks with the inanimate are taking her in another direction: to a world without risk and without caring.

Automated Psychotherapy

We create machines that seem human enough that they tempt us into conversation and then we treat them as though they can do the things humans do. This is the explicit strategy of a research group at MIT that is trying to build an automated psychotherapist by "crowdsourcing" collective emotional intelligence. How does this work? Imagine that a young man enters a brief (one- to three-sentence) description of a stressful situation or painful emotion into a computer program. In response, the program divides up the tasks of therapy among "crowd workers." The only requirement to be employed as a crowd worker is a command of basic English.

The authors of the program say they developed it because the conversations of psychotherapy are a good thing but are too expensive to be available to everyone who needs them. But in what sense is this system providing conversation? One worker sends a quick "empathic" response. Another checks if the problem statement distorts reality and may encourage a reframing of the problem. Or a reappraisal of the situation. These, too, are brief, no more than four sentences long. There are people in the system, but you can't talk to them. Each crowd worker is simply given an isolated piece of a puzzle to solve. *And indeed, the authors of the program hope that someday the entire process—already a well-oiled machine—will be fully automated and you won't need people in the loop at all, not even piecemeal.*

This automated psychotherapist, Tara's conversations with Siri, and the psychiatrist who looks forward to the day when a "smarter" Siri could take over his job say a lot about our cultural moment. Missing in all of them is the notion that, in psychotherapy, conversation cures because of the relationship with the therapist. In that encounter, what therapist and patient share is that they both live human lives. All of us were once children, small and dependent. We all grow up and face decisions about intimacy, generativity, work, and life purpose. We face losses. We consider our mortality. We ask ourselves what legacy we want to leave to a next generation. When we run into trouble with these things—and that kind of trouble is a natural part of every life—that is something a human being would know how to talk to us about. Yet as we become increasingly willing to discuss these things with machines, we prepare ourselves, as a culture, for artificial psychotherapists and children laying out their troubles to their iPhones.

When I voice my misgivings about pursuing such conversations, I often get the reaction "If people say they would be happy talking to a robot, if they want a friend they can never disappoint, if they don't want to face the embarrassment or vulnerability of telling their story to a person, why do you care?" But why not turn this question around and ask, "Why don't we all care?" Why don't we all care that when we pursue these conversations, we chase after a fantasy? Why don't we think we deserve more? Don't we think we can have more?

In part, we convince ourselves that we don't need more—that we're comfortable with what machines provide. And then we begin to see a life in which we never fear judgment or embarrassment or vulnerability as perhaps a good thing. Perhaps what machine talk provides is progress—on the path toward a better way of being in the world? Perhaps these machine "conversations" are not simply better than nothing but better than anything?

There Are No People for These Jobs

A cover story in *Wired* magazine, "Better than Human," celebrated both the inevitability and the advantages of robots substituting for people in every domain of life. Its premise: Whenever robots take over a human function, the next thing that people get to do is a more human thing. The story was authored by Kevin Kelly, a self-declared techno-utopian, but his argument echoes how I've found people talking about this subject for decades. The argument has two parts. First, robots make us more human by increasing our relational options because now we get to relate to *them*, considered as a new "species."

Second, whatever people do, if a robot can take over that role, it was, by definition, not specifically human. *And over time, this has come to include the roles of conversation, companionship, and caretaking.* We redefine what is human by what technology can't do. But as Alan Turing put it, computer conversation is "an imitation game." We declare computers intelligent if they can fool us into thinking they are people. But that doesn't mean they are.

I work at one of the world's great scientific and engineering institutions. This means that over the years, some of my most brilliant colleagues and students have worked on the problem of robot conversation and companionship. One of my students used his own two-year-old daughter's voice as the voice of My Real Baby, a robot doll that was advertised as so responsive it could teach your child socialization skills. More recently, another student developed an artificial dialogue partner with whom you could practice job interviews.

At MIT, researchers imagine sociable robots—when improved—as teachers, home assistants, best friends to the lonely, both young and old. But particularly to the old. With the old, the necessity for robots is taken as self-evident. Because of demography, roboticists explain, "there are no people for these jobs."

The trend line is clear: too many older people, not enough younger ones to take care of them. This is why, roboticists say, they need to produce "caretaker machines" or, as they are sometimes called, "caring machines."

In fairness, it's not only roboticists who talk this way. In the past twenty years, the years in which I've been studying sociable robotics, I've heard echoes of "There are no people for these jobs" in conversations with people who are not in the robot business at all—carpenters, lawyers, doctors, plumbers, schoolteachers, and office workers. When they say this, they often suggest that the people who are available for "these jobs" are not the right people. They might steal. They might be inept or even abusive. Machines would be less risky. People say things like, "I would rather have a robot take care of my mother than a high school dropout. I know who works in those nursing homes." Or, "I would rather have a robot take care of my child than a teenager at some day-care center who really doesn't know what she's doing."

So what are we talking about when we talk about conversations with machines? We are talking about our fears of each other, our disappointments with each other. Our lack of community. Our lack of time. People go straight from voicing reservations about a health-care worker who didn't finish high school to a dream of inventing a robot to care for them, just in time. *Again, we live at the robotic moment, not because the robots are ready for us, but because we are counting on them.*

One sixteen-year-old considered having a robot as a friend and said it wasn't for her, but thought she understood at least part of the appeal:

> *There are some people who have tried to make friends and stuff like that, but they've fallen through so badly that they give up. So when they hear this idea about robots being made to be companions, well, it's not going to be like a human and have its own mind to walk away or ever leave you or anything like that.*

Relationship-wise, you're not going to be afraid of a robot cheating on you, because it's a robot. It's programmed to stay with you forever. So if someone heard the idea of this and they had past relationships where they'd always been cheated on and left, they're going to decide to go with the robot idea because they know that nothing bad is going to happen from it.

The idea has passed to a new generation: Robots offer relationship without risk and "nothing bad is going to happen" from having a robot as a friend or, as this girl imagines it, a romantic partner. But it's helpful to challenge the simple salvations of robot companionship. We will surely confront a first problem: The time we spend with robots is time we're not spending with each other. Or with our children. Or with ourselves.

And a second problem: Although always-available robot chatter is a way to never feel alone, we will be alone, engaged in "as-if" conversations. What if practice makes perfect and we forget what real conversation is and why it matters? That's why I worry so much about the "crowdsourced" therapist. It is presented as a path toward an even more automated stand-in and is not afraid to use the word "therapist" or "conversation" to describe what it offers.

Smart Toys: Vulnerability to the As-If

In the late 1970s, when I began my studies of computers and people, I started with children. A first generation of electronic toys and games (with their assertive displays of smarts) were just entering the mass market. In children's eyes, the new toys shared intelligence with people, but as the children saw it, people, in contrast to computers, had emotions. People were special because they had feelings.

A twelve-year-old said, "When there are computers who are just as smart as the people, the computers will do a lot of the jobs, but there will still be things for the people to do. They will run the restaurants, taste the food, and they will be the ones who will love each other, have families, and love each other. I guess they'll still be the only ones who will go to church." And in fact, in the mid-1980s and early 1990s, people of all ages found a way of saying that *although simulated thinking might be thinking, simulated feeling is never feeling, simulated love is never love.*

And then, in the late 1990s, there was a sea change. Now computer objects presented themselves as having feelings. Virtual pets such as Tamagotchis, Furbies, and AIBOs proposed themselves as playmates that asked to be cared for and behaved as though it mattered. And it was clear that it did matter to the children who cared for them. We are built to nurture what we love but also to love what we nurture.

Nurturance turns out to be a "killer app." Once we take care of a digital creature or teach or amuse it, we become attached to it, and then behave "as if" the creature cares for us in return.

Children become so convinced that sociable robots have feelings that they are no longer willing to see people as special because of their emotional lives. I've interviewed many adults who say of children's attachment to as-if relationships: "Well, that's cute, they'll grow out of it." But it is just as likely, more likely in fact, that children are not growing out of patterns of attachment to the inanimate, but growing *into* them.

What are children learning when they turn toward machines as confidants? A fifteen-year-old boy remarks that every person is limited by his or her life experience, but "robots can be programmed with an unlimited amount of stories." So in his mind, as confidants, the robots win on expertise. And, tellingly, they also win on reliability. His parents are divorced. He's seen a lot of fighting at home. "People," he says, are "risky." Robots are "safe." The kind of reliability they will provide is emotional reliability, which comes from their having no emotions at all.

An Artificial Mentor

To recall Marvin Minsky's student, these days we're not trying to create machines that souls would want to live *in* but machines that we would want to live *with*.

From earliest childhood, Thomas, now seventeen, says that he used video games as a place of emotional comfort, "a place to go." Thomas came to the United States from Morocco when he was eight. His father had to stay behind, and now Thomas lives with his mother and sister in a town that is more than an hour from his suburban private school. He has family all over the world and he keeps up with them through email and messaging. His relationship with his mother is quite formal. She holds down several jobs and Thomas says he doesn't want to upset her with his problems. Now, he says that when he has a problem, the characters in his video games offer concrete advice.

Thomas provides an example of how this works. One of his friends at school gave him a stolen collector's card of considerable value. Thomas was tempted to keep it but remembered that a character in one of his favorite games was also given stolen goods. In the game, Thomas says, the character returned the stolen items and so he did too. "The character went and did the right thing and returned it. And in the end, it would turn out good. So I just said, 'Yeah, that's good. I should probably return it, yeah.'"

Inspired by the character's actions, Thomas returned the stolen card to its rightful owner. The game helped Thomas do the right thing, but it did not offer a chance to talk about what had happened and how to move forward with his classmates, who steal with apparently no consequence and who now have reason to think he steals as well. Thomas says that at school he feels "surrounded by traitors." It's a terrible feeling and one where talking to a person might help. But Thomas doesn't see that happening any time soon. On the contrary, in the future, he sees himself increasingly turning to machines for companionship and advice. When he says this, I feel that I've missed a beat. How did he make the leap to artificial friendship? Thomas explains: Online, he plays games where he sometimes can't tell people and programs apart.

Thomas has a favorite computer game in which there are a lot of "non-player characters." These are programmed agents that are designed to act as human characters in the game. These characters can be important: They can save your life, and sometimes, to proceed through the game, you have to save theirs. But every once in a while, those who designed Thomas's game turn its world upside down: The programmers of the game take the roles of the programmed characters they've created. "So, on day one, you meet some characters and they're just programs. On day two, they are people. . . . So, from day to day, you can't keep the robots straight from the people."

When we meet, Thomas is fresh from an experience of mistaking a program for a person. It's left a big impression. He's wondering how he would feel if a "true bot"—that is, a character played by a computer program—wanted to be his friend. He cannot articulate any objection. "If the true bot actually asked me things and acted like a natural person," says Thomas, "then I would take it as a friend."

In the Turing "imitation game," to be considered intelligent, a computer had to communicate with a person (via keyboards and a teletype) and leave that person unable to tell if behind the words was a person or a machine. Turing's test is all about behavior, the ability to perform humanness. Thomas lives in this behaviorist world. There is a "Thomas test" for friendship. To be a friend, you have to *act* like a friend, like a "natural person."

For Thomas makes it clear: He is ready to take the performance of friendship for friendship itself. He tells me that if a bot asked him, "How are you? What are you feeling? What are you thinking?" he would answer. And from there Thomas has an elaborate fantasy of what personalities would be most pleasing in his machine friends. Unlike the kids he doesn't get along with at school, his machine friends will be honest. They will offer companionship without tension and difficult moral choices. The prospect seems, as he puts it, "relaxing."

This is the robotic moment, "relaxing" to a seventeen-year-old who has been befriended by young thugs. If Thomas accepts programs as confidants, it is because he has so degraded what he demands of conversation that he will accept what a game bot can offer: the *performance* of honesty and companionate interest.

And then there is the question of how much we value "information." By the first decade of the 2000s, it was easy to find high school students who thought it would be better to talk to computer programs about the problems of high school dating than to talk to their parents. The programs, these students explained, would have larger databases to draw on than any parent could have. But giving advice about dating involves identifying with another person's feelings. So that conversation with your father about girls might also be an occasion to discuss empathy and ethical behavior. If your father's advice about dating doesn't work out, hopefully you'll still learn things from talking to him that will help things go better when you have your next crush.

Saying that you'll let a machine "take care" of a conversation about dating means that this larger conversation won't take place. It can't. And the more we talk about conversation as something machines can do, the more we can end up devaluing conversations with people—because they don't offer what machines provide.

I hear adults and adolescents talk about infallible "advice machines" that will work with masses of data and well-tested algorithms. When we treat people's lives as ready to be worked on by algorithm, when machine advice becomes the gold standard, we learn not to feel safe with fallible people.

When I hear young people talk about the advantages of turning to robots instead of their parents, I hear children whose parents have disappointed them. A disengaged parent leaves children less able to relate to others. And when parents retreat to their phones, they seem released from the anxieties that should come from ignoring their children. In this new world, adding a caretaker robot to the mix can start to seem like not that big a deal. It may even seem like a solution. Robots appeal to distracted parents because they are already disengaged. Robots appeal to lonely children because the robots will always be there.

The most important job of childhood and adolescence is to learn attachment to and trust in other people. That happens through human attention, presence, and conversation. When we think about putting children in the care of robots, we forget that what children really need to learn is that adults are there for them in a stable and consistent way.

From Better than Nothing to Better than Anything

The bonds of attachment and the expression of emotion are one for the child. When children talk with people, they come to recognize, over time, how vocal inflection, facial expression, and bodily movement flow together. Seamlessly. Fluidly. And they learn how human emotions play in layers, again seamlessly and fluidly.

Children need to learn what complex human feelings and human ambivalence look like. And they need other people to respond to their own expressions of that complexity. These are the most precious things that people give to children in conversation as they grow up. No robot has these things to teach.

These are the things that we forget when we think about children spending any significant amount of time talking with machines, looking into robotic faces, trusting in their care. Why would we play with fire when it comes to such delicate matters?

But we do. It's part of a general progression that I've called "from better than nothing to better than anything." We begin with resignation, with the idea that machine companionship is better than nothing, as in "there are no people for these jobs." From there, we exalt the possibilities of what simulation can offer until, in time, we start to talk as though what we will get from the artificial may actually be better than what life could ever provide. Child-care workers might be abusive. Nurses or well-meaning mothers might make mistakes. Children say that a robotic dog like the AIBO pet will never get sick, and can be turned off when you want to put your attention elsewhere. And, crucially, it will never die.

Grown-ups have similar feelings. A robot dog, says an older woman, "won't die suddenly, abandon you, and make you very sad."

In our new culture of connection, we are lonely but afraid of intimacy. Fantasies of "conversation" with artificial beings solve a dilemma. They propose the illusion of companionship without the demands of friendship. They allow us to imagine a friction-free version of friendship. One whose demands are in our control, perhaps literally.

I've said that part of what makes our new technologies of connection so seductive is that they respond to our fantasies, our wishes, that we will always be heard, that we can put our attention wherever we want it to be, and that we will never have to be alone. And, of course, they respond to an implied fourth fantasy: that we will never have to be bored.

When people voice these fantasies, they are also describing, often without realizing it, a relationship with a robot. The robot would always be at attention, and it would be tolerant of wherever your attention might take you. It certainly wouldn't mind if you interrupted your conversation to answer a text or take a call. And it would never abandon you, although there is the question of whether it was ever really there in the first place. As for boredom, well, it would do its best to make boredom, for you, a thing of the past.

If, like Tara, we choose to share our frustrations with robot friends because we don't want to upset our human friends with who we really are and what we're really feeling, the meaning of human friendship will change. It may become the place you go for small talk. You'd be afraid that people would be tired out by big talk. This means that there won't be any more big talk because robots won't understand it.

Yet so many people talk to me about their hope that someday, not too far down the road, an advanced version of Siri will be like a best friend. One who will listen when others won't. I believe this wish reflects a painful truth I've learned in my years of research: The feeling that "no one is listening to me" plays a large part in our relationships with technology. That's why it is so appealing to have a Facebook page or a Twitter feed—so many automatic listeners. And that feeling that "no one is listening to me" makes us want to spend time with machines that seem to care about us. We are willing to take their performances of caring and conversation at "interface value."

When roboticists show videos of people happy to engage with sociable robots, the tendency is to show them off as moments of exalted play. It is as though a small triumph is presented: We did it! We got a person to talk happily with a machine! *But this is an experiment in which people are the "reengineered" experimental subjects.* We are learning how to take as-if conversations with a machine seriously. Our "performative" conversations begin to change what we think of as conversation.

We practice something new. But we are the ones who are changing. Do we like what we are changing into? Do we want to get better at it?

Turning Ourselves into Spectators

In the course of my research, there was one robotic moment that I have never forgotten because it changed my mind.

I had been bringing robots designed as companions for the elderly into nursing homes and to elderly people living on their own. I wanted to explore the possibilities. One day I saw an older woman who had lost a child talking to a robot in the shape of a baby seal. It seemed to be looking in her eyes. It seemed to be following the conversation. It comforted her. Many people on my research team and who worked at the nursing home thought this was amazing.

This woman was trying to make sense of her loss with a machine that put on a good show. And we're vulnerable: People experience even pretend empathy as the real thing. But robots can't empathize. They don't face death or know life. So when this woman took comfort in her robot companion, I didn't find it amazing. I felt we had abandoned this woman. Being part of this scene was one of the most wrenching moments in my then fifteen years of research on sociable robotics.

For me, it was a turning point: I felt the enthusiasm of my team and of the staff and the attendants. There were so many people there to help, but we all stood back, a room of spectators now, only there to hope that an elder would bond with a machine. It seemed that we all had a stake in outsourcing the thing we do best—understanding each other, taking care of each other.

That day in the nursing home, I was troubled by how we allowed ourselves to be sidelined, turned into spectators by a robot that understood nothing. That day didn't reflect poorly on the robot. It reflected poorly on us and how we think about older people when they try to tell the stories of their lives. Over the past decades, when the idea of older people and robots has come up, the emphasis has been on whether the older person will talk to the robot. Will the robot facilitate their talking? Will the robot be persuasive enough to do that?

But when you think about the moment of life we are considering, it is not just that older people are supposed to be talking. *Younger people are supposed to be listening.* This is the compact between generations. I was once told that some older cultures have a saying: When a young person misbehaves, it means that "they had no one to tell them the old stories." When we celebrate robot listeners that cannot listen, we show too little interest in what our elders have to say. We build machines that guarantee that human stories will fall upon deaf ears.

There are so many wonderful things that robots can do to help the elderly—all those things that put the robot in the role of the cavalry. Robots can help older people (or the ill or homebound) feel greater independence by reaching for cans of soup or articles of clothing on high shelves; robots can help shaky hands cook. Robots can help to lower an unsteady body onto a bed. Robots can help locate a mislaid pair of glasses. All of these things seem so much for the good. Some argue that a robot chatting with an older person is also unequivocally for the good. But here, I think we need to carefully consider the human specificity of conversation and emotional care.

Sociable robots act as evocative objects—objects that cause us to reflect on ourselves and our deepest values. We are in the domain of that fourth chair where we consider nature—our natures and the second natures we have built. Here, talking with machines forces the question:

What is the value of an interaction that contains no shared experience of life and contributes nothing to a shared store of human meaning—and indeed may devalue it? This is not a question with a ready answer. But this is a question worth asking and returning to.

It is not easy to have this kind of conversation once we start to take the idea of robotic companionship seriously. Once we assume it as the new normal, this conversation begins to disappear.

Right now we work on the premise that putting in a robot to do a job is always better than nothing. The premise is flawed. If you have a problem with care and companionship and you try to solve it with a robot, you may not try to solve it with your friends, your family, and your community.

The as-if self of a robot calling forth the as-if self of a person performing for it—this is not helpful for children as they grow up. It is not helpful for adults as they try to live authentically.

And to say that it is just the thing for older people who are at that point where they are often trying to make sense of their lives is demeaning. They, of all people, should be given occasions to talk about their real lives, filled with real losses and real loves, to someone who knows what those things are.

Finding Ourselves

We are positioned to have these conversations. Sometimes I fear they may not happen.

As I was concluding work on this book I attended a large international meeting that had a session called "Disconnect to Connect." There, psychologists, scientists, technologists, and members of the business community considered our affective lives in the digital age. There was widespread agreement that there is an empathy gap among young people who have grown up emotionally disconnected while constantly connected to phones, games, and social media. And there was much enthusiasm in the room for how technology might help. Now, for people who show little empathy, there will be "empathy apps" to teach compassion and consideration. There will be computer games that will reward collaboration rather than violence.

The idea is that we've gotten ourselves into trouble with technology and technology can help us get out of it. It's that image of the cavalry. Where we once dreamed of robots that would take care of our physical vulnerabilities, now apps will tend to our emotional lapses. If we have become cold toward each other, apps will warm us. If we've forgotten how to listen to each other, apps will teach us to be more attentive. But looking to technology to repair the empathy gap seems an ironic rejoinder to a problem we perhaps didn't need to have in the first place.

I have said that it can be easier to build an app than to have a conversation. When I think of parents who are drawn to their email instead of a dinner conversation with their children, I am not convinced that there is a technological fix for the emotional distance that follows. Yes, we should design technology to take account of our vulnerabilities—those phones that release us rather than try to hold us—but to bridge the empathy gap, I think of things that people can do. I think of parents who experiment with sacred spaces and technology time-outs to reclaim conversation with their children and each other. I think of the college students and CEOs who put their phones away to pay full attention to friends and colleagues. I think of the new enthusiasm for meditation as a way to be present in the moment and discover the world we hold within. When people give themselves the time for self-reflection, they come to a deeper regard for what they can offer others.

The moment is right. We had a love affair with a technology that seemed magical. But like great magic, it worked by commanding our attention and not letting us see anything but what the magician wanted us to see. Now we are ready to reclaim our attention—for solitude, for friendship, for society.

Caring machines challenge our most basic notions of what it means to commit to each other. Empathy apps claim they will tutor us back to being fully human. These proposals can bring us to the end of our forgetting: Now we have to ask if we become more human when we give our most human jobs away. It is a moment to reconsider that delegation. It is not a moment to reject technology but to find ourselves.

This is our nick of time and our line to toe: to acknowledge the unintended consequences of technologies to which we are vulnerable, to respect the resilience that has always been ours. We have time to make the corrections. And to remember who we are—creatures of history, of deep psychology, of complex relationships. Of conversations artless, risky, and face-to-face.

Acknowledgments

In this book, I study something I think is slipping away: a certain kind of face-to-face talk. Unplanned. Open-ended. The kind that takes time. You study what isn't there by studying what is. So to investigate the conversations that were not happening, I asked people what they were talking about, who they were talking with, and how it was going. To answer this question, a lot of people reached for their laptops and phones to show me their latest exchanges. But then, when I said I also wanted to talk with them, they were gracious. My argument about conversation is based on talking to people, face-to-face, many of whom admitted that this usually wasn't easy for them. My thanks to them is all the more heartfelt.

In this work, I had help over the years from two research colleagues. For interviews of students and young adults, I worked with Emily Carlin. For interviews within the business community, I worked with Erica Keswin. In many places, the scaffolding of my argument grew out of conversations with them, and then even more conversations contributed immeasurably to the interpretation of what we found.

Additionally, Carlin was my research assistant throughout this project; she broadened the scope of materials I read as well as serving as the best kind of dialogue partner. In this collegial group was also Kelly Gray, whose taste and wonderful ideas have sustained my efforts to understand things and thinking since I began the MIT Initiative on Technology and Self in 2001. Gray was crucial to that effort and to the shaping of every one of the books that have emerged from it. This is the sixth.

I thank Katinka Matson, Susan Pollak, Nancy Rosenblum, Merilyn Salomon, Natasha Schüll, Susan Silbey, Daniel Stern, and Susan Stern, who helped in the formulation of this project. I also thank Mel Blake, Rogers Brubaker, Jackson Davidow, Amira Eltony, Emily Grandjean, Alice Kurtz, Herb Lin, Nelly Mensah, Chris Meyer, Stan Rogow, Benjamin Sherman, Elizabeth Thys, Rodanthi Vardouli, and Theodora Vardouli for helpful comments as the writing progressed. Conversations with Richard Giglio and Diane Hessan were an inspiration; Jean Rhodes was a generous friend to this project with practical help and new ideas. A conversation with Paul Reitter was the best kind of academic exchange: I left it with new questions and new ideas! I thank Aziz Ansari for our conversations about romance in the digital age. I thank Louis C.K. for giving me permission to cite his poetry about solitude, empathy, and cell phones. Judith Spitzer and Randyn Miller provided the competent and calming administrative backup that every author dreams of. Additionally, the meticulous Ms. Spitzer was able to track down the peskiest of citations that I had noted on little slips of yellow paper whose location became elusive at critical moments. My editor at Penguin Press, Virginia Smith, responded to a first draft with a letter for which I shall always be grateful, one that offered clear directions for what to do next. The review of the manuscript by Veronica Windholz at Penguin Press was a treasured gift. To Drs. Andrew Chen and Leslie Fang I owe deep gratitude for their tenacious work on my migraines so that I could be equally tenacious about my book.

My daughter, Rebecca, read an early draft with a stern and constructive editorial eye. And then she read a final draft and held me to a higher standard. I marvel that I have raised a loving daughter who is also a fearless editor.

MIT and my home in the STS program have been a wonderful environment in which to work on this project. The students in my STS seminar, Technology and Conversation, were a sounding board as I shaped this book. I thank the students in that class (and all of my students from 2010 to 2015 who lived with a professor preoccupied with talk!) and hope they recognize how seriously I took their ideas.

As I worked on this project I was faced daily with the irony that for someone writing about a flight from conversation, this book brought me some of the most memorable conversations of my life.

Sherry Turkle
Boston, May 2015

Notes

THE EMPATHY DIARIES

4 **we often find ourselves bored:** A 2015 Pew Research study reported that younger users of mobile phones "stand out prominently when it comes to using their phones for two purposes in particular: avoiding boredom, and avoiding people around them." Aaron Smith, "U.S. Smartphone Use in 2015," Pew Research Center for Internet, Science, and Technology, April 1, 2015, http://www.pewinternet.org/2015/04/01/us-smartphone-use-in-2015.

4 **a word in the dictionary called "phubbing":** *Macmillan Dictionary,* Buzz-Word section, "Phubbing," http://www.macmillanthedictionary.com/us/buzzword/entries/phubbing.html.

4 **we find traces of a new "silent spring":** Rachel Carson, *Silent Spring* (Boston: Houghton Mifflin, 1962).

4 **moment of recognition:** *I Forgot My Phone,* a short film directed by Miles Crawford, written by and starring Charlene deGuzman, exemplifies the new recognition. It was posted online in August 2013. It presents the following narrative, a cautionary tale about our flight from conversation:

Imagine a day when a young woman's daily routine unfolds normally, with one exception: She forgot her phone. She wakes up in the arms of her lover who idly strokes her arm as he does his email. At a birthday party, guests fuss over getting a picture of the cake. When it's time for a celebratory toast, the focus is on taking photographs of the champagne. A lunch with friends is silent—everyone is on a phone. When she goes bowling and makes a strike, none of her friends give her a high five; they're all texting. She can't share a moment of laughter with her boyfriend when they go out to a comedy club. He has replaced actual laughter with a post "about laughter" that he shares with his online friends.

Within six months of the film's release, it had almost 40 million online views. To me, its popularity suggests reason for cautious optimism. People recognize themselves in its disturbing scenario and are perhaps ready to rethink their relationship with their phones. See *I Forgot My Phone*, https://www.youtube.com/watch?v=OINa46HeWg8.

4   **even a silent phone:** Andrew Przybyliski and Netta Weinstein, "Can You Connect with Me Now? How the Presence of Mobile Communication Technology Influences Face-to-Face Conversation Quality," *Journal of Social and Personal Relationships* (2012): 1–10, doi:10.1177/0265407512453827; Shalini Misra, Lulu Cheng, Jamie Genevie, et al., "The iPhone Effect: The Quality of In-Person Social Interactions in the Presence of Mobile Devices," *Environment and Behavior* (2014): 124, doi:10.1177/0013916514539755.

6   **the precautionary principle:** This phrase is on a mural about cancer prevention in Cambridge, Massachusetts; it was how those who contributed to the mural synthesized the precautionary principle. Genevieve Howe, "Cambridge Mural Cries Out Against the Cancer Epidemic," *Peacework Magazine* (March 1999), http://www.peaceworkmagazine.org/pwork/0399/039904.htm.

6   **to explore the self:** For my early work on children and digital culture, see Sherry Turkle, *The Second Self: Computers and the Human Spirit* (Cambridge, MA: The MIT Press, 2005 [1984]), and *Life on the Screen: Identity and the Age of the Internet* (New York: Simon and Schuster, 1995).

10   **in his cabin:** Henry David Thoreau, *Walden* (Princeton, NJ: Princeton University Press, 2004 [1854]), 140.

10   **But after just six minutes:** Timothy D. Wilson, David A. Reinhard, Erin C. Westgate, et al., "Just Think: The Challenges of the Disengaged Mind," *Science* 345, no. 6192 (2014): 75–77, doi:10.1126/science.1250830.

11   **their ability to identify the feelings of others:** For example, in one study children who had spent five days without devices were able to read facial emotions and correctly identify the emotions of actors in videotaped scenes significantly more than a control group. The authors write: "The results suggest that digital screen time, even when used for social interaction, could reduce time spent developing skills in reading nonverbal cues of human emotion." Yalda T. Uhls, Minas Michikyan, Jordan Morris, et al., "Five Days at Outdoor Education Camp Without Screens Improves Preteen Skills with Nonverbal Emotional Cues," *Computers in Human Behavior* 39 (2014): 387–92, doi:0.1016/j.chb.2014.05.036.

12   **somehow more lonely:** For example, a 2006 study showed that the number of Americans who feel they have no one to discuss important matters with tripled from 1985 to 2004. Miller McPherson, Lynn Smith-Lovin, and Matthew E. Brashears, "Social Isolation in America: Changes in Core Discussion Networks over Two Decades," *American Sociological Review* 71 (2006): 353–75, doi:10.1177/000312240607100301. Robert Putnam's *Bowling Alone* (New York: Simon and Schuster, 2001) describes the deterioration

of American communal life. A May 2012 article by Steven Marchie in *The Atlantic* that considered social media and social isolation sparked a debate on "the Internet paradox." More connecting can make us feel more alone. "Is Facebook Making Us Lonely?" http://www.theatlantic.com/magazine/archive/2012/05/is-facebook-making-us-lonely/308930.

12   **children are less empathic:** See Sara Konrath, Edward H. O'Brien, and Courtney Hsing, "Changes in Dispositional Empathy in American College Students over Time: A Meta-Analysis," *Personality and Social Psychology Review* 15, no. 2 (May 2011): 180–98, doi:10.1177/1088868310377395.

14   **this will degrade the performance:** Faria Sana, Tina Weston, and Nicholas J. Cepeda, "Laptop Multitasking Hinders Classroom Learning for Both Users and Nearby Peers," *Computers and Education* 62 (March 2013): 24–31, doi:10.1016/j.compedu.2012.10.003.

15   **"a national conversation":** In the Bible, the word *conversation* meant one's relation to a community as a citizen. In the mid-fourteenth century, it still derives from words about "living together, having dealings with others," and also "manner of conducting oneself in the world." Dictionary.com, Online Etymology Dictionary, Douglas Harper, historian, http://dictionary.reference.com/browse/conversation.

16   **To take the measure of these:** Many hundreds of conversations about conversation make up the primary source material for this book. I begin with the "one-chair" conversations of solitude and self-reflection and then the "two-chair" conversations of friendship and intimacy (conversations with family, friends, and lovers). I then move out to the "three-chair" worlds of our social connections: the conversations we have about education, work, and politics. Unless otherwise noted, all the interviews I cite were conducted between 2010 and 2015. Unless I quote from the public record or a public meeting, I disguise the identities of the people I interviewed and the institutions (schools, universities, corporations) I visited.

To consider "one- and two-chair" conversations, I talked with over 150 young people from their teens to early thirties, some interviewed in groups, some individually, and some in family settings. I held most of the group conversations in an office or conference room. But some were "cabin chats" with children at summer camp, usually gatherings of ten campers in their bunks before lights-out. Additionally, twenty-seven adults shared their most memorable conversations with me. And I also interviewed sixty-four middle school and high school educators—teachers, counselors, psychologists, and school administrators. In a few places, for a sense of recent history, I look back at the voices of young people I interviewed in 2008–2010. There, I worked with over three hundred interviews that document the not-so-distant days when texting and social media were new.

My chapters on "three-chair conversations" focus on higher education and work. For the education chapter, I interviewed college and university professors, administrators, and students. Here, the number of people I interviewed is hard to add up because I drew on conversations over decades of working in a university.

For my chapter on work, I spoke with a range of professionals including lawyers, doctors, architects, consultants, and members of the financial services community. In a software company I call HeartTech, a design firm I call Stoddard, and a consulting company I call ReadyLearn, I was able to run focus groups as well as have individual interviews with a wide range of employees, from engineers and programmers to financial executives, architects, and administrative assistants. For the chapter on work I spoke with 202 individuals.

When I talk about the conversations of the public square, my emphasis is the emerging political sensibilities of those who grew up with smartphones, and I return primarily to my data on adolescents and young adults.

16   **We have built machines that speak**: I have been studying our conversations with intelligent machines for over three decades. Hundreds of subjects, child and adult, have been involved in this work. For a review of earlier studies, see my *Alone Together: Why We Expect More from Technology and Less from Each Other* (New York: Basic Books, 2011).

THE FLIGHT FROM CONVERSATION

19   "*My guess—and I think*": The Fletcher School, "Eric Schmidt and Jared Cohen on 'The New Digital Age,'"

February 26, 2014, YouTube video, https://www.youtube.com/watch?v=NYGzB7uveh0.

19   "*Don't all these little tweets*": The Colbert Report, January 17, 2011.

21   **Studies show that the mere presence of a phone**: Andrew Przybyliski and Netta Weinstein, "Can You Connect with Me Now? How the Presence of Mobile Communication Technology Influences Face-to-Face Conversation Quality," *Journal of Social and Personal Relationships* (2012): 1–10, doi:10.1177/0265407512453827.

21   **each feels less connected to the other**: Shalini Misra, Lulu Cheng, Jamie Genevie, et al., "The iPhone Effect: The Quality of In-Person Social Interactions in the Presence of Mobile Devices," *Environment and Behavior* (2014): 124, doi:10.1177/0013916514539755. This study takes the theme of "Can You Connect with Me Now?," a laboratory experiment, and investigates it in a natural setting with similar results.

21   **a trend that researchers link to the new presence of digital communications**: Psychologist Sara Konrath collated evidence from seventy-two studies that suggested that empathy levels among U.S. college students are 40 percent lower than they were twenty years ago. She notes that in the past ten years there has been an especially sharp drop. She and her team speculate that this may be due to the increase in mediated communication—"with so much time spent interacting with others *online* rather than in reality, interpersonal dynamics such as empathy might certainly be altered." See Sara Konrath, Edward H. O'Brien, and Courtney Hsing, "Changes in Dispositional Empathy in American College Stu-

dents over Time: A Meta-Analysis," *Personality and Social Psychology Review* 15, no. 2 (May 2011): 180–98, doi:10.1177/1088868310377395.

22 **when children hear less adult talk:** D. A. Christakis, J. Gilkerson, J. A. Richards, et al., "Audible Television and Decreased Adult Words, Infant Vocalizations, and Conversational Turns: A Population-Based Study," *Archives of Pediatrics and Adolescent Medicine* 163, no. 6 (June 2009): 554–58, doi:10.1001/archpediatrics.2009.61.

23 **In-person conversation led to the most emotional connection:** In this study, not surprisingly, video chat was second and audio chat third in providing feelings of connection. L. E. Sherman, M. Michikyan, and Patricia Greenfield, "The Effects of Text, Audio, Video, and In-Person Communication on Bonding Between Friends," *Cyberpsychology: Journal of Psychosocial Research on Cyberspace* 7, no. 2, article 1 (2013), doi:10.5817/CP2013-2-3.

23 **we become most human to each other:** The philosopher Emmanuel Levinas writes that the presence of a face calls forth the human ethical compact. See *Alterity and Transcendence*, Michael B. Smith, trans. (London: Athlone, 1999).

23 **will only know how to be lonely:** This idea is treated in the work of psychoanalyst Donald W. Winnicott; see especially "The Capacity to Be Alone," *International Journal of Psychoanalysis* 39, no. 5 (September–October 1958): 416–20.

24 **our culture of continual performance:** Brené Brown's TED presentation on the power of vulnerability is one of the most viewed TED talks. Delivered in June 2010, by February 2015 it had been watched on the TED site over 20 million times. http://www.ted.com/talks/brene_brown_on_vulnerability?language=en.

25 **depression and social anxiety:** Mark W. Becker, Reem Alzahabi, and Christopher J. Hopwood, "Media Multitasking Is Associated with Symptoms of Depression and Social Anxiety," *Cyberpsychology, Behavior, and Social Networking* 16, no. 2 (November 5, 2012): 132–35, doi:10.1089/cyber.2012.0291.

25 **difficulty reading human emotions:** Media psychologist Clifford Nass at Stanford was working on social media and empathy before his death in 2013. See Elizabeth Cohen, reporting on Clifford Nass's resesarch: "Does Life Online Give You 'Popcorn Brain'?," CNN, June 23, 2011, http://www.cnn.com/2011/HEALTH/06/23/tech.popcorn.brain.ep/index.html. When multitaskers are shown pictures of faces, they have a hard time identifying what the people in the pictures are feeling. When you read stories to multitaskers, they have difficulty identifying the emotions of the people in the stories and saying what they would do to make the people in the stories feel better. See Clifford Nass, "Is Facebook Stunting Your Child's Growth?," *Pacific Standard*, April 23, 2012, http://www.psmag.com/culture/is-facebook-stunting-your-childs-growth-40577. See also Eyal Ophir, Clifford Nass, and Anthony Wagner, "Cognitive Control in Media Multitaskers," *PNAS (Early Edition)* 106, no. 37 (2009): 1–5, doi:10.1073/pnas.0903620106.

25 **greater self-esteem and an improved ability to deal with others:** Roy Pea, Clifford Nass, Lyn Meheula, et al.,

"Media Use, Face-to-Face Communication, Media Multitasking, and Social Well-Being Among 8- to 12-Year-Old Girls," *Developmental Psychology* 48, no. 2 (2012): 327–36, doi:10.1037/a0027030.

27   **the presence of a phone on the landscape:** The study in which even a phone turned off on a table "changes the topic" is Przybyliski and Weinstein, "Can You Connect with Me Now?" As noted, a second study took the theme of "Can You Connect with Me Now?," a laboratory experiment, and investigated it in a natural setting with similar results. It was in this second study that the phone on the landscape led to lesser feelings of empathic connection between people in the conversation. Misra, Cheng, Genevie, et al., "The iPhone Effect."

28   **Are we depriving them of skills:** We know that children from different socioeconomic backgrounds develop different language abilities. Those from less advantaged backgrounds know fewer words and have slower language-processing speeds. They start out behind in their ability to express themselves. If parents from all walks of life don't feel that conversation is important, all children will begin life with a language deficit and a deficit in the interpersonal skills that we learn through language. See Anne Fernald, Virginia A. Marchman, and Adriana Weisleder, "SES Differences in Language Processing Skill and Vocabulary Are Evident at Eighteen Months," *Developmental Science* 16, no. 2 (2013): 234–48.

30   **"continuous partial attention":** This term was coined by technology expert Linda Stone. See "Continuous Partial Attention," http://lindastone.net/qa/continuous-partial-attention.

36   **the most powerful path to human connection:** Mark R. Dadds, Jennifer L. Allen, Bonamy R. Oliver, et al., "Love, Eye Contact, and the Developmental Origins of Empathy Versus Psychopathy," *British Journal of Psychiatry* 200 (2012): 191–96, doi: 0.1192/bjp.bp.110.085720.

37   **"gradual completion of thoughts while speaking":** There are many translations of this essay and this sentiment. See, for example, Heinrich von Kleist, *On the Gradual Production of Thoughts Whilst Speaking,* David Constantine, ed. and trans. (Indianapolis: Hackett Publishing, 2004), 405.

37   **love and politics:** In fact, as an example of how conversation brings us to our best ideas, Kleist uses Mirabeau's declaration of the rights of a nation at the start of the French Revolution. Mirabeau stumbles toward eloquence because he has an interlocutor. You can sense that he thrills his audience and himself.

37   **In the new communications culture:** That there is a cognitive and emotional side to our desire for interruption was pointed out by Nicholas Carr. He said: "We want to be interrupted, because each interruption brings us a valuable piece of information. To turn off these alerts is to risk feeling out of touch, or even socially isolated." Carr, following Cory Doctorow, called the experience of being at a computer being "plugged into an ecosystem of interruption technologies." See *The Shallows: What the Internet Is Doing to Our Brains* (New York: W. W. Norton, 2010), 133–34, 91.

39   **"Scandal! Caught playing iPhone":** Alex Kantrowitz, "John McCain Unapologetic After Playing iPhone Poker During Syria Hearing," *Forbes,*

September 3, 2013, http://www
.forbes.com/sites/alexkantrowitz/
2013/09/03/john-mccain-unapolo
getic-after-playing-iphone-poker
-during-syria-hearing/.

39 **open screens degrade the perfor-
mance:** Faria Sana, Tina Weston,
and Nicholas J. Cepeda, "Laptop
Multitasking Hinders Classroom
Learning for Both Users and Nearby
Peers," *Computers & Education* 62
(March 2013): 24–31, doi:10.1016/j
.compedu.2012.10.003.

39 **the experience of boredom is directly
linked to creativity:** Sandi Mann and
Rebekah Cadman, "Does Being
Bored Make Us More Creative?,"
Creativity Research Journal 26, no. 2
(2014): 165–73. For an overview on
this point, see Scott Adams, "The
Heady Thrill of Having Nothing to
Do," *Wall Street Journal*, August 6,
2011, http://online.wsj.com/article/
SB100014240531119034545045764
86412642177904.html.

39 **What our brains want is new input:**
For more on the neural reward systems involved in information-seeking
behavior: Kent C. Berridge and
Terry E. Robinson, "What Is the
Role of Dopamine in Reward: He-
donic Impact, Reward Learning, or
Incentive Salience?," *Brain Research
Reviews* 28 (1998): 306–69. The
public conversation of how the brain
itself is changed by online life
has been shaped by the work of
Nicholas Carr in *The Shallows*. The
argument is that the more one lives a
life online, the more one is incapable
of quiet reverie (and by extension,
deep reading and full-attention conversation).

40 **emotional life of teenage girls:** Nass
studied the online life of young women,
aged eight to twelve—a critical time in
the building of identity and a stable
sense of self. One result of that work was
this coauthored paper: Pea, Nass, Meheula, et al., "Media Use, Face-to-Face
Communication, Media Multitasking,
and Social Well-Being Among 8- to
12-Year-Old Girls."

41 **you are not focusing on your own
feelings either:** Simon Baron-Cohen,
an empathy researcher, made this
point: "Empathy often goes hand-in-
hand with self-awareness. The people who are good at empathy are not
only good at picking up on other
people's feelings, but they—they're
also good at reflecting on their
own behavior." See "Does Empathy
Explain Cruelty?," *Science Friday*,
September 30, 2011, http://www
.sciencefriday.com/guests/simon
-baron-cohen.html#page/full-width
-list/1. For Baron-Cohen's argument
on the decline in empathy as a cause
of personal and social cruelty, see *The
Science of Evil: On Empathy and the
Origins of Cruelty* (New York: Basic
Books, 2012).

41 **capacities for self-reflection:** Nass,
"Is Facebook Stunting Your Child's
Growth?" For a review of people's
tendency to recall negative events
more strongly than positive ones: Roy
F. Baumeister, Ellen Bratslavsky, and
Catrin Finkenauer, "Bad Is Stronger
than Good," *Review of General Psychology* 5, no. 4 (2001): 323–70, doi:
10.1037//1089-2680.5.4.323. The
work of Antonio Damasio and
colleagues suggests that certain
emotions—for example, admiration
and compassion—actually take longer to process at a neural level than
responses to physical pain. See Mary
Helen Immordino-Yang, Andrea
McColl, Hanna Damasio, et al.,
"Neural Correlates of Admiration

and Compassion," *PNAS* 10, no. 19 (2009): 8021–26. In environments of mediated communication, this matters because interactions happen too quickly to elicit empathic responses. This study's lead researcher, Immordino-Yang, a former junior-high teacher, summed up this finding in an interview: "If things are happening too fast, you may not ever fully experience emotions about other people's psychological states and that would have implications for your morality." A team led by Antonio Damasio also uncovered a link between compassion and the default mode network, the same region that is activated when people are alone with their thoughts. Admiration for virtue as well as compassion for social or psychological pain are processed in the default mode. Both are slower-processed responses, the kind that we are speeding ourselves out of in a life of good news. See Rick Nauert, "Twitter Tweets, Texting May Lack Compassion," Psych Central, April 14, 2009, http://psych central.com/news/2009/04/14/twitter-tweets-texting-may-lack-compassion/5317.html).

42 **"a sentimental education"**: Nass, "Is Facebook Stunting Your Child's Growth?"

42 **every six and a half minutes**: This statistic is from a widely reported study of mobile phone usage commissioned by Nokia in 2013. For example, see "Mobile Users Can't Leave Their Phone Alone for Six Minutes and Check It up to 150 Times a Day," *Mail Online*, http://www.dailymail .co.uk/news/article-2276752/Mobile -users-leave-phone-minutes-check -150-times-day.html.

42 **There are now baby bouncers**: This is known as the iPad Apptivity Seat, made by Fisher-Price. Here is how it is described on Amazon: "It's a grow-with-me seat for baby that's soothing, entertaining, and has a touch of technology, too." It should be noted that the seat did draw pushback from the public. http://www.commercial freechildhood.org/action/tell -fisher-price-no-ipad-bouncy-seats -infants.

42 **within five minutes of waking up**: Marketers rely on this fact—these numbers come from a report co-released by Ipsos MediaCT and Wikia (a web hosting and wiki farm site): "Generation Z: The Limitless Generation Study of 1,200 Teen Wikia Users by Wikia and Ipsos MediaCT," PR NewsWire, March 19, 2013, http://www.wikia.com/ Generation_Z:_A_Look_at_the _Technology_and_Media_Habits _of_Today's_Teens.

42 **send one hundred texts a day**: Amanda Lenhardt, "Teens, Smartphones, and Texting," Pew Research Center's Internet & American Life Project, March 19, 2012, http://www .pewinternet.org/2012/03/19/teens -smartphones-texting.

42 **sleep with their phones**: Amanda Lenhardt, Rich Ling, Scott Campbell, et al., "Teens and Mobile Phones," Pew Research Center's Internet & American Life Project, April 20, 2010, http://www.pewin ternet.org/2010/04/20/teens-and -mobile-phones.

42 **do not "unplug," ever**: "Generation Z: The Limitless Generation Study of 1200 Teen Wikia Users by Wikia and Ipsos MediaCT," PR NewsWire.

42 **six or seven simultaneous streams**: This finding is from research conducted by the LEGO company. It was

brought to my attention by Sasha Strauss's presentation at the Milken Institute's conference in May 2014. "Capturing the 'Cool Factor' in Consumer Tech," *Currency of Ideas*, May 2014, http://currency-of-ideas.tumblr .com/post/84355392003/capturing -the-cool-factor-in-consumer-tech.

42   **likely to be using four at a time**: The top 25 percent of Stanford students are using four media at one time whenever they are using media. Clifford Nass, "The Myth of Multitasking," narrated by Ira Flatow, *Talk of the Nation*, National Public Radio, May 10, 2013, http://www.npr.org/ 2013/05/10/182861382/the-myth -of-multitasking.

42   **degrades our performance**: Ophir, Nass, and Wagner, "Cognitive Control in Media Multitaskers." New research suggests that a small percentage of the population—1 to 2 percent—are able to multitask. For the other 98 to 99 percent of the world, every new task degrades performance, and there is a further irony: The more you multitask, the worse you get at multitasking. Maria Konnikova, "Multitask Masters," *The New Yorker*, May 7, 2014, http://www .newyorker.com/online/blogs/maria konnikova/2014/05/multitask-masters .html?utm_source=tny&utm_medi um=email&utm_campaign=dailye mail&mbid=nl_Daily%20(173).

42   **it makes us less productive**: Zheng Wang and John M. Tchernev, "The 'Myth' of Media Multitasking: Reciprocal Dynamics of Media Multitasking, Personal Needs, and Gratifications," *Journal of Communication* 62 (2012): 493–513, doi: 10.1111/j.1460-2466.2012.01641.x.

42   **depression, social anxiety**: Becker, Alzahabi, and Hopwood, "Media Multitasking Is Associated with Symptoms of Depression and Social Anxiety."

42   **problems with self-esteem**: Pea, Nass, Meheula, et al. "Media Use: Face-to-Face Communication, Media Multitasking, and Social Well-Being Among 8- to 12-Year-Old-Girls."

43   **"the seeking drive"**: Washington State University neuroscientist Jaak Panskepp coined this term. Jaak Panskepp, *Affective Neuroscience: The Foundations of Human and Animal Emotions* (Oxford: Oxford University Press, 1998), 151. For a generalist's concerned view about the neuroscience of technology use, see Emily Yoffe, "Seeking How the Brain Hardwires Us to Love Google, Twitter, and Texting. And Why That's Dangerous," *Slate*, August 12, 2009, http://www.slate.com/articles/ health_and_science/science/2009/ 08/seeking.html.

44   *design for vulnerability*: I owe this evocative phrase to a conversation with Emily Carlin.

44   **"a deliberate action"**: Giles M. Phillips, "Are Mobile Users More Vigilant?," *Proceedings of the 2014 ACM Conference on Web Science* (2014): 289–90, doi:10.1145/2615569 .2615642.

44   **health and emotional well-being**: There are signs that within the technology industry, a new generation of designers is converging on this theme. See, for example, Justin Rosenstein, the inventor of Facebook's "like" button, and Tristan Harris, currently working at Google, arguing for design that does not seize and capture our attention but helps us live our fullest lives. This is design that would measure the success of an app, as Harris puts it, not by time spent but by "time well spent." See Rosenstein in May

2014, http://techcrunch.com/video/ do-great-things-keynote-by-justin -rosenstein-of-asana/518220046/ and Harris in December 2014, https:// www.youtube.com/watch?v=jT5r Rh9AZf4. Harris hopes that "time well spent" could become a new branding standard, much as the label "organic" is something that consumers look for. Personal communication with author, April 6, 2015.

44   words that mean: *Oxford English Dictionary* (Oxford University Press, 2015, http://www.oed.com). http:// www.oed.com/view/Entry/40748?rs key=URvqon&result=1&isAdvanced =false#eid.

46   may not even know: For a review of how universities are trying to put conversation on the curriculum, see "The University: The Social Emotional Well-Being of College Students," Aspen Ideas Festival, July 1, 2014, http://www.aspenideas.org/ session/social-emotional-well-being -college-students.

47   spare parts to support our fragile selves: Writing long before constant connectivity was on the radar, the psychoanalyst Heinz Kohut described fragile people—he called them narcissistic personalities—who are characterized not by a love of self but by a damaged sense of self. They try to shore themselves up by turning other people into what Kohut calls "selfobjects." In the role of selfobject, another person is experienced as part of oneself, thus in perfect tune with a fragile inner state. New communications technology makes it easier to serve up people as slivers of self, providing a sense that to get what you need from others you have multiple and inexhaustible options. On the psychology that needs these "slivers,"

see Paul Orenstein, ed., *The Search for Self: Selected Writings of Heinz Kohut (1950–1978)*, vol. 2 (New York: International Universities Press, 1978).

47   meals shared with their families: The dinners protect from delinquency and drug addiction. They predict academic success. For a review of this research, see Barbara H. Fiese and Marlene Schwartz, "Reclaiming the Family Table: Mealtimes and Child Health and Well-Being," Society for Research in Child Development, *Social Policy Report* 22, no. 4 (2008), http://srcd.org/ sites/default/files/documents/22-4 _fiese.pdf.

48   interrupt dinner *ourselves*: The Facebook ad, with its tongue-in-cheek attack on conversation, signals our cultural moment. So does an altogether serious op-ed in the *New York Times*, "Is Family Dinner Overrated?" The article begins with the well-known litany of positive outcomes associated with dinner. And then it points out the obvious: It isn't dinner that makes the difference, it's whether parents "use the time to engage with their children and learn about their day-to-day lives." The author's summation: "If you aren't able to make the family meal happen on a regular basis, don't beat yourself up: just find another way to connect with your kids."

The intent of the op-ed is to remind parents that connecting with their children is essential. If you can't do it at dinner, do it elsewhere. Between the lines, its message reads: Since we all know dinner is important, but we aren't really eating it together, perhaps we should start connecting elsewhere. That's fair. But if you take away dinner, you have to open up another space. For social scientists to make the point that what matters at dinner is the conversation, not the food, does not mean that dinner doesn't matter. Dinner matters a great deal because it is traditionally the time that our culture set aside for families to talk to one another. Perhaps it is easier to have a fantasy that there will be "another time" to connect with your kids than to do the work of making the kitchen and dining room a "sacred space" for conversation—the first advice I give parents who ask me how to raise a relational child in a digital world. Ann Meier and Kelly Musick, "Is the Family Dinner Overrated?," *New York Times*, June 29, 2012, http://www.nytimes.com/2012/07/01/opinion/sunday/is-the-family-dinner-overrated.htm.

48 **good for the bottom line:** Benjamin N. Waber, *People Analytics: How Social Sensing Technology Will Transform Business and What It Tells Us About the Future* (Upper Saddle River, NJ: FT Press, 2015), and Benjamin N. Waber, Daniel Olguin Olguin, Taemie Kim, et al., "Productivity Through Coffee Breaks: Changing Social Networks by Changing Break Structure," *Proceedings of the Thirtieth International Sunbelt Social Network Conference*, Trento, Italy (2010), http://papers.ssrn.com/sol3/papers.cfm?abstract_id=1586375.

48 **learning more "efficient":** In summer 2011, I attended a retreat for administrators in higher education that was focused on "productivity" in higher education. It was clear that this group saw the problem as how they would respond to demands to "prove" that their system was cost effective. At the center of their deliberations: how online courses would help them quantify student participation and student learning according to standard measures.

51 **magic of simulated feelings:** And in China, Microsoft has released XiaoIce, a sophisticated artificial intelligence designed to chat with you on your phone. A September 5, 2014, blog post gives the flavor of the ambitions of this project: "By simply adding her to a chat, people can have extended conversations with her. But XiaoIce is much more evolved than the chatbots you might remember. XiaoIce is a sophisticated conversationalist with a distinct personality. She can chime into a conversation with context-specific facts about things like celebrities, sports, or finance but she also has empathy and a sense of humor. Using sentiment analysis, she can adapt her phrasing and responses based on positive or negative cues from her human counterparts. She can tell jokes, recite poetry, share ghost stories, relay song lyrics, pronounce winning lottery numbers and much more. Like a friend, she can carry on extended conversations that can reach hundreds of exchanges in length. . . . Since launch, she has had 0.5 billion conversations. People were amazed . . . by her personality and sense of humor. XiaoIce has been ranked as Weibo's top influencer, and currently has over 850,000 followers on the service." From the blog post of Stefan Weitz, senior director of Bing, "Meet XiaoIce, Cortana's Little Sister," September 5, 2014, http://blogs.bing.com/search/2014/09/05/meet-xiaoice-cortanas-little-sister.

51 **exemplars of "affective computing":** See, for example, the seminal work in

this field by Rosalind W. Picard, *Affective Computing* (Cambridge, MA: The MIT Press, 2000).

52 **function, not a feeling:** For more on this, see Sherry Turkle, *Alone Together: Why We Expect More from Technology and Less from Each Other* (New York: Basic Books, 2011), 106.

53 **problem in the first place:** This issue is the theme of technology critic Evgeny Morozov's *To Save Everything, Click Here: The Folly of Technological Solutionism* (New York: Public Affairs, 2013), where he calls this fallacy "solutionism."

55 **take a "smartphone-free" night:** For an example of how one company insisted that its consultants take "predictable time off" from their phones during the workweek, see the case of the Boston Consulting Group (BCG), a large international consulting company. Notably, it was important that the program also included time spent talking in your collegial group, your team, to plan work and support the group. See Leslie A. Perlow, *Sleeping with Your Smartphone* (Cambridge, MA: Harvard Business Review Press, 2012).

55 **Sabbaths, and sabbaticals:** See, for example, digitaldetox.org. There, the rules are: "No digital technology. No phones, Internet or screens. No FOMO (fear of missing out)."

55 **"No one ever pulled out an iPad":** "Steve Jobs didn't let his children use iPhones and here's why." *Inquisitr*, September, 11, 2014, http://www.inquisitr.com/1468612. Apple's chief designer, Jonathan Ive, also limits his children's screen time. See Ian Parker, "The Shape of Things to Come," *The New Yorker*, February 23, 2015, http://www.newyorker.com/magazine/2015/02/23/shape-things-come.

56 **encourage empathic habits:** Sara Konrath, "Harnessing Mobile Media for Good," *Psychology Today*, December 18, 2013, http://www.psychologytoday.com/blog/the-empathy-gap/201312/harnessing-mobile-media-good.

56 **when we allow ourselves to be vulnerable:** This simple statement is an example of something that people don't always want to acknowledge but know "by heart." As evidence of this, again, see the popularity of Brené Brown's TED talk on the power of vulnerability, viewed 20 million times, http://www.ted.com/talks/brene_brown_on_vulnerability?language=en.

SOLITUDE

59 **"being a person":** "Louis C.K. Hates Cell Phones," September 20, 2013, YouTube video, *Conan O'Brien*, posted by Team CoCo, September 20, 2013, https://www.youtube.com/watch?v=5HbYScltf1c.

60 **don't want to get a phone for my kids:** ibid.

60 **important for introverts:** Susan Cain, *Quiet: The Power of Introverts in a World That Can't Stop Talking* (New York: Crown, 2012).

61 **"default mode network":** For an overview of the past thirty years of research on the default mode, see Randy L. Buckner, Jessica R. Andrews-Hanna, and Daniel L. Schacter, "The Brain's Default Network: Anatomy, Function, and Relevance to Disease," *Annals of the New York Academy of Sciences* 1124 (2008): 1–38, doi:10.1196/annals.1440.011. The authors write that "the default mode network is active when individuals are engaged in internally focused tasks including autobiographi-

cal memory retrieval, envisioning the future, and conceiving the perspectives of others." They also discuss potential connections between disruptions in the default mode network and autism spectrum disorder: For them, disruption in the default mode "might result in a mind that is environmentally focused and absent a conception of other people's thoughts": 26.

61 **culture of continual sharing:** A 2012 study reported that the median number of texts (i.e., the midpoint user in a sample) sent on a typical day by teens 12–17 rose from 50 in 2009 to 60 in 2011. For girls 14–18, that number is 100. Amanda Lenhardt, "Teens, Smartphones & Texting," March 19, 2012, Pew Research Center for Internet, Science, and Technology, http://www.pewinternet.org/2012/03/19/teens-smartphones-texting.

62 **building a false self:** Donald W. Winnicott, "The Capacity to Be Alone," *The Maturational Processes and the Facilitating Environment: Studies in the Theory of Emotional Development* (London: The Hogarth Press and the Institute of Psycho-Analysis, 1965), 32.

62 **we live too "thickly":** Henry David Thoreau, *Walden* (Princeton, NJ: Princeton University Press, 2004 [1854]), 136.

62 **reveries of solitude:** See, for example, Kalina Christoff, Alan M. Gordon, Jonathan Smallwood, et al., "Experience Sampling During fMRI Reveals Default Network and Executive System Contributions to Mind Wandering," *Proceedings of the National Academy of Sciences* 106, no. 21 (May 26, 2009): 8719–24, doi:10.1073/pnas.0900234106; see also the overview of "mindwandering" research in

John Tierney, "Discovering the Virtues of Mind Wandering," *New York Times* (June 28, 2010), http://www.nytimes.com/2010/06/29/science/29tier.html?pagewanted=all&_r=0, and Josie Glausiusz, "Devoted to Distraction," *Psychology Today,* March 1, 2009, http://www.psychologytoday.com/articles/ 200903/devoted-distraction.

62 **tends to worship sociality:** For an overview of our love affair with the gregarious, to the point that we have turned it into a civic virtue, see Susan Cain, *Quiet.*

62 **people thinking on their own:** In *Quiet,* Susan Cain tells this compelling story: The original work that extolled brainstorming, getting together to generate ideas, was done by Alex F. Osborn in the 1940s and reported in *Your Creative Power* (New York: Scribner, 1948). In Keith Sawyer's *Group Genius: The Creative Power of Collaboration* (New York: Basic Books, 2007), Sawyer reviews Osborne's studies: They show that although brainstorming leads to *more* ideas, it also leads to more *bad ideas.* People are moved to go along with bad ideas to feel part of a group process.

63 **rise of playground accidents:** CDC statistics indicate that nonfatal injuries to children under five rose by 12 percent from 2007 to 2010. This is a reversal of a decrease in accidents over the previous decade. See Ben Worthen, "The Perils of Texting While Parenting," *Wall Street Journal,* September 29, 2012, http://online.wsj.com/news/articles/SB100008723963904447724045775896 83644202996.

64 **time and stillness:** Erik Erikson, *Identity and the Life Cycle* (New York:

W. W. Norton, 1980 [1952]), and *Childhood and Society* (New York: Norton, 1950).

64   **build their own games:** See, for example, work in the "constructionist" tradition of children beginning as programmers developed at MIT in the group around Seymour Papert's Learning and Epistemology Group. The classic statement of this position was in Papert's *Mindstorms: Children, Computers, and Powerful Ideas* (New York: Basic Books, 1980). This tradition of constructivist work continues at MIT in the Lifelong Kindergarten Group and development of the Scratch programming language by Mitchel Resnick at MIT. http://scratch.mit.edu/info/research.

65   **an attentive other:** Winnicott, "The Capacity to Be Alone," 29–37.

65   **"dialogue of thought":** That is, thought requires solitude. It is the conversation that the self has with the self. Hannah Arendt, *The Origins of Totalitarianism* (New York: Harcourt Brace Jovanovich, 1974), 174.

65   **"Language . . . has created the word 'loneliness'":** Paul Tillich, *The Eternal Now* (New York: Scribner, 1963), 17–18.

65   **Loneliness is painful:** "Deprive us of the attention of a loving, reliable parent and, if nothing happens to make up for that lack, we'll tend toward loneliness for the rest of our lives. Not only that, but our loneliness will probably make us moody, self-doubting, angry, pessimistic, shy, and hypersensitive to criticism." Judith Shulevitz, "The Science of Loneliness: How Isolation Can Kill You," *New Republic*, May 13, 2013, http://www.newrepublic.com/article/113176/science-loneliness-how-isolation-can-kill-you.

66   **"solitude is everything":** As quoted in Sy Safransky, ed., *Sunbeams: A Book of Quotations* (Berkeley, CA: North Atlantic Books, 1990), 42.

66   **"wants to move out of it":** Rainer Maria Rilke, *Letters to a Young Poet*, Stephen Mitchell, trans. (New York: Vintage Books, 1984 [1929]), 54.

66   **facilitates healthy development:** Reed Larson, "The Emergence of Solitude as a Constructive Domain of Experience in Early Adolescence," *Child Development* 68, no. 1 (1997): 80–93.

67   **finding some for ourselves:** Here I see some reason for optimism. The growing interest in meditation and practices of "mindfulness"—as a personal practice and, increasingly, something introduced in business settings—is itself an expression of people and organizations wanting to develop the capacity for solitude. On the enthusiasm for mindfulness in business, see David Gelles, *Mindful Work* (New York: Houghton Mifflin, 2015), and David Hochman, "Mindfulness—Getting Its Share of Attention," *New York Times*, November 1, 2013, http://www.nytimes.com/2013/11/03/fashion/mindfulness-and-meditation-are-capturing-attention.html?pagewanted=all.

67   **We have testimony about solitude:** See http://zenhabits.net/creative-habit.

67   **"freedom from interruption":** Cain continues: "Sixty-two percent of the best performers said their workspace was acceptably private compared to only 19 percent of the worst performers; 76 percent of the worst programmers but only 38 percent of the top performers said that people often interrupted them needlessly." Cain, *Quiet*, 84.

69   **infer emotional states:** David Comer

Kidd and Emanuele Castano, "Reading Literary Fiction Improves Theory of Mind," *Science* 342, no. 6156 (October 18, 2013): 377–80, doi: 10.1126/science.1239918. P. Matthijs Bal and Martijn Veltkamp, "How Does Fiction Reading Influence Empathy? An Experimental Investigation on the Role of Emotional Transportation," *PLOS ONE*, January 30, 2013, doi:10.1371/journal.pone.0055341.

69 **"see things through"**: University of Pennsylvania psychologist Angela Duckworth has researched and popularized the idea of "true grit" as a predictor for success. Angela Lee Duckworth and Lauren Eskreis-Winkler, "True Grit," *Association for Psychological Science Observer* 26, no. 4 (2013), http://www.psychological science.org/index.php/publications/observer/2013/april-13/true-grit.html.

71 **signal developmental achievement**: Winnicott is known for his focus on the child's "capacity to be alone." See Winnicott, "The Capacity to Be Alone," 29–37. For an eloquent elaboration of Winnicott's perspective on boredom, see Adam Phillips, *On Kissing, Tickling, and Being Bored: Psychoanalytic Essays on the Unexamined Life* (Cambridge, MA: Harvard University Press, 1998), 69.

73 **"*being* that machine"**: Natasha Dow Schüll, *Addiction by Design* (Princeton, NJ: Princeton University Press, 2012), 173.

73 **the "Facebook zone"**: Alexis Madrigal, "The Machine Zone: This Is Where You Go When You Can't Stop Looking at Pictures on Facebook," *The Atlantic*, July 31, 2013, http://www.theatlantic.com/technology/archive/2013/07/the-machine-zone -this-is-where-you-go-when-you -just-cant-stop-looking-at-pictures -on-facebook/278185.

74 **sense of self**: Mihaly Csikszentmihalyi, *Flow: The Psychology of Optimal Experience* (New York: Harper, 2008 [1990]).

74 **"what we want you to be doing"**: The Fletcher School, "Eric Schmidt and Jared Cohen on 'The New Digital Age,'" YouTube video, February 28, 2014, https://www.youtube.com/watch ?v=NYGzB7uveh0.

76 **"*presents itself to the mind*"**: Henri Poincaré, "Mathematical Creation," *The Monist* 20 no. 3 (1910): 321–35.

76 **fast and routine work**: David Levy, a computer scientist and philosopher at the Information School at the University of Washington, has tried to systematize Poincaré's intuition. He has researched the link between slow and deliberate effort and creativity's "lightbulb moments," drawing on accounts of scientists, artists, and philosophers.

Levy points out that philosophers have long made the distinction between fast, routine thought and slow, deeper efforts. And Levy traces the fast/slow distinction from the medieval scholastics who distinguished between *ratio* (discursive thought) and *intellectus* (simply looking) to Vannevar Bush's distinction of logical processes (those that happen "along an accepted groove") and mature and creative processes. See David Levy, "No Time to Think: Reflections on Information Technology and Contemplative Scholarship," *Ethics and Information Technology* 9, no. 4 (2007): 237–49, doi:10.1007/s10676-007-9142-6.

77 **"thing in its environment"**: Jonathan Schooler, cited in Josie Glausiusz,

"Devoted to Distraction," *Psychology Today*, March 1, 2009, http://www.psychologytoday.com/articles/200903/devoted-distraction.

77   **a threat in the wild**: Maggie Jackson's *Distracted: The Erosion of Attention and the Coming Dark Age* (New York: Prometheus Books, 2008) touches on the psychological and social underpinnings of our distracted lives—see in particular pp. 45–127. See also Emily Yoffe, "Seeking How the Brain Hardwires Us to Love Google, Twitter, and Texting. And Why That's Dangerous," *Slate*, August 12, 2009, http://www.slate.com/articles/health_and_science/science/2009/08/seeking.html.

77   **come up with new solutions**: Jonathan Schooler, cited in Glausiusz, "Devoted to Distraction."

77   **to find their identity**: Erikson, *Identity and the Life Cycle* and *Childhood and Society*.

78   **"a cloud of electronic and social input"**: William Deresiewicz, "Solitude and Leadership: If You Want Others to Follow, Learn to Be Alone with Your Thoughts," *American Scholar*, March 1, 2010, http://Theamericanscholar.Org/Solitude-And-Leadership/#.Vdf1b-Erhx4.

SELF-REFLECTION

80   **those who have mattered most to us**: See, for example, how the philosopher Charles Taylor captures the notion of what psychoanalysis would call internalized objects: "We define our identity always in dialogue with, sometimes in struggle against, the things our significant others want to see in us. Even after we outgrow some of these others—our parents, for instance—and they disappear from our lives, the conversation with them continues within us as long as we live." Charles Taylor, *Multiculturalism: Examining the Politics of Recognition* (Princeton, NJ: Princeton University Press, 1994 [1992]), 37.

81   **quantified or algorithmic self**: This phrase was first used by the anthropologist Natasha Dow Schüll, who is working on an ethnography of self-tracking. *Keeping Track: Personal Informatics, Self-Regulation, and the Data-Driven Life* (New York: Farrar, Straus and Giroux, forthcoming 2016).

84   **experiment with identity**: Sherry Turkle, *Life on the Screen: Identity in the Age of the Internet* (New York: Simon and Schuster, 1995). See also Amy Bruckman, "Identity Workshops: Emergent Social and Psychological Phenomena in Text-Based Virtual Reality," unpublished essay (Media Lab, Massachusetts Institute of Technology, 1992), ftp://ftp.cc.gatech.edu/pub/people/asb/papers/identity-workshop.ps.

85   **Privacy . . . At what cost?**: Just the perception of being observed can lead to feelings of low self-esteem, depression, and anxiety. So it is not surprising that the more people give up their privacy, the less happy they feel. Kate Murphy, "We Want Privacy but Can't Stop Sharing," *New York Times*, October 4, 2014, http://www.nytimes.com/2014/10/05/sunday-review/we-want-privacy-but-cant-stop-sharing.html. Social penetration theory sketches out the reciprocal patterns of disclosure that in the face-to-face world protect privacy and lead to intimacy. These patterns are disrupted online. New mores take over. See Irwin Altman and Dalmas

Arnold Taylor, *Social Penetration: The Development of Interpersonal Relationships* (New York: Holt, 1973). But even with diminished privacy, people stay on social media, afraid of being out of the game. And once we are on social media, our natural inclinations about the pace of self-disclosure become confused. People worry that they share "too much" online, but they do it because these are the new norms. There are starting to be some changes in how Americans behave online in the post-Snowden years, with some people showing greater reticence. See Lee Rainie and Mary Madden, "Americans' Privacy Strategies Post-Snowden," Pew Research Center for Internet, Technology, and Society, March 16, 2015, http://www.pewin ternet.org/2015/03/16/americans -privacy-strategies-post-snowden.

87   **"watch the football?"**: Jamie Bartlett, "Brand You: Why Facebook and Twitter Are Deliberately Turning Us into Narcissists," *The Telegraph,* December 27, 2013, http://blogs.telegraph.co.uk/ technology/jamiebartlett/100011912/ why-facebook-google-and-twitter -are-deliberately-turning-us-into -narcissists. Facebook was not alone here. Google and Twitter offer similar compilations—also with background music.

88   **"nice musical transition in between"**: Reactions to the "year in review" feature were in the news at the close of 2014. The six-year-old daughter of web design consultant and author Eric Meyer died in June. When he received his Facebook collage, he was upset. His daughter was featured prominently, surrounded by jolly balloons and dancing cartoons. Meyer wrote on his blog: "This inadvertent algorithmic cruelty is the result of code that works in the overwhelming majority of cases, reminding people of the awesomeness of their years, showing them selfies at a party or whale spouts from sailing boats or the marina outside their vacation house. But for those of us who lived through the death of loved ones, or spent extended time in the hospital, or were hit by divorce or losing a job or any one of a hundred crises, we might not want another look at this past year."

Meyer suggested simple fixes. Facebook could hold off on making a picture until it was sure a user wanted it. And don't "push" the app on people. "Maybe ask them if they'd like to try a preview—just a simple yes or no. . . . It may not be possible to reliably pre-detect whether a person wants to see their year in review, but it's not at all hard to ask politely—empathetically—if it's something they want." Facebook apologized. Meyer ends his blog with a call for the industry to think more about the people they touch. That argument, writ large, touches on the larger themes of this book. Meyer says, "If I could fix one thing about our industry, just one thing, it would be that: to increase awareness of and consideration for the failure modes, the edge cases, the worst-case scenarios." http://meyerweb.com/eric/thoughts/ 2014/12/24/inadvertent-algorith mic-cruelty.

88   **The Facebook algorithm:** Facebook did its curation project as a special ten-year anniversary project. Other apps are dedicated to this kind of curation as their sole purpose. One, Timehop, sends users a snapshot of what they were doing a year ago. It describes itself as "A time capsule of you." It

puts this information in the context of the "I share, therefore I am" sensibility, assuming that you will "Celebrate the best moments of the past with your friends!" See www.timehop.com for details.

89   or degree of focus: Of course, some people are more committed to the idea of a quantified self than others. As in any movement, there are different levels of participation. Some simply track their exercise program on a mobile app and find it useful for staying with a weight loss program. Some bring the data from their devices to meetings for help with its analysis; some work to develop more perfect tracking devices and ways of elaborating what this all means for thinking about the self.

91   wanted to understand the algorithm: Technology critic Evgeny Morozov describes the opacity problem in this model of self: If you don't understand the algorithm that produced your output, "it doesn't necessarily translate into any holistic understanding of the self who is behaving." Evgeny Morozov, interviewed by Natasha Dow Schüll, Public Books, 2013, http://www.publicbooks.org/interviews/the-folly-of-technological-solutionism-an-interview-with-evgeny-morozov. See also Gideon Lewis-Kraus, "Numerical Madness," Harper's, September 2013, http://harpers.org/archive/2013/09/numerical-madness.

91   which words had "triggered": 750words.com uses the text-analysis system Regressive Imagery Dictionary to report on a user's emotional state. See http://www.kovcomp.co.uk/wordstat/RID.html.

91   tempted to stop there: Evgeny Morozov, To Save Everything, Click Here: The Folly of Technological Solutionism (New York: Public Affairs, 2013).

93   "just an element in a narrative process?": Natasha Dow Schüll, interviewing Morozov for Public Books.

93   psychologist at the Intel Corporation: Examples of the research of Morris and her team include Margaret Morris, Quasi Kathawala, Todd K. Leen, et al., "Mobile Therapy and Mood Sampling: Case Study Evaluations of a Cell Phone Application for Emotional Self-Awareness," Journal of Medical Internet Research 12, no. 2 (2010), doi:10.2196/jmir.1371, and Margie Morris and Farzin Guilak, "Mobile Heart Health: Project Highlight," IEEE Pervasive Computing 8, no. 2 (2009), doi:10.1109/MPRV.2009.31.

94   "spark conversations along the way": Margaret E. Morris, personal communication to the author, July 3, 2014.

95   the chemicals associated with happiness: Tara L. Kraft and Sarah D. Pressman, "Grin and Bear It: The Influence of Manipulated Facial Expression on the Stress Response," Psychological Science 23, no. 11 (2012): 1372–78, doi:10.1177/0956797612445312.

96   to say what comes to mind without self-censorship: Avoiding self-censorship at the end of the Victorian age was one of the reasons that, originally, the psychoanalytic conversation avoided the face-to-face. The idea was that if the analyst sat behind the analysand, he or she would feel more comfortable saying whatever came to mind, and the analyst, too,

would be free to let his or her mind move beyond the literal. In a session, the analyst follows the patient's train of associations with a free-floating attention of her own. The idea is to help both analysand and analyst engage the unconscious.

98   **"solitude for two"**: Adam Phillips, *On Kissing, Tickling, and Being Bored: Psychoanalytic Essays on the Unexamined Life* (Cambridge, MA: Harvard University Press, 1998).

FAMILY

105   **development depends on the environment**: Recall the study that shows that children from different socioeconomic backgrounds develop different language abilities. Those from less advantaged backgrounds know fewer words and have slower language-processing speeds. They start out behind in their ability to express themselves. Anne Fernald, Virginia A. Marchman, and Adriana Weisleder, "SES Differences in Language Processing Skill and Vocabulary Are Evident at Eighteen Months," *Developmental Science* 16, no. 2 (2013): 234–48.

108   **"harder to learn later on"**: Personal communication, email to author, July 2, 2014.

108   **paid more attention to their phones:** Sixteen of the fifty-five adults in the study did not use a phone and four shared something on their phone with a child. Jennifer Radesky, Caroline J. Kistin, Barry Zuckerman, et al., "Patterns of Mobile Device Use by Caregivers and Children During Meals in Fast Food Restau-

rants," *Pediatrics* 133, no. 4, doi: 10.1542/peds.2013-370. Some fast-food restaurants are building tablets with touch screens into dining room tables. The idea is that customers will be able to order from these screens and then children can use them to play games. With this innovation, restaurants could become places of near silence. Patrons won't have to speak to a server to get food, and, as this study shows, already caregivers and children don't do much talking.

108   **Infants deprived of eye contact:** Edward Tronick, Heidelise Als, Lauren Adamson, et al., "The Infant's Response to Entrapment Between Contradictory Messages in Face-to-Face Interaction," *Journal of the American Academy of Child Psychiatry* 17, no. 1 (1978): 1–113, doi:10.1016/S0002-7138(09)62273-1. See also Lauren B. Adamson and Janet E. Frick, "The Still Face: A History of a Shared Experimental Paradigm," *Infancy* 4, no. 4 (October 1, 2003): 451–73, doi:10.1207/S15327078IN0404_01.

108   **all of the attendant damage:** James Swain, Sara Konrath, Carolyn J. Dayton, et al., "Toward a Neuroscience of Interactive Parent-Infant Dyad Empathy," *Behavioral and Brain Sciences* 36, no. 4 (2013): 438–39, doi:10.1017/S0140525X12000660.

110   **"We become, neurologically, what we think"**: Nicholas Carr, *The Shallows: What the Internet Is Doing to Our Brains* (New York: W. W. Norton, 2010), 33.

111   **read to children and with them:** For Maryanne Wolf's treatment of reading and the plasticity of the brain, see *Proust and the Squid: The Story and Sci-*

ence of the Reading Brain (New York: Harper, 2007). Nicholas Carr was inspired by Wolf's research in his treatment of the more general notion of "your mind on Google." For coverage of Wolf's more recent work in progress, see Michael S. Rosenwald, "Serious Reading Takes a Hit from Online Skimming, Researchers Say," *Washington Post*, April 6, 2014, http://www .washingtonpost.com/local/serious -reading-takes-a-hit-from-online -scanning-and-skimming-researchers -say/2014/04/06/088028d2-b5d2 -11e3-b899-20667de76985_story.html.

111   **talking back to the television**: When computers are used in this "family hearth" spirit, they, too, can bring families together. The popularity of the Wii—the video game console that turned a TV screen into a virtual tennis court or bowling alley or golf course—was in part due to families' and friends' being able to play it together. This is a very different way of using a screen from Leslie's description of a "chain reaction," where each person slips away to his own life on his own phone.

113   **"I shall be fed"**: Erik Erikson, *Childhood and Society* (New York: W. W. Norton, 1950).

114   **a device-free summer camp**: My visit took place in the summer of 2013. All of the adolescents I spoke with at camp were fourteen and fifteen. I interviewed them in six groups of around ten each. Of course, these "bunk chat" interviews took place in a special setting, a place where campers check in their phones at the beginning of a month-long session. So these campers were self-selected as teens willing to do without their phones for at least that long.

125   **wait for the responses to come in**:

"Louis C.K. Hates Cell Phones," YouTube video, *Conan O'Brien*, posted by Team CoCo, September 20, 2013, https://www.youtube.com/ watch?v=5HbYScltf1c.

131   **new conversations about the self**: See, for example, Sherry Turkle, *Alone Together* (New York: Basic Books, 2011). And John Hamilton, "The World Wide Web," Kim Leary, "Cyberplaces," and Marsha Levy-Warren, "Computer Games," in *The Inner History of Devices*, Sherry Turkle, ed. (Cambridge, MA: The MIT Press, 2008).

132   **Communities of practice form**: Jean Lave and Etienne Wegner, *Situated Learning: Legitimate Peripheral Participation* (Cambridge, UK: Cambridge University Press, 1991).

135   **Instead of talking**: Here, in the family, an issue comes up that mirrors questions of privacy on a larger scale, something to which I'll return. See "The Public Square."

FRIENDSHIP

137   **eyes on your phone**: *Macmillan Dictionary*, BuzzWord section, "Phubbing," http://www.macmillandictionary.com/ us/buzzword/entries/phubbing.html.

139   **including face-to-face communication**: By 2012, a Pew Research Center report found that "63 percent of all teens say they exchange text messages every day with people in their lives. This far surpasses the frequency with which they pick other forms of daily communication, including phone calling by cell phone (39 percent do that with others every day), face-to-face socializing outside of school (35 percent), social network site messaging (29 percent), in-

stant messaging (22 percent), talking on landlines (19 percent) and emailing (6 percent)." Amanda Lenhart, "Teens, Smartphones & Texting," Pew Research Center's Internet & American Life Project, March 19, 2012, http://www.pewinternet.org/2012/03/19/teens-smartphones-texting. By 2015, 88 percent of teens had access to cell phones or smartphones and 90 percent of those teens texted daily. Lenhart, "Teens, Social Media & Technology Overview 2015," Pew Research Center's Internet, Science, and Technology Project, April 9, 2015, http://pewinternet.org/2015/04/09/teens-social-media-technology-2015.

139   **self-destructing text messages:** In this case, the receiver can choose to save a message, but the sender will be notified if they do.

145   **Fear of Missing Out:** Studies have shown that when users passively follow the photos and postings of other people, as opposed to actively writing their own posts and uploading their own photos, they tend to experience more envy and feelings of loneliness. For example, see Edson C. Tandoc, Patrick Ferrucci, and Margaret Duffy, "Facebook Use, Envy, and Depression Among College Students: Is Facebooking Depressing?" *Computers in Human Behavior* 43 (2015): 139–46, doi:10.1016/j.chb.2014.10.053. For a general overview of research on Facebook and unhappiness, see Maria Konnikova, "Why Facebook Makes Us Unhappy," *The New Yorker*, September 10, 2013, http://www.newyorker.com/tech/elements/how-facebook-makes-us-unhappy.

146   **Riesman's "other-direction":** David Riesman, *The Lonely Crowd, Revised Edition: A Study of the Changing*

American Character (New Haven, CT: Yale University Press, 2001 [1950]).

148   **shaped by their phones:** In 2012, the Pew Research Center reported that nearly one in four American teens had a smartphone (as opposed to a cell phone)—by 2013, this had risen to half of all American teens. In 2015, Pew found that 88 percent of American teens have access to a cell phone of some kind, with 73 percent having smartphones. For 2012 numbers, see Amanda Lenhart, "Cell Phone Ownership," Pew Research Center's Internet & American Life Project, March 19, 2012, http://www.pewinternet.org/2012/03/19/cell-phone-ownership. For 2013 numbers, see Mary Madden, Amanda Lenhart, Maeve Duggan, et al., "Teens and Technology 2014," Pew Research Center's Internet & American Life Project, March 13, 2013. For 2015 numbers, see Lenhart, "Teens, Social Media, and Technology Overview 2015."

151   **Susan Sontag wrote:** Sontag writes that her own formulation is an update of Mallarmé's nineteenth-century assertion that "Today, everything exists to end in a book." Susan Sontag, *On Photography* (New York: Picador, 2001 [1973]).

152   **everything from glasses:** Google Glass is one example of wearable technology that will display messages directly in a wearer's visual field. For more information on one of the tap bracelets, see http://www.usemagnet.com.

157   **we keep conversations light:** Andrew Przybyliski and Netta Weinstein, "Can You Connect with Me Now? How the Presence of Mobile Communication Technology Influences Face-to-Face Conversation Quality,"

Journal of Social and Personal Relationships (2012): 1–10, doi:10.1177/0265407512453827. See also Shalinni Misra, Lulu Cheng, Jamie Genevie, et al., "The iPhone Effect: The Quality of In-Person Social Interactions in the presence of Mobile Devices," *Environment and Behavior* (2014): 124, doi: 10.1177/00139165 1453975.

157 **can still sting:** A recent study shows that people's perceptions of their relationships are not adversely affected by mobile phone use as long as both people are on the same page about the norms governing that use. It doesn't matter if people think that larger societal rules about mobile phones are being followed. What matters is if they share an understanding about the rules they will follow together. Jeffrey Hall, Nancy Baym, and Kate Miltner, "Put Down That Phone and Talk to Me: Understanding the Roles of Mobile Phone Norm Adherence and Similarity in Relationships," *Mobile Media & Communication* 2, no. 2 (May 1, 2014): 134–53, doi:10.1177/2050157913517684. But the study leaves a question unanswered. Even if you give a friend "permission" to use a phone and drop out of an ongoing conversation, even if you say that it doesn't upset you, your relationship may be changing in ways that a self-report survey cannot capture. For example, "Can You Connect with Me Now?" and "The iPhone Effect" report on studies that show that the mere presence of a phone on a social landscape affects what people talk about. These studies suggest that you may not feel angry with a friend for interrupting a conversation to make a call, but that doesn't mean

the nature of your conversation hasn't changed.

164 **"if they don't get satisfaction":** This way of thinking about friendship treats it as an "app." This sensibility is discussed by Howard Gardner, a professor of developmental psychology and education at Harvard, and Katie Davis, a professor at the University of Washington Information School, in *The App Generation: How Today's Youth Navigate Identity, Intimacy, and Imagination in a Digital World* (New Haven, CT: Yale University Press, 2013). Gardner and Davis distinguish between "app-dependent" and "app-enabled." We are app-dependent when our sense of what is possible is constrained by an app and when we approach only problems for which there is an app solution. We are app-enabled when we use apps as time-savers so we can focus on what is important to us, or as starting points for new directions. Gardner and Davis are concerned that young people may be tending more toward app dependence.

166 **spike in self-confidence:** Keith Wilcox and Andrew T. Stephen, "Are Close Friends the Enemy? Online Social Networks, Self-Esteem, and Self-Control," *Journal of Consumer Research* 40 (November 27, 2012), doi:10.1086/668794.

166 **insecure in their attachments:** Sara H. Konrath, William J. Chopik, Courtney K. Hsing, et al., "Changes in Adult Attachment Styles in American College Students Over Time: A Meta-Analysis," *Personal Social Psychology Review* (2014): 1–23, doi:10.1177/1088868314530516.

168 **an ever more sophisticated archive:** There have been extensive experiments in technologies for life cap-

ture. Beginning in the mid-1980s, Steve Mann of the MIT Media Lab wore wearable devices to record the experience of everyday life. Mann's intent was both to make a statement about surveillance—by doing surveillance on his own environment—and to experiment with computation and remembrance. On his experience, see Steve Mann, with Hal Niedzviecki, *Digital Destiny and Human Possibility in the Age of the Wearable Computer* (New York: Random House, 2001). Thad Starner, also of the cyborg group at the Media Lab, worked on the Remembrance Agent, a tool that would sit on your computer desktop (or now your mobile device) and not only record what you were doing but also make suggestions about what you might be interested in looking at next. See Bradley J. Rhodes and Thad Starner, "Remembrance Agent: A Continuously Running Personal Information Retrieval System," *Proceedings of the First International Conference on the Practical Application of Intelligent Agents and Multi-Agent Technology (PAAM '96)*, 487–95, www.bradley-rhodes.com/Papers/remembrance.html). These ideas were taken up by Gordon Bell, who, along with Jim Gemmell, developed a system, MyLifeBits, whose aspiration was—by providing the user with a wearable camera and microphones—to record a life as it unfolded. See Gordon Bell and Jim Gemmell, "A Digital Life," *Scientific American* 296, no. 3 (March 2007): 58–65, http://www.scientific american.com/article/a-digital-life. Bell and Gemmell published a book-length discussion of this project, *Total Recall: How the E-Memory Revolution Will Change Everything*

(New York: Dutton, 2009). Google Glass is a more recent incarnation of this long-standing technological dream.

169 **take on the visual perspective of others**: Google has canceled the Glass project for now, but while it distributed the product to its beta testers, known as Glass "explorers," I heard many variations on the idea that Glass would serve as an empathy prosthetic or empathy supplement or empathy trainer. One Glass explorer, a man of twenty-six, talks about providing Glass to those who have done acts of violence against minorities so that they could see the racial violence from the point of view of the victims. He knows that there are programs, such as Facing History and Ourselves, that get people talking about violence, genocide, victims, and perpetrators and about putting yourself in the place of the other. But he thinks that technology will be more effective than "that kind of thing." Why? "Seeing is more powerful than listening. People get bored with words nowadays. They want to see things. They don't want a long story." As he sees it, in place of the long talks of the past that we relied on to develop empathy and a moral code, we will take this shortcut: an empathy machine. Is a first-person view of violence what our racially and economically divided society is missing? Or is it simply what we can give ourselves with technology? I am moved by the hopefulness of Glass explorers: Their technology is wondrous and they want it to be useful for serious human problems. But having a technology does not mean that it is useful for every human job. For some human jobs, we may have

the appropriate technology already: people in conversation.

170   turn it into a way of life: Enthusiasm among Glass users is high for using this technology to support those on the autism spectrum, certainly as a support for those with Asperger's. With Glass, one can replay interactions and conversations again and again that were not fully understood the first time.

170   it needs eye contact: Mark R. Dadds, Jennifer L. Allen, Bonamy R. Oliver, et al., "Love, Eye Contact, and the Developmental Origins of Empathy Versus Psychopathy," British Journal of Psychiatry 200 (2012): 191–96, doi:0.1192/bjp.bp.110.085720.

170   what a moment of eye contact accomplishes: Daniel Siegel, cited in Mark Matousek, "The Meeting Eyes of Love: How Empathy Is Born in Us," http://www.psychologytoday .com/blog/ethical-wisdom/201104/ the-meeting-eyes-love-how-em pathy-is-born-in-us.

171   "to read the other person's brain": At Sushi Senji cited in Kate Murphy, "Psst. Look Over Here," New York Times, May 16, 2014, http://www .nytimes.com/2014/05/17/sunday -review/the-eyes-have-it.html.

171   a 40 percent drop in empathy: This is drawn from the paper in which psychologist Sara Konrath collated evidence from seventy-two studies that suggests that empathy levels among U.S. college students are 40 percent lower than they were twenty years ago. She notes that in the past ten years there has been an especially sharp drop. See Sara Konrath, Edward H. O'Brien, and Courtney Hsing, "Changes in Dispositional Empathy in American College Students over Time: A Meta-Analysis," Personality and Social Psychology Re-

view 15, no. 2 (May 1, 2011): 180–98, doi:10.1177/1088868310377395.

171   the resourcefulness of the young: The most persuasive formulation of this argument comes in Internet scholar danah boyd's book on social networks and teens. danah boyd, It's Complicated: The Social Lives of Networked Teens (New Haven, CT: Yale University Press, 2014).

171   Since Socrates lamented the movement: Plato, Phadedrus, Christopher Rowe, trans. (New York: Penguin Classics, 2005).

172   In a series of 2014 lectures: Rowan Williams, "The Paradoxes of Empathy," Tanner Lectures on Human Values, Cambridge, MA, April 8–10, 2014.

173   "from a relationship to a feeling": William Deresiewicz, "Faux Friendship," Chronicle of Higher Education, December 6, 2009, 2014, http:// chronicle.com/article/Faux-Friend ship/49308.

174   They accomplish "what everyone likes": Mihaly Csikszentmihalyi, Flow: The Psychology of Optimal Experience (New York: Harper Perennial Modern Classics, 2008 [1990]), 186.

175   "My friend is one": Henry David Thoreau, The Writings of Henry David Thoreau, Bradford Torrey, ed., Journal IV, May 1, 1852–February 27, 1853 (Boston: Houghton Mifflin and Company, 1906), 397.

175   "any increase in complexity entails": Csikszentmihalyi, Flow, 189.

ROMANCE

180   where you trust and share your life: Sara H. Konrath, William J. Chopik,

Courtney K. Hsing, et al., "Changes in Adult Attachment Styles in American College Students over Time: A Meta-Analysis," *Personal Social Psychology Review* (2014): 1–23, doi: 10.1177/1088868314530516.

182 **"paradox of choice"**: Barry Schwartz and Andrew Ward, "Doing Better but Feeling Worse: The Paradox of Choice," *Positive Psychology in Practice* (New York: John Wiley and Sons, 2004). My discussion follows Schwartz's analysis of choice and its stresses. I found the dynamic he describes reflected in interviews where the conversation was about dating.

183 **leads to depression and feelings of loneliness**: cited in ibid., 108–110.

183 **something they have committed to**: Increasingly, people live in smaller familial and communal circles. As noted, one study comparing data from 1985 and 2004 found that the mean number of people with whom Americans can discuss matters of importance to them dropped by nearly one third. The number of people who said they had no one with whom to discuss such matters more than doubled. The survey found that both family and nonfamily confidants dropped, with the loss greatest in nonfamily connections. See Miller McPherson, Lynn Smith-Lovin, and Matthew E. Brashears, "Social Isolation in America: Changes in Core Discussion Networks over Two Decades," *American Sociological Review* 71, no. 3 (June 1, 2006): 353–75, doi: 10.1177/000312240607100301.

183 **more satisfied with how the chocolates tasted**: Sheena Iyengar and Mark R. Lepper, "When Choice Is Demotivating: Can One Desire Too Much of a Good Thing?" *Journal of*

Personality and Social Psychology 79, no. 6 (December 2000): 995–1006, doi:10.1037//0022-3514.79.6.995.

192 **to make space for them**: Sociologist Jeremy Birnholtz suggests that in their online practices, people sometimes rely on so-called butler lies—a strategy for availability management—to get around the downside of constant communication. For example, if a woman doesn't want to text with a particular suitor, she might respond to a text by saying, "Can't talk now. I'm at the movies." See, for example, Lindsay Reynolds, Madeline E. Smith, Jeremy P. Birnholtz, et al., "Butler Lies from Both Sides: Actions and Perceptions of Unavailability Management in Texting," in *Proceedings of the 2013 Conference on Computer Supported Cooperative Work* (2013): 769–78, doi:10.1145/2441776.2441862.

192 **distracted by their mobile phones**: Forty-two percent of cell-owning eighteen- to twenty-nine-year-olds in serious relationships say their partners have been distracted by their mobile phones while they were together (25 percent of all couples say this). Amanda Lenhart and Maeve Duggan, "Couples, the Internet, and Social Media," Pew Research Center's Internet & American Life Project, February 11, 2014, http://www.pewinternet.org/2014/02/11/couples-the-internet-and-social-media/. A 2015 British study had one quarter of cell phone users taking calls during sex. http://www.yourtango.com/201165808/shocking-stat-25-percent-people-answer-phone-during-sex. In America, a 2013 Harris poll had 20 percent of eighteen- to thirty-four-year-olds answering the phone during sex. http://

www.cbsnews.com/news/cell-phone-use-during-sex-believe-it/.

195   "they'd agreed to type, not talk": Tao Lin, *Taipei* (New York: Vintage Contemporaries Original, 2013), 241.

195   "fight tracking" apps: Examples include "Marriage Fight Tracker" for the iPhone.

201   can be a place for personal growth: These are the themes of my earlier work on identity and the Internet, where for over a decade I studied people who created online avatars. Sherry Turkle, *Life on the Screen: Identity in the Age of the Internet* (New York: Simon and Schuster, 1995).

202   He tried to live it out: On the issue of dependencies facilitated by digital media—and how this affects relationships—see Jeffrey K. Hall and Nancy K. Baym, "Calling and Texting (Too Much): Mobile Maintenance Expectations, (Over)dependence, Entrapment, and Friendship Satisfaction," *New Media & Society* 14, no. 2 (March 1, 2012): 316–31, doi:10.1177/1461444811415047.

EDUCATION

211   "*From what I hear*": Anant Agarwal, cited in Jeffrey R. Young, "The New Rock-Star Professor," *Slate*, November 6, 2013, http://www.slate.com/articles/technology/future_tense/2013/11/udacity_coursera_should_celebrities_teach_moocs.html.

213   we add to the mix: And if we don't do a worse job, it takes us longer. Carrie B. Fried, "Laptop Use and Its Effects on Student Learning," *Computers and Education* 50 (2008): 906–14, doi:10.1016/j.compedu.2006.09.006.

213   how to organize their time: Eyal Ophir, Clifford Nass, and Anthony D. Wagner, "Cognitive Control in Media Multitaskers," *Proceedings of the National Academy of Sciences* (2009), doi:10.1073/pnas.0903620106.

213   said that they text: Deborah R. Tindell and Robert W. Bohlander, "The Use and Abuse of Cell Phones and Text Messaging in the Classroom: A Survey of College Students," *College Teaching* 60, no. 1 (January 2012): 1–9, doi:10.1080/87567555.2011.604802.

215   when students are in class multitasking: Faria Sana, Tina Weston, and Nicholas J. Cepeda, "Laptop Multitasking Hinders Classroom Learning for Both Users and Nearby Peers," *Computers and Education* 62 (March 2013): 24–31, doi:10.1016/j.compedu.2012.10.003.

215   A series of ads: "AT&T Commercial—It's Not Complicated, 'Dizzy,'" YouTube video, posted by CommercialCow, February 4, 2013, https://www.youtube.com/watch?v=yYaS1_VgqbE.

215   the novelist Zadie Smith: See the acknowledgments in Zadie Smith, *NW: A Novel* (New York: Penguin Press, 2013).

217   to be unhelpfully nostalgic: Katherine N. Hayles, "Hyper and Deep Attention," *Profession* (2007): 187–99.

218   "change that environment to fit the students": ibid., 195.

218   "*on the material being presented*": ibid., 196.

219   "we've got to work on that": The Fletcher School, "Eric Schmidt and Jared Cohen on 'The New Digital Age,'" YouTube video, February 28, 2014, https://www.youtube.com/watch?v=NYGzB7uveh0.

219   how technology will "reshape" people: Eric Schmidt and Jared Cohen, *The New Digital Age: How Technology*

Is *Reshaping the Future of People, Nations, and Business* (New York: Knopf, 2013).

221 **are being produced at six minutes:** Philip J. Guo, Juho Kim, and Rob Rubin, "How Video Production Affects Student Engagement: An Empirical Study of MOOC Videos," *Proceedings of the First ACM Conference on Learning @ Scale Conference* (2014), doi:10.1145/2556325.2566239. See also Philip J. Guo, "Optimal Video Length for Student Engagement," edX (blog), November 13, 2013, https://www.edx.org/blog/optimal-video-length-student-engagement#.U71MsxZFFBW.

221 **what she calls "deep reading":** Michael S. Rosenwald, "Serious Reading Takes a Hit from Online Scanning and Skimming, Researchers Say," *Washington Post*, April 6, 2014, http://www.washingtonpost.com/local/serious-reading-takes-a-hit-from-online-scanning-and-skimming-researchers-say/2014/04/06/088028d2-b5d2-11e3-b899-20667de76985_story.html.

221 **depending on how attention is allocated:** Wolf has a developmental argument for how capacity can be lost: "The act of going beyond the text to analyze, infer and think new thoughts is the product of years of formation. It takes time, both in milliseconds and years, and effort to learn to read with deep, expanding comprehension and to execute all these processes as an adult expert reader. When it comes to building this reading circuit in a brain that has no preprogrammed set-up for it, there is no genetic guarantee that any individual novice reader will ever form the expert reading brain circuitry that most of us form. The reading circuit's very plasticity is also its Achilles' heel. It can be fully fashioned over time and fully implemented when we read, or it can be short-circuited—either early on in its formation period or later, after its formation, in the execution of only part of its potentially available cognitive resources. Because we literally and physiologically can read in multiple ways, how we read—and what we absorb from our reading—will be influenced by both the content of our reading and the medium we use." Maryanne Wolf, "Our 'Deep Reading' Brain: Its Digital Evolution Poses Questions," *Nieman Reports*, Summer 2010, http://www.nieman.harvard.edu/reports/article/102396/Our-Deep-Reading-Brain-Its-Digital-Evolution-Poses-Questions.aspx. And Wolf's argument for plasticity gives her a specific anxiety: "My major worry is that, confronted with a digital glut of immediate information that requires and receives less and less intellectual effort, many new (and many older) readers will have neither the time nor the motivation to think through the possible layers of meaning in what they read. The omnipresence of multiple distractions for attention—and the brain's own natural attraction to novelty—contribute to a mind-set toward reading that seeks to reduce information to its lowest conceptual denominator. Sound bites, text bites, and mind bites are a reflection of a culture that has forgotten or become too distracted by and too drawn to the next piece of new information to allow itself time to think." See Maryanne Wolf and Mirit Barzillai, "The Importance of Deep Reading," *Educational Leadership* 66, no. 6 (March

2009): 32–37, http://www.ascd.org/ publications/educational-leadership/ mar09/vol66/num06/The-Impor tance-of-Deep-Reading.aspx.

222 **a new style of learner**: John Palfrey and Urs Gasser, *Born Digital: Understanding the First Generation of Digital Natives* (New York: Basic Books, 2010).

222 **The web is their "information prosthetic"**: Internet researcher danah boyd argues that the most important skill is now knowing how to look things up rather than knowing things. Her position implies that you need your phone with you at all times as an information prosthetic. See danah boyd, "Participating in the Always-On Lifestyle," in *The Social Media Reader*, Michael Mandiberg, ed. (New York: New York University Press, 2012). boyd makes the case that what you find on the phone allows you to make sense of things by connecting the dots. "Creativity," she says, "is shaped more by the ability to make new connections than to focus on a single task." The educators I interviewed suggest another view. It is important to have some material that you have made "your own," by interest, in advance. The idea that all you need to do is "look up the relevant things" implies that you know what you are looking for, which, in the creative process, you often don't. And you need time to process material—you'll be able to do that with things you know "by heart."

223 **the presentation carries its own way of thinking**: On this point, I follow the work of Yale statistician and computer scientist Edward Tufte.

Edward R. Tufte, *The Cognitive Style of PowerPoint: Pitching Out Corrupts Within* (Cheshire, CT: Graphics Press, 2006 [2003]).

224 **what one philosopher calls "E-memory"**: See Robert W. Clowes, "The Cognitive Integration of E-Memory," *Review of Philosophy and Psychology* 4, no. 1 (2013): 107–33, doi:10.1007/s13164-013-0130-y. Also see Annie Murphy Paul in her weekly newsletter on the science of learning: Annie Murphy Paul, "Your Two Kinds of Memory: Electronic and Organic," *The Brilliant Report*, August 6, 2014, http:// anniemurphypaul.com/2014/08/ your-two-kinds-of-memory -electronic-and-organic.

224 **their first choice for answering clinical questions**: Randall S. Edson, Thomas J. Beckman, Colin P. West, et al., "A Multi-Institutional Survey of Internal Medicine Residents' Learning Habits," *Medical Teacher* 32, no. 9 (2010): 773–75, doi: 0.3109/01421591003692698. Cited in Paul, "Your Two Kinds of Memory: Electronic and Organic."

224 **Quick, accurate judgments depend on**: Jennifer K. Phillips and her colleagues write of the relationship of expertise and decision making: "Experts have a broader and deeper knowledge base than journeymen and novices. They understand the dynamics of events in their domain. . . . Experts simply know more facts, more details." See Jennifer K. Phillips, Gary Klein, and Winston R. Siek, "Expertise in Judgment and Decision Making: A Case for Training Intuitive Decision Skills," *Blackwell Handbook of Judg-*

ment and Decision Making, Derek J. Koehler and Nigel Harvey, eds. (Malden, MA: Blackwell Publishing, 2004), 297–315. The authors point out that this category of factual knowledge corresponds to John Anderson's "declarative knowledge"; see John Anderson, *The Architecture of Cognition* (Cambridge, MA: Harvard University Press, 1983).

224 **doctors used to build their own:** Jerome Kassirer, "We Should Encourage Browsing," *British Medical Journal* 342 (2011), doi:http://dx.doi.org/10.1136/bmj.d2182. See also Curtis A. Olson, "Focused Search and Retrieval: The Impact of Technology on Our Brains," *Journal of Continuing Education in the Health Professions* 32, no. 1 (2012), doi: 10.1002/chp.21117.

224 **"information that may be critically useful later":** Quoted in Paul, "Your Two Kinds of Memory: Electronic and Organic."

225 **"Outsource memory, and culture withers":** Nicholas Carr, *The Shallows: What the Internet Is Doing to Our Brains* (New York: W. W. Norton, 2010), 197.

225 **"trying to establish transcripts":** Research on using computers to take notes supports this classroom experience. People who take notes on a computer turn into something close to transcribers. They have a hard time staying engaged with the content of the material. This suggests that there is a virtue in the "inefficiency" of taking notes by hand, a method that forces you to decide what to take down and what not. See Pam Mueller and Daniel M. Oppenheimer, "The Pen Is Mightier

than the Keyboard," *Psychological Science* 25, no. 6 (2014), doi:10.1177/0956797614524581.

227 **massive open online courses:** In September 2011, Stanford put three computer science courses online. The first was Sebastian Thrun and Peter Norvig's Introduction to AI. Thrun went on to found Udacity, a company to deliver online courses. Another of Stanford's first online courses was Machine Learning, taught by Andrew Ng. When it is offered at Stanford, it usually draws over 400 students; 100,000 students signed up when the course was offered online. By January 2012, Ng and Daphne Koller, one of his computer science colleagues, had spun off a company, Coursera. It soon formed a partnership with Stanford, the University of Pennsylvania, Princeton, and the University of Michigan with the goal of producing online courseware. MIT soon allied with Harvard to form edX, their online consortium. Other schools soon joined them, among them UC Berkeley, the California Institute of Technology, the University of Chicago, and Cornell. By the summer of 2014, edX had over fifty participating institutions; Coursera had over eighty.

228 **the year of the MOOC:** Laura Pappano, "Massive Open Online Courses Are Multiplying at a Rapid Pace," *New York Times*, November 2, 2012, http://www.nytimes.com/2012/11/04/education/edlife/massive-open-online-courses-are-multiplying-at-a-rapid-pace.html.

228 **you can easily test the result:** MOOCs were hailed as a unique environment to learn about learning.

Any instructional change can be tried on hundreds of thousands of students at a time. But, of course, the only pedagogical changes that can be tried are those that can take place on a MOOC.

228 **more dynamic than what students had before**: The movement for on-line education contains multitudes—those who see it as a way of getting more conversation into classrooms by freeing up teachers to spend more time away from the lectern, and those who imagine teachers as research professionals whose "rote" teaching jobs can be more efficiently done by machines. At a day of reflection on MOOCs at MIT in 2012, one presenter, very positive about online education, said that he thought a machine could replace professors in presenting content to students. But he didn't know if it could respond to students' questions. For him, the future of MOOCs depended on developing this artificial intelligence. You could never have enough professors to converse with the number of students who would want to take MOOCs.

228 **some called it a tsunami**: Stanford's president, John Hennessy, described online education as a tsunami in a *New Yorker* article about the relationship between Stanford and Silicon Valley. Ken Auletta, "Get Rich U," *The New Yorker*, April 30, 2012, http://www.newyorker.com/reporting/2012/04/30/120430fa_fact_auletta?currentPage=all.

228 **"thinking about something"**: Seymour Papert, "You Can't Think About Thinking Without Thinking About Thinking About Something," *Contem-*

porary Issues in Technology and Teacher Education 5, no. 3 (2005): 366–67.

229 **"Ancient Greek Hero"**: The website for this ongoing community is hour25.heroesx.chs.harvard.edu.

230 **includes face-to-face encounters**: The principal investigator, Shanna Smith Jaggars, is assistant director of Columbia University's Community College Research Center. Her research compared online-only and face-to-face learning in studies of community-college students and faculty in Virginia and Washington. Among her findings: In Virginia, 32 percent of students failed or withdrew from for-credit online courses, compared with 19 percent for equivalent in-person courses. Shanna Smith Jaggars, cited in Geoffrey A. Fowler, "An Early Report Card on Massive Open Online Courses," *Wall Street Journal*, October 8, 2013. http://www.wsj.com/articles/SB100014240527023037596045790934000834738972.

230 **"interpersonal interaction and support"**: Shanna Smith Jaggars, cited in Fowler, "An Early Report Card."

230 **what classrooms teach**: Andrew Ng, cited in Emma Green, "What MOOCs Can't Teach," *The Atlantic*, December 16, 2013, http://www.theatlantic.com/education/archive/2013/12/what-moocs-cant-teach/282402. Andrew Ng sums up the MOOC experience: "We do not recommend selecting an online-only experience over a blended learning experience." Cited in Fowler, "An Early Report Card."

230 **"What's striking is how similar"**: Lawrence Summers, "The Future of X: Lawrence Summers on Higher

Education," *The Atlantic* (video), July 9, 2012, http://www.theatlantic .com/video/index/259430/the -future-of-x-lawrence-summers-on -higher-education.

231 **"When a question is asked"**: Daphne Koller, "The Online Revolution— Learning Without Limits," You-Tube video, posted by CCNMTL, April 17, 2013, https://www.youtube .com/watch?v=Fc8Yl094KOA.

231 **no one in the front row who will upstage you**: Some students tell me that online lectures are preferable because they don't have to deal with students who ask the professor off-topic questions or who talk just for the sake of talking. But perhaps this is a skill that, along with overcoming shyness, it is good to go to classrooms to learn.

232 **"confined to a computer screen and digitized feedback"**: Nwadiuto Amajoyi, "Can Online Courses Replace Classrooms?," *SF Gate*, February 15, 2013, http://www .sfgate.com/opinion/article/Can -online-courses-replace -classrooms-4283110.php.

232 **you might see something unexpected**: Physicists work hard to create "the reality effect" in their lectures. This is the illusion that they are thinking on their feet because most often they are not. Why do they try to create the reality effect? They are trying to model the way creative moments in science happen. You make a mistake, you take the wrong path, you go back and make a correction, you see something new. They want their students to see how this happens in real time. Arthur Zajonc, a professor of physics at Amherst, tries to capture what creative moments in science are and are not: "People have a wrong kind of idea of how discoveries happen in science. They think you kind of calculate your way towards the discovery. It never happens that way. You know, you may embed yourself in the math, you may study it thoroughly, you may have data sets that you're poring over, but the insight comes in a flash." "Holding Life Consciously," narrated by Krista Tippett, *On Being*, National Public Radio, November 10, 2011, http:// www.onbeing.org/program/hold ing-life-consciously/transcript/293.

233 **nothing he wrote on the discussion board**: Bucciarelli notes: "You may well wonder about the value of this experience. What have I learned? I read, watch a video lecture clip, respond with what I value as creative commentary—but how good is it? Is it sophomoric, impulsive, a-historical, all-been-said-before? I don't know. I have attracted no critique. And besides, if a fellow student does offer praise or take me to task—how do I judge the worth of that? It's clear what is needed—a teacher's response. . . . Here lies the Achilles' heel of the MOOC. *A MOOC's massive number of registrants work against students' opportunities for real learning through exchange with faculty and staff*. . . . Knowledge as information, no matter how artfully, dramatically, convincingly, portrayed online is not the driver in the education of youth. It's what the students themselves bring to the show, how they engage the material, under the guidance of an experienced teacher that matters. The discussion forum moves the stu-

dents to write, the talking head may enlighten, but if the student[s] [are] to learn, they must be challenged to reflect on their contributions. For this a teacher is essential to encourage critical thinking, reflecting, (and rewriting)." Louis Bucciarelli, *MOOC Thread Commentary I*, unpublished manuscript, 2014.

235   **They saw the classroom as a place:** For more on the Athena experience and its lessons, see Sherry Turkle, *Simulation and Its Discontents* (Cambridge, MA: The MIT Press, 2009).

237   **Bettelheim is a controversial figure:** See, for example, Richard Pollak, *The Creation of Dr. B.* (New York: Simon and Schuster, 1997).

238   **why not an actor indeed?:** Online classes have already experimented with using models as students. Apparently, it is easier to watch a beautiful set of student "learners," even if they are not learners at all. Models were used for a videotaped class with Harvard Business School's Clay Christensen. The "students" had instructions to look puzzled when he spoke about something complex, to nod when he clarified it, and seem fascinated when he did anything to explain it. Jerry Useem, "Business School, Disrupted," *New York Times*, May 31, 2014, http://www.nytimes.com/2014/06/01/business/business-school-disrupted.html.

239   **set aside for reflections on teaching:** MIT, "MacVicar Day 2013," MIT Video, March 17, 2013, http://video.mit.edu/watch/mac-vicar-day-13993.

240   **might not be worked through or popular:** As I make this point about the importance of visibility, I am respectful that anonymity on the Internet has been important to allow the fullest expression of thoughts for people who feel or who are unsafe in their communities.

240   **his biggest challenge as a professor:** Lauren Berlant and Lee Edelman, "Sex, or the Unbearable: Lauren Berlant and Lee Edelman in Conversation About Their New Book" (discussion, Tufts University, Somerville, MA, February 28, 2014).

241   **life repays close, focused attention:** Not everyone characterizes the lecture this way. I am intrigued to discover that if you equate biometric measures of arousal with pedagogic success, experiments on the lecture show it to be under par. A group of students wore wristbands for a week that measured skin conductance as an index of "the arousal associated with emotion, education, and attention." The sensor recorded regular, strong spikes during periods of study, lab work, and homework, but the readout flatlined during two activities: attending class and watching television. From Eric Mazur, et al. "Blended Models of Learning: Bringing Online to On-Campus," MIT, March 21, 2013, citing Ming-Zher Poh, N. C. Swenson, and R. W. Picard, "A Wearable Sensor for Unobtrusive, Long-Term Assessment of Electrodermal Activity," *IEEE Transactions on Biomedical Engineering* 57, no. 5 (May 2010): 1243–52, doi:10.1109/TBME.2009.2038487.

246   **amounted to a love letter to conversation:** Daniel Kahneman and Vernon L. Smith, "Daniel Kahneman—Biographical," in *Les Prix Nobel (The Nobel Prizes), 2002*, Tore Fraängsmyr, ed. (Stockholm: Nobel Foundation, 2003). Full text available at: http://

www.nobelprize.org/nobel_prizes/economic-sciences/laureates/2002/kahneman-bio.html.

246 one of the founding documents: Amos Tversky and Daniel Kahneman, "Judgment Under Uncertainty: Heuristics and Biases," *Science* 185 (1974): 1124–31.

247 not virtual contact, but live contact: Adam F. Falk, "In Defense of the Living, Breathing Professor," *Wall Street Journal*, August 28, 2012, http://online.wsj.com/news/articles/SB100008723963904443272045776 15592746799900.

247 students don't show up for office hours: MIT, "MacVicar Day 2014," MIT TechTV (video), March 14, 2014, http://techtv.mit.edu/collections/duevideos/videos/28190 -macvicar-day-2014.

247 Students avoid faculty: The complaint about students abandoning office hours goes beyond MIT. And faculty can't think of how to turn this around other than by making coming to office hours mandatory for a final grade.

248 the presence of one strong figure: Laura Vivienne and Jean Rhodes, "Someone Who 'Gets' Me: Adolescents' Perceptions of Relational Engagement with Key Adults" (manuscript under review, 2014).

WORK

249 Alan Johnson Miller and Associates: As previously noted, all of the names of companies and institutions in this chapter have been changed. And all of the names of people as well.

250 clear link between sociability and employee productivity: The casual conversations Lister is talking about are part of the "water cooler effect," a combination of social bonding and information sharing that depends on being physically together in a workplace. Ben Waber's work with sociometric badges—measuring productivity and where people were in social space—shows the power of that water cooler: Employee interaction improves productivity. See, for example, Benjamin N. Waber, Daniel Olguin Olguin, Taemie Kim, et al., "Productivity Through Coffee Breaks: Changing Social Networks by Changing Break Structure," *Proceedings of the Thirtieth International Sunbelt Social Network Conference*, Trento, Italy (2010), http://papers.ssrn.com/sol3/papers.cfm?abstract_id=1586375. See also Benjamin N. Waber, *People Analytics* (New Jersey: FT Press, 2013).

252 is also associated with reduced stress: ibid.

252 The "conversation effect": Lynn Wu, Benjamin N. Waber, Sinan Aral, et al., "Mining Face-to-Face Interaction Networks Using Sociometric Badges: Predicting Productivity in an IT Configuration Task," *Proceedings of the International Conference on Information Systems* (2008), http://papers.ssrn.com/abstract=1130251.

252 "those conversations are worth it": "Presence vs. Productivity: How Managers View Telecommuting," narrated by Neil Conan, *Talk of the Nation*, National Public Radio, February 27, 2013, http://www.npr.org/2013/02/27/173069965/presence-vs-productivity-how-managers-view-telecommuting.

253 **asked employees to work from home whenever possible:** ReadyLearn is trying to streamline its organization by replacing employees who work in more expensive salary markets with employees who work in less expensive salary markets. So almost all teams are global teams and require Skype communication.

254 **take another phone call:** Gretchen Gavett, "What People Are Really Doing When They're on a Conference Call," *Harvard Business Review*, August 19, 2014, http://blogs.hbr .org/2014/08/what-people-are-really -doing-when-theyre-on-a-confer ence-call/?utm_source=Social flow&utm_medium=Tweet&utm _campaign=Socialflow.

257 **puts us into a state similar to vigilance:** Giles M. Phillips, "Mobile Users Are More Vigilant than Situated Users," in *Human-Computer Interaction, Part III, HCI 2014, LNCS 8512*, Masaaki Kurousu, ed. (Switzerland: Springer International Publishing, 2014): 166–77.

257 **the most rudimentary arguments:** Eyal Ophir, Clifford Nass, and Anthony D. Wagner, "Cognitive Control in Media Multitaskers," *Proceedings of the National Academy of Sciences* (2009), doi:10.1073/pnas.0903620106.

257 **distracts everyone around the machine:** Faria Sana, Tina Weston, and Nicholas J. Cepeda, "Laptop Multitasking Hinders Classroom Learning for Both Users and Nearby Peers," *Computers and Education* 62 (March 2013), 24–31, doi:10.1016/j .compedu.2012.10.003.

259 **with the attention that their problems deserve:** Rattan's experience is not unusual. In a survey of 1,215 workers worldwide, 66 percent say they aren't able to focus on one thing at a time and 70 percent say they don't have regular time at work for creative or strategic thought. But the 20 percent who were able to focus on one task at a time were 50 percent more engaged in their work. The authors cite the rise of digital technology as the greatest influence on loss of thinking time because when information and requests come in, "we feel compelled to read and respond to [them] at all hours of the day and night." The authors of the study, Tony Schwartz and Christine Porath of the Energy Project, wrote about their findings in "Why You Hate Work," *New York Times*, May 30, 2014, http://www.nytimes.com/2014/ 06/01/opinion/sunday/why -you-hate-work.html. For a fuller report of their work, in partnership with the *Harvard Business Review*, see Tony Schwartz, Christine Porath, "The Power of Meeting Your Employees' Needs," *Harvard Business Review*, June 30, 2014, https://hbr .org/2014/06/the-power-of-meeting -your-employees-needs.

261 **a "Tabless Thursday":** James Hamblin, Katherine Wells, and Paul Rosenfeld, "Single-Tasking Is the New Multitasking," *The Atlantic* (video), June 19, 2014, http://www.theatlan tic.com/video/index/373027/single tasking-is-the-new-multitasking.

264 **those who have experienced the change:** In one tradition of studying communications of the voice and body (focusing on when people are discussing likes and dislikes, feelings and attitudes), the psychologist Albert Mehrabian has come up with a "7 percent, 38 percent, 55 percent rule." When we are together in the same room, 7 percent of how we feel is conveyed by words, 38 percent is

conveyed through our tone of voice, and 55 percent through our body language. Albert Mehrabian, *Silent Messages: Implicit Communication of Emotions and Attitudes* (Belmont, CA: Wadsworth, 1981).

269 **'Why are we doing this?':** Business theorist Clay Christensen writes about the importance of disruptive innovation to the long-term health of a firm. To make radical, creative change people need data, but they also need time to think and talk. They can't be looking too anxiously at short-term results. Short-term thinking leads corporations to allocate resources to things that have already been successful. It doesn't open space for disruptive innovation.

In Christensen's terms, Tripp feels that his company has made it harder for disruptive innovation to happen because it has destroyed the places it was most likely to come from. That was the relationship among people who worked together every day, who talked together every day about problems and how to solve them. Tripp's company responded to short-term financial results and so is not as likely to get what Christensen calls "market-creating" change, the kind of change that makes the real difference. See, for example, Clayton Christensen, "The Capitalist's Dilemma," *Harvard Business Review,* June 2014, http://hbr.org/2014/06/the-capitalists-dilemma/ar/1.

269 **to increase their productivity and creativity:** While one tradition of work measures productivity in relation to interactions of workers on site, other research tracks the numbers of times a scholarly work is cited and links this to the physical proximity of its authors. Collocation is shown to increase the impact of collaboration.

See, for example, Kyungjoon Lee, John S. Brownstein, Richard G. Mills, et al., "Does Collocation Inform the Impact of Collaboration?" *PLOS ONE* 5, no. 12 (2010), doi:10.1371/journal.pone.0014279.

271 **more productive when they talk more:** Waber, Olguin, Kim, et al., "Productivity Through Coffee Breaks."

281 **whether it was time well spent:** "Time spent vs. time well spent" is the phrase used by Tristan Harris at Google to talk about his vision of a new consumer/industry alliance to build technology that will better serve humanity. In his December 2014 TEDx presentation in Brussels, Harris compared your phone to a slot machine that offered two sad choices: Either you are distracted or you have a fear of missing out. https://www.youtube.com/watch?v=jT5rRh9AZf4.

282 **treating the "iPatient":** Abraham Verghese, "Treat the Patient, Not the CT Scan," *New York Times*, February 26, 2011, http://www.nytimes.com/2011/02/27/opinion/27verghese.html?pagewanted=all, and "Culture Shock—Patient as Icon, Icon as Patient," *New England Journal of Medicine* 359, no. 26 (2008): 2748–51, doi:10.1056/NEJMp0807461.

282 **all of these are being discussed:** For example, see Robert Wachter, *The Digital Doctor: Hope, Hype, and Harm at the Dawn of Medicine's Computer Age* (New York: McGraw-Hill, 2015).

283 **doctors can more easily engage with patients:** On the invention of the profession of medical scribes, see Katie Hafner, "A Busy Doctor's Right Hand, Ever Ready to Type," *New York Times*, January 12, 2014, http://www.nytimes.com/2014/01/14/health/a-busy-doctors-right-hand-ever-ready-to-type.html.

284   **complete important tasks one by one**: For one advocate of slowing things down, see David Levy, "No Time to Think: Reflections on Information Technology and Contemplative Scholarship," *Ethics and Information Technology* 9, no. 4 (2007): 237–49, doi:10.1007/s10676-007-9142-6.

284   **be more intentional about the use of technology**: In January 2015, a New York City–based campaign, "Bored and Brilliant," enlisted thousands to give up aspects of their smartphone use every day. It began from the premise that boredom inspires brilliance and the observation that when you have a smartphone, you don't allow yourself to be bored. When the organizers assessed the results they found that the greatest impact of the challenge was to increase awareness of how phones shape our sensibilities. http://www.wnyc.org/series/bored-and-brilliant. In other words, the impact of the challenge was intentionality.

286   **in an open floor plan**: For an overview of research on the social, psychological, and economic implications of the open office plan, see Maria Konnikova, "The Open-Office Trap," *The New Yorker*, January 7, 2014.

286   **a "quiet car" for productivity**: It is relevant to recall the striking finding about the power of privacy to maximize productivity among programmers. Susan Cain sums it up this way: "Sixty-two percent of the best performers said their workspace was acceptably private compared to only 19 percent of the worst performers; 76 percent of the worst programmers but only 38 percent of the top performers said that people often interrupted them needlessly." Susan Cain, *Quiet: The Power of Introverts in a World That Can't Stop Talking* (New York: Crown, 2012), 84.

286   **twenty-three minutes to get back on track**: These findings from the work of attention researcher Gloria Mark and her research team were reported in Rachel Emma Silverman's "Workplace Distrations: Here's Why You Won't Finish This Article," *Wall Street Journal*, December 11, 2012, http://www.wsj.com/articles/SB10001424127887324339204578173252223022388. It is significant that Mark's findings include managers, financial analysts, and software developers. Silverman's article also summarizes the efforts of companies that are trying to enforce policies of forced attention. One company has done away with email altogether. Others set aside special times for creative thinking. In one case, there is a no-email policy; in another, there are special hours when email is not allowed and which are deemed as times for creative thinking. For a bibliography of Mark's work on "interruption science," see http://mail.free-knowledge.org/references/authors/gloria_mark.html.

286   **we learn to interrupt ourselves as well**: Laura Dabbish, Gloria Mark, and Victor Gonzalez, "Why Do I Keep Interrupting Myself? Environment, Habit and Self-Interruption," CHI 2011, *Proceedings of the SIGCHI Conference on Human Factors in Computing Systems* (New York: ACM Press): 3127–30, https://www.ics.uci.edu/~gmark/Home_page/Research_files/CHI%202011%20Self-interruption.pdf.

287   **predictable time off**: Leslie Perlow, "Predictable Time Off: The Team Solution to Overcoming Constant Work Connection," *Fast Company*, May 2012, http://www.fastcompany.com/1837867/predictable-time

-team-solution-overcoming-constant -work-connection. See also Perlow, *Sleeping with Your Smartphone: How to Break the 24/7 Habit and Change the Way You Work* (Cambridge, MA: Harvard Business Review Press, 2012).

287   **the place where new thinking begins:** On solitude and its importance, including in business settings, see Cain, *Quiet*.

THE PUBLIC SQUARE

293   **the ideas we think our followers want to hear:** Keith Hampton, Lee Rainie, Weixu Lu, et al., "Social Media and the 'Spiral of Silence,'" Pew Research Center for Internet, Technology, and Society, August 26, 2014, http://www.pewinternet.org/ 2014/08/26/social-media-and-the -spiral-of-silence.

296   **those in political power ultimately surrender:** Anthony Wing Kosner, in a blog post on Forbes.com, writes about this model as a game changer: "12 Lessons from KONY 2012 from Social Media Power Users," *Forbes* (blog), March 9, 2012, http://www .forbes.com/sites/anthonykosner /2012/03/09/12-lessons-from-kony -2012-from-social-media-power -users.

296   **"Go out and rock it":** "KONY 2012," YouTube video, posted by Invisible Children, March 5, 2012, https:// www.youtube.com/watch?v=Y4 MnpzG5Sqc.

297   **a direct source of political change:** Malcolm Gladwell refers to Clay Shirky's *Here Comes Everybody* (New York: Penguin Press, 2008) as the "bible of the social media movement," though Shirky is not alone in extolling the utopian possibilities of social media for political action. Malcolm Gladwell, "Small Change: Why the Revolution Will Not Be Tweeted," *New Yorker*, October 4, 2010, http://www.newyorker.com/ magazine/2010/10/04/small -change-3. The Kony video also got its share of negative press, most of it critical of its "slacktivism," the way it turned activism into the feeling of activism. See, for example, Michael Deibert, "The Problem with 'Invisible Children: Kony 2012,'" *Huffington Post*, March 7, 2012, http://www.huffingtonpost .com/michael-deibert/joseph-kony -2012-children_b_1327417.html. Some of the critical literature is summarized in Eleanor Goldberg, "Invisible Children, Group Behind 'Kony 2012,' Closing Because of Funding Issues," *Huffington Post*, December 16, 2015, http://www .huffingtonpost.com/2014/12/16/ invisible-children-closing _n_6329990.html.

297   **nominated for the Nobel Peace Prize:** Mark Pfeifle, cited in Gladwell, "Small Change."

297   **the State Department asked Twitter:** Ibid.

297   **The power of weak ties is awesome:** Gladwell does not minimize what you can accomplish with weak ties. Among other things, he notes that studies show that "our acquaintances—not our friends—are our greatest source of new ideas and information." Gladwell, "Small Change." Here, Gladwell cites Stanford sociologist Mark Granovetter's work on weak ties. See, for example, Mark Granovetter, "The Strength of Weak Ties," *American Journal of Sociology* 78, no. 6 (1973): 1360–80, http://www.jstor.org/stable/2776392.

But the civil rights movement became effective as it turned bloody and dangerous. Gladwell asks, "What makes people capable of this kind of activism?" To answer this question, one place Gladwell looks is to a study that compared those who stuck with the Freedom Summer movement and those who dropped out. Those who stayed in were likely to have close personal friends who were going to Mississippi. In "Small Change" Gladwell concludes that high-risk activism is a "strong-tie" phenomenon.

298 **"was flanked by his roommate"**: Gladwell, "Small Change."

302 **Is there free thought without privacy?**: The Fourth Amendment to the United States Constitution makes citizens immune from unreasonable search and seizure of their possessions. The amendment applies to their books and papers. Now that our books and papers are digital, should they be fair game?

304 **"Where do you want to go today?"** Evgeny Morozov, "The Death of the Cyberflâneur," *New York Times,* February 4, 2012, http://www.nytimes.com/2012/02/05/opinion/sunday/the-death-of-the-cyberflaneur.html?pagewanted=all&_r=0.

305 **searches of ordinary Americans are monitored**: A write-up of a cache of intercepted conversations given to the *Washington Post* by Edward Snowden revealed that "nine of ten account holders . . . were not the intended surveillance targets but were caught in a net the agency had cast for somebody else." Barton Gellman, Julie Tate, and Ashkan Soltani, "In NSA-Intercepted Data, Those Not Targeted Far Outnumber the Foreigners Who Are," *Washington Post,* July 5, 2014, http://www.washingtonpost.com/world/national-security/in-nsa-intercepted-data-those-not-targeted-far-outnumber-the-foreigners-who-are/2014/07/05/8139adf8-045a-11e4-8572-4b1b969b6322_story.html.

305 **is out of sync**: You are in a new kind of space; the term "hyper-public" has been used in an effort to capture the kind of space it is. Harvard's Berkman Center for Internet and Society hosted "Hyper-Public: A Symposium on Designing Privacy and Public Space in the Connected World," in June 2011. The symposium website has background information and video footage from the conference, http://www.hyperpublic.org.

In May 2015, a federal appeals court found that some of the NSA searches, in particular the bulk collection of data on individuals, is illegal. This area of law is fast-moving, in line, I believe, with my hypothesis that it is time to rethink where we are on these matters. Charlie Savage and Jonathan Weisman, "NSA Collection of Bulk Call Data Is Ruled Illegal," *New York Times,* May 7, 2015.

305 **Bentham's image of panopticon surveillance**: Michel Foucault, *Discipline and Punish*, Alan Sheridan, trans. (New York: Pantheon Books, 1977 [1975]).

306 **the feeling that we are cared for**: Rob Horning, "No Life Stories," *New Inquiry,* July 10, 2014, http://thenewinquiry.com/essays/no-life-stories, a review of Marc Andrejevic's *Infoglut: How Too Much Information Is Changing the Way We Think and Know* (London: Routledge, 2013).

306 **can provide "natural data" to the system**: Zeynep Tufecki, "Engineering the Public: Big Data, Surveillance,

and Computational Politics," *First Monday* 19, no. 7 (2014), http://first monday.org/ojs/index.php/fm/article/view/4901/4097.

307 **It places us in a particular world:** Eli Pariser, *The Filter Bubble: How the New Personalized Web Is Changing What We Read and How We Think* (New York: Penguin Press, 2013). Also on this topic, see Rob Horning, "No Life Stories." The degree to which the net polarizes is an important and researchable topic. As this book goes to press, a new study has been published, done by Facebook investigators and published in *Science*, that suggests that the polarization effects of the Facebook News Feed are less significant than expected. Almost 29 percent of the news stories displayed by Facebook's News Feed presents views that conflict with the user's own ideology. Eytan Bakshy, Solomon Messing, and Lada Adamic, "Exposure to Ideologically Diverse News and Opinion on Facebook," *Science*, May 2, 2015. doi: 10.1126/science.aaa1160. The discussion of this study centers on the fragility of this hopeful finding: The algorithm for what shows up in the News Feed is after all determined by Facebook and can be changed by Facebook. (Most recently, Facebook has given users greater control over what appears in their timeline— again, an intriguing corporate decision in the direction of transparency but one that can be reversed.) The new study about the diversity of what we see in a Facebook News Feed is in dialogue with other studies, such as the 2014 Pew study that suggested that online we read what we agree with and post what we think our followers will want to hear, the idea of a

"spiral of silence." Keith Hampton, Lee Rainie, Weixu Lu, et al., "Social Media and the Spiral of Silence," Pew Research Center's Internet & American Life Project, August 26, 2014, http://www.pewinternet.org/2014/08/26/social-media-and-the-spiral-of-silence.

307 **just not to you:** Jonathan Zittrain, "Facebook Could Decide an Election Without Anyone Ever Finding Out," *New Republic*, June 1, 2014, http://www.newrepublic.com/article/117878/information-fiduciary-solution-facebook-digital-gerrymandering.

307 **"The most successful tyranny":** Allan Bloom, *The Closing of the American Mind* (New York: Simon and Schuster, 2008 [1987]), 249.

307 **actively constructs its version of you:** Sara M. Watson, "Data Doppelgängers and the Uncanny Valley of Personalization," *The Atlantic*, June 16, 2014, http://www.theatlantic.com/technology/archive/2014/06/data-doppelgangers-and-the-uncanny-valley-of-personalization/372780.

We have become what the social philosopher Gilles Deleuze called "dividuals," to denote entities comprised of multiple parcels of data that can be bought, sold, and traded in the new marketplace. The dividual is an aggregate of recorded preferences, histories, and tastes. If we are disoriented and unsure in our new situation, Deleuze would say this is natural. We have never been dividuals before. Gilles Deleuze, "Postscript on the Societies of Control," *October* 59 (1992): 3–7, http://jstor.org/stable778828.

308 **"evolves out of its wooden brain":** Karl Marx, *Capital, Volume 1: A Critique of Political Economy* (New York: Penguin Classics, 1992 [1867]).

308 "a line has been crossed": Watson, "Data Doppelgängers."

308 reached its conclusion about her: Watson comes to understand that the study is targeting all women in her age group. Ibid.

308 And how can she challenge: In this, Watson is like respondents in a 2014 Pew study of privacy and the Internet. They didn't think they had enough privacy, but they didn't know what to do about it. Eighty percent of those who use social networking sites like Facebook, Twitter, and LinkedIn are concerned about advertisers and businesses accessing the information they share on the sites. Two-thirds of them think the government should do more to regulate those advertisers. Mary Madden, "Public Perceptions of Privacy and Security in the Post-Snowden Era," Pew Research Center's Internet & American Life Project, November 12, 2014, http://www.pewinternet.org/2014/11/12/public-privacy-perceptions/.

308 "knows us better than we know ourselves": Watson, "Data Doppelgängers."

309 "rather go to a movie": Zuckerberg said this during an interview with Charlie Rose, noted by Morozov, "The Death of the Cyberflâneur." He is cited in Neil M. Richards, "The Perils of Social Reading," Georgetown Law Journal 101, no. 689 (2013): 691, http://ssrn.com/abstract=2031307.

309 "and even thinking": ibid.

309 blogging as a regular part of her academic program: Molly Sauter, "Curiosity, Being Yourself, and Being Bad at Things," Odd Letters: The Online Home of Molly Sauter (blog), December 5, 2013, http://oddletters

.com/2013/12/05/curiosity-being-yourself-and-being-bad-at-things.

310 friends might disagree with them: Hampton, Rainie, Lu, et al., "Social Media and the 'Spiral of Silence.' "

310 "Crowdsourcing" your reading preferences: Richards, "The Perils of Social Reading."

310 easy not to think about something: On a cognitive level, problems that are not clearly defined are nearly impossible for people to care about as moral problems. Researchers have studied how this is true of climate change—a problem that is "complex, large-scale and unintentionally caused." Ezra M. Markowitz and Azim F. Shariff, "Climate Change and Moral Judgment," Nature Climate Change 2 (2012): 243–47, doi:10.1038/nclimate1378. See also Matthew C. Nisbet, "Communicating Climate Change: Why Frames Matter for Public Engagement," Environment: Science and Policy for Sustainable Development 51, no. 2 (2009): 12–23, doi:10.3200/ENVT.51.2.12-23.

312 a blizzard of acronyms: On teenagers' strategies for preserving their privacy from parents and others in their communities, see danah boyd, It's Complicated: The Social Lives of Networked Teens (New Haven, CT: Yale University Press, 2013).

312 experts tell us that this is not true: In one classic example from 1997, Carnegie Mellon computer scientist Latanya Sweeney reidentified the medical record of William Weld—then-governor of Massachusetts—using only data on gender, date of birth, and home zip code. "No Silver Bullet: De-Identification Still Doesn't Work" (unpublished), http://randomwalker.info/publications/no

-silver-bullet-de-identification.pdf. Other, more recent studies have shown that many personal characteristics—including sexual orientation, ethnicity, religious views, and political views—can be predicted by nothing more than Facebook "likes": Michal Kosinski, David Stillwell, and Thore Graepel, "Private Traits and Attributes Are Predictable from Digital Records of Human Behavior," *Proceedings of the National Academy of Sciences* 110, no. 15 (2013): 5802–5, doi:10.1073/pnas.1218772110, cited in Zeynep Tufecki, "Engineering the Public: Big Data, Surveillance, and Computational Politics," *First Monday* 19, no. 7 (2014), http://firstmonday.org/ojs/index.php/fm/article/view/4901/4097.

312 **you will also activate "full tracking":** Patrick Tucker, "If You Do This, the NSA Will Spy on You," *Defense One,* July 7, 2014, http://www.defenseone.com/technology/2014/07/if-you-do-nsa-will-spy-you/88054/?oref=d-topstory. See also Sean Gallagher, "The NSA Thinks Linux Journal Is an 'Extremist Forum'?" *ArsTechnica,* July 3, 2014, http://arstechnica.com/security/2014/07/the-nsa-thinks-linux-journal-is-an-extremist-forum/.

314 **manipulation of votes by social media:** Zittrain, "Facebook Could Decide an Election Without Anyone Ever Finding Out," *New Republic,* June 1, 2014, http://www.newrepublic.com/article/117878/information-fiduciary-solution-facebook-digital-gerrymandering.

314 **to see if this changed their moods:** Adam D. I. Kramer, Jamie E. Guillory, and Jeffrey T. Hancock, "Experimental Evidence of Massive-Scale Emotional Contagion Through Social Networks," *Proceedings of the National Academy of Sciences of the United States of America* 111, no. 24 (2014): 8788–90, doi:10.1073/pnas.1320040111. For comprehensive coverage of this story, see "Everything We Know About Facebook's Secret Mood Manipulation Experiment," *The Atlantic,* June 28, 2014, http://www.theatlantic.com/technology/archive/2014/06/everything-we-know-about-facebooks-secret-mood-manipulation-experiment/373648.

315 **knows a lot more about them:** During an April 2015 interview with Edward Snowden, the comedian and TV host John Oliver pursued an "objects to think with" strategy. He told Snowden that Americans have a hard time relating directly to the idea that the government has the ability to listen to their phone calls but care deeply if the government has the right to look at photographs of their private parts that they post online or send as a JPEG file attached to an email or text. The comedian had come to the interview with a photograph of his genitals that now resided online. Snowden was then asked which surveillance programs would give the government legal cover to look at Oliver's naked self. "John Oliver Interviews Edward Snowden," *Last Week Tonight with John Oliver,* HBO, April 6, 2015, https://www.youtube.com/watch?v=XEVlyP4_11M.

316 **"The way to deal is to just be good":** Talking about using Google services that will monitor your home, Eric Schmidt's position was "If you don't like it, don't use it." The Fletcher

School, "Eric Schmidt and Jared Cohen on 'The New Digital Age,'" YouTube video, February 28, 2014, https://www.youtube.com/watch?v=NYGzB7uveh0. Eric Schmidt made his first remark about controlling individual behavior rather than worrying about controlling privacy to CNBC. The video is available at Ryan Tate, "Google CEO: Secrets Are for Filthy People," *Gawker*, December 4, 2009, http://gawker.com/5419271/google-ceo-secrets-are-for-filthypeople. An earlier and much-quoted variant of this sentiment was voiced by Scott McNealy, then-CEO of Sun Microsystems, when he said at a press event for a launch of its Jini technology in 1999, "You have zero privacy anyway. Get over it." The incident was widely reported. See, for example, Sally Sprenger, "Sun on Privacy: Get Over It," *Wired*, January 26, 1999. http://archive.wired.com/politics/law/news/1999/01/17538.

316   **this conversation about technology, privacy, and democracy**: I first made this argument in *Alone Together*. Over time, I believe it has taken on greater urgency. Sherry Turkle, *Alone Together: Why We Expect More from Technology and Less from Each Other* (New York: Basic Books, 2011).

THE NICK OF TIME

317   *"what we refuse to destroy"*: John Sawhill, cited in E. O. Wilson, *The Future of Life* (New York: Knopf, 2002), vi.

317   **pushed his chairs to its far corners**: Henry David Thoreau, *Walden* (Princeton, NJ: Princeton University Press, 2004 [1854]), 141.

317   **begin to recover their empathic**

capacity: Yalda T. Uhls, Minas Michikyan, Jordan Morris, et al., "Five Days at Outdoor Education Camp Without Screens Improves Preteen Skills with Nonverbal Emotional Cues," *Computers in Human Behavior* 39 (2014): 387–92, doi: 0.1016/j.chb.2014.05.036.

318   **they atrophy if not exercised**: Clifford Nass, "Is Facebook Stunting Your Child's Growth?," *Pacific Standard*, April 23, 2012.

319   **A first step is to slow down**: For one example of writing on this theme, see David Levy, "No Time to Think: Reflections on Information Technology and Contemplative Scholarship," *Ethics and Information Technology* 9, no. 4 (2007): 237–49, doi:10.1007/s10676-007-9142-6.

320   **a mechanical "Memex" would free us**: Vannevar Bush, "As We May Think," *Atlantic Monthly*, July 1945, 101–6, http://www.theatlantic.com/magazine/archive/1945/07/as-we-may-think/303881.

320   **to return to the spirit of Bush's original idea**: On this point, Arianna Huffington has encouraged and supported the conversation. See Arianna Huffington, *Thrive: The Third Metric to Redefining Success and Creating a Life of Well-Being, Wisdom, and Wonder* (New York: Harmony, 2014).

320   **to encourage thought, talk, and new ideas**: "Go Inside Google Garage, the Collaborative Workspace That Thrives on Crazy, Collaborative Ideas," *Fast Company* (video), http://www.fastcompany.com/3017509/work-smart/look-inside-google-garage-the-collaborative-workspace-that-thrives-on-crazy-creat.

322   **they fear their followers will disagree**: The study also showed, surprisingly, that social media users were also less

willing than nonusers to discuss their views offline. Keith Hampton, Lee Rainie, Weixu Lu, et al., "Social Media and the 'Spiral of Silence,'" Pew Research Center's Internet & American Life Project, August 26, 2014, http://www.pewinternet.org/2014/08/26/social-media-and-the-spiral-of-silence. I have noted that a new study by Facebook scientists, published in *Science*, challenges the strength of this effect. Eytan Bakshy, Solomon Messing, and Lada Adamic, "Exposure to Ideologically Diverse News and Opinion on Facebook," *Science*, May 2, 2015. doi:10.1126/science.aaa1160.

322 **who do not share their views:** Rebecca Ellen Turkle Willard, "The Irrelevant Opposition: Reference Groups in the Formation of Political Attitudes Among Partisan College Students" (undergraduate dissertation, Harvard College, 2014).

322 **Even a small amount of common ground can nurture a conversation:** And to nurture conversation, it would help to break the habit of bringing data sets to the table as a substitute for discussing the substance of issues. More than ever, data can deceive. We have so much data now that we can do correlational studies that support every and any position. Famously, recent correlational studies linked intelligence to a love of curly fries. What this correlation lacked—and this is "Big Data's" threat to reasoned conversation—is a rationale, a hypothesis, a theory. It showed only that with enough data you can show anything. Michal Kosinski, David Stillwell, and Thore Graepel, "Private Traits and Attributes Are Predictable from Digital Records of Human Behavior," *Proceedings of the National Academy of Sciences* 110, no. 15 (2013): 5802–5, doi:10.1073/pnas.1218772110.

323 **grew up with phones in hand:** Howard Gardner and Katie Davis, *The App Generation: How Today's Youth Navigate Identity, Intimacy, and Imagination in a Digital World* (New Haven, CT: Yale University Press, 2013).

325 **require eye contact for emotional stability and social fluency:** For example, Atushi Senju and Mark H. Johnson, "The Eye Contact Effect: Mechanisms and Development," *Trends in Cognitive Sciences* 13, no. 3 (January 3, 2009): 127–34, doi:10.1016/j.tics.2008.11.009, and Laura Pönkänen, Annemari Alhoniemi, Jukka M. Leppänen, et al., "Does It Make a Difference If I Have Eye Contact with You or with Your Picture? An ERP Study," *Social Cognitive and Affective Neuroscience* 6, no. 4 (September 1, 2011): 486–94, doi:10.1093/scan/nsq068.

326 **It can bring us back to ourselves and others:** This point was made when the author Sebastian Junger tried to find meaning in years of overseas combat with a group of veterans returned home. His choice was to take a long walk with them in order to share solitude in difficult, intimate conversations. They took a walk across America, "a 300-mile, 400-mile conversation about war, and how it affects you and why so many young men miss it when it's over." Gisele Regato, "A 300 Mile Walk to Talk About War," WNYC News, October 23, 2014, http://www.wnyc.org/story/300-mile-walk-talk-about-war.

326 **walking was a kind of shared solitude:** Adam Gopnik writes about walking as a form of Western meditation and shared solitude in "Heaven's Gaits:

What We Do When We Walk," *The New Yorker*, September 10, 2014, http://www.newyorker.com/magazine/2014/09/01/heavens-gaits. The article reviews Frédéric Gros, *A Philosophy of Walking*, John Howe, trans. (New York: Verso, 2014 [2009]). Gros says, "for solitude too can be shared, like bread and daylight."

Thoreau's comments on walking as a way to "shake off the village" are from a June 1, 1862, essay, "Walking," originally published in *The Atlantic*. They are cited by Arianna Huffington in *Thrive*, 100. Huffington also cites Nilofer Merchant, a Silicon Valley executive who has walking meetings instead of meetings at her desk. There is no phone to distract. In Merchant's TED talk on walking, she calls it "walking the talk." Nilofer Merchant, "Got a Meeting? Take a Walk," TED mainstage, February 2013, http://www.ted.com/talks/nilofer_merchant_got_a_meeting_take_a_walk?language=en. In a *New York Times* article on walking, quoted by Huffington, Merchant expands: "What I love is that you're literally facing your problem or situation together when you walk side by side with someone. . . . I love that people can't be checking email or Twitter during walking meetings. You're awake to what's happening around you, your senses are heightened and you walk away with something office meetings rarely give you—a sense of joy." David Hochman, "Hollywood's New Stars: Pedestrians," August 16, 2013, http://www.nytimes.com/2013/08/18/fashion/hollywoods-new-stars-pedestrians.html?pagewanted=1&_r=2.

327 **we are very interested indeed**: One survey reports that only 35 percent of eighteen- to twenty-four-year-olds will say they are interested in privacy matters in regard to mobile communications, with those over forty years old showing only slightly greater interest. See "Can Data Become a New Currency?," *Amdocs Survey*, 2013, http://www.amdocs.com/vision/documents/survey-highlights.pdf. But when people were surveyed about a *particular* surveillance activity—"Do you think the government should be able to monitor everyone's email and other online activities if officials say this might prevent future terrorist attacks?"—52 percent of respondents were against the practice. "Majority Views NSA Phone Tracking as Acceptable Anti-Terror Tactic," Pew Research Center for the People and the Press, June 10, 2013, http://www.people-press.org/files/legacy-pdf/06-10-13%20PRC%20WP%20Surveillance%20Release.pdf.

327 **we don't know how to object**: Sara M. Watson, "Data Doppelgängers and the Uncanny Valley of Personalization," *The Atlantic*, June 16, 2014, http://www.theatlantic.com/technology/archive/2014/06/data-doppelgangers-and-the-uncanny-valley-of-personalization/372780.

328 **information we share with them**: Jack Balkin, "Information Fiduciaries in the Digital Age," *Balkinization* (blog), Yale Law School, March 5, 2014, http://balkin.blogspot.com/2014/03/information-fiduciaries-in-digital-age.html, cited in Jonathan Zittrain, "Facebook Could Decide an Election Without Anyone Ever Finding Out," *New Republic*, June 1, 2014, http://www.newrepublic.com/article/117878/information-fiduciary-solution-facebook-digital-gerrymandering.

329 we adapt to rules we actually object to: One study showed a group of Facebook users how the service decides what does and does not show up on their newsfeed. More than half of the participants began the study unaware that their newsfeed was curated at all. They thought that everything their friends said would show up on the feed. They objected to the curation. But a follow-up showed that once people knew about the "objectionable" rules for curation, their idea of redress was to try to get the curation to work in their favor. They tried to second-guess Facebook. There are many ways to game the system: You can use brand names in your posts so that they get noticed. You can try to increase the number of posts from family members that show up in the newsfeed by remembering to always "like" family posts.

On this, see Christian Sandvig, Karrie G. Karahalios, and Cedric Langbort, "Uncovering Algorithms: Looking Inside the Facebook Newsfeed," Berkman Luncheon Series, Harvard Law School, Cambridge, MA, July 21, 2014. Full video available at http://cyber.law.harvard.edu/interactive/events/luncheon/2014/07/sandvigkarahalios. Also see Tarleton Gillespie, citing a personal communication with danah boyd in "The Relevance of Algorithms," *Media Technologies: Essays on Communication, Materiality, and Society*, Tarleton Gillespie, Pablo J. Boczkowski, and Kirsten A. Foot, eds. (Cambridge, MA: The MIT Press, 2014).

330 "using parks and gardens as buffers against traffic": Evgeny Morozov, "Only Disconnect," *The New Yorker*, October 28, 2013, http://www.newyorker.com/magazine/2013/10/28/only-disconnect-2.

330 uncontrolled access to data: Here, on technology and its desires, I have been influenced through my career by the work of Bruno Latour. See, for example, *Science in Action: How to Follow Scientists and Engineers Through Society* (Cambridge, MA: Harvard University Press, 1999 [1987]); *Aramis, or the Love of Technology*, Catherine Porter, trans. (Cambridge, MA: Harvard University Press, 2002 [1996]).

332 the rise of a "public sphere": See Jürgen Habermas, *The Structural Transformation of the Public Sphere: An Inquiry into a Category of Bourgeois Society* (Cambridge, MA: The MIT Press, 1991 [1962]). Cited in Steven Miller, *Conversation: A History of a Declining Art* (New Haven, CT: Yale University Press, 2007), 91.

332 "seats of English liberty": Cited in ibid, 90.

333 "the Man I conversed with": Cited in ibid., 91.

333 "*to improve the nick of time*": Henry David Thoreau, *Walden* (Princeton, NJ: Princeton University Press, 2004 [1854]), 17.

THE END OF FORGETTING

337 he calls it his withdrawing room: Henry David Thoreau, *Walden* (Princeton, NJ: Princeton University Press, 2004 [1854]), 141.

337 substitute for humans in conversation: For practice with job interviews, see Mohammed (Ehsan) Hoque, Matthieu Corgeon, Jean-Claude Martin, et al., "MACH: My Automated Conversation coacH," http://web.media.mit.edu/~mehoque/Publications/13.Hoque-etal

-MACH-UbiComp.pdf. For an automated psychotherapist, albeit one that still uses human input but hopes to do away with that system limitation as soon as possible, see Rob Morris and Rosalind Picard, "Crowdsourcing Collective Emotional Intelligence," *Proceedings of CI* 2012, http://www.robertrmorris.org/pdfs/Morris_Picard_CI2012.pdf. For a first look at a robot that aspires to be a social and emotionally competent constant companion, note Jibo, developed by Cynthia Breazeal, one of the world's leading researchers in sociable robotics, http://www.myjibo.com.

338   a "robotic moment": For a fuller discussion of "the robotic moment," see Sherry Turkle, *Alone Together: Why We Expect More from Technology and Less from Each Other* (New York: Basic Books, 2011), 23–147.

341   a computer program called ELIZA: Joseph Weizenbaum's original paper on ELIZA was written in 1966: Joseph Weizenbaum, "ELIZA: A Computer Program for the Study of Natural Language Communication Between Man and Machine," *Communications of the ACM* 9, no. 1 (January 1966): 36–45. Ten years later his book, *Computer Power and Human Reason: From Judgment to Calculation*, was deeply critical of the AI enterprise. The ELIZA experience had chastened him.

341   remember your name: For overviews of sociable robotics by two leaders in the field, see Rodney Brooks, *Flesh and Machines: How Robots Will Change Us* (New York: Pantheon, 2002), and Cynthia Breazeal, *Designing Sociable Robots* (Cambridge, MA: The MIT Press, 2002).

341   The man finds Kismet so supportive: See, for example, this interaction with the robot Kismet: MIT CSAI, "Kismet and Rich," MIT AI video, http://www.ai.mit.edu/projects/sociable/movies/kismet-and-rich.mov.

341   Machines with voices have particular power: Anthony DeCasper, "Of Human Bonding: Newborns Prefer Their Mothers' Voices," *Science* 208, no. 4448 (1980): 1174–76, doi: 10.1126/science.7375928.

342   distinguish human speech from the machine-generated kind: Judith Shulevitz brought together an array of facts about our vulnerability to machine talk, including this one. See Judith Shulevitz, "Siri, You're Messing Up a Generation of Children," *New Republic*, April 2, 2014, http://www.newrepublic.com/article/117242/siris-psychological-effects-children.

342   when we observe others acting: For an overview, Giacomo Rizzolatti, Laila Craighero, "The Mirror-Neuron System," *Annual Review of Neuroscience* 27 (2004): 169–92, doi:10.1146/annurev.neuro.27.070203.144230.

342   has no meaning when we feel it: Emmanuel Levinas, "Ethics and the Face," *Totality and Infinity: An Essay on Exteriority*, Alphonso Lingus, trans. (Pittsburgh, PA: Duquesne University Press, 1969).

342   I worked at the MIT Artificial Intelligence Laboratory: I worked with Cynthia Breazeal and Brian Scasellati, the chief designers of Kismet and Cog, to study children's responses to these sociable robots. The stories about children and robots that follow are drawn from my report of that work. See Turkle, *Alone Together*, 84–101.

346   Sharing a few words at the checkout: And research suggests this kind of

small talk is not just an act of kindness to other people; it makes people happier. Nicholas Epley and Juliana Schroeder, "Mistakenly Seeking Solitude," *Journal of Experimental Psychology: General*, advance online publication (2014), http://dx.doi.org/10.1037/a0037323.

347 **trying to build an automated psychotherapist**: For a description of the system, see Morris and Picard, "Crowdsourcing Collective Emotional Intelligence."

347 **description of a stressful situation**: The three-sentence limit is an example of how we reduce conversation because of the limitations of technology and then reframe the reduced conversation as a feature rather than a bug. The authors of the automated psychotherapy program say, "By limiting the text entry to three sentences, we help users compartmentalize their stressors. Also, shorter text entries are easier to read and are therefore more manageable for the online workers." Ibid.

348 **increasingly willing to discuss these things with machines**: This is unfolding in a context where fewer people ask for talk therapy and fewer professionals suggest it. And in a context where cultural expectations of what a therapist might provide have shifted. We used to expect that therapists would want to learn about our families, where we were from, the details of our life situations. Now we are likely to content ourselves with medication if it will make us feel better, and often our professional consultations are by telephone or Skype. Of course, all of these have a place. They are sometimes useful, often necessary. See Gardiner Harris, "Talk Doesn't Pay, So Psychiatry Turns Instead to Drug Therapy," *New York Times*, March 5, 2011,

http://www.nytimes.com/2011/03/06/health/policy/06doctors.html?ref=health. University of Pennsylvania researcher Steven C. Marcus has documented the decline of psychotherapy in recent years. See, for example, Steven C. Marcus and Mark Olfson, "National Trends in the Treatment for Depression from 1998 to 2007," *Archives of General Psychology* 67, no. 12 (2010): 1265–73, doi:10.1001/archgenpsychiatry.2010.151. See also Mark Olfson and Steven C. Marcus, "National Trends in Outpatient Psychotherapy," *American Journal of Psychiatry* 167, no. 12 (2010): 1456–63, doi:10.1176/appi.ajp.2010.10040570.

But in our enthusiasm for the new, convenience becomes custom. We are too ready to forget the power of face-to-face presence. Gillian Isaacs Russell, a British-trained psychoanalyst now working in the United States, embraced computer-mediated psychoanalytic treatment and had a long-distance practice with patients in China, the United Kingdom, and Central America. She writes this about her experience: "I met for over three years with a small peer group of practitioners who were doing treatments in China. Initially we met to navigate the cross-cultural territory, but found increasingly that we were concerned with the limitations of the medium itself." Her work is a powerful argument for presence and an argument against those who believe that in psychoanalytic practice there was an equivalence between what could be accomplished face-to-face and over the Internet. Gillian Isaacs Russell, *Screen Relations: The Limits of Computer-Mediated Psychoanalysis* (London: Karnac Books, 2015).

Among the things that translate poorly online are the bodily experiences that are part of the therapeutic experience. We come to treatment with our whole selves. As do therapists. So therapists explain that when they are listening to a patient, they may have a bodily experience of the patient's words. They may feel sleepy, get a headache, a backache, experience nausea. That bodily experience is part of the countertransference, a reaction that demonstrates again and again the connection between body and mind. In an analytically oriented therapy, the therapist sees his or her job as putting these bodily sensations back into words: an interpretation, an intervention that hopefully reframes what is happening in a way that will be useful to the patient. On this point, see Patrick Miller, *Driving Soma: A Transformational Process in the Analytic Encounter* (London: Karnac Books, 2014).

349 **"Better than Human"**: Kevin Kelly, "Better than Human: Why Robots Will—and Must—Take Our Jobs," *Wired*, December 24, 2012, http://www.wired.com/2012/12/ff-robots -will-take-our-jobs/all.

349 *include the roles of conversation*: Computer scientist David Levy argues that robots should even be given their chance to become our spouses. *Love and Sex with Robots: The Evolution of Human-Robot Relationships* (New York: HarperCollins, 2007). *Love and Sex* is a personal favorite of mine in the escalation of the "simple salvations" literature because it is dedicated to Anthony, a hacker I used as a case study in my 1984 *The Second Self: Computers and the Human Spirit*

(Cambridge, MA: The MIT Press, 2005 [1984]). Levy thought that Anthony, lonely and somewhat isolated, might appreciate a robot lover since he had trouble in the human romance department. My reading of Anthony's story shows him yearning for relationship. It's a world he has trouble with, but he wanted in. To me, Levy had missed the point in his haste to solve Anthony's "problem" with a robot. Levy was suggesting replacing the person with a machine instead of increasing the potential of the person.

To me, David Levy's *Love and Sex* is a companion piece to Kevin Kelly's *Wired* cover story. For Levy, having a robot as a lover would not diminish Anthony. In Kelly's piece, if Anthony will accept a robot in the job, then by definition it was a job that not only people were meant to do.

349 **computer conversation is "an imitation game"**: Alan Turing, "Computing Machinery and Intelligence," *Mind* 59 (1950): 433–60.

349 **robot conversation and companionship**: For so generously sharing their work, robots, and ideas, special thanks to my colleagues Lijin Aryananda, Rodney Brooks, Cynthia Breazeal, Aaron Edsinger, Cory Kidd, and Brian Scasellati.

349 **But particularly to the old**: There is controversy about the economic benefit of substituting robots for humans in service jobs. See Zeynep Tufecki, "Failing the Third Machine Age," The Message, Medium, 2014, https://medium.com/message/failing-the -third-machine-age-1883e647ba74.

350 **produce "caretaker machines"**: See, for example, Timothy W. Bickmore

and Rosalind W. Picard, "Towards Caring Machines," in *CHI 04 Extended Abstracts on Human Factors and Computer Systems* (New York: ACM Press, 2004).

I have studied Paro, a robot in the shape of a baby seal, designed as a companion to the elderly. Publicity films for Paro show older men and women who live with Paro having breakfast with it, watching television with it, taking it to the supermarket and out to dinner. In interviews about life with Paro, people say they are happy for its company, that it is easier to take care of than a real pet, and they are reassured to have a pet that will not die. See the Paro website at www.parorobots .com. On Paro, see Sherry Turkle, William Taggart, Cory D. Kidd, et al., "Relational Artifacts with Children and Elders: The Complexities of Cybercompanionship," *Connection Science* 28, no. 4 (2006): 347–61, doi: 10.1080/09540090600868912. See also Cory D. Kidd, William Taggart, and Sherry Turkle, "A Sociable Robot to Encourage Social Interaction Among the Elderly," *Proceedings of the 2006 IEEE International Conference on Robotics and Automation* (2006): 3972–76.

351 **engaged in "as-if" conversations**: In this context, I use the term "as-if" in the spirit of Helene Deutsch's work on the as-if personality: Helene Deutsch, "Some Forms of Emotional Disturbance and their Relationship to Schizophrenia," *Psychoanalytic Quarterly* 11 (1962): 301–21.

351 **People were special**: For my early work on computational objects, the question of aliveness, and what made people "special" in this context,

see Turkle, *The Second Self*. My work on aliveness continued with a second generation of computational objects and was reported in Turkle, *Life on the Screen: Identity in the Age of the Internet* (New York: Simon and Schuster, 1995). My inquiry, with an emphasis on children's reasoning rather than their answers, is inspired by Jean Piaget, *The Child's Conception of the World*, Jean Tomlinson and Andrew Tomlinson, trans. (Totowa, NJ: Littlefield, Adams, 1960).

355 **better to talk to computer programs**: See Turkle, *Alone Together*, 50–52.

356 **one for the child**: From the earliest ages, children thrive on getting emotional feedback from the faces of their caretakers. In infant studies, when infants encounter "still-faced" and silent mothers, they become agitated, do everything possible to reengage the mother, and then, if not successful, become withdrawn and despondent, shriek, and lose control of their body posture. A silent mother is a pathological mother and a pathology-inducing mother. See Edward Tronick, Heidelise Als, Lauren Adamson, et al., "The Infant's Response to Entrapment Between Contradictory Messages in Face-to-Face Interaction," *Journal of the American Academy of Child Psychiatry* 17, no. 1 (1978): 1–113, doi:10.1016/S0002 -7138(09)62273-1. See also Lauren B. Adamson and Janet E. Frick, "The Still Face: A History of a Shared Experimental Paradigm," *Infancy* 4, no. 4 (October 1, 2003): 451– 73, doi:10.1207/S15327078IN0404 _01. For a video of the phenomenon, see "Still Face Experiment: Dr. Edward Tronick," YouTube video,

posted by "UMass Boston," November 30, 2009, https://www.youtube.com/watch?v=apzXGEbZht0.

358   **videos of people happy to engage:** One classic sequence with Kismet is "Kismet and Rich," MIT AI video, http://www.ai.mit.edu/projects/sociable/movies/kismet-and-rich.mov.

361   **there will be "empathy apps" to teach compassion and consideration:** See, for example, the work of Richard J. Davidson of the University of Wisconsin, who, with the support of the Bill and Melinda Gates Foundation, is developing handheld games to teach a range of skills, from attention to empathy. For the announcement of this work, see Jill Sakai, "Educational Games to Train Middle Schoolers' Attention, Empathy," *University of Wisconsin-Madison News*, May 21, 2012, http://www.news.wisc.edu/20704. On the work of the center, see http://www.investigatinghealthyminds.org/cihmProjMeditation.html. Mindfulness training is a large part of the curriculum.

Index

cultivating capacity for, 65, 66–67, 77, 81

first chair and, 10–11, 16, 46–47

Internet surfing as, 61, 74–75

loneliness and, 23, 65–66, 265, 286–87, 346

playing alone, and, 65, 71

self and, 61

virtues of, 60–62, 79

vulnerability to feeling alone, 152–53

work and, 287

Sontag, Susan, 151

Spectator, 333

spontaneity, 4, 22, 53,143

Stanford University, 40, 138, 230, 231

Starbucks, 285

strangers, conversations with, phone as "security blanket," 152–53

stress,

emotional exposure as, example, 264–66

of family life, 117–18

work and, 250, 253, 277-278, 280

of being "always-on," 278–79

see also anxiety

strong and weak ties, 297

students, *see* college students; schools, schoolchildren

summer camps, device-free, 11, 26, 104, 114–16, 175–76, 317–18

Summers, Lawrence, 230

suveillance, 50, 86, 304, 305, 312–13, 315

self-, 304–6

see also privacy

Syria, senate hearings on, 39

Tabless Thursday, 261

Taipei (Tao Lin), 194–95

talk therapy (psychodynamic), 96–99

teachers, 5-6, 231–32, 241-244

actors as (for online courses), 211, 238

see also Holbrooke School, Radway School,

technological affordances, 43–44, 111, 126, 261

technology,

addiction to, 126, 215–16

and choosing right tool for the job, 324–25

conflicts about role of, learning from 325

"coping," a metaphor with problems, 171

and forgetting what we know about life, 13, 23, 232, 325–26

human values and, 7, 319, 321, 359

vulnerabilities and, 25, 27, 30, 44, 114, 126, 124, 135, 171, 216, 261, 358, 360, 361

telecommuting, 269, 270

teleconferences, 268

telephone calls, *see* phone calls and conversations

television, 111–12, 115

terrorism, 300, 311

September 11 attacks, 299, 300

see also catastrophe culture

texting and messaging, 4, 11–13, 19–20, 21-24 , 42, 139, 140, 141, 144–46, 152

apologies and, 32–33

breakups and, 25, 196–97

in classrooms, 164–65, 212–14, 215, 243

collaboration on, 189

as commitment, 160

consolation and, 155, 156, 172